D1063843

The Passion of Ayn Rand's Critics

James S. Valliant

DURBAN HOUSE

The Passion of
Ayn Rand's
Critics

Printed in the United States of America.

For information address:
Durban House Publishing Company, Inc.
7502 Greenville Avenue, Suite 500, Dallas, Texas 75231

Library of Congress Cataloging-in-Publication Data
Valliant, James S., 1963 –

The Passion of Ayn Rand's Critics / James S. Valliant

Library of Congress Control Number: 2004115671

p. cm.

ISBN 1-930654-67-1

First Editions

10 9 8 7 6 5 4 3 2 1

Cover art by Michael Limber

Visit our Web site at
http://www.durbanhouse.com

The private journals of Ayn Rand are reproduced here with the kind permission of the Estate of Ayn Rand.

For Holly

Acknowledgments

The author gratefully acknowledges the invaluable editorial assistance of Robert W. Middlemiss, Robert Begley, David Hayes, Jeff Britting, Kate Jones, Shawn Michael Fisher, Phil Steele, and—most especially—Casey Fahy. The entire staff at the Ayn Rand Archive deserves thanks for their generous assistance, and Allan Gotthelf provided a swift response to my inquiry. Wayne Valliant, Michael Limber, Jeffrey Young, August Meyer, Steven Carver, and—most importantly—Holly Valliant must also be thanked for their unyielding encouragement—without which this project would never have been completed. Above all, the author wishes to thank the Estate of Ayn Rand for granting unconditional access to the private journals of Ayn Rand and for generously allowing their use in the present volume.

Table of Contents

Introduction

AYN RAND, the greatest iconoclast of the Twentieth Century, has herself become a cultural icon.

Half a century after their first appearance on "Best Seller" lists, Ayn Rand's novels are still popular. The novel *Atlas Shrugged*, despite having been in continuous hard and paperback editions for forty-four years, sold more than 120,000 copies in the year 2001 alone. Total sales of her titles have reached half a million copies annually—more than a generation after the death of their author.

Equally noteworthy has been Ayn Rand's steady ascension to that high shelf alongside the great philosophers of history. Recent years have seen a veritable Renaissance of scholarly interest in her philosophy, Objectivism.

Rand's image has even been celebrated on a U.S. Postage Stamp. (1)

If Rand has achieved an impressive influence, she has also been the most unfairly misunderstood thinker of the Twentieth Century. Rand was a lucid writer, and not even her critics have faulted her for a lack of clarity in presenting her ideas—quite the opposite, in fact. Yet, a diverse collection of famous writers, of every political stripe, have been taken to task for obviously—even willfully—getting those ideas wrong in each of their attempted critiques of her philosophy. (2) Unfortunately, this trend dominated criticism of Rand's ideas during her lifetime, following the publication of *Atlas Shrugged* in 1957. To some degree, it still persists.

Of greater concern is the more recent trend toward personal attack against Rand in order to dismiss her ideas—and how often the philosopher's sex life is brought up in discussions of her epistemology or political theory.

As James Arnt Aune puts it in the pages of *The Journal of Ayn Rand Studies*, Ayn Rand's critics are "curious what Rand scholars think about...

claims that Rand enthusiasts appear mired at an adolescent stage of psychological development, that her style is peculiarly authoritarian... and that the particulars of her private life call into question the validity of her moral philosophy." (3) While these comments are far less sophisticated than any of the harshest words Rand ever wielded, it is *Rand* who such critics routinely tar as uncivil and "peculiarly authoritarian." Such crude *ad hominem* attacks by Rand's critics are themselves never seen as "authoritarian" or anything less than civil discourse—even by the editors of professional journals of philosophy.

But Professor Aune is not the author of these allegations. The principal cause of this particular form of Rand-bashing, the root of this trend, can be traced to two persons: Nathaniel and Barbara Branden. (4)

At first, the Brandens were Rand's most ardent apologists and, ironically, the first to adopt a policy of blind sycophancy towards Rand. Following Rand's famous break with the Brandens in 1968, their stated perspective on Rand changed radically. Later, in biography and memoir, each would promote a dark picture of an "authoritarian" Rand whose personal and psychological problems—and whose hypocrisy—they would now claim, made both the Brandens and Rand herself utterly miserable.

From scholarly journals to allegedly historical novels, from an episode of *The Simpsons* to a cable-television movie, from cocktail party conversations to university lectures, both of the Brandens' accounts set the agenda for most public discussions of Rand and her ideas today.

The truth of Rand's philosophy is, of course, untouched by their allegations, one way or another. They are distracting and troublesome not simply because they are almost always irrelevant, but most importantly because they are historically inaccurate. To date, no detailed analysis of the Brandens' accounts, one which addresses all of the major themes of their work, has appeared. Such an analysis is clearly overdue. Too much of the discussion of Rand and her ideas has been—and continues to be—based solely on the accounts of two sources whose very reputations hinge on how history will interpret their roles in the events they purport to relate.

Part I of the present volume is an analysis of the Brandens' main biographical works about Ayn Rand, *The Passion of Ayn Rand* by Barbara Branden, and *My Years With Ayn Rand* by Nathaniel Branden (previously titled *Judgment Day: My Years With Ayn Rand*).

Biography and philosophy are two distinct subjects. Logicians since Aristotle have been at pains to demonstrate that an attack on the person cannot suffice as an attack on that person's beliefs. Whatever Sir Isaac Newton's vices—or virtues—his science stands or falls on its own merits. To confuse the person with his position is to commit the logical fallacy *ad hominem*, which means, literally, "against the man," as opposed to "against his argument."

One obvious reason for this distinction is that a person can be right about one thing and still be obnoxiously wrong about others. Some famous composers of music have been unpleasant (even vicious) human beings.

Another reason to evaluate the person and his ideas separately is that a discoverer of new knowledge may not appreciate the import of his own work. He may leave his new ideas in books, and the ideas that govern his behavior may only be the traditional ideas he has inherited. He might even be a hypocrite.

However, the importance of biography cannot be overlooked. The practical effects of a man's *operative* ideas can be seen playing out in his life, in triumph and disaster. Among writers, for example, the personal lives of Victor Hugo, Feodor Dostoevsky, Mark Twain, and Ernest Hemingway stand as important footnotes to their work.

Ayn Rand was an artist as much as she was a philosopher. She sought to give her vision reality in both her art and her life. Rand once characterized her own life as a "postscript" to her work consisting of the phrase, "*And I mean it.*" (5) As Rand herself would have acknowledged, if she did *not* mean it—if her personal life contradicts this statement—it is worthy of interest to the biographer, and, perhaps, of at least passing interest to the philosopher.

A novel is an intimate experience. To create characters and situations that can engage the reader's emotions, a good writer must bare his own soul and reveal the deepest workings of his heart and mind. The reader's response is just as personal.

This is especially true of Ayn Rand's major novels, *Atlas Shrugged* and *The Fountainhead.* They are philosophically comprehensive, and written with such obvious sincerity that the sensitive reader cannot help but learn a great deal about their author and her character.

But there is no substitute for personal, first hand knowledge. While the Brandens were associated with Rand for over eighteen years, I never met Rand. Although Rand had said that the Brandens were dishonest, for me to have known just from the pages of *Atlas Shrugged* that the portraits which they drew of its author must be *entirely* flawed would have taken an intelligence I did not possess.

Leonard Peikoff, the foremost authority on Rand's thought, and many others who were closely associated with Rand, have declared the Brandens' biographies to be nothing more than arbitrary assertions, and on that basis they have dismissed these books without further consideration. Peikoff defines an arbitrary claim as one for which there is no evidence, that is, "a brazen assertion, based neither on direct observation nor an attempted logical inference therefrom." (6) Because of Peikoff's wholesale dismissal of these books—and a general disgust for the Brandens among Rand's defenders—no comprehensive critical response to these books has yet appeared in print.

However, only an analysis of the biographies themselves makes possible the conclusion that they are largely arbitrary and often demonstrably false. For those of us who never met Rand, to dismiss entirely and without consideration those critics of Rand who knew her would be a mistake—no matter how much credibility Rand has earned from her readers.

Moreover, even if there is no truth to be gleaned from these works and they are wholly arbitrary, the necessary dirty work of exposing them remains, since they are published as historical records by primary sources, and future generations will not have the benefit of Rand's contemporaries to dispute their specific allegations.

For myself, such an analysis was necessary, and I would not be stopped even by the sincere and prescient advice of Leonard Peikoff.

During my own 1995 interview of Peikoff for the television show *Ideas in Action*, he admitted that, while Rand was, indeed, the person she had to be in order to have written *Atlas Shrugged*, it is impossible "to project" all that Rand was "from just reading her work." (7)

Yet her work had made me want to know more of what she was, to glimpse more of the genius who had achieved such greatness in the very act of defending human greatness. I was curious to know more about Rand, for the sheer inspiration and fascination and delight of it, and my projection of what kind of soul she must have had gave me confidence that even her critics could not help but provide valuable observations of what must have been a remarkable and unique human being.

I had no illusions that Rand would be without fault or flaw. We will see that Rand herself admitted to being mistaken about something (or someone) on more than one occasion, and even her staunchest defenders have admitted that Rand's anger could sometimes be unjust.

My mind was certainly open to what Rand's critics had to say.

Nathaniel Branden was the first of Rand's former associates with whom I became personally acquainted. In 1982, the year of Rand's death, I was a teenager attending the University of California at San Diego. (8) Because of my interests, a campus newspaper sent me to Beverly Hills to interview Nathaniel Branden at his home. While my focus was on his and Rand's ideas, I was certainly aware of the negative things Rand had written about him.

The interview went well, and when I invited him to speak at the University he anxiously agreed, saying that "there *was* something" he had been "wanting to say about Rand..."

It was I who introduced him at the speech he delivered there for the first time, "The Benefits and Hazards of the Philosophy of Ayn Rand." Following the lecture, I asked the written questions submitted by the audience—a procedure Mr. Branden insisted upon, incidentally. I was to use my own judgment in screening the questions.

I did not ask the question we received inquiring whether he and Rand had had an affair. The question seemed unintellectual and rude.

After the event, walking back to his car, Branden asked if any questions had been screened out. When I told him what the question had been, a long, embarrassed silence followed. My own suspicions in this area therefore emerged *before* either of the Brandens' biographies were published. These suspicions never distracted me from my interest in Rand's work. I knew that I was in no position to judge a situation about which I knew next to nothing.

About a year later, an acquaintance of mine introduced me to Ms. Branden, taking me to her home in Hollywood. It was a brief meeting in which Ms. Branden inquired about the impact Rand's books had had on my life and the lives of some of my friends. She indicated then that she was writing a book on Rand and was nearly finished.

When I continued my studies at New York University, I became acquainted with many who had known Rand, both Libertarians and Objectivists, including Murray Rothbard and Leonard Peikoff. The former only encouraged my skepticism regarding the Brandens, the latter almost never spoke of them.

But when I first opened the pages of the Brandens' books, I was fully prepared to learn about the negative side of Rand's ledger, and I presumed that the Brandens, so close to Rand for many years, would be the ones to reveal it.

What I found upon careful examination and comparison of both of these authors' works, however, was that they had erected monuments of dishonesty on a scale so profound as to literally render them valueless as historical documents—and that Rand's critics have been building on a foundation of historical sand in their widespread reliance on these works.

Despite the claims these biographers make that their memoirs are drawn from personal experience, it will be seen that their intense personal animosity towards Rand—which emanates from that experience—has scarred all aspects of their work.

We shall see that rhetorical maneuvering, insinuation, failure to name sources, uncorroborated, self-serving assertion, and extensive internal contradiction, render even the positive things the Brandens have to say about Rand—which might be regarded as credible considering the authors' obvious hostility toward her—of little value as well. Any praise they offer seems, in the end, a mere acknowledgement of the observations of far more honest sources.

An earlier version of the present analysis was available on the Internet from March of 2002 until February of 2003 on the website of my friend, Casey Fahy, under the title "The Passion of Ayn Rand's Critics," and this, along with some additions, comprises Part I of the present volume. During the time that it was posted (and since) several additions and alterations were made to the text, in large measure, due to the critical e-mail response which it generated and the efforts of sensitive editors, for which I am most grateful. However, I had not consulted with Leonard Peikoff, the Estate of Ayn Rand, or the Ayn Rand Institute in any way about my essay.

The original analysis had urged the publication of the unpublished portions of Ayn Rand's private journals if they should prove relevant to my subject.

In May of 2003, the Estate of Ayn Rand granted me unprecedented access to these same unpublished journals. At that time, only a small handful of people, and certainly not the Brandens, had even seen many of these journal entries, and their contents were the subject of considerable speculation.

Rand's private journals turn out to shed enormous light on the events related in the Brandens' works, and this again prompted several additions to the original essay, and these will be apparent. As with the previous modifications, I found that this material only strengthened the original analysis, exposing still more flaws in the Brandens' accounts of the very kind already identified, and confirming several of the original theses. In particular, this material demonstrated the degree to which the Brandens have suppressed information vital to a fair assessment of their own behavior and Rand's, and, far from revealing personal hypocrisy on Rand's part, are testimony to Rand's integrity and consistency.

Even more, these journals provide the fascinating account of how an extraordinary mind systematically unmasked the systematic deceit of a rather extraordinary deceiver, and they provide a tragic chronicle of how a romantic soul was cruelly manipulated by a man to whom she had given her highest trust and affection.

Most critically, these journals provide Rand's only means of posthumous response to the Brandens' allegations, the only window into her perspective on this issue. For this reason alone, Rand's students and admirers must be grateful to the Estate of Ayn Rand for making them available—without fee or royalty of any kind—for this analysis.

In the process of attempting to understand Mr. Branden's various psycho-pathologies, Rand has also left us many invaluable insights into human psychology that will no doubt be of more lasting value than the exposure of the Brandens' deceptions.

Since nearly all of this private journal material is directly relevant to the Brandens' accounts of Rand's final break with Mr. Branden—and since none of this material has been previously available—the bulk of it has been reproduced, with extensive commentary, in Part II. The single longest of these entries, that of July 4, 1968, is the best summary of Rand's diagnosis of Mr. Branden (we shall see that she was officially acting as his therapist at this point), and this entry has been reproduced almost in its entirety and without significant interruption.

The acuity of Rand's mind—and the intensity of her anger—on the topic of Nathaniel Branden is bracingly apparent in these journal entries; frequently, and despite the pain this topic involved for Rand, they sparkle with a crystal clarity and radiate a ruthless honesty so familiar to Rand's readers.

It must be remembered, however, that these private journals were written by Rand *for herself,* in order to clarify her own thinking, and that Rand never intended that they be published. For that reason, they cannot be considered definitive statements of Rand's philosophy, Objectivism. Nevertheless, they provide important insight into Rand's own perspective on the Brandens and her break with them—the very perspective which the Brandens uniformly ignore. Indeed, it is upon ignorance of this perspective that the Brandens' theses critically depend.

For reasons that will be made obvious, the inclusion of material from either of the Brandens' biographies in no way implies that any of the events related actually took place, or, if they did, that the Brandens are believed to be credible sources regarding those events. My object is only to demonstrate why the picture the Brandens seek to draw of Ayn Rand should not be accepted as even partially trustworthy, as many today do, simply for the fact that the Brandens' biographies have existed in a vacuum.

In the course of what follows, we will also find something else: the profound truth about Ayn Rand and the meaning of her life, the very truth in danger of being lost to the character of a legend invented by the Brandens.

PART I: *Biography and Myth*

I. Less Than Zero

AMONG THE MANY TROUBLING ASPECTS of the biographical works of Nathaniel and Barbara Branden, the "who's-less-objective-than-who" contest between Rand's two leading critical biographers must be our first concern.

In the Introduction to *The Passion of Ayn Rand*, Barbara Branden writes:

> Over the years, many people have suggested to me that it was time for me to write Ayn Rand's biography. But I had come to believe that I would never do so, that I could not again immerse myself in those days of wonder and pain and again struggle to emerge from them whole. For some time after the ending of our relationship, I doubted that I had achieved the necessary objectivity to write about a woman and a life that had so powerfully affected and altered my own life. (1)

But, Ms. Branden reports, the positive feelings finally won out, and the "necessary objectivity" must have been achieved, at least in the author's mind, since she did write the book.

Nathaniel Branden in the 1989 version of his memoir, *Judgment Day: My Years With Ayn Rand*, takes issue with Ms. Branden's claim to objectivity:

> Contrary to what Barbara says in *The Passion of Ayn Rand*, where she suggests that not long after the break her feelings of anger at Ayn faded and her love reasserted itself, she and I remained at loggerheads over this issue for eleven years. On an evening in 1979, in the living room of my home, Barbara began to speak with great pain and anger—once again—about how Ayn had almost ruined her life. Losing patience, I said sharply, "*Stop seeing yourself as a victim!*" (2)

Ms. Branden, suggesting that she is not alone in her continued feelings of persecution, writes that, "[r]egrettably, Nathaniel [Branden]'s anger against Ayn and against his former friends who rejected him appears not to have diminished but rather to have escalated during the years since 1968; too often, he has characterized and described them in terms that can only be called unjust." (3)

By "former friends" Ms. Branden cannot be referring to those among her own former friends whom she gives short shrift to, especially Leonard Peikoff, who is inadequately discussed in her biography, considering his important role in Rand's life and the Objectivist movement, as Rand would designate Peikoff her heir. An outside observer of this intellectual history can hardly be satisfied by the few references given to Peikoff, who is also her first cousin, which is one notable example of Ms. Branden's employing a dubious historical/memory selectivity of her own.

Perhaps sensing that this entire exchange paints both Brandens as biased reporters, the 1999 edition of Nathaniel Branden's memoir, now less righteously titled *My Years With Ayn Rand*, attempts to soften the scene depicted above, and Branden interestingly omits his own angry retort to Ms. Branden. (4) These are not the only changes, and Branden, crediting the help of his former wife, has rewritten his previous position on some of his "former friends." The portrait of Rand herself remains largely the same. (5)

Branden admitted in a 1999 interview that a certain lingering "pain" had "showed up in the writing" of which he claims not even to have been consciously aware in 1989. So he rewrote the past, he says, "to make a book that would be... more positive and more kind." (6)

In the process, some of the memoir's original fire has been dimmed, but much remains—Allan Blumenthal, for example, is still a "eunuch," (7) for daring to suggest that Branden was a bit obsessed with sex.

This is the calm version, written after thoughtful reflection.

Nathaniel Branden's revised edition also accuses Leonard Peikoff of a "display of imaginativeness that few people would have anticipated" in "converting the Rand legacy into personal cash" by publishing Rand's private journals. (8)

Despite Branden's bizarre contention that "few would have anticipated" the publication of such material, the practice of publishing the notes of literary figures is quite common, and many generations of scholars to come will appreciate this fact, if Branden does not. Before the publication of the present volume, those portions of Rand's journals which her estate had made public were almost entirely of a philosophic or literary nature. Finally, of course, Peikoff, as Rand's heir, has the moral and legal right to do so, and in fact Rand's permission.

Given the history of Mr. Branden's own career and the subject of the book in which he makes this statement, one cannot help thinking that Branden doth protest too much about financial exploitation. (Readers of Part II will be able to identify many possible causes of Mr. Branden's alarm at the possibility—now realized—of Rand's private journals reaching publication.)

Among the most disturbing changes between the two versions of Branden's memoir are the differing accounts of his own state of mind during episodes about which he writes. In 1989, Branden tells us that after *Atlas Shrugged* was published in 1957, he felt as if the spotlight of history were upon him. In 1999, Branden tells us that he really felt foolish.

Attempting to explain the obvious contradiction, Branden says that it was the "surface arrogance" that he was projecting at the time to Rand and others which was still affecting his mind in the 1980s. He reports "almost going into an altered state to recapture the nuances of what I [really] felt..." (9)

As necessary, our analysis will note where other important changes have been made from one edition to another. Yet this example serves to illustrate a notable tendency in the Brandens' recollections. Both of the Brandens' works—in any edition—suffer from manic-bipolar swings in the authors' attitudes. It is their very closeness to their subject—which they claim gives them such insight—that causes fatal distortions of their objectivity.

And if this kind of closeness does not, in itself, render their judgments entirely dubious, the way they parted company from Rand (discussed at length in chapter four) should surely amplify our concerns about their objectivity.

The Brandens' readers cannot help but notice that a large part of their motive in recounting events in which they played leading roles involves rescuing their own reputations. As they themselves make clear, despite the obvious spin they attempt to put on these facts, their behavior towards Rand—and others—in the course of these events was grotesquely dishonest and manipulative.

Dishonesty is apparent not merely from the Brandens' general approach but from countless smaller issues. As a case in point, we are treated to an unnecessary fabrication concerning how Rand chose her name. While it is a minor point, it is an ominous foreshadowing of the dishonesty of the Brandens' main theses.

Born Alice (or Alyssa) Rosenbaum in 1905 in St. Petersburg, Russia, the novelist adopted the name "Ayn Rand" in order to protect her family still living in the Soviet Union. Rand's first novel, *We the Living*, is a powerful critique of dictatorship based on Rand's own experiences in Russia. It was published in America while Rand's family lived under the shadow of Stalin's reign of terror.

A controversy has arisen regarding the origins of the name Rand selected. It is said that she once joked that criminals and writers should keep their original initials, and, hence, the "A.R." Other suggestions have been largely speculation.

In her 1986 biography of Rand, Ms. Branden quotes Rand's cousin, Fern Brown, as her source for the claim that Rand had been inspired by the name of her American typewriter—a Remington-Rand.

Ms. Branden also tells us: "Ayn never told her family in Russia her new name... they never knew she had become 'Ayn Rand.'" (10) Ms. Branden may be trying to insinuate that Rand was being neurotically secretive, perhaps even turning her back on her family. This is the sort of vague impression we will see the Brandens persistently attempt to create. Ms. Branden certainly claims that this was an important reason why Rand lost contact with her family shortly before World War II—they did not know her name.

However, this is demonstrably false. Anyone who has seen the biographical documentary, *Ayn Rand: A Sense of Life*, has seen the letter from Rand's proud Russian family with the hand-drawn name "Ayn Rand" on a big marquee in neon lights. (11) Given Ms. Branden's fictionalizing on this issue, could the rest of her name-story be false?

Nathaniel Branden goes so far as to quote Rand as telling an undetermined "us" that she had adopted the name from her typewriter. (12) If so, it is curious that Ms. Branden did not report Rand's words—or Rand as her source—since she is the only other person likely to have been included in Mr. Branden's "us" at that early stage in his story.

Ms. Branden and Ms. Brown both say that Rand chose her name when she was staying with Ms. Brown's family in Chicago. Rand left for Hollywood near the end of August of 1926, since her contemporaneous private notes indicate that she saw a movie in Chicago on August 28 of that year. Professor Allan Gotthelf has observed, however, that the Rand Kardex Company (which never made typewriters) had not merged with the Remington Typewriter Company until 1927 and did not make typewriters labeled "Remington-Rand" for several more years after that. Since there was as yet no such thing as a "Remington-Rand," Ms. Brown's story must be entirely dismissed.

The evidence does demonstrate that Rand had adopted her name at some point *before* coming to work in Hollywood—for example, she kept a studio pass for the DeMille Studio which was stamped "September 4, 1926" and which had been issued to a person with the name of "Rand." She simply cannot have been inspired by the name of any typewriter then being manufactured. (13)

Moreover, it has come to light that there exist letters to Rand from her Russian family which use the name "Rand" but which also predate any previous communication from Rand in America. The origins of her name must go back to a very early stage in Rand's career.

Michael Berliner and Richard Ralston, scholars at the Ayn Rand Institute, have also observed that in the Russian, or Cyrillic, alphabet letters which look similar to our letters R, a, n and d can be found in the Cyrillic version of "Alice Rosenbaum" and that letters similar to the three Roman letters a, y, n (or m) appear in similar sequence as the last three Cyrillic letters of Rosenbaum. (14)

The new evidence appears to confirm what Rand told *The New York Evening Post* in 1936 and *The Saturday Evening Post* in the November 11, 1961, edition, namely, that "Ayn Rand" is an "abbreviation" of her Russian name.

It seems that both of the Brandens may have been sold a bill of goods from cousin Fern and then each did a bit of embellishing on their own. The new evidence also demonstrates that Mr. Branden has no compunction against putting statements into the mouth of Ayn Rand which are, in fact, products of his own imagination.

As we proceed, Mr. Branden will be seen to invent implausible, improbable, and impossible quotations for Rand—again and again. Ms. Branden will be seen to make bold assertions even in the face of conclusive evidence to the contrary—again and again. The Brandens' books are themselves replete with evidence that this kind of dishonesty pervades all aspects of their "biographical" efforts.

II. Rand and Non-Rand, at the Same Time and in the Same Respect

BETWEEN AND WITHIN BOTH AUTHORS' BIOGRAPHIES OF AYN RAND, and even between differing editions of those biographies, are obvious contradictions and distortions that demonstrate that neither author has achieved the objectivity necessary to depict Rand in a reliable way. Their mission, therefore, strikes the reader as one of vengeance and tastes of financial exploitation.

And as their own accounts certainly substantiate, this would not be the first time they had so exploited Ayn Rand.

Most helpfully for her readers, Ms. Branden wears her own distorting prejudices on her sleeve. The portrait of Rand that she paints is so filled with contradictions, both explicit and implicit, that they form a striking spectacle of their own that focuses the eye away from Rand and on a disturbing portrait of Ms. Branden painted with impressions of Rand refracted through the prism of her conflicted mind. Just as in non-objective art, the prism of Ms. Branden's mind soon becomes the focus, since what is reflecting through it is clearly impossible.

Take, for example, the issue of intelligence to Rand. Ms. Branden writes:

> [Ayn Rand] placed on intelligence what can only be termed a *moral* value; intelligence and virtue were to become inextricably linked in her mind and emotions; where she saw no unusual intelligence... she saw no value that meant anything to her in personal terms. (1)

Oddly enough, Ms. Branden also reveals that:

> Throughout [Rand's] life, she often said that the simplest
> of men, the least educated, had the power to grasp
> complex ideas if they were led through the necessary
> logical steps. It was a view that gave her infinite patience
> with minds slower and less competent than hers, so long
> as she believed the mind was honest and seeking... She
> believed that such people had a capacity for logic, for
> understanding, an intellectual integrity uncorrupted by
> what she contemptuously called "modern education";
> her patience and respect for the uncorrupted "common
> man" made her superbly able, in her personal dealings and
> through her writings, to reach him. (2)

A personality can be complex—it can even contain contradictory
elements—especially the personality of a creative artist like Ayn Rand. But
the Law of Non Contradiction, which Ms. Branden still claims to believe,
remains true. Either Rand was a person who had a universal contempt for
the less intelligent or she was a person who had "infinite patience" and
"respect" for them—she cannot have been both.

The latter view is confirmed by Nathaniel Branden, who writes:

> [Rand] had a great talent for establishing intellectual
> rapport with "ordinary people"—a cleaning woman, a
> taxi driver, a telephone installer. She was very proud of the
> fact that in conversation she could make her ideas clear to
> almost everyone... (3)

The following passage is from Rand's private journals, never intended
for publication, dated July 13, 1945, prior to ever meeting the Brandens:

> The moral man is not necessarily the most intelligent, but
> the one who independently exercises such intelligence as
> he has. (4)

In her biography of Rand, Ms. Branden tells us as early as page 49:

[Rand] could no longer live in the present, no longer stop to notice it, no longer remove her mental focus from tomorrow. Several of the people who knew her most intimately in later years commented that they never once saw her fully enjoy an event or activity that was here and now.

"Never once" is a long time. Certainly longer than the nineteen pages between that and page 68:

Whatever the mud and the dross of the years, that capacity for enjoyment... never wholly left her.

And one only has to wait until page 71 for this:

[Rand's] relatives recalled that Ayn seemed happy. Minna [an aunt] explained: "She sang a lot around the house... she'd dance around the room [to her favorite song]. She loved it." Ayn *was* happy; something inside her was blazing with a fierce, exultant joy.

Ms. Branden also quotes Rand's husband, Frank O'Connor, on page 87 as follows:

[Ayn] had a tremendous capacity for enjoyment. Whether it was a piece of music she liked or a story or some present I bought her that cost a dollar—she was so expressively and radiantly delighted...

This zest for life lasts at least up to page 239, where Ms. Branden reports the following observation from her own early experiences with Rand:

When we entered the living room, it was to the sight of this serious, austere woman, interested only in the most crucial issues of human life and thought, dancing around the room, spinning in circles and laughing, her head thrown back in a gesture of cheerful defiance, waving a baton that Frank had bought for her—like a child to whom life was an endlessly joyous adventure.

We are told by Ms. Branden that: "Ayn had very little humor in her psychological make up, and was suspicious of humor on principle." (5)

We are then surprised to read that Rand "laughed uproariously" at her favorite comedian's jokes, that she enjoyed the humorous stories of O. Henry, and that her husband, Frank, had a delightful wit which Rand appreciated.(6) Among the many other examples in her book which contradict the idea that Rand was almost utterly humorless on principle (including humorous passages from Rand's novels!) are the following:

At [a friend's] urging, Ayn gave her first talk in Hollywood at a Books and Authors group—at which the attendance established a record for the organization... She spoke for a few minutes, then asked for questions. At the first question [her friend] cringed with embarrassment. "Miss Rand," a woman said, "the sex scenes between Roark and Dominique are so wonderful! Do they come from your own experience? What is their source?" Ayn brought down the house when she replied in two words: "Wishful thinking." Ayn gave another talk during this period [to the American Association of Architects]... During the question period, a man said, "You present Howard Roark as unconventional—but he wasn't really—he was, after all, faithful to one woman all his life!" Ayn replied, "Do you call *that* conventional?"—and the audience burst into laughter and applause. (7)

Nathaniel Branden reports that while Rand preferred small, informal gatherings, he attended at least one larger party at Rand's home in California before they moved to New York. He describes Rand at that party as possessing "great charm, warmth, and even humor..." (8) In a modest upgrade from his former wife's contention, he suggests that, while Rand was no comedienne, she was certainly not humorless.

It is true that Rand was "suspicious" of certain uses of humor. In *The Romantic Manifesto*, Rand writes, "Humor is not an unconditional virtue; its moral character depends upon its object. To laugh at the contemptible, is a virtue; to laugh at the good, is a hideous vice. Too often humor is used as the camouflage of moral cowardice." (9) Even from this passage, however, it is clear that Rand regarded humor as a "virtue," and, from all the actual evidence, one she comfortably practiced.

Another issue Ms. Branden succeeds in confusing pertains to Rand's alleged insensitivity to "personal context." After relating Rand's disappointment with her peers in her early school days, Ms. Branden says:

> Nothing could be more typical of... Ayn Rand... the instantaneous judgment... the failure to ask any other questions, to consider the possibility of a legitimate context not known to her... [Rand's] psychological nature [was] arrogant, demanding, dogmatically wedded to its first passionate perceptions [and] would make her, in the realm of human relationships, *impatient* with methodology, with the calm and painstaking pursuit of hidden truth... in the realm of social dealings, there would be for her no subtleties, no context, no hidden meanings... (10)

In Rand's "philosophy," Ms. Branden concedes, there were plenty of "subtleties" but, it is insisted, never in her understanding of other people.

But, Ms. Branden also tells us that, "[a]n important part of the powerful effect of Ayn's personality on everyone who met her was that she appeared to have an acute sensitivity to the particular concepts most relevant to whomever she was addressing, a special antenna that gave her a direct line to what would be especially meaningful; many of her acquaintances had commented on this phenomenon, as many more were to do so throughout her life." (11)

And, it is clear from both Branden biographies that Rand's alleged insensitivity to a "context not known to her" did not prevent either of the Brandens from repeatedly soliciting Rand's counsel on personal and psychological issues—even up to the last months of their association. The remarkable extent of this counseling will become ever more apparent as we proceed in this analysis.

Was Rand ever sensitive to a person's context, or was she callously and "dogmatically wedded" to her "passionate" snap judgments about people? Apparently Ms. Branden would have it both ways since she reports the following from her own experience, on pages 237 and 238:

> Sometimes, on a bright afternoon, Ayn and I would walk together along the paths of the ranch, past the cages of Frank's exquisite preening peacocks and along the alfalfa field, while she scanned the ground for the colorful rocks she loved to collect. As we walked, I would tell her about the problems on my mind... all the difficulties of a young girl on the verge of adulthood. Where I saw no avenue of solution, she would point out what I had overlooked, with *a sensitive, non-judgmental understanding of my context and needs.* I have never forgotten those sunlit walks and those equally sunlit discussions. (12)

Yet, she seems to have forgotten them—again—only three pages later, on page 241:

> The special softness, the need to touch and be touched, the concern with day-to-day activities, the non-judgmental tenderness, the unconditional acceptance that one associates with motherhood, were alien to Ayn.

Somehow, once again, on page 357, Ms. Branden is still able to remember "Ayn's smile whenever I entered the door, and the touch of her hand when something was troubling me... [and Ayn] blowing a kiss whenever we parted."

Breathtaking.

Words like "never" and "alien" have specific meanings, perhaps not those Ms. Branden has in mind, but did no one at Doubleday even read the book?

Nathaniel Branden meanwhile describes at least one conversation with Ms. Branden in which "[t]here was no sound of reproach in Ayn's voice, just a gentle, persistent probing, encouraging Barbara to explore and voice her feelings." (13)

The Passion of Ayn Rand's internal confusion can be seen in many smaller issues, as well. For example, we are left perplexed when Ms. Branden asserts that Rand's arrival in Berlin in 1926 represented her "first sight of a major European city," (14) after telling us that (apart from being a native of St. Petersburg and having previously seen Moscow) Rand had walked "along a London street with her governess" in 1914. (15)

A biographer's subject, as mentioned earlier, can be complex and contradictory, but it is the biographer's duty to sort these aspects out into something at least comprehensible. As described in Ms. Branden's book, Rand is not only hard to understand but impossible to have existed.

The Brandens' portraits of Rand are nothing if not complex. Along with their many criticisms of Rand's psychology and behavior are mixed significant complimentary references. They both concede that there is much for which Rand must be praised—using Rand's own standards. Rand was a woman of fierce independence, brilliant and dedicated to her ideas and to her craft.

All this fails to assure the skeptic, however, regarding the Brandens' objectivity, but, rather, highlights the persistent need both authors have to justify their own conduct in the events they relate and to justify their own, however temporary, admiration of Rand. Their critique, at face value, is overblown and overstated, carried by the obvious passions and prejudices they both still exhibit.

But even when taken at face value the total picture they paint of Rand, good and bad, strikes one with the contrast it creates to the lives of other widely respected writers and philosophers.

In *Intellectuals*, Paul Johnson's biographical survey of many of the most influential thinkers of the past couple of centuries, a fascinating series of case studies offer a dramatic comparison.

Bertrand Russell, for example, while he was taking "free love" to promiscuous new heights with "chambermaids, governesses, any young and pretty female whisking about the house," complained bitterly when his second wife, Dora, had an affair of her own. (16)

Russell was a socialist, but, like his friend Clough Williams-Ellis, Russell's inherited wealth permitted him a more than comfortable existence that included lavish gifts. However, Russell also exhibited at times a "meanness and avarice." (17) Russell's response to charges of hypocrisy was simple: "I'm afraid you got it wrong. Clough Williams-Ellis and I are socialists. We don't pretend to be Christians." (18)

Russell was also a pacifist, "but there were times when he loved force," as when he stated his desire to murder British Prime Minister Asquith. (19) So detached from physical reality was Russell that "the simplest mechanical device"—or even making tea—was well beyond his capacity. (20)

Then, of course, there is Ernest Hemingway, who was an alcoholic, and who, under the influence, would often beat his wives or anyone else who happened to be within arm's reach, that is, when he wasn't describing, in some detail, his wife's genitals or boasting of his own pretended sexual prowess to the other guy at the bar. His own son, Gregory, reports how Hemingway so "tortured" his second wife, who had the nerve to object to "his drinking and the brutality it engendered" (21), that Hemingway "finally destroyed all her love for him." (22)

A Communist Party sympathizer, Hemingway was also a frequent and grandiose liar about everything from his own accomplishments (e.g., he claimed to have been the first person to enter liberated Paris in 1944) to the role of the communists in the Spanish Civil War. Papa ended his life with a shotgun.

Karl Marx rarely bathed, and though he got the nursery maid pregnant ("the only member of the working class that Marx ever knew at all well") and refused to acknowledge any responsibility, he got his patron-sucker, Engels, to assume it.

Jean-Paul Sartre, who compared America to the Nazis, but was all talk and no action during World War II and the French Resistance Movement, was also said to have consumed a quart of alcohol, 200 milligrams of amphetamines, and several grams of barbiturates a day, in addition to various other chemicals.

Every significant fact about Lillian Hellman's life—except her enduring sympathy for Stalin—was a fabrication, such that Mary McCarthy said of Hellman, "every word she ever writes is a lie, including 'and' and 'the.'" (23) (Hellman was also a vicious critic of Rand.)

The other lives Johnson relates in *Intellectuals* tell much the same story. With principles that cannot be lived in practice, each, in one way or another, became an ugly hypocrite, or a tortured idealist, or a bit of both.

From the ferocity of the Brandens' attack, one would assume that Rand was far worse than any of these celebrated figures. And, yet, an objective comparison—using the Brandens' own works—suggests a contrast to these "giants" of another kind.

Ayn Rand came to America at the age of 21—a young woman, alone in the 1920s—half-way around the world to a country where she still barely spoke the language, determined to become a writer, an artist, in that new language. Less than twenty years later, after the publication of *The Fountainhead*, she was selling the movie rights to her best-selling novel, which was being praised by *The New York Times* for its literary mastery.

Rand's novels represent a remarkable achievement. They involve complex plots that can last over a thousand pages and which are explained in long and complex philosophical passages. Yet, they are still "best-sellers" that keep readers in page-turning suspense through exciting twists and turns across vast and thrilling tableaux.

We the Living, Rand's searing indictment of the Soviet Union—indeed, any dictatorship—was based in part on her own experience in Russia. First published in 1936, it predates the assassination of Leon Trotsky by four years, the publication of Boris Pasternak's *Doctor Zhivago* by two decades, and that of Alexander Solzhenitsyn's work by two-and-a-half decades. Of course, with respect to their philosophies these authors are miles apart, and Rand, in contrast to so many anti-communist writers, opposed both socialism and mysticism in *any* form. Although Rand was certainly not the first Russian to complain about Russia's experience with communism, she was among the earliest to gain an audience outside of that country.

Anthem, Rand's depiction of a future totalitarian dark age in which the word "I" has been removed from the human vocabulary, was first published in 1938, eleven years before the publication of George Orwell's *Nineteen Eighty-Four*, and seven years before *Animal Farm*. Unlike Orwell, Rand labored under no illusion that a totalitarian state could long remain a technologically advanced society, and, again, she seemed uniquely able to perceive the dictatorship implicit in *any* form of collectivism. (24)

Ayn Rand saw much more clearly, and much sooner, than even

its most celebrated critics the nature and causes of Twentieth Century totalitarianism.

These novels were just etudes in relation to the concerto that would follow, but *The Fountainhead* would be rejected by a dozen publishers. Despite all the advice she received to temper her views, Rand refused to compromise and held fast to her controversial positions. With very little help, Rand was almost entirely a "self-made" success.

Conservatives hated Rand for her atheism, liberals for her defense of capitalism, and everyone objected to her egoism, but Rand refused to modify or moderate her views to please the critics, and she stuck to her beliefs through thick and thin. The battles she waged over her innovative play, *The Night of January 16th*, and the widely anticipated film version of *The Fountainhead* show how hard she was willing to fight, like her hero Howard Roark, for her artistic integrity—as the Brandens admit.

That Rand never surrendered her controversial stances for popularity would be tested again and again throughout her life—as when a "Texas oil man once offered her up to a million dollars to use in spreading her philosophy, if she would only add a religious element to it to make it more popular." (25) She refused.

Rand astonished her own publishers by getting them to agree to print every word she wrote in her magnum opus, *Atlas Shrugged*. With the same energy and acumen, Rand had gotten Jack Warner to film every single word of the climactic courtroom speech of her hero, Howard Roark, in the film version of *The Fountainhead*.

Clearly, Rand could be as "hard-thinking" (Peikoff's term for Rand), hard working and fiercely independent as any of the characters in her novels.

The Brandens contend that Rand was blind—perhaps even dishonest—when it came to certain "personal areas," especially in her relationship with the Brandens. Mr. Branden says that keeping his affair with Rand a secret involved an otherwise undefined "network of lies and deception." (26) That Rand and Branden worked closely together—and (at the time) had the highest admiration for one another—was certainly no secret, however. If nothing else, the original dedication of *Atlas Shrugged* to both O'Connor and Branden makes this obvious.

Actually, the extent to which Rand was serious about honesty can be seen from the fact that only with the full knowledge and consent of both of their respective spouses did Rand begin her affair with Nathaniel Branden.

We shall return to these "personal areas" shortly. On all other matters, they provide substantial evidence of Rand's impressively rigorous honesty.

Ms. Branden repeatedly tells us that a strict respect for the facts was Rand's normal policy, both in theory and in practice. Ms. Branden even reveals that she was "always impressed with the range and exactitude of [Rand's] memory," a capacity Ms. Branden elsewhere calls "remarkable." (27)

Through their research, even scholars who are critical of Rand have almost entirely verified the truth of Rand's various assertions regarding her education and youth, long a subject of doubt and speculation in some quarters. (28) Despite such verification, these scholars persist in treating Rand's statements skeptically while they simultaneously fail to subject the Brandens' assertions to the same testing of credibility. Indeed, most uncritically (and often extensively) rely on them in their own work.

Describing his first impressions of Rand, her husband, Frank O'Connor, is quoted by Nathaniel Branden as follows: "One of the most striking things about [Ayn] was the absence of any trace of deviousness. The total honesty..." (29)

Branden writes that "[w]ith the exception of certain personal areas where she could be appallingly unconscious, [Rand] had the most profound and passionate respect for the facts." (30) More than this, he concedes, Rand was an honest writer who strove for clarity, lucidity and precision. Rand wrote exactly what she meant, getting straight to her point, pulling no punches.

Rand was also true to her values, an attitude which today is regarded as downright rude in dry, academic circles. If Rand admired something, her praise was an exultant hymn—when she admired someone, she hero-worshipped. Conversely, if Rand did not think highly of something or someone, her attack could be merciless. Her sense of justice demanded this attitude, according to all sources.

It seems that Rand embodied in her very personality—as well as in her philosophy—a passionate concern for truth and justice.

By Ms. Branden's account, Rand got intoxicated exactly once in her entire life, at the final dress-rehearsal of the disastrous stage adaptation of her first novel, *We the Living*, titled *The Unconquered*, in 1940. She did not like the effects of alcohol, but she did not object to the social drinking of others.

It also seems, from her account, that Rand had sex with just two men in her life, both in serious, committed and long-term relationships.

According to the Brandens, Rand only became at all violent, if that's even a correct description here, on exactly one occasion in her life—when she slapped Nathaniel Branden's face upon learning, not that their affair was over (as we shall see, that had been clear to both of them for several weeks, if not months, by that point), but about Branden's four-year, eight-month deception of Rand with yet *another* woman. (31)

Outside of the Brandens' own (brief) dispute with Rand, the Brandens seem to concede that Rand never violated anyone's legal rights in her entire life. It seems that it was her constant policy to respect the persons and property of others. And, in their own case, the Brandens' claims to the contrary prove empty, as we shall see.

Rand was no socialist; in fact, she regarded taxes as immoral. Yet, unlike many a socialist hypocrite, she was, going by the Brandens' accounts, a tax-paying, law-abiding citizen. (As an egoist, Rand was dubious of self-made martyrs.)

Rand is also repeatedly described by both Brandens as being remarkably generous to others with both her time and her money. Ms. Branden writes that, "Ayn often was warm and generous with her friends, generous with her concern, her time, her attention..." (32) She also relates that an old friend of Rand's recalled "that Ayn and Frank, despite their difficult financial circumstances [at the time], loaned small sums of money to out-of-work writers who were having an even more difficult time." (33) We also hear that, in later years, Rand "gave gifts of money, informal scholarships to young people who could not otherwise complete their education and in whom she saw intelligence and promise." (34) Each of the Brandens reports experiencing Rand's various kinds of generosity, personally.

Rand's gratitude was apparently no less than her generosity, "so much so that people who knew her were often startled by the extent of her gratitude, when they did her the smallest of services..." (35). Rand's charm, brilliance and, especially, her gratitude were the very attributes Rand's publisher, Bennett Cerf, most recalled of Rand in his own memoir, *At Random*. (36) Ms. Branden reports that this graciousness and charm were felt by people even in the last decade of her life. (37)

Despite her atheism, and surprisingly to those who might not grasp her concept of egoism, Rand loved Christmas, "an excuse to give parties and exchange gifts with friends." (38)

In comparison to the "great minds" Johnson writes about, and even the average Joe, Ayn Rand was a sober, non-promiscuous, peaceful, rights-respecting, honest, hard-working and generous individual. Rand also exhibited a degree of integrity unknown to a majority of the "giants" of modern intellectual history.

The Brandens all but say that Ayn Rand was a genius of the ages, but they fail to give comparison to others who are said to have achieved that status. Was Ayn Rand harsh to questioners following a lecture, as they report? In comparison to Beethoven's social manner, Rand was a pussycat. Was Rand alienated from her culture and those around her? In comparison to Van Gogh, Rand was a party animal. Was Rand authoritarian with her students? Mullah Rand?

To justify what they were willing to "tolerate," Rand must be portrayed as a genius. To justify their break with Rand, Rand must be portrayed as a monster. Ms. Branden writes of Rand that both her "virtues" and her "shortcomings" were "larger than life." (39) The whole enterprise is suspect in light of their obviously similar agendas.

The Brandens' criticisms of Rand are, mostly, but not exclusively, personal and psychological rather than philosophical. They briefly review several of Objectivism's principal ideas, not always in the language Rand herself used to explain those ideas, but they do so in a generally laudatory manner. In fact, they appear to be repeatedly assuring their readers that they still support most of Rand's ideas—and that they had good reason to be caught up in Rand's spell, as it were. Their thrust is that Rand often did not live up to her own stated ideals because of deep psychological issues which Rand herself never acknowledged.

There are some significant philosophical differences, however. Mr. Branden rejects the use of the term "validate" with regard to metaphysical axioms, thinks Rand's novels subtly but pervasively encourage psychological repression, (40) and thinks Rand gave insufficient attention to benevolence. (41)

Still more profoundly, Branden endorses such assertions as Haim Ginott's "labeling is disabling." (42) Without disputing that it may be counterproductive in a psycho-therapeutic context to pour concrete onto a patient's current self-estimate, surely even the field of psychology is conceptual, and Branden seems to have veered sharply away from the author of *Introduction to Objectivist Epistemology*, if not the necessity and objectivity of concepts themselves.

Branden also now generally rejects making Rand-style ethical judgments about others, and he says that he prefers a non-judgmental, psychological approach to human evaluation. For example, he now rejects the normative evaluations of the great philosophical systems in history— and some of their originators—which Rand had developed in *For the New Intellectual*. (43) Branden does not argue with Rand's evaluations, but he nonetheless claims Rand's approach unnecessarily alienates intellectuals.

Branden asserts that the severity of Rand's moral judgments was a relic of religious thinking—which he had, he suggests, purged from his own psychology completely. He prefers now to see things simply as "harmful" or "beneficial," rather than "good" or "bad." (44) Branden thus appears to accept the modern notion that passionate normative evaluation is "unscientific" or non-objective, hence, religious. Ironically, it is the psychological dimension of evaluations, i.e., emotions, which Branden now emphatically rejects.

Branden's own confessions to having slavishly and "violently" suppressed his "true self" in order to identify with Rand (discussed in chapters three and four) do not suggest any disturbing religiosity on his own part to Branden. Nor does his self-defined role as Rand's "enforcer" (also discussed in chapter three) strike him as "a remnant" of anything of the sort. The fact that in those days Branden could be what he regards as too "judgmental" and "intolerant" does not suggest anything about his own psychology to the famous psychologist, either.

For her part, Ms. Branden uses concepts that Rand would have wholeheartedly rejected. She refers, for example, to Rand's "feminine instincts," (45) the "intuitive aspects of her nature," (46) and areas of "subjective preference." (47) Rand herself would have demanded definitions of these concepts—whether used about her or anyone else—and almost certainly would have rejected the terminology. Ms. Branden does not give definitions and leaves it up to the reader to rely on what Rand herself would have regarded as sloppy modern thinking. It is not too much to ask that Ms. Branden should explain her philosophically contentious terminology to, say, the average student of Rand's philosophy.

In any case, the thrust of their critique is not aimed at Rand's philosophy, but rather at her failure to live up to it. But they do concede that Rand had remarkable qualities, that she was a woman of rationality, artistic integrity and independence, that she conscientiously read her critics but never yielded to them. She made it her policy to respect the rights of her fellow man and to be an exactingly honest person.

And she was exciting to be around. New ideas flowed daily from a mind with a seemingly unlimited range. Her brilliance and charm could be irresistibly compelling. That is why, they say, they devoted their lives to the woman as well as her ideas.

However, in her dealings with her students and followers, they tell us, Rand could be oppressively authoritarian. It is claimed that Rand demanded absolute agreement. They say that her penchant for constant moralizing created a rigid atmosphere which stifled creativity and spontaneity. Her habit of ascribing behavior—or even artistic preferences—with which she did not agree to a psychological disease or moral failure encouraged an all-encompassing emotional repression of any desire or attitude not sufficiently in line with Rand's views. During question-and-answer periods following a lecture, they tell us, Rand could get angry and, sometimes very unfairly, alienate or humiliate the questioner. We will examine each of these issues in the next chapter.

To explain this kind of behavior, Ms. Branden provides a detailed psychological profile of Rand. Nathaniel Branden apparently concurs with most of her conclusions. In the "Introduction" to the new edition of his own biography, Mr. Branden says that "in order to let the story speak for itself" he "offer[s] very little psychological analysis" of Rand. (48) However, though Branden draws few firm conclusions of any kind, psychological analysis is implicit throughout his book.

Rand was a deeply repressed and alienated woman, both Brandens write, alienated from the culture in which she lived and from the material world itself. Such repression was the result of Rand's burying a childhood, indeed, a lifetime, of emotional pain: parental rejection, surviving the Russian Revolution and its aftermath, including periods of near-starvation, an intense professional struggle and the unjust rejection by many critics of her titanic efforts.

According to the Brandens, this resulted in a pronounced psychological need for Rand to be "in control," as much as possible, hence, a moralizing "authoritarian."

In every case, the Brandens' assertions on these topics are presented with little or no evidence to support them.

Rand was certainly in one sense very alienated from the world around her. She was at times depressed, angry and harsh. Presumably, she was, at times, tense, irritable and demanding—as, I fear, most of us are.

Rand's fierce anger, however, was an unusually intense and major part of her personality—of this, there can be no doubt.

One does not have to be a psychologist to know that inappropriate or misplaced anger often does indicate repressed feelings of pain and injustice. This, of course, assumes that the anger is misplaced or inappropriate. Otherwise, anger is simply a healthy response to injustice.

In developing her psychological profile of Rand, Ms. Branden stretches well past the range of the evidence. Ms. Branden's entire portrait is, in fact, simply a compilation of specious logic supported by virtually no evidence, at all, despite her prolonged personal history with Rand.

For example, it is exclusively from a family photograph that Ms. Branden divines that Rand's maternal grandmother, about whom there is almost no other evidence or mention, was "clearly the feared matriarch and the soul of her family." (49)

That Rand's parents are "leaning in opposite directions," in this lone, innocuous snapshot from the awkward post-daguerreotype days of photography, is somehow grounds to conclude that "they are avoiding" each other.

From the "model" of their relationship, principally deduced from this photograph, Ms. Branden is able to see the same "pattern" that would emerge in Rand's own marriage. Yet, from the evidence, the only similarity between O'Connor and Rand's father is a quiet disposition. Claims of "passivity" or any other psychological conclusions are simply impossible to achieve from such a paucity of data. (50)

The absurd extent to which Ms. Branden claims to be able to draw deductive conclusions from this single photograph is remarkable and must raise a bright red flag about her objectivity in general.

Ms. Branden is also convinced, not from witness statements or circumstantial evidence, but from her own deductions that Rand experienced comprehensive rejection from her parents.

The actual circumstances suggest otherwise.

The Rosenbaums clearly gave their children considerable attention, providing a comfortable home with servants and the best education they could obtain for them. As she matured, Alyssa Rosenbaum, who would later take the name Ayn Rand, developed a real friendship with her father. Whatever their disagreements, it was her mother who had the sensitivity to her daughter's needs to have sold the last of her jewelry to get Rand out of Russia. True, her father exhibited the reserve typical of the period, and her mother's ideas and personality were anathema to Rand.

This hardly justifies the following:

> Her father's seeming indifference to her and her mother's disapproval had to be sources of anguish to the child. Yet as an adult she always spoke as if they were simple facts of reality, of no emotional significance to her then or later. *One can only conclude* that a process of self-protective emotional repression—which was so clearly to characterize her adult years—was becoming deeply rooted even in early childhood. (51)

There is an obvious response which leaps to mind: no, one can more easily conclude that Rand had come to terms with these "facts," even assuming that their attitude can be described as "seeming indifference" and "disapproval," for which there is no real evidence provided.

Ms. Branden fails to consider the possibility that Rand was not somehow deeply disturbed by things she spoke of as "simple facts of reality." But what would the state of the evidence look like if Rand had somehow managed to deal with such childhood issues as she had in a psychologically healthy way? Wouldn't she, then, be able to talk about them without getting emotional—as Ms. Branden reports was just the case?

Rand was born to Jewish parents in Russia in 1905. The idea that she confronted anti-Semitism at an early age is at least plausible. Rand herself attached no significance to her race or ethnic heritage for both philosophical and psychological reasons, as Ms. Branden concedes.

Now, consider Ms. Branden's psycho-epistemology in overdrive:

> In all my conversations with Ayn Rand about her years in Russia, she never once mentioned to me—nor, to the best of my knowledge, to anyone else—any encounter she might have had with anti-Semitism. It is all but impossible that there were not such encounters. *One can only assume* that, as with the pain caused by the indifference of her parents [notice that both are now "indifferent"], the pain and terror of anti-Semitism was ultimately blocked from her memory—in both cases, perhaps, because the memory would have carried with it an unacceptable feeling of humiliation. (52)

The idea that anti-Semitism may not have touched her childhood in any dramatic way, or that Rand was simply able to deal with whatever level of bigotry she faced, is just not considered by Ms. Branden. "One can only assume" proves—even suggests—nothing.

But, Ms. Branden claims that since Rand spoke of her parents in a matter-of-fact way, we may conclude that she was highly repressed, and, from the fact that Rand never mentioned an anti-Semitic experience in Russia, that she was psychologically "blocking." Rarely, if ever, has so much psycho-theory been built on so little reality.

Perhaps because of his background in psychology, Nathaniel Branden shies away from any detailed analysis of a family and childhood he knows little about. Nevertheless, he generally agrees with his ex-wife's psychological assessments, while providing no more evidence for such conclusions than Ms. Branden does. Mr. Branden invariably uses the same, useless examples she does, and we are provided little or no additional detail when he recycles the same material. Merely adding a second voice to repeat the same foundationless assertions does not give the unproven any greater reality.

In fact, reiterating the same examples suggests a coordinated story, for we must remember that Branden suffers from the same highly biased position to his subject as his ex-wife does. Although long-estranged afterwards, in the immediate wake of their break with Rand in 1968 they did, in fact, coordinate their responses to Rand. (53)

As with so much else, Branden does not attempt to demonstrate these theories about Rand but simply *insinuates* them. As he told an interviewer, the suggestions he makes in his memoir are not "claims of knowledge" but, rather, possible or "partial" explanations of Rand's behavior. (54) A more artfully vague escape clause for any defects which might be found in his memoir is hard to imagine.

Mr. Branden tells us that "somehow [he] felt certain" that no adult had ever "cuddled" Rand as a child. (55) Despite his professional training as a psychologist and his closeness to Rand, that "somehow" is never specified. That Rand herself could be warm and affectionate—even "cuddly" with her husband—becomes apparent from both Brandens' descriptions of Rand. We are simply left to ponder Mr. Branden's "intuitions."

As proof that Rand experienced a "tension over practical affairs," Ms. Branden cites the fact that "[a]lthough [Rand] was an excellent cook, she worked painfully slowly, her movements awkwardly overprecise..." (56)

This is hardly surprising as Rand was then writing full-time, according to Ms. Branden. A "tension over practical matters" is hardly indicated by a professional adult's awkwardness in the kitchen (apart from a professional chef, of course), even one who might fall short of being described as an "excellent cook," like Rand.

While he does not report any "awkward overprecision," Nathaniel Branden does claim that Rand once gave him "a brief monologue on her hatred for cooking; for [Rand], cooking evidently required a form of concentration she found particularly onerous." (57) Rand is not quoted here, and whether Rand actually used the word "hate" is not at all clear. What is clear is that Rand often cooked—"hate" it or not—and that she gave it, like everything else she did, her full "concentration." Her efforts apparently resulted in "excellent" meals.

Branden concurs that Rand was a talented cook and reports that the novelist-philosopher's culinary skills introduced him to a couple of his favorite dishes (including even his "number-one favorite" or his "absolute favorite," depending on which edition you read)—in his own words, giving him "a new appreciation for Russian culture." (58) Curious results from a chef who "hates" cooking. Such results, one might have supposed, would have also excused a degree of "awkward overprecision."

Ms. Branden tells us that Rand worked in the wardrobe department at RKO Studios during the Depression. The job involved "filing, purchase supervising, keeping track of the costumes and accessories and seeing that the actors got the right costumes." (59) Bertrand Russell, it goes without saying, would not have lasted a week, while Rand became head of the department within a year. This, too, is hard to reconcile with the notion of a Rand helpless in the face of "practical matters."

Rand was alienated not just from the practical, according to the Brandens, but from the physical itself. To demonstrate this, Ms. Branden notes that Rand abhorred physical exercise. As a child she did enjoy climbing around the Alps, and, in her sixties, Rand took dancing lessons and seems to have enjoyed these, too. Despite this, we are told that Rand "loathed" physical activity from early childhood. (60)

Ms. Branden relates the painful hunger and desperate privations of Rand's youth, yet fails to mention that a childhood that involves periods of *near starvation* is usually not conducive to the development of good, lifetime exercise habits.

According to one source, Rand told Professor John Hospers that, as a child, she once had to walk from St. Petersburg to Kiev, a distance of 600 miles as the crow flies, in order to avoid such starvation. Hospers said that Rand recalled "going up hills and walking across rocks in broken shoes, at age twelve or thirteen." (61)

Maybe this had something to do with it, too.

With regard to Rand's alleged alienation from the physical world, Nathaniel Branden reveals that one of the interesting things which Rand taught the cerebral young Branden was that the "physical is not unimportant" in relation to the differences between men and women. (62) This fact is a little more obvious to some than to others, it seems.

By Branden's own description—if not admission—it was Rand who initially set him on the course to look for mind-body integration and the potential harmony of reason and emotion. By his own account, it was Rand who first got Branden in touch with his own "physical" side, both sexually and philosophically.

One can only imagine, then, how "estranged from physical reality"

Nathaniel Branden was himself when he first met Ayn Rand.

From Rand's own analysis of Mr. Branden's psychology (which is the subject of Part II), we will see that Rand, in fact, believed Branden to be overly "cerebral" and "rationalistic," and, simultaneously, that he was attempting to compensate for this by making a lurch in what might seem to be the opposite direction—"crude materialism"—in the last years of their association together.

Despite all of this, Nathaniel Branden agrees with Ms. Branden that Rand was "estranged from physical reality." Branden relates that he "was sometimes astonished at the intensity of [Rand's] exasperation over such trivia" as "[l]ocks that jammed, toasters that malfunctioned, blouses with missing buttons, dresses with falling hems—all seemed to be malevolent adversaries whose sole intention was to frustrate and thwart her." (63) One wonders whether Branden, as a man, ever deals with hems, buttons or toasters at all—and whether Branden would so criticize a career-minded male writer. These things *are* irritating distractions for someone as busy as Rand seems to have been, and it was not Rand who declared that these things were "malevolent adversaries" to her—it is Branden allegedly getting that grandiose impression.

Once again, we are given no evidence or incidents or quotations, only Mr. Branden's hostile and baseless impressions to consider.

As Ms. Branden does, Nathaniel Branden places great importance on the fact that a writer born in Russia at the turn of the Twentieth Century never learned to drive an automobile.

For Ms. Branden, Rand was simply "unable" to learn to drive, as she found "mechanical objects impossible to master" (64), despite the fact that it is clear from her own account that Rand competently used typewriters, ovens and several other mechanical devices—including (under supervision) the engine of the Twentieth Century Limited locomotive (except for Rand, no one else even "touched a lever" of the engine, we are told.) (65)

Ms. Branden reports that Rand's husband, Frank O'Connor once tried to give his wife driving lessons. But, Ms. Branden asserts, these were abandoned in "mutual enraged despair." (66) The "enraged despair" is not quoted from either of the O'Connors and seems to be simply the author's own dubious evaluation of a situation to which she was not herself a witness. In any event, however, being unable to drive after an undisclosed number of very amateur lessons does not make a person "estranged from physical reality"—it could simply make her husband charmingly paranoid for his wife's safety.

Mr. Branden also suggests an alternative explanation, if one is really needed. Rand worshipped her husband. Although Rand was not a servile person in most respects, she was submissive to her husband in many respects. As Ms. Branden tells us, "...no one who knew Ayn and Frank ever saw her refuse him a firmly expressed wish." (67) When it came to driving, Rand may simply have been complying with her husband's wishes. If there is a necessity for psychological speculation, which is already an enormous stretch here, then perhaps at some level Rand wanted to depend on O'Connor for this.

There are other possibilities as well. The idea that O'Connor may simply have been a bad driving teacher—just to cite one of the more obvious contrary possibilities—does not occur to either Branden. All of these theories, of course, including the Brandens', are sheer speculation.

Moreover, there is plenty of evidence to suggest that Rand was definitely not "estranged from physical reality," in this sense. Years later, Rand was up for dancing lessons, a skill which she learned "with remarkable speed" according to her teacher. (68) While dancing is a whole lot safer than driving, it can be far more physically demanding, especially at sixty-two.

As proof that Rand had a neurotic self-image, the Brandens cite the fact that Rand was not happy with her own appearance.

They remain undeterred from this notion though they report that Rand did take apparent pride in her own "shapely legs, which she cheerfully flaunted in short skirts," and that Rand "delighted in compliments," to use Ms. Branden's words. Nathaniel Branden says that Rand was "very proud" both of her "beautiful legs" and enormous eyes. (69)

The Brandens also concede that jealousy was utterly alien to Rand. Ms. Branden says that Rand's open delight in the beauty of other women had "no tinge of jealousy." Mr. Branden says that "[n]ot once did I ever sense in [Rand] the slightest jealousy about anyone's attractiveness." (70)

The Brandens point to hastily applied make-up and snagged stockings to suggest that Rand had some kind of neurosis about her appearance. Ms. Branden does not seem to appreciate that her own descriptions of Rand as being "impeccably groomed" on more formal occasions (71) provide the important context on this issue.

We should suppose, Ms. Branden seems to be saying, that since Rand did not always obsess like a model over her clothing and make-up, she must have been alienated from the material world itself. In fact, Rand, at least at home, sounds a lot like the young Howard Roark, with buttons missing on his shirt, only neater. What the evidence does not indicate, however, is a neurotic self-image.

Mr. Branden says that "left to her own devices, [Rand] was more or less unconcerned with what she wore—because her writing, she said, 'leaves no space in my brain for such things.'" (72) If Rand actually said this about herself, then Rand—who purchased and wore the theatrical fashions of Gilbert Adrian years before she met the Brandens (73)—is obviously being a little rough on herself, unless "left to her own devices" meant when she was at home immersed in the context of her writing. If the context were attending the Academy Awards, the Brandens themselves suggest she would happily have embraced the glamour of high fashion.

Another breathlessly reported instance of Rand's psychological illness was that Rand did not travel by airplane until 1963, when she flew to Oregon to receive an honorary Doctorate of Humane Letters from Lewis and Clark College. This claim is made despite the fact that air travel was not a commonplace until about the middle of the Twentieth Century.

Rand's "powerful need for control, her need to run her own life, her abhorrence of ever dropping the reins and putting herself in the hands of someone else, was at the root of her fear [of flying]."

Yet, "[a]ll through the flight—which was, at times, unpleasantly bumpy—[Rand] thoroughly enjoyed herself." It seems that it was "typical of Ayn that, once she made the commitment to fly, she was no longer nervous..." Rand later did "occasionally travel by air," as well. (74)

Unless standards of mental health have dramatically changed, this appears to be the description of a normal, indeed, a healthy psychology, hardly proof of an obsessive "need to be in control."

However, this is the *kind* of evidence the Brandens find compelling in establishing their shared thesis.

Branden does not commit himself to many clear opinions about Rand—positive or negative—but he does adeptly insinuate several which are quite dubious.

As a professional psychologist who knew Rand in both personal and professional contexts, Mr. Branden cannot say that Rand was clinically paranoid, but he does claim that in "her grandiosity and suspiciousness, [Rand's] behavior bordered *at times* on paranoia." (75) What behavior Mr. Branden believes actually "bordered on paranoia"—or even how it seemed to—he does not share. Branden may be making the unwarranted assumption that these conclusions are apparent from the allegedly "authoritarian" behavior he attributes to Rand (discussed in the next chapter), but he nowhere explicitly draws this connection himself.

Evidence of "suspiciousness" seems to be confined to how "closed [Rand] typically was to any new knowledge that seemed to clash with her familiar paradigms." (76) Control issues are involved again, it seems.

One must say "seems" as Branden never clarifies whether he actually agrees with many of the theories he develops in his book. Indeed, these theories may not even be, to use his own words, "claims of knowledge" but merely hypotheses.

Given the ample evidence which Branden supplies that *refutes* these same theories, he elects to merely suggest the worst without committing himself.

It "seems" to Branden that hypnosis, non-Darwinian theories of evolution, the ideas of Arthur Koestler, and biological causation in various kinds of depression "clash" with Rand's "familiar paradigms." Objectivism, of course, is Rand's paradigm and—rejecting any kind of philosophical cosmology—it explicitly has no position on evolution, Darwinian or otherwise. Likewise, Objectivism does not try to explain hypnosis or the physiological components and causes of emotion. It leaves all such things to the various fields of science, and—within the rather broad parameters of the "Primacy of Existence" and the Law of Identity (Objectivist metaphysics)—it cannot "clash" with scientific theories. (77)

Just why it seems to Branden that non-Darwinian theories of evolution "seem" to threaten Rand's philosophy—or how they ever could— he does not explain, nor does Branden tell us that Rand ever disapproved of his own experiments with hypnosis. Branden does suggest that Rand was dubious of the potentially fraudulent uses of hypnosis (Past-Life Regression comes to mind), but, it seems, she remained on the fence, as it were, about various other claims made about hypnosis.

Curiously, Rand's private journals from July 4, 1968, reveal that Branden's self-reported "love" for "scientific discovery" was one of the qualities she most admired in him. (78)

Going by his own account, Rand did occasionally express an understandable irritation when Branden, her co-editor of *The Objectivist*, began spending time on these subjects, which time Rand believed should have been given to Objectivism. This, of course, has nothing to do with being "open" or "closed" to new ideas. The allegation that Rand was "closed" to new ideas appears to have been one of Mr. Branden's key rationalizations for his growing drift from Objectivism, which we will take up in chapter four.

Set against all the many passionate odes to the discoverers of new knowledge—philosophers, scientists, inventors, creative artists—found in Rand's work, Branden's examples are paltry evidence of a "closed mind." Regarding Rand, the most that Branden's evidence yields is a lack of interest on certain narrow, scientific subjects. If Rand did not express an interest in neuropharmacology, is she supposed to have been "closed" to new ideas? Given the astonishing range of Rand's achievement—as Branden himself describes it—this criticism borders on the ridiculous.

Mr. Branden does not say that Rand was a megalomaniac, but he insinuates much the same thing, claiming that Rand was given to making "grandiose" statements about herself. Of course, when it comes to examples, Branden provides nearly none. Comparing her own novel, *The Fountainhead* to other novels (including her own first novels), Branden does quote Rand as saying: "Everything I've liked has had some inconsistencies, some contradictions. *The Fountainhead* doesn't have any." Branden goes on, "This was said impersonally, with no implication of boasting, but merely as a self-evident fact. I had grown accustomed to hearing her discuss herself and her work in this way." (79) That Rand was fully satisfied with *The Fountainhead*, philosophically, is hardly surprising—after all, she wrote it. After *We the Living, The Night of January 16th* and *Anthem*, Rand had fully found her unique voice, literarily, with *The Fountainhead*. This is simply a fact that Rand would have been blind not to have seen.

If a writer is not writing the best thing that he can imagine being written, it is hard to imagine any readers will ever think so. If this is wild boasting, then to be an artist of any quality one must be a wild boaster.

As for Rand's actual, historical significance, Branden himself states that he and others were "profoundly convinced that Ayn was bringing an inestimable value to the world—intellectually, literarily, socially—and that it would be virtually impossible for people not to recognize this fact." (80) Branden claims to have retained his belief in at least the first part of this assertion, but still says that Rand was neurotic for believing precisely the same thing—although, even here, he cannot quote Rand as saying this much.

On the issue of Rand's allegedly oversized self-estimate, it is interesting to note that Rand is quoted by Branden as saying, "The difference between me and other people is that I am more honest." Branden even says that Rand "resisted the idea that her powerful intelligence was at least as important as her honesty." (81) If anything, Rand did not fully appreciate her unique talents. And, indeed, much of Rand's anger at intellectuals stemmed from her conviction that they should have known better—as she had—and that, in Rand's own mind, there was nothing "special" about her except honesty.

It is in this light that we should consider Rand's most notoriously "grandiose" assertion: "I've never had an emotion I couldn't account for." (82) Rand believed that anyone could access their own subconscious and do the same (except, perhaps, psychotics).

Ms. Branden does not tell us how she was able to determine that Rand meant by this "that the total contents of her subconscious were instantly available to her conscious mind, that all of her emotions had resulted from deliberate acts of rational thought, and that she could name the thinking that had led her to each feeling." (83) In fact, Rand did not believe the first two propositions at all, and even here she seems only to be making the third assertion.

However, this statement is not so wild a boast as it might appear. When we are angry, scared or sad we usually know *why*. That part is typically not the mystery for most people other than the highly neurotic.

Branden quotes Rand as saying about her leadership role: "I never wanted to be a general, let alone a commander in chief. My dream has always been to be an ideal lieutenant—to my kind of man." Rand explains elsewhere, "A man, conceivably, could adjust to the knowledge that he was at a higher level than those around him, although no rational man could possibly enjoy that perspective; but to a woman it would be intolerable." (84)

These are not the statements of a megalomaniac of any sort, but actually those of a rather "simple and modest" woman, as her publisher, Bennett Cerf, described her. (85)

Mr. Branden says of Rand: "[w]ith the exception of certain personal areas where she could be appallingly unconscious, [Rand] had the most profound and passionate respect for the facts." In a contradiction worthy of his former wife, Branden elsewhere complains of Rand's "manipulative dishonesty," and even calls hers "a life of lies and deception." (86)

Yet, apart from his highly dubious account of the events surrounding his affair and subsequent break with Rand (discussed in chapter four), actual evidence of any dishonesty on Rand's part is wholly absent.

Branden recalls Rand once telling a group of people that "no one had ever helped her," (87) a claim he observes that Rand also made in the autobiographical sketch included at the end of *Atlas Shrugged*. This, he believes, is an obvious example of "grandiose" dishonesty.

Branden does not, however, reproduce the full context of Rand's assertion. Rand writes, "I had a difficult struggle, earning my living at odd jobs, until I could make a financial success of my writing. No one helped me, nor did I think at any time that it was anyone's duty to help me." (88)

Speaking of honesty, the honest reading of this passage is a bit more complex than the one Branden has suggested. Anyone reading it must suppose that Rand had received help from her publisher in printing her books and from her parents when she was a baby.

What could she mean?

Atlas Shrugged, the novel one has presumably just read, contains an extensive discussion of *altruism*. The author has just denounced any kind of "help" which involves self-sacrifice. In that book, the model for all human relations is "the trader," for Rand believed that in spiritual as well as in commercial matters, human relationships must be an exchange of values—that is, Rand did not approve of any "help" that was not a selfish act on the part of the giver.

In this context, it is much more likely that Rand simply meant that she got no *altruistic* help, such as welfare. Thus, she did not "think at any time" that it was anyone's "duty" to help. One must presume that Rand had received some selfish "help" at some point—she could not have set the type *and* poured the ink *and* run the printing machines that produced copies of *Atlas Shrugged* all by herself, that much is clear. One must also presume that Rand knew that we must presume this; if Rand had wanted to lie, she could have been a lot less obvious.

She also might have avoided repeatedly acknowledging—both publicly and privately—her gratitude for the help she received from a number of people. *Who Is Ayn Rand?*, the Brandens' first book, and its biographical essay by Ms. Branden, were sourced directly from interviews of Rand and were published with Rand's approval. The inclusion of material there represents the very things that Rand wanted the world to know about her. There, Rand tells how it was primarily her mother's efforts that got her to America, how relatives in Chicago put Rand up when she first arrived, how the Studio Club in Hollywood provided her affordable housing when she arrived there, and how Archibald Ogden even staked his career on *The Fountainhead*. (89)

Ms. Branden, in *The Passion of Ayn Rand*, also notes Rand's gratitude to her mother who had sold the last of her jewelry to get Rand out of Russia; she also quotes Rand as saying of her Chicago relatives that "they saved my life"; and, she reveals that Rand wrote an "open letter" to the Studio Club in which she spoke of their "great work which is needed so badly—help for young talent." (90)

Rand's published letters confirm her profound need to offer gratitude and acknowledgment to those whom Rand knew had helped her. Still in her twenties, Rand wrote to Cecil B. DeMille that if she had "achieved any kind of success, I owe it to your instructions." In the same year, she wrote to H. L. Mencken to express "why I appreciate your kindness in helping me to put my book [*We the Living*] before the public." In 1936, she wrote to Gouverneur Morris to express her gratitude for "the wonderful things you've said about me" and to the director of the Studio Club to "thank you and the other officers of the Studio Club for all your kindness and help at a time when I needed it so badly." In 1942, she wrote Archibald Ogden to tell him that his work on both *We the Living* and *The Fountainhead* had been helpful to her, and that "you have analyzed my work better than I could have explained it myself." In another letter, Rand catalogs the various other ways Ogden's help was critical to *The Fountainhead*. (91)

Finally, although this hardly completes the inventory of Rand's openly expressed gratitude, in the "Introduction" to the Twenty-fifth Anniversary Edition of *The Fountainhead,* Rand most publicly and permanently credited her husband, Frank O'Connor, with no less than having "saved" the novel. (92)

The notion that Rand had any difficulty acknowledging what she regarded as appropriate "help," or that Rand ever sought to deny or minimize this kind of help is simply absurd, as the Brandens know well.

Mr. Branden also tells us that he was "shocked" to see several of Ludwig von Mises' ideas "frankly condemned" by Rand in the margins of her personal copy of *Human Action.* Branden calls the language used "abusive," and he believes it betrays hypocrisy since, in person, Rand was "never... anything but friendly, respectful, [and] admiring" towards Mises. (93)

Rand's occasional frustration while reading Mises is understandable. From Rand's perspective, what classical liberal defenders of the free market, from Adam Smith and John Stuart Mill to Mises and F. A. Hayek—whatever their other virtues—all so desperately needed was a systematic *moral* defense of the profit motive, i.e., selfishness, something Rand's philosophy distinctively provides.

More critically, Rand believed, they needed methodological foundations more secure than the skeptical philosophy of David Hume or the philosophical subjectivism of Immanuel Kant, influences that capitalism's defenders seemed unable to shake until Rand.

If Rand thought Mises was a "goddamned fool" for some position he took, Rand is supposed to have been a hypocrite for otherwise being polite to the brilliant old economist? She could not still admire his other accomplishments?

And, if Rand had used such language with Mises himself, or did not still admire his work, wouldn't that have been some real proof of her irrational intolerance? Or, is Rand not supposed to get passionate about ideas—even in private notes to herself?

Rand's margin notes on this book and over twenty others are now available, so we can now make up our own minds on this issue. (94)

That Mr. Branden is every bit as small and petty as is his former wife could not be more apparent—but criticizing Rand for her margin notes reaches a new low.

Not to be outdone, Ms. Branden uncritically repeats the allegation that Rand was a hypocrite because—despite being an enemy of mysticism—she kept a little gold watch which she called her "good-luck watch." (95)

Such instances not only reveal the emotional animus behind the attack, but also the degree of distortion from which their perceptions suffer.

Ms. Branden has alleged still another area of Rand's self-delusion in an attack that is surely the Brandens' most substantive.

When Rand prepared her first novel, *We the Living*, which had originally been published in 1936, for its new release in 1959, she made some editorial changes. In her "Foreword" to the new edition, Rand calls these "editorial line-changes." While she admits cutting even whole paragraphs of material which were "so confusing in their implications" that they had to be removed, Rand tells us that she neither "added or eliminated to or from the content of the novel." (96)

Ms. Branden and other critics have not been satisfied with Rand's statement. In the original version, the heroine, Kira, tells the communist Andrei that "I loathe your ideals. I admire your methods," that if one is right one shouldn't have to wait to convince a million fools, "one might as well force them." Indeed, at one point Kira suggests that it would be appropriate to "sacrifice millions for the sake of the few," knowing "no worse injustice than justice for all."

It may be said that Rand meant by this that if millions were to gang up and threaten the rights of the few, it would be more just that the gang should be "forced" than their victims, a point she would certainly elaborate on and clarify in *Atlas Shrugged*, where the few sabotage the intentions of the millions who would enslave them. Since this was not clear in the passage from *We the Living* and needed greater working out, it may be perfectly understandable that Rand would not allow the statement to stand unclarified in the earlier novel and rely on herself to make the same impassioned point more completely in subsequent writings. The delivery, and not the point, may well be all that she abandoned here.

However, to some Rand critics this sounds like the unmodified philosophy of Friedrich Nietzsche, famous for his lack of squeamishness when it came to the use of force and violence.

On the other hand, even in the original, Kira also says that she does not know "whether I'd include blood in my methods," and that she does not want to fight *for* the people or *against* the people, she just wants "to be left alone." (97) And, of note, "left alone" to be an *engineer*, the only job left where she will not have to "lie."

Although it is the Russian, not the American, version of "justice for all" which Kira is complaining about, the influence of Nietzsche on this passage is apparent. Rand admitted to the influence of Nietzsche on her own intellectual development while repudiating many of that thinker's most fundamental ideas.

Rand was certainly right in calling this passage "so confusing in its implications" that it had to go.

Ms. Branden even agrees that Rand did not think that literally "forcing fools" would be a good idea, even "at the time of writing *We the Living*," but implicitly gives credence to the notion that—at some earlier phase in her thinking—Rand might have actually been a full-fledged authoritarian under the skin.

But Rand is clearly not expressing a Nietzschean "will to power," as some have asserted, and until it can be shown that Rand at that point in her thinking held an unreformed Nietzschean position, there is no basis to assert that she was being in any way dishonest.

As the recently published private journals of Rand reveal, she was already questioning many of Nietzsche's most important ideas (the Will to Power, determinism, "instinct," and, most importantly, knowledge as personal interpretation and the role of logic) in her very first notes of an explicitly philosophical nature, which were written when she was just twenty-nine. It is also clear from this evidence that if Rand was ever operating within a largely Nietzschean context it was during the period of her earliest extant literary notes in English, her notes for a proposed novel, *The Little Street*, which were written when Rand was just twenty-three—a project she quickly abandoned. (98)

And of course, by her thirties, when Rand wrote *The Fountainhead*, Nietzsche's influence had become a negative and polemical one; he had by then, if not earlier, become a foil and a foe in Rand's mind, quite explicitly. In the character of Gail Wynand, Rand's own break with Nietzsche was completed, her critique of the "Will to Power" fully embodied.

Far from impugning it, Rand's admission of her early confusion enhances her credibility.

It also must be remembered that Rand wrote *We the Living* in her twenties, that she had not yet been in America for ten years when it was first published, and that she was still becoming familiar with a new language. Already fluent in Russian and French, and able to read German, Rand's earliest notes in English demonstrate the remarkable speed with which she mastered English. But the process did take time and effort, something also to be seen in the progression of those early journal entries.

Ms. Branden alleges that dishonest grandiosity is apparent in Rand's claim that "the only thinker in history from whom she had had anything to learn" was Aristotle. This is something for which Rand "should have been challenged," according to Ms. Branden, who also claims that Rand "dismissed" as worthless, if not immoral, the whole "history of philosophy, with the sole significant exceptions of Aristotle and aspects of Thomas Aquinas..." (99)

It is simply a fact that Rand was influenced by very few thinkers when it came to philosophical fundamentals. Does Ms. Branden wish to imply that Rand *should have been* more influenced by others?

And, as usual, what Rand had said, at least in print, was more than slightly different from what is being claimed. Rand explicitly acknowledged the influence that Nietzsche had had on her intellectual development in *Who Is Ayn Rand?*—by Barbara Branden. In that book, Ms. Branden had written:

> In [Rand's] readings in philosophy [in her late teens], she discovered Nietzsche's *Thus Spoke Zarathustra*. Because Nietzsche revered the heroic in man, because he defended individualism and despised altruism, she thought she had found a spiritual ally. But she was made uneasy by the implication that a great man would seek power, not over nature, but over other men; to rule, she thought, was an unworthy occupation for a hero; a hero would not degrade himself by spending his life enslaving others.
>
> As she read further in Nietzsche's writings, her hope

gradually changed to disappointment. And, when she discovered, in *The Birth of Tragedy*, an open denunciation of reason, she knew that any value she might find in his works could only be partial and selective; she saw that in their basic premises, Nietzsche and she were philosophical opposites. (100)

Ms. Branden even tells us that Rand only "gradually" changed from thinking of Nietzsche as an actual ally. While Rand would come to disagree with just about every aspect of his basic philosophy—and, hence, he cannot be regarded as a positive contributor to Objectivism, like Aristotle—Rand was certainly not concealing Nietzsche's influence in the areas where his influence lingered.

In her "Introduction" to the Twenty-fifth Anniversary Edition of *The Fountainhead*, Rand went so far as to reference her continued—if highly qualified— appreciation for Nietzsche. There, she tells us that she almost attached a quotation from Nietzsche to the original edition of *The Fountainhead*. Able to qualify her comments, Rand indicated that she was "glad" to restore it for the new edition. The quotation was: "The noble soul has reverence for itself." (101)

Rand was *advertising* his influence.

In *Atlas Shrugged*'s "About the Author," Rand does acknowledge Aristotle as the only one to whom she owed a *philosophical* debt, (102) but it is also clear that had Rand included Nietzsche on that list, a truly misleading impression would have been created. Nietzsche was, after all, proud of his opposition to systematic and principled morality *as such*, i.e., Rand's very project and aim in ethics. At his own repeated insistence, Nietzsche must be regarded as a philosophical bulldozer—Rand was an architect.

Despite Ms. Branden's assertions, Rand's appreciation of the Aristotelian tradition itself extended further than just Thomas Aquinas—as is apparent from her review of *Aristotle* by Professor John Herman Randall. (103)

As Ms. Branden also knows, America's Founding Fathers were given great praise by Rand. Rand also acknowledged the important role of the philosopher John Locke, whose political philosophy the first Americans largely adopted. In *Capitalism: The Unknown Ideal*, Rand includes Locke in her account of that "long struggle" to achieve political freedom which had "stretched from Aristotle to Locke to the Founding Fathers." (104)

The claim that Rand was trying to hide the influence of these great thinkers, or to somehow magnify her own originality, is refuted by Rand's own published comments. It is simply that Rand did not believe that either Locke or Nietzsche deserved the same kind of credit that Aristotle did and that she did not trace her *fundamentals* to their philosophies, as she did Aristotle's.

Rand disagreed with many fundamental aspects of the philosophies of both Locke—a Christian who endorsed the "representationalist" theory of perception—and Nietzsche—whose own passion decayed into raw emotionalism. She believed that their virtues—i.e., the parts of their philosophies with which she did agree—had their roots in Aristotle himself, as she suggests, for example, in repeatedly calling Aristotle America's first "Founding Father." Locke's focus on man's nature in political theory and his belief that all human knowledge derives from sense-perception do owe much to Aristotle. The (largely unadmitted) influence of Aristotle's egoism on Nietzsche's egoism has been observed by no less than Walter Kaufmann, one of the foremost Nietzsche scholars of the Twentieth Century. (105)

Who else would Ms. Branden nominate for Rand's admittedly sparse list? Even stretching to add these two figures still makes for a pretty quick read.

To celebrate the publication of *Atlas Shrugged*, Random House threw Rand a surprise party. O'Connor was instructed to tell Rand to expect a special dinner out—just the two of them. According to the Brandens, Rand was not happy about the surprise party that ensued, and she made that quite clear at the time.

Nathaniel Branden says that Rand complained: "I do *not* like surprises."

Barbara Branden quotes Rand as not "approving" of surprises. (106)

Although Rand really enjoyed the custom cigarette case she was given that night, and although Bennett Cerf was later able to cheer her up, and although Ms. Branden admits that then "one saw again the childlike charm in the woman who a moment ago had been so sternly disapproving," Rand's initial reaction to being misled and surprised, it seems, is further proof of her controlling, repressed nature.

Mr. Branden concurs and again claims to possess special (i.e., unverifiable) knowledge: "Only I, and possibly Barbara, could know how many times in the months and years ahead Ayn would refer to this evening chastisingly, with an appalling lack of benevolence and grace, for our daring to take any action without her say-so." (107) Barbara Branden, too, questions Rand's gratitude in this instance.

It is interesting to note that in his own memoir, *At Random*, Bennett Cerf does not mention the incident (although Random House threw the party), and, indeed, he goes into some detail regarding Rand's unusually intense gratitude at the smallest of favors. (108)

In other contexts the Brandens themselves note Rand's normally strong sense of gratitude. This should have—but did not—give them pause before launching into an attack on Rand's graciousness.

Had the Brandens first inquired into whether Rand—the supposed beneficiary of the party—liked surprise parties or not, they would not themselves have been the ones who got surprised, and they would have discovered that Rand had a definite view on the subject. Rand later explained this to her stamp-collecting friend, Charles Sures, who reported her position in his own memoir:

> First and foremost is that it puts the recipient in the position of having to suddenly switch his context and deal with an unplanned for, unexpected situation. What, she asked, is the value of that? This is what we do in cases of emergency, she said. We shouldn't be put in the position of doing it for a celebration. She objected to being 'put in a position' by someone else, of being deprived of choice in the matter. The giver mistakenly thinks that the shock of the surprise will be more appreciated than a planned-for party. On the contrary, [Rand] said. The recipient gets no benefit whatever from the surprise element. It adds

no value over and above what would be derived from a planned-for occasion. Instead, it detracts from the value of the occasion, because the recipient is put in the position of being a guest of honor and a host at the same time. He has to put his shock aside and greet people he had not expected to see (or perhaps not wanted to see), he is expected to be grateful to the party givers who study him for his reactions, he is expected to be gracious and charming when he may feel annoyance, or anger, or [be] overwhelmed by the situation.... [Rand] made additional points. The giver has no right to be the final unilateral authority on how anyone's achievement is celebrated. And the giver has no right to be the sole arbiter to determine who the guests are. Most important, the giver has no right to be the one who determines how any evening out of the life of the recipient is to be spent. That's up to the recipient.

Added to all this is that the recipient is deprived of the pleasure of anticipation, which adds greatly to the enjoyment of the celebration.

Sures was asked whether some people do not simply enjoy surprise parties:

That may be. She couldn't see any valid reason for them. But that's something the giver should find out in advance, if the pleasure of the recipient is the first consideration. And, she said, it should be. (109)

Rand was not seeking to "control" anyone's context here but her own. It was the Brandens who were part of the effort to "control" Rand's context through deception—Rand was merely objecting to the deception. (We shall see that this will not be the last time they will attempt to do this, merely one of the less important times.)

The Brandens do occasionally mention a psychologically interesting fact about Rand. One or two, at least, are corroborated by more credible witnesses. But they always make much more of the point than is merited.

If Rand picked up from her mother a mild fear of germs and a habit of washing dishes a certain way—her mother is said to have disinfected every toy before it came into the nursery—(110) one can hardly criticize her, given the mortality statistics from diseases like typhus and cholera in Russia following the Revolution when Rand was a young woman, facts Ms. Branden herself mentions.

Like a lot of Russians of the period, Rand's family barely survived. With this background, it is impossible to say that running the water before using it was even a symptom of neurosis, or, indeed, any more than a grim habit learned early and hard. Rand had a very rough youth. Other conclusions are unwarranted, but Ms. Branden forges ahead without benefit of evidence into the realm of sheer speculation, sensing in this, too, a neurotic need by Rand to "be in control."

Ms. Branden also reports that Rand expressed concern if her friends failed to dress warmly when the weather was cold, that she kept a certain distance if her companion was ill, and that she, like modern dish washing machines, would "scald her dishes in boiling water." (111)

Apart from running the tap, all of these are common practices—even for many who have not experienced a childhood marked by fatal plagues and Russian winters. And it seems that her "phobia" manifested itself in no other symptoms. Indeed, at other times in her book, Ms. Branden provides clear evidence that Rand was otherwise no clean-freak, much less a compulsive hand-washer. (112)

Rand spoke to a crowded venue just weeks before her death.

Nevertheless, Ms. Branden, true to form, has no problem conjuring up the image of a reclusive Howard Hughes, with uncut fingernails, fighting germs both real and imagined from this one unusual habit.

The level of Ms. Branden's desperation for evidence can be measured by the fact that she speculates in a footnote that the low-dosage diet pill that Rand was prescribed by her doctor "may" have resulted in "paranoid symptoms." Ms. Branden does so despite also conceding that the pills probably only had a "placebo effect" after just a short time. Nor is Ms. Branden in any way dissuaded by the fact that Rand easily discontinued their use, again, on medical advice. (113)

Though Ms. Branden draws no "conclusion" herself, she encourages her readers to speculate further within the vacuum of evidence provided. As with so much else, the reader is, in fact, only left trying to fathom why Ms. Branden even mentioned it.

Nathaniel Branden has elevated mention of the prescribed diet pill from the mere footnote which Ms. Branden had given it and has proudly introduced it into his text. However, Branden chose not to share with his readers the dosage, the possible "placebo effect" or the easy discontinuation of it, that is, the context which, at least, Ms. Branden had the fairness to provide. (114) The Brandens are sometimes inconsistent in their suppression of important information, and, in this case, it helps to highlight that process in Mr. Branden's writing.

What is clear is that the Brandens are willing to relate *any* information, however shaky in substance, that might reflect negatively upon Rand's character and psychology. The weakness of the Brandens' case is matched only by the pettiness they exhibit in making it. This should not be surprising from a biographer who still "sees herself as a victim" of Rand, and her ex-husband, whose own continued fury is barely concealed.

The Brandens' claims of a highly "repressed" Rand fly in the face of their own testimony: Rand was often warm and cuddly, soft and affectionate, but also angry, sharp and harsh—she sometimes got depressed at the state of things, but she was also "blazing" with a "fierce joy"—she "openly delighted" in the beauty of others, but she also delighted in compliments—she was often worshipful and reverent, but she was also proud and self-assertive. In other words, Rand seems to have been passionately emotional about everything that mattered to her.

Rand did have a lot of pain and suffering to deal with in her life. Yet, even if—as unwarranted as that "if" may be—the Brandens' accounts can be credited, Rand appears to have dealt with this pain remarkably well, for she emerges looking much better than her detractors do, simply from their own renderings of Rand.

The Brandens were close to Rand for eighteen years, and they have demonstrated every desire to criticize her on every possible count, no matter how tenuous, frivolous or contradictory. In short, this must be the *very best* case to be made against Ayn Rand.

III. Mullah Rand?

Both Nathaniel and Barbara Branden concede that Ayn Rand did not "rule" the Objectivist movement by force or threats of force. Rand's "authoritarian" nature revealed itself in harsh words and the avoidance of certain adversaries.

Scary stuff.

If the Brandens' characterizations are to be believed, however, comparisons to the medieval church, perhaps even to Stalin, are appropriate. Indeed, it is their assertions in this regard that have provided the main foundation for this often repeated characterization.

Given the Brandens' demonstrated penchant for drawing conclusions from nearly non-existent evidence, one should view with considerable skepticism the portrait they draw of the "Authoritarian" Ayn Rand of the many "Purges," the moralizer and psychologizer. This is especially true, since both Brandens regard themselves as the very persons most seriously victimized by the Authoritarian Rand.

Ms. Branden relates the visit Rand once paid to Taliesen East, Frank Lloyd Wright's school of architecture. The legendary architect had become an admirer of *The Fountainhead*. Wright wrote Rand a letter in praise of the novel, kept the book on his nightstand and recommended it to his students—almost every one of whom read it, according to Ms. Branden. Wright later designed a home for Rand that was never built.

Rand described Taliesen to her friends as a "feudal establishment." She felt "the buildings were magnificent" but the school itself repressive. Rand was "startled" to learn that Wright's students who lived at Taliesen had to pay for the privilege of being servants as well as students in a somewhat monastic existence. They took communal meals, with Wright and his guests on a raised dais eating a better menu than the serf-students below.

Rand complained:

> Almost all his students seemed like emotional, out-of-focus hero-worshippers. Anything he said was right, there was an atmosphere of worshipful, awed obedience. When [Wright] and I began to argue about something, the students were against me instantly; they bared their teeth that I was disagreeing with the master. They showed me some of their work, which was badly imitative of Wright. What was tragic was that he did not want any of that...

Ms. Branden notes what she believes are the parallels between Wright and Rand here. Ms. Branden says that "it was clear to her listeners that [Rand] was describing, unknowingly, conflicting aspects of her own attitude: the emotional need and demand for total agreement always at war with the equal, simultaneous longing for an independent response." (1)

What *is* clear from her own comments is that Rand's conscious attitude toward such authoritarianism (if that's what it should be called) was quite negative.

It is also clear that the Objectivist movement, at its worst, including its manifestation in NBI (the Nathaniel Branden Institute), never required Rand's students to wait on her, nor were they ever put into a monastic setting with communal meals, much less a raised dais and separate menus. In all these ways, at least, Rand compares very favorably with Wright, and Ms. Branden's example has something of the opposite effect it was meant to have.

In none of her writings, of course, did Rand ever make a "demand for total agreement." In private, Rand disliked even the idea of having "followers."

"I don't like the personal adulation or any of the 'fan' atmosphere," Branden quotes her as saying. (2)

Nonetheless, the Brandens insist that Rand required "absolute agreement" from her students. But, here, the Brandens raise the white flag and admit their total lack of evidence, which does not stop them, however, from making the accusation.

Ms. Branden, for example, says that Rand "made it *implicitly* clear that any criticism of her was an act of treason to reason and morality." (3)

Nathaniel Branden asserts that there were certain "implicit premises" which were somehow "transmitted" to the students at NBI, and among these were the beliefs that a "good Objectivist" admires and condemns whatever Rand admired and condemned, and that Rand was the "supreme arbiter of what was rational, moral, or appropriate to man's life on earth." (4)

Both use the term "implicit," presumably to convey the fact that these dictums were never explicitly stated, as they were surely never stated in print or on tape by Rand or any of her associates. Mr. Branden even tells us that among these unspoken premises was the stipulation that "it is best not to say these things explicitly..." (5)

In other words, no one ever said these things, including Rand herself.

Still Branden is able to assert that what "Rand made *overpoweringly clear* to us was that the ultimate test and proof of one's idealism were one's loyalty to her work and to her personally." (6) What Branden seems unable to make even slightly clear to his readers is *how* Rand did so—at least, he does not cite for us statements or actions which even suggest Rand communicated this.

Now, it is certainly true that the periodicals which Rand and Mr. Branden edited did nothing but praise Rand and criticize her ideological opponents. To the simple-minded, perhaps, this is cause to conclude all of these alleged "implicit premises." But Rand herself reminded her readers, quite explicitly and on more than one occasion, that no human being is either omniscient or infallible.

It should also be remembered that it was the Brandens themselves who were singing Rand's praises the loudest in those days. Are they now confessing that they were, in fact, that simple-minded?

There is a single occasion where Nathaniel Branden alleges in contradiction to his otherwise consistent use of the word "implicit" that Rand did privately reveal to him her expectation that she be her circle's "highest loyalty so far as other people are concerned, if it ever comes to a conflict." (7) What exactly this was supposed to mean is left to the various imaginations of Branden's readers.

From his own description, this was said to Branden alone and in private, and, therefore, we have no unbiased corroboration. With Branden as our only witness, we require such corroboration.

Given the scant factual information which the Brandens are willing to provide for any of their claims, it is not hard to imagine that Branden would feel the need to amplify the evidence a little here.

Moreover, the statement is highly improbable. Branden has here put the prediction of a future "conflict" with members of her circle into Rand's mind, which does not seem likely. Branden quotes Rand as saying in 1961 that she believed a future dispute—at least between the two of them—to be "hardly likely," when the suggestion was first made in legal planning for *The Objectivist Newsletter.* (8) None of the context is given: where, when, in response to what, etc. Just, "Rand, just once, said this to me privately— although she said and wrote the opposite lots of other times." To use Rand's own words, "hardly likely."

Consider what we know Rand actually did say about having "followers":

> I never wanted and do not now want to be the leader of a "movement." I do approve of a philosophical or intellectual movement, in the sense of a growing trend among a number of independent individuals sharing the same ideas. But an organized movement is a different matter. NBI was not quite either; it was intended as a purely educational organization, but it did not function fully as such, and, at times, it became a professional embarrassment to me. (9)

Mr. Branden even tells us that Rand was dubious about NBI's prospects from the beginning and that NBI was named after Branden, rather than Rand or Objectivism, precisely in order to establish "a certain distance" between Rand and that organization. (10)

Such attitudes are not easily reconciled with a single statement that Branden claims Rand once made to him privately.

In an introductory note preceding his book, Branden says that when he reproduces a conversation, "I am not suggesting that all the words reported are verbatim," although he is confident, he says, that he was faithful to "the spirit and mood of the occasion." (11) This is simply insufficient, given Branden's predilection for ax-grinding and contradiction.

As we shall see in Part II, Rand's private journals demonstrate that—far from "demanding" such "loyalty" from anyone, including Branden—Rand was actually appalled by the fact that Branden himself seemed to require her "sanction" for all of his decisions, including those involving his sex life. (12)

Despite the Brandens' assertions to the contrary, Rand did have certain profound insights into how the human mind works outside of pure "theory," but, in the Brandens' view, Rand was a "psychologizer," one who uses psychological rationalizations to condemn unfairly other persons or their ideas, a practice that was identified by Ayn Rand and one she explicitly condemned in her essay, "The Psychology of 'Psychologizing.'" (13)

The Brandens would never "psychologize," of course.

On many occasions in her writing, and it is to be believed in her private life, Rand did ascribe psychological motives to her adversaries. But, as with her moral judgments, Rand could provide specific reasons, indeed, an entire philosophical framework, to justify her conclusions. Nor could she have been more forthright in expressing them.

The Brandens' principal evidence for Rand the Psychological Inquisitor, as opposed to Rand the Constant Moralizer, are the so-called "trials"—of which we are given but one example between them.

Ms. Branden tells us that a young student of Objectivism was having "personal problems in her romantic relationship" with another young Objectivist. No other details on the "problems" are given. Whether the girl was in therapy or with whom is not mentioned. The circumstances of her life are not related.

But, we are told, noted psychologist Nathaniel Branden "called her in for a discussion of her psychology." The Brandens, the two young students, along with O'Connor and Rand, were present. Ms. Branden indicates that "[s]uch evenings were becoming commonplace in Ayn's dealings." (14)

Whether or not "group-therapy" is even a psychologically valid technique, if Ayn Rand were truly the genius the Brandens still claim that she was, then who would not have paid dearly to take part in a small group therapy session which included Rand—provided, of course, that the psychologist conducting it was trustworthy.

Anyone who has observed group therapy can attest that the group sometimes has to come down on an individual pretty hard. It is said that this is part of the power of "group" as a therapeutic technique. It is also sometimes all too easy to be too hard on the individual being "grouped." It is always a difficult line for even the best-trained clinician to draw.

Ms. Branden says that while "Ayn exhibited a lack of human empathy that was astonishing...," it was Nathaniel who "conducted" the discussion. It was Branden who delivered the merciless verdict, which apparently included a diagnosis of "social metaphysics," but, if he would make a good point, Rand would occasionally chuckle or clap. (15)

This is all the information we are provided about what was said that night. Based on this one example, Ms. Branden would have us believe that psychology was a weapon which Rand used "as an inquisitor might use fire and the rack." (16)

To judge Rand from even the single case Ms. Branden presents, however, is impossible, given the tiny amount of information that is provided. What was said, what was "chuckled at," how actually sensitive this unnamed girl was that night, how did her problems turn out, etc.? All these questions need to be answered before any judgment by Ms. Branden's reader—all of us who were not present—can be made of Rand's behavior. Of course, all of these questions remain unanswered by Ms. Branden.

Ms. Branden was herself present, and these details could have been supplied. We must, therefore, ask why they were left out.

In any event, without such details, this anecdote is nearly useless to the historian; given Ms. Branden's lack of credibility on so many other issues, the reader may well demand that she supply more than her own summary conclusion.

If it is unfair to characterize this "discussion" as "group-therapy" from the information provided, then it is equally unfair to call it a "trial," as Ms. Branden does. Apparently, the only "verdict" was Mr. Branden's diagnosis. After the discussion, the girl wrote a paper about her state of mind. She was clearly experiencing distressingly low self-esteem, although, again, all the specifics are left out.

One thing is clear: the girl was not sent to Siberia.

Even taking the unwarranted step of assuming the truth of this information, it seems that the worst to be said of Rand is that she "astonished" Ms. Branden one evening by her "lack of empathy." This consisted of clapping and chuckling during a discussion of someone's psychology being conducted by Mr. Branden. From this, one can hardly leap to the conclusion that Rand used psychology "like a torturer uses the rack." The facts she has presented as her evidence simply do not warrant the opinions Ms. Branden would have us draw from them. It must be emphasized that, for some odd reason, this is the only specific example of such a "trial" that either of the Brandens mentions. We are simply told that there were others.

Nathaniel Branden admits: "I looked for alternative ways to reassure Ayn of my devotion. I became her 'enforcer.' If someone in our group did something to offend Ayn, or the 'cause'... I would invite that person to lunch and in a quiet but deadly voice I would inform him or her of the nature of the transgression." (17)

Branden not only reveals that these meetings were *his idea*, he also tells us that only if the offense was "big enough" would others, presumably sometimes including Rand, even be involved. He does not say that Rand even knew about any of these private discussions, and he almost certainly would have told us if she had known of these. In other words, as Rand's self-appointed "enforcer," Branden was acting, without Rand's knowledge, to create a culture of conformity which he would later blame Rand for creating.

Such "trials," Branden claims, could involve charges of "gossiping" about another close associate of Rand's, or "being friendly" with a critic of Rand. (18) But, of course, no examples are provided, nor are we entrusted with any of the details regarding these instances, even assuming that Branden is referring to actual events.

Did the "gossip" amount to slander or merely a rude invasion of privacy? Just who was the critic of Rand—and just how "friendly" did the person become with him or her?

Omitting these details and distinctions, Branden suggests that the very idea of questioning what someone says about other people—or with whom someone is friendly—is authoritarian in itself. By implication, he suggests that Rand should have had no problem with a teacher of her ideas getting married to a Nazi or Communist, or with one member of her circle falsely accusing another of child molesting. Without the specifics we can only assume that Rand would be criticized just the same.

But, of course, this assumes that Mr. Branden is telling the truth about these things. Telling us so little may simply mean that there is very little to tell.

Branden does tell us that Ms. Branden "sometimes played the role of Lord High Executioner herself," whatever that concretely means, an idea that readers of Ms. Branden's own biography will find surprising. (19)

Since the Brandens both chose the very same "trial" to present, it must represent their strongest case—otherwise, we must also ask how they happened to choose the same lonely example. In light of the extensive counseling Rand provided the Brandens themselves over the years (just how extensive is made clear in Part II) it is curious that no example or detail of such torment could be produced from any these sessions.

As we have observed, the accounts of this single "trial" obviously lack any of the relevant data to make a fair assessment of even that situation. If absolutely no one was willing, decades later, to waive whatever therapy-privilege might be involved in order to be named, much less interviewed about these "trials," at least one of the Brandens should say so. If they never tried, they should tell us that, too. "Well, you just had to be there" is insufficient for the historian. With only their conclusions to go on, we are left actually knowing no more than before we read their books.

Notice, too, it was Nathaniel Branden that "called" the discussion and "conducted it," and that such meetings were his idea in the first place. It was he who delivered the "diagnoses." This, at least, is credible, as neither of the Brandens suggests that Rand would ever have conducted such a group discussion of *anyone's* psychology at her own instigation. And, if it got out of hand, surely, it was Branden's—the trained therapist's—job to correct the situation.

Which brings us to Nathaniel Branden's curiously different account of that evening. Of course, it is different only in its conclusory description, for the only additional detail he provides is the name of one of the young people involved. (Apparently, the privacy or legal privileges of the people involved are no concern to Branden.) That's it.

As Barbara Branden herself observed, in Branden's version it is no "discussion" of someone's psychology—it is a meeting convened by Branden to hear ethical "charges." These are even less specific than Ms. Branden's psychological issues, which were at least suggested to have involved "social metaphysics."

It seems that, as the "prosecutor" in these meetings, as well as a psychotherapist, Branden realizes that if these meetings were, indeed, psychological in nature, then any mental anguish caused is principally the result of his own "professional" conduct. (20) If they were an indistinguishable mixture of the two, it casts Branden in no better professional light.

As Branden is fond of pointing out, Rand repeatedly disclaimed any specialized knowledge of—or interest in—clinical psychology. (21)

From the combined evidence of both Brandens, it is quite impossible to say which characterization of these meetings is more accurate—or that these meetings (or even just the one referred to) were somehow inappropriate. They (more accurately, it) may or may not have been.

In interviews published since the release of *The Passion of Ayn Rand*, Ms. Branden has not added new examples or details, but she has somewhat augmented the picture of Branden as "persecutor"—with Rand largely on the sidelines even in this single instance. Ms. Branden now suggests that, rather than wielding excessive "control" over the situation, if anything, Rand gave Branden too much latitude. (22)

Of course, most large, private organizations have a protocol for "in-house" disciplinary proceedings and often a code of ethical standards governing the membership. Upon an allegation of code violations, some kind of informal hearing is usually part of the "due process" that is believed to be necessary to ensure fairness to all concerned.

NBI and *The Objectivist* had both employees and management. Presumably, they had internal rules, including, thanks to Rand herself, an entire code of ethics. (Regulations need not be posted in the lunchroom.)

Were any of these "trials" proceedings of this sort? It is impossible to say from the Branden account. The Brandens seem to imply that, since an ethical judgment is being made in the context of an informal hearing, this is somehow in itself proof of a Stalinist show-trial or "kangaroo court." (All you attorneys can stop laughing now.)

Unfortunately, neither of the Brandens reveals the actual nature of their complaint. Is it: A) The very fact of such meetings; B) The ethical and/or psychological standards Mr. Branden used at such meetings; C) The way Mr. Branden conducted the meetings; or, D) The way Rand chuckled at one of them? These issues are all so blurred that the reader cannot tell.

Perhaps the Brandens are simply organizational anarchists. We don't know, and they never tell us.

But defining these issues is the necessary precondition before any determination can be made that some line had been crossed. Otherwise, it is impossible to say whether something inappropriate was going on at this meeting or not.

The only certainty is that the Brandens are more eager to imply that the Objectivist movement, with Rand's tacit approval, had gotten out of hand than they are capable of substantiating their own claim.

What they reveal without intending to is that Mr. Branden's behavior, if anyone's at all, was by far the worst.

Branden says that "Ayn and I caused a great deal of guilt and suffering." But he still seems not to have come to terms with the extent of the specific blame he, as opposed to Rand, might have had in the suffering of others. Although he called these meetings, "prosecuted" them and "delivered the verdicts," and although Rand was apparently most times not even present, he was just being Rand's "enforcer," a role that she had never asked him to assume and the particulars of which she was kept largely unaware.

Mr. Branden even admits that, compared to him, Rand "was often the freest in communicating positive feelings toward her friends; in some moods she was kinder and more emotionally expressive than anyone else in our group." (23) He does not appear to recognize the implications of this for his own arguments.

As indicated, this single example of such a "trial" hardly proves that Rand used psychological theories to torture people—or moral theories to persecute people. Everyone present was an adult, who was there voluntarily; of that there is no dispute.

And, if this was the extreme—perhaps astonishing—case of Ayn Rand's "lack of empathy" with her students, then, on balance, the woman looks to have been a saint.

Another indication, the Brandens tell us, that Rand was a psychological tormentor is the extent to which a number of Rand's students found themselves repressing their "true selves," in order to live up to the alleged ideals of Objectivism.

Ms. Branden relates that once she mentioned to Rand that she liked to look at the mountains and ocean. Rand asked why, and Ms. Branden explained that their changelessness gave her a sense of peace. Rand noted that she preferred "man made" things like skyscrapers and suggested that the preference for nature over man stems from a tragic "dust in the wind" sense of life. Although Ms. Branden knew "that some part of what [Rand] said was true," she felt uncomfortable at the discussion of her own psychology.

Another evening, Ms. Branden relates, she expressed an admiration for novelist Thomas Wolfe, about whom Rand had very definite opinions. "With devastating logic... [Rand] demonstrated Wolfe's shortcomings with regard to precisely the elements of fiction I had agreed were essential." (24)

Both of these events occurred quite early in her relationship with Rand.

Ms. Branden reports, however, that she was never able "to tear out of myself my passionate response to Thomas Wolfe's novels." Instead, she says, she learned to repress her true artistic tastes and, indeed, many of her natural emotions. What she told Rand was "I agree"; what her heart told herself was, "But I don't!" In plain English: she lied to Rand about her feelings.

Ms. Branden claims that Rand later began to demand agreement "even in areas of subjective preference," if not explicitly, then implicitly. (25) Nathaniel Branden confirms that from the very beginning of his relationship with Rand, it was clear that Rand attached a deep significance to a person's aesthetic tastes.

If someone expressed an artistic value not shared by Rand, she might actually say things like: "not my kind of person," or "not my sense of life." Rand even once said of a student who enjoyed Mozart and Beethoven, "That's why there will always be a wall between us. Our souls are essentially different." (26)

The fascist implications speak for themselves.

Both Brandens tell us that many of Rand's students found themselves becoming comprehensive emotional repressors, smothering their "true selves" in an effort to be properly "Objectivist." (27)

If so, was this Rand's fault? If, as they say, they knew from the outset that Rand attached significance to these matters, then was it not for them to be honest about their own feelings, rather than smile and nod their agreement? Whatever psychological label they place on it, the effect on Rand was dishonesty. If they deceived themselves, they surely also—by their own admission—systematically deceived Rand, as well.

Notice, too, that, as in the case of the Mozart lover, such differences did not cause a "break." They apparently did not even cause the moral condemnation for which Rand was allegedly famous. According to the Brandens' own reports, the only quoted reaction Rand had was one of personal dislike, "not my kind of person," and such. Why did the Brandens feel the need to repress? Simply in order to be regarded by Rand as "one of her kind of people" and in order to claim to Rand that they shared with her a certain spiritual affinity.

This cannot be ascribed to any "authoritarian" tendencies of Rand, but rather to the dishonest and sycophantic tendencies of the Brandens.

An entirely different account of how Rand approached esthetic differences is given by Mary Ann Sures in her memoir, *Facets of Ayn Rand*. Mrs. Sures relates that she liked a certain painting by Cezanne but "couldn't put [her] finger" on what she liked about it. So she asked Rand, who she knew definitely did *not* like Cezanne. Mrs. Sures tells us that this is what happened:

> [Rand] asked me if I could tell her why I liked it. I don't remember all that I said. I recall talking about two things: the secluded, peaceful setting, and the sharp contrast between the sunlight and shade in the painting—what [Rand] called "stylized sunlight." [Rand] said she could understand why I was responding to that aspect of it...
>
> The value of that discussion was her stress on the importance of understanding the reasons behind artistic preferences. Doing so puts you in touch with yourself, and you identify your basic values in the process. (28)

So, as the Brandens and their friends were suppressing their true selves in order to impress Rand as being "her kind of person," Mrs. Sures, not trying to impress, was actually discovering her true self—and not resenting Rand in the process.

Leonard Peikoff insightfully refers to those former associates of Rand who "chafed under the necessity of suppressing their real sel[ves] in order to keep up the pretense of intellectual passion." (29)

Ms. Branden states the obvious when she frankly admits "we could've said: 'Enough!' and walked away." (30) The Brandens' credibility as witnesses against Rand the Authoritarian would have been greatly enhanced if they had done so. Instead of the Brandens' leaving Rand with the exasperated comment, "I can't take all this moralizing and this implicit demand for absolute agreement," it was the Brandens who were both shown the door by Rand. It was Rand who chose not to "oppress" the Brandens, anymore.

Another of the terrible psychological weapons in Rand's arsenal was *praise*, and here we can see Rand at her most cruel, it seems.

Ms. Branden reports that Rand once told her that she expected "world shaking achievements... miracles" from Ms. Branden and that she was convinced that Ms. Branden was "going to be a great writer."

Ms. Branden says that no one, "not even Ayn," could have seen a "great" writer from what she had shown Rand. (31) This is surely true, but does Ms. Branden now resent the generous encouragement she was being given by a famous writer?

Nathaniel Branden recalls that Rand once described him as John Galt, the hero of *Atlas Shrugged*, "except for a few blemishes." He actually blames Rand's obviously unrealistic view of him for the "erratic behavior [he exhibited] with Ayn during this period." (32)

And Edith Efron, an associate of Branden in those days, agrees that he was "murdered by flattery," that is, he was a *social metaphysician* (one whose beliefs and values are determined, not by one's own judgment, but by that of others) as the noted psychologist—who helped to articulate this term—might have diagnosed himself.

Rand's opinion was clearly in error, but Branden himself was in a better position to know just how much Rand was mistaken here. It was his responsibility to correct Rand in this matter rather than to continue what he knew to be a fraud for several more years, as he did, and then, after her death, to characterize her unconsciousness of certain personal facts as "appalling."

Efron also calls Branden a "con man." (33)

Rand is attacked not just because she denounced people so harshly but also because she praised them so effusively. This kind of polar reaction was true for all Rand's values—not just people—and it is, therefore, unfair to regard this as a kind of conscious manipulation, as Efron implies.

It seems that Rand just can't win.

The principal evidence which Ms. Branden can produce that Rand ever made any "implicit demand" for total agreement consists of the so-called "purges" of certain close associates, those occasions when Rand terminated her association with a friend or student for ethical or ideological reasons. The Brandens, themselves, of course, fall into this category.

While it is true that most people will rarely, if ever, consciously terminate a relationship on the grounds of ethics or, more accurately, rarely label it in that fashion, people will frequently break up over insults, lies, infidelities, slights to one's dignity, and generally losing one's respect for the other person. Without the philosophically explicit concepts to which Rand related everything in her life, this is called "human nature," and it is not usually compared to Stalin's behavior, no matter how harshly it is verbalized.

Another chief difference was that Rand made her reasons clear, and left no doubt in those concerned as to the cause of the break. And it was a clear *break*. There was no cruel snubbing, no cowardly backstabbing, no secretive blacklisting. In this sense, Rand gave those she passionately disagreed with the respect of an explanation of her reasons and a complete context to her position, something quite uncommon.

Ayn Rand was a philosopher. And she was a philosopher who believed that philosophy mattered to life on earth—from art and politics to the most prosaic and everyday concerns. Rand strove for integrity, and so she applied her thinking to everything in her life.

Rand was, in particular, a moralist. Her philosophy, in large part, explicates a new system of ethics. In her writing and lecturing, and, certainly, in her private life, Rand was given to making moral judgments. The gusto with which Rand judged people was certainly no greater than many of the writers of our morally-relativistic age. For example, Norman Mailer's and Susan Sontag's condemnations of America in the wake of 9-11, because they are on the left of the spectrum, are not regarded as moralistic or intolerant. (34)

In any event, Rand, at least in print, always gave the specific reasons for her judgments, which could often, at first blush, appear harsh. Her clarity, though, gave every reader the option to accept or reject these judgments for themselves.

Moral judgment is a complex business with any code of ethics, and Ayn Rand had just articulated a revolutionary new code. Rand was acutely aware of the necessity to pass moral judgments only on the voluntary actions of those who actually had a choice. She realized that a person's emotions are outside of the person's direct volitional control, and they are, thus, outside of the province of moral condemnation or praise. In her books, Rand made it a moral principle to distinguish between "errors of knowledge" and "breaches of morality." (35) In principle, only conscious evil and willful evasion actually merited Rand's angry denunciation. And, in many cases, passing judgments can be a difficult matter, requiring information about an individual's particular context of knowledge and circumstances, as Rand repeatedly acknowledges.

A passage from Rand's private notes to herself eloquently expresses her approach to moral judgment in this respect, here in the context of her growing doubts about Nathaniel Branden:

> If I know that I cannot accept his present attitude, why don't *I* break with him now? *Because I do not understand his attitude.* Because I must first understand. (36)

For Rand, *understanding* was the *sine qua non* of ethical evaluation.

Rand also understood the absurdity of any attempt to force a mind. She argued that force and mind were opposites. Thinking, she believed, was a capacity only possessed by an individual. Each of us must think for ourselves and not yield our judgment to anyone or anything, even if, like Howard Roark, the hero of *The Fountainhead*, we must stand alone against the entire world.

Rand was articulating a new philosophy, one that was being continually misrepresented by the media in what both of the Brandens acknowledge were grossly unfair ways. In one of the great moments of journalistic mendacity, *The National Review*, for example, reviewing *Atlas Shrugged*, compared Rand's ideas to Nazism, when, of course, Rand was a passionate advocate of freedom and herself a refugee from totalitarianism. (37) Rand was justifiably concerned with giving the media any cause to be right, and she took great care with respect to her ideological endorsements.

There were unauthorized attempts to use the names of the heroes of Rand's novels in commercial projects, and a few of Rand's former students, most notably Murray Rothbard, began advocating anarchism as a political doctrine. Under such circumstances, it was hardly paranoid on Rand's part to explicitly announce who did and did not have her sanction, who could speak for Rand and who was only "a student of Objectivism," whatever resentments this might engender.

Such resentment is curious in itself. If Rand really was a monster— or if Rand was just wrong about something—then why resent Rand for calling the relationship off? Accept the fact, *vive la difference*, and move on. Even, perhaps, be grateful.

When Rand broke with someone, she usually did it privately, as with the Rothbard faction—the sole exception (apart from the Brandens) being the brief note in *The Objectivist* which informed readers that Edith Efron was no longer associated with Rand or Objectivism in 1967. Rand thereafter declined further comment. Only the case of the Brandens' would cause Rand to write an extensive piece, which we will consider in chapter four. But then, the Brandens, too, were not to be heard about again, apart from a brief "Legal Notice" regarding the later marketing of the Brandens' NBI courses.

It should be repeated that Rand could have significant personal or ideological differences with someone she had known and still praise that person's work. When she ended a relationship, it did not always end with any kind of formal "break." Ms. Branden herself says that John Chamberlain, Henry Hazlitt, William Mullendore and Albert Mannheimer are just some of those with whom Rand's deteriorating relationships are better described as "losing contact" but remaining on friendly terms with them. In all of these cases and others, if a writer was involved, Ms. Branden acknowledges that Rand continued to praise and recommend their books, whatever her past differences with these people had been, for the rest of her life.

Nathaniel Branden agrees that although Rand had become estranged from Isabel Paterson, with whom she had been quite close, this "in no way diminished Ayn's appreciation of [Paterson's] book." On the other hand,

Rand's disillusionment with Mannheimer, Branden concedes, did not "occasion a permanent rift." He points out that Rand could admire an artist's skill even while having profound objections to his philosophy—and even if she disliked the work, as in the case of Tolstoy and others. He observes that Rand, quite explicitly, did not seek ideological agreement from her business associates, such as her publisher. He points out that, even during the heyday of the "movement," Rand was quite capable of a friendship with composer and music critic Deems Taylor, "without requiring that he be a convert." (38)

As many others have observed, it was only with closer intellectual associates, those to whom Rand had given a higher ideological endorsement, that "official" breaks happened—and for perfectly understandable reasons.

The Brandens both assert that Rand was "constantly moralizing." (39) But the moral judgments which most concern the Brandens, and the ones, they say, that reveal the most about Rand, are the ones Rand passed on the people she knew best, starting with the Brandens themselves.

"Ayn was often warm and generous with her friends, generous with her concern, her time, and her attention. But when, in her view, a line had been crossed, when she saw an action as unjust to her, or as intellectually dishonest, or as morally wrong, she became an avenging angel and the relationship ended in a burst of rage." (40) Several people "crossed that line," among her students and later intellectual associates.

Professor Murray Rothbard, Edith Efron and Professor John Hospers all "suffered" such "excommunications" in the years while the Brandens were still with Rand. Mr. Branden, of course, tells us that he participated in each of these.

Then came the break with the Brandens themselves. Several others would follow them.

The proceeding years saw the emergence of the Libertarian Party, which Rand denounced from the outset for many reasons, including its lack of a philosophical base, indeed, its apparent contempt for philosophy as such, and its alliances with anarchists, foreign policy appeasers and various other questionable persons. (41) Many of Rand's former students and exponents now found a home there, completing their own journeys away from "orthodox Objectivism." Hospers became that Party's first presidential candidate and Rothbard its most ardent propagandist.

The Brandens, along with many others, believe that Rand was intolerant and "close-minded" because she denounced the Libertarian Party. To them this Party's domestic platform seems to be so close to Rand's own views that her failure to endorse it can only be construed as overly suspicious, perhaps even authoritarian. Rand's failure to endorse (or even read) the writings of former associates, and others, whose work appears related to Rand's own work—if not actually based on it—strikes Ms. Branden as "perhaps the clearest" evidence of Rand's "underlying despair and pessimism." (42)

But whoever Ms. Branden believes should have gotten it, Rand held her endorsement, her "sanction," dear.

Unlike Libertarians, Rand could not make common-cause with anarchists and those who would unilaterally disarm America. Nor could Rand continue to endorse the work of people she personally knew to be dishonest—like the Brandens. Nor would Rand cozy up to the close colleagues of such people. In all these ways Rand certainly had a "closed mind." She was an intellectual individualist, not a fellow traveler.

These "differences" are not so trivial as the critics suppose. They were certainly not trivial to Rand. But, rather than simply disagreeing with Rand over, say, the importance of systematic honesty in forming political and intellectual alliances, they accuse Rand of "intolerance."

Owing so much to her, Libertarian disappointment over Rand's failure to endorse their efforts is understandable. Predictable accusations that Rand was "closed-minded," "suspicious" and "authoritarian," from the same quarter nonetheless still seem childishly petulant (and rather ironic), coming from the party of so-called "individualists."

Precisely what kind of "individualist" is it who would feel compelled to swallow all of her principles and convictions in order to be considered "open minded"—or who must join the crowd in order to avoid the risk of being called "intolerant"?

Murray Rothbard (43), apart from being an anarchist, was clearly using ideas he got from Rand in scholarly articles without crediting his own source for the material, and he continued to do so throughout his career. (44)

In his own defense, Professor Rothbard would dig up an isolated point from some previous philosopher, usually very obscure, who had said something similar to Rand on a topic such as free will—but Rothbard's own first source for the point was invariably (and quite obviously) Rand.

From Rand's philosophical perspective, either his anarchism or his plagiarism would each and together seem to justify her break with Rothbard.

Professor John Hospers, according to the Brandens, was taken to task for certain "sarcastic" and "professorial" criticisms of Rand in an academic setting, although, once again, neither of the Brandens chooses to relate any of the specifics. (45) Although still unable to provide the relevant details, Hospers himself was more forthcoming, although hardly satisfying.

In a 1990 interview, Hospers said that he was merely being "challengingly exegetical if not openly critical of Rand," but he was still no more obliging than the Brandens had been about the content of that challenge. However, eight years later, Hospers admitted that it had included certain "mild criticisms" of Objectivism.

In that 1998 article, Hospers, a specialist in esthetics, recalled being "publicly" critical of Rand's view that every work of art conveys a "sense of life" (i.e., that art expresses some view of reality, a "metaphysics," even if that view is conveyed in purely emotional terms and held only subconsciously—even by the artist himself.) Apparently, Hospers had also maintained that "what we say about sense of life depends on the language we use" to convey it (i.e., that our understanding of metaphysics—reality—"depends on" language.)

Hospers conceded that these were topics which he had been discussing with Rand for some time—indeed, from their first meetings—and that he knew that such a "linguistic" approach to ideas was fundamentally abhorrent to Rand. Hospers also says that he remains mystified as to specifically what had triggered Rand's reaction. He tells us, "I never discovered what there was about my remarks that made her 'go ballistic.'" (46) We are, thus, still left almost entirely in the dark as to Rand's perspective on this event.

Hospers does not give us the smallest clue as to what Branden might have found "sarcastic."

The relevant details cannot be such a mystery to the Brandens, for it was Mr. Branden himself who proceeded to "read the riot act" to Hospers according to Branden's own account. (Of course, neither Hospers nor Branden provide us with any of the specifics of that "riot act"—which might at least have provided *some* insight into Rand's position at the time—Hospers does not even mention Branden's complaints.) Mr. Branden's total failure to provide any of the actual content of the issues involved in her break with Hospers is another glaring instance of Branden suppressing important evidence.

From the published portions of their correspondence, what is clear is that Ayn Rand and John Hospers had profound differences in the field of epistemology regarding all of its most basic questions. (47) With methodological approaches at such variance, it is not surprising that they eventually separated. This is especially predictable, given the enormous importance which Rand attached to epistemological issues. They are no less than the fundamental preconditions of further thought or discussion, in Rand's view.

Unfortunately, we may never know the specifics behind their break.

As for Efron, neither of the Brandens says they can even remember why they split with her at all. Branden merely relates his own distress at Efron's "anger and sarcasm"—but leaves it there. (48)

It seems that the clarity of the Brandens' memory depends upon how friendly they later were with the individuals involved, for while Ms. Branden later reconciled with Hospers and Efron, as Branden later did with Hospers, neither were ever associated with Rothbard again. But, from the historian's perspective, all the key evidence is entirely lacking in the Brandens' accounts of the Efron and Hospers cases. (Unfortunately, Rand's private journal entries throw no additional light on these issues, either.)

Hospers and the Brandens all stop at the observation that intellectual views could cause moral indignation on Rand's part, if she knew the person's context of knowledge, the context which informed the person's behavior. This seems to them overly moralistic on the face of it. But not to Rand.

According to Objectivism, believing something is an act of will—assenting to logic and evidence is a moral decision. Going "out of focus" or evading is all too common, but it can be volitionally corrected. An intellectual position can, therefore, be immoral if it is a product of such evasion. (49)

To determine in any particular case whether someone's belief in false ideas stems from a moral failure or not, of course, requires knowledge about the person involved. What does the person know—e.g., has a communist lived in a cave for the last century or is he aware of the slaughter of millions and the enslavement of millions more under the various experiments with communism? In common parlance, should the person "know better?"

There is no point continuing a conversation with someone who cannot or will not acknowledge reality—as opposed to someone who is willing but struggling.

With Rothbard, the case is clear: intellectual larceny and anarchism. With Hospers and Efron, the missing details, never offered, are obviously crucial.

As usual, the Brandens' failure to recollect or to be specific is telling. They both dismiss any actual reasons Rand might have had for such a break, and chalk it up to Rand's unfair and authoritarian nature, the same nature that "persecuted" them. They assume that the policy of breaking with someone in a permanent way is in itself somehow authoritarian. "My gosh, for purely *ideological* reasons?"

Of course, it is not, and the reasonableness of such an action depends upon all of the circumstances—the very circumstances left out of the Brandens' accounts. They do not let the reader judge for himself, and it is specifics that are essential for us to make any final judgment regarding Rand's alleged "implicit demands for absolute agreement," much less hypocrisy on Rand's part. We should not have to take the Brandens and their friends on faith.

As indicated, both Brandens seem to assume that such a "break" constitutes some form of persecution. Ayn Rand does not want to see you anymore, and, therefore, your rights have been violated. Rand may have had more to give and/or receive from these relationships, but she surely did not have to accept the exchange on any terms other than her own. And, according to Objectivism, this is not for anyone but her to determine.

Ms. Branden complains that "however much [Rand] previously had projected love and affection, one was always potentially on trial with her. At any time, an action, an emotion, a conviction that she deemed irrational, could result in an explosion of anger," and that one "teetered constantly on the edge of moral depravity." (50)

However overstated, though, such is the nature of human volition. No matter how good someone has been in the past, he is still capable of bad behavior. No matter how bad, he is still capable of a good deed. It is true that people get into habits, develop character, such that you can begin to predict someone you know well. But even then, you can be surprised.

And you can also be deceived.

Nathaniel Branden writes that when someone had done something to displease Rand, "it was as if all history and context vanished... She gave her unconditional acceptance to no one." In Ms. Branden's words, "Rand retroactively demoted" or "rewrote" the history of a friendship that had gone sour. (51) One can only wonder if Nathaniel Branden ever grasps the irony of his own *literal* rewrite of his former friends.

But when you discover that a friend has systematically deceived you—for example, when he misleads you into thinking that he is something he is not—a total reevaluation is in order. By the Brandens' accounts, it seems, Rand could never have been wrong about a person's character, as she surely was wrong about the Brandens. Any new or corrected opinion must be a dishonest, retroactive "demoting."

So, although the Brandens concede that Rand's original opinion of them was way too high, they also bitterly complain when Rand corrects that view. History has been rewritten, in other words, if I'm no longer John Galt.

In addition, Nathaniel Branden seems to have forgotten that "unconditional love" is a contradiction to the entire ethics of Objectivism. Branden's apparent rejection of so fundamental a point requires a better account than he gives of it.

Following the Brandens' departure, to which we will turn our attention in the next chapter, there were several more "breaks," among which were: Allan and Joan Blumenthal, Erika and Henry Mark Holzer, Philip and Kay Nolte Smith.

In many of these cases, it is clear that profound intellectual differences were emerging between Rand and the person involved, if it is not entirely clear that those differences were the proximate cause of the split with Rand.

For example, Henry Holzer, an attorney and legal scholar, has forthrightly endorsed the conservative "strict interpretation" of the U.S. Constitution, like Robert Bork. (52) In contrast, Rand endorsed a more expansive view of the unenumerated rights, such as abortion. (53) Allan

Blumenthal, a psychiatrist, has asserted that literally "all of Objectivism" was the product of Rand's efforts to cope with her own psychology. He thus appears to have endorsed a form of psychological determinism—entirely rejecting, it seems, the possibility of objective cognition, a rather fundamental tenet of Objectivism. (54)

Such differences, while they certainly would have justified Rand in breaking with these men—if only to defend and protect the integrity of Objectivism—do not appear to have been decisive. Indeed, it was not Rand who ended the relationship with either of them. (55) One could never have guessed it from reading Ms. Branden's book, but it was they who left Rand.

These can hardly be called "excommunications," but somehow they are still evidence, in Ms. Branden's view, of *Rand's* intolerance.

In lectures and interviews, both the Blumenthals and the Holzers have endorsed the portrait drawn by Ms. Branden of Rand the Authoritarian. This has not deterred the Blumenthals from their own policy of ostracizing Nathaniel Branden (who is Dr. Blumenthal's first cousin)—in 1996, they severed all association with an organization which had invited Branden to speak. And Professor Holzer, at least in the Sixties, is described by Branden as having a particularly zealous approach to Objectivism and "a style that made even Ayn appear tame by comparison." (56)

Intolerance, it seems, is everywhere.

As for the Smiths, their story is curiously absent from Ms. Branden's account.

In the 1970s the Smiths produced an off-Broadway revival of Rand's play, *Penthouse Legend.* When the play had been originally produced under the title, *The Night of January 16th*, about forty years previously, Rand had waged a difficult battle to keep her dialogue intact. This history was well known to the Smiths.

Presumably, they also knew that Rand had convinced Jack Warner himself to order Gary Cooper to deliver each word of Rand's screenplay for *The Fountainhead.* Rand had even threatened to dissociate herself from the production if *The Fountainhead* was not shot exactly as written.

Such a famous reputation might be counted on to provide caution to those who would take liberties with this author's text. Not so with Kay Nolte Smith and her husband, who, in an act exhibiting unbelievably reckless judgment, changed the dialogue in their production of *Penthouse Legend* without authorization from Rand. (57) In such an instance of systematic and personal betrayal, a break was at least understandably in order, simply on the basis of their callous indifference to Rand's personal history, if not to her artistic integrity.

While Ms. Branden relates the story of the play's production and the role of the Smiths on that production, we are told nothing about the actual causes of this break. We are told that Rand broke with them—"how typical of Ayn"—but we are not given the benefit of Rand's side.

This is simply one more thing Ms. Branden clearly knew but decided not to include in her account.

It should come as no surprise that this list of "former" Rand-associates, Rothbard, Efron, Hospers, the Blumenthals, the Holzers and the Smiths, while they may not have gotten along with one another afterwards, all helped to contribute to Ms. Branden's biography, as her "Acknowledgments" indicate.

Understandably, those who remained friendly with Rand did not make themselves available for Ms. Branden to interview.

All those with whom Rand had a "break" share precisely the same bias and precisely the same interest in presenting Rand as an "authoritarian" as do the Brandens. Ms. Branden's book appears to have been the receptacle for all the stories most likely to demonstrate Rand's alleged injustices to each of them individually and collectively, but none that might explain Rand's side.

Thus, the information sources used by Ms. Branden share a distinct perspective on Rand. Rather than mitigating the effect of the author's personal bias, their contributions merely magnify it.

While most of these individuals have themselves given talks or have been interviewed about their relationships with Rand, none of them appears able (or willing) to provide any facts or details that cannot also be found in Ms. Branden's biography, apart from two or three new anecdotes.

Even the missing anecdotes appear to have been weighed carefully for possible inclusion before being omitted. *The Passion of Ayn Rand* seems to represent their collective "best shot" at Rand.

Those anecdotes, however, are interesting, not in what they reveal about Rand so much as what they reveal about Rand's critics and the similarity of their perspectives.

Kay Nolte Smith relates that she once hosted a New Year's Eve Party to which Rand and her husband were invited. Smith decided that they should play the party game where the guests are challenged to identify their fellow guests from baby pictures. Smith recalls the exaggerated concern Rand expressed for the photo of her husband—it was apparently the only baby picture of him that she possessed.

According to Smith, Rand expressed a worry that the picture would be damaged in duplication, that Smith might be robbed, and even that Smith could be hit by a taxi crossing the street with it. Smith's conclusion: "[Rand] really was paranoid about practical reality." (58)

The familiar Brandenian diagnosis does not necessarily fit the evidence here, and perhaps this is why even Ms. Branden did not share the experience—or Mrs. Smith's conclusion—with her readers.

Such a diagnosis might be plausible within a pattern of similar behavior in other matters, but Rand's alleged alienation from "practical reality" is a rather forced explanation of Rand's fear for the photo. It is more easily explained by her intense romantic attachment to her husband, of whom she possessed only one irreplaceable baby photo. A different mentality might actually be touched by the story.

But, of course, any psychological "explanations" here are merely guesses. Mrs. Smith's guesses are guesses of the identical sort that the Brandens have published, even if they don't quite fit.

Edith Efron recalls that Rand once launched into "a thunderous tirade" during a door-to-door magazine pitch. "Do you expect me to finance them after the slime they've printed about me?" (59)

Rand had a definite set of negative epithets (whim-worshiper, etc.). The word "slime" is not a word Rand commonly used, indeed, used more than once or twice in her vast corpus of writings. This uncharacteristic language casts intrinsic doubt on the accuracy of Efron's account. Moreover, the story does not reveal the "insanity" that Efron suggests, even if it is credible. Many of us might have acted the same way.

As previously noted, Rand was being compared in those days to the Nazis by America's foremost conservative magazine, *The National Review*. Rand's overreaction may have had an undeserved effect on the magazine salesmen, but Rand certainly had an honest gripe against many magazines. In my view, door-to-door solicitors must surely be prepared for a lot worse.

The same distorting pettiness and ax-grinding which the Brandens have perfected to an art can be detected in Miss Efron's case, as well.

Does the sheer number of Rand's personal breaks in itself indicate that Rand was too judgmental? It is important to recall that Rand's breaks with her "non Objectivist" associates did not involve permanent "excommunications" nor the total rejection of their work. As previously indicated, only those who might themselves be confused with Rand or her ideas drew such denunciations. Even then, it was rare for Rand to publish comment about it.

The answer seems to be that many of Rand's radical ideas and methodology could not be easily grasped even by some of her brightest students, and that Rand strove hard not to be confused with those with whom she had developed philosophical disagreements.

By far the Brandens' strongest case, at least their best documented case, for Rand the Intellectual Tyrant—believe it or not—involves Rand's occasionally harsh answers during question-and-answer periods following a lecture. The Brandens not only provide examples, they provide different examples in some detail. Moreover, these events were witnessed by others. Readers of the Branden biographies will appreciate that this is a remarkably rare alignment of factors and, therefore, something worth examining.

Ms. Branden concedes: "In the first years of the lectures, Ayn's appearance at question periods was an event eagerly anticipated by the students. She was usually courteous, considerate, and painstaking in her response if a question seemed to her valid and intelligent; the students recognized the enormous compliment to them which her attitude projected, her assumption that they required and would respond only to a rational argument." (60)

And Mr. Branden, after acknowledging that Rand's presence was "enormously helpful" to the early success of NBI, reluctantly admits: "There were, of course, question-and-answer sessions when Ayn was warm, friendly, benevolent, charming. Once, when a student apologized for the naiveté of some question, she told him encouragingly, 'There are no stupid questions, only stupid answers.'" (61)

In Rand's view, there were, however, *dishonest* questions.

Mr. Branden says: "In the question periods following my lectures, she often became angry with any question she felt should not have been asked, perhaps because it had been answered in *Atlas Shrugged*, or perhaps because she believed that any honest person would figure it out for himself. Most of our students seemed to love her; but sometimes she could be terrifying." (62)

Ms. Branden continues: "But if [Rand] did not believe the question to be valid and intelligent, she was scathing in her denunciation; her anger, she would insist, was rationally justified moral indignation. A young man asked: 'How can you expect everyone to be rational and to arrive at correct philosophical conclusions, if they have not been taught rationality and have not been exposed to a philosophy of reason?' Ayn exploded, '*I* did it myself! No one taught *me* how to think!' The student later said to his friends, 'How can she have it both ways? How can she consider herself a great innovator, yet insist that everyone should arrive at the conclusions she did?'" (63)

It is possible that the questioner had not grasped that Rand's morality does not require the understanding of complex or innovative ideas in order for a person to be judged as being moral. Rand believed that everyone— not just intellectual giants—could absorb the virtues of rationality, and honesty, and a respect for the rights of others.

Of course, every great discoverer of knowledge, from Aristotle to Newton, had every right "to expect that everyone should arrive" at his improved conclusions, even though he was also a "great innovator"— he was right. It was the discoverer's contemporaries who should have demonstrated patience, not the innovators.

It is more likely that the questioner did understand all of these things and was simply balking at Rand's claim to have actually discovered a fully rational code of ethics. The hostility apparent in the follow-up question also suggests the hostility latent in the first inquiry. Did the questioner really expect to be answered?

Sensing this potential dishonesty in the question, Rand reacted with emotion.

As we have previously seen, Rand did not regard her achievement as resulting from her unusual intelligence, but her unusual honesty. And while Rand was convinced of her own historical significance, she did not go around calling herself "a great innovator." This modesty was precisely the cause of her indignation.

Ms. Branden herself believes that Rand's behavior in this regard is among the very gravest charges against her. She says that "[i]t was the question period... that gradually became the arena in which Ayn was especially bewildering and damaging to her students" as she would become, in Ms. Branden's words, "enraged by an innocent questioner" and "lash out furiously at the hapless questioner." (64)

If this was "the arena" in which Rand was especially damaging to her students, then the notion that Rand was an intellectual authoritarian seems quite farfetched.

And, while Rand's response was angry and sharp, the provided case is not an example of Rand being "enraged" or "lashing out" at "the hapless" at all. Ms. Branden cites the wife of Ludwig von Mises expressing her agreement that Rand was too harsh in her responses to students and tells us that Rand was gradually phased out of the question periods at NBI for this reason. (65) Rand did, however, continue to answer questions following lectures—both her own and Leonard Peikoff's—for several years to come.

Ms. Branden's tendency for exaggeration is made clear from her descriptions of other Rand appearances. A good example is Rand's first appearance on *The Phil Donahue Show*. Ms. Branden says:

> It was a disaster. A young woman in the audience asked a question which made it clear that she thought her former admiration for Rand's work had been an aberration of youth—and Ayn, offended and insulted, pounced angrily, shouting at the girl; a substantial part of the show was devoted to their exchange. (66)

Fortunately, the videotape of this appearance is still available through The Ayn Rand Bookstore.

The "girl" in the audience was clearly an adult. The "girl" started to ask a question about ITT's allegedly monopolistic control over "everything," but interrupted herself to say, "Fifteen years ago, I was impressed with your books, and I sort of thought your philosophy was proper. Today, I am more educated, and I find that if a company—"

Without "shouting," Rand interrupted, "This is what I don't answer."

To which Donahue replied, "Wait a minute, you haven't heard the question yet—"

Rand: "She's already estimated her position on my work—incidentally, displaying the quality of her brain. If today she says she is 'more educated' than..."

"Girl": "I am more educated than I was fifteen years ago, before I went to college, before I read the newspapers..."

Rand: "I am not interested in your biography, in the context..." (At which the audience audibly moaned.)

The "girl" then proceeded to assert that in a free market "ITT and Nazi Germany" are somehow able to do "whatever they damn well please" because "ITT owns everything."

When Donahue called upon the now silent Rand "to contribute," she offered to answer the question if only someone else would ask it, saying, "I will not answer anyone who is impolite." This elicited audience laughter.

Rand explained: "I do not sanction impoliteness, and I am not a victim of hippies." (More laughter.) "That's where it started, this dropping of politeness in manners."

Failing to see the insult implied by the question, Donahue took the position that Rand was equating any disagreement with impoliteness and proceeded to praise the questioner.

Going to commercial, Donahue cried out to Rand, "Don't be so sensitive!"

Rand called back, "I am going to be—I intend to be!"

In response to a later question asking how a woman "as intelligent" as Rand could be "so emotional in her approach," Rand's response was calm and insightful: "I did not come here to be judged. I came here to answer questions. A question asked in the following form: 'I used to agree with you, but now that I am more educated, I don't,' is an insult which I cannot sanction. I am not interested in the woman's history. She didn't have to begin it that way, and that's what I want to register my protest against."

In total, the exchange could not have accounted for 10% of the show's time.

The fact that Donahue was blind to the gratuitous *ad hominem* within a question about ITT is not surprising. It is less understandable how Rand's comment about "the quality" of the questioner's brain should be taken as insult but not the "more educated" crack. It is a strange "one-way" street on which Donahue directed traffic.

In any event, Rand did not "shout" at "a girl," but only refused to answer the condescending question of a grown woman. The appearance was not such a "disaster" as to prevent Rand from being invited back the following year. That appearance cannot boast even this type of minor "moment."

Even more to her credit—and despite the obvious temptations—Rand is not said to have ever exploded at Phil Donahue or any other interviewer.

There were occasions when Rand could regret the intensity of her responses, according to Mr. Branden:

> I recall an incident in which a man with a thick Hungarian accent began his question, "In his speech, Galt contends that—" He never got any further because Ayn exploded. "Galt does not *contend*," she shouted, "if you have read *Atlas Shrugged*, if you profess to be an admirer of mine, then you should know that Galt does not 'strive,' 'debate,' 'argue,' or 'contend.'" The man looked stricken. He pleaded, "But Miss Rand, all I meant was—" Ayn thundered back at him, "If you wish to speak to me, first learn to remember to whom and about what you are speaking!" Ayn was obsessed with clarity and precision... but I did not feel sympathy for the passion in this instance; I thought it totally misapplied. The man sunk into his chair, embarrassed and defeated... Later when we were alone, I pointed out that the man had a foreign accent and probably was not aware of the nuances of meaning contained in the word "contend." "I never thought of that," Ayn replied, with a look of astonished, childlike innocence.

Rand quickly added, however, that she could not promise that it would not happen again. (67)

Nor was this an isolated case, according to Branden. "Sometimes, Ayn would apologize for her outbursts." (68) In another context, Branden unwittingly sheds some light:

> [Rand] was convinced that ideas ruled the world and, consciously or subconsciously, ruled the life of every individual... Ideas *mattered* to her. No one could understand her who did not understand her conviction concerning the supreme importance of philosophy. If, for example, she heard a statement to the effect that man had no right to exist for his own sake, but exists only to serve society, or the state, or the race, or the planet—or if she heard a statement to the effect that reason is impotent to know reality, or that all value judgments are ultimately arbitrary, or that notions of good and evil are merely expressions of subjective emotion—she saw, concretely and specifically, the oceans of human blood that were spilled as a consequence of such beliefs—she saw Nazi Germany and Soviet Russia—and she reacted accordingly. (69)

It is revealing that this observation is made in the context of observing that this "conviction concerning the importance of ideas could lend [Rand] enormous patience in intellectual discussions." (70)

Rand saw the error of moral relativism—and the moral cowardice that it implies. She realized that America's resolve and determination were sapped by such ideas. When anthropologists and historians come to a stage where they can no longer criticize the Aztec practice of human sacrifice, Rand knew something fatal had gone wrong.

As a prophylactic, Rand threw every ounce of her justifiable "intolerance"—every sincere ethical judgment she could muster—into the promiscuously "tolerant" culture she perceived around her.

The Brandens' real problem with Rand is her moral (they would say "moralistic") perspective. Just as Nathaniel Branden prefers "beneficial" and "harmful" to "good" and "bad" these days, so he reveals his distaste for most of Rand's ethical judgments.

Branden takes issue with Rand's approach in the "Introduction" to *The Virtue of Selfishness*. Rand states that she had been asked why she used the word "selfish" to denote virtue when many people might be alienated by it. "For the reason that makes you afraid of it," was her response. (71)

Branden asks, "What is accomplished by sounding a note of abusiveness on the first page?" (72)

For anyone familiar with Rand's work, the answer is so apparent that Branden can only be intentionally omitting it. Rand is asking her readers for considerable moral courage to question the moral consensus of their age. She is asking them to join her in taking a position that has been stigmatized as evil itself.

And, if there is no word in the English language for the rational, principled pursuit of one's actual long-term interests, then isn't something being insidiously defined out of existence in the process? To anyone but the most spineless, Rand's approach can only be appreciated for its clarity.

Branden says this is merely a "mild version" of the same attitude Rand brought to the question periods. (73) What he and his former wife actually object to is the field of ethics, the subject about which one might expect them to be most uncomfortable—given the revelations to come.

Leonard Peikoff has conceded that Rand's anger was sometimes "not justified," and Peikoff admits that he was sometimes angered by this himself. However, he adds: "...I never saw her hold an unadmitted grudge. Her anger never festered unexpressed or turned into devious, brooding hatred. It was an immediate, open storm of indignant protest—then it was over. In this respect, she was the easiest person in the world to know and to deal with." (74)

And Charles Sures has said, "[Rand's] expressions of anger were not the outbursts of someone run by wild and uncontrolled emotions. She didn't use anger to intimidate people, as bullies do. When she got angry it was precisely because she was a thinker and an evaluator who was certain of her convictions."

Sures agrees with Peikoff that Rand did not "simmer and stew"—she "came to an immediate boil"—and that "the anger didn't last. It was over almost as soon as it began." (75)

When asked about Rand's anger, Mary Ann Sures has said:

> One of the things I miss most [about Rand] is what we've been talking about—her anger and righteous

indignation, and what it came from. I miss knowing that there is someone in the world who always speaks out, unequivocally, against irrationality and injustice, and who not only denounces evil but who defends the good. She was mankind's intellectual guardian, a soldier in the battle of ideas. Her banner was always flying high. When she died, someone made the following comment: now anger has gone out of the world. And I thought, it's true, and it's the world's loss, and mine.

To which Charles added, "And mine." (76)

It should also come as no surprise that nearly all of those who do not miss Rand's anger are now also admirers of Ms. Branden's biography, for Ms. Branden's tale of Rand the Repressive, Moralizing Monster is one to which all of these people can comfortably repair.

But, precisely to the extent that they have endorsed Ms. Branden's deeply flawed account, they are subject to an identical critique of their own distorted objectivity.

Pleasant or unpleasant, according to Objectivism, it is morally necessary to make appropriate ethical judgments of others. If this is what the Brandens and their friends now dispute, then they no longer believe in the basics of Rand's ethics and should say so far more plainly, rather than accuse Rand of hypocrisy.

It is the Brandens' responsibility as Rand biographers to provide us with all the significant examples of Rand's unjust or inappropriate moral assessments. The examples must include enough information for their readers to pass their own judgment. Otherwise, we have nothing on which to base our agreement or disagreement, except the Brandens' credibility and judgment—which we have seen, and will continue to see, is simply too suspect to provide a credible basis.

We have seen that each of the Brandens will distort and exaggerate the evidence, and that they have repeatedly suppressed vital evidence, and even that they will employ creativity in recollecting it. Both exhibit internal confusions and numerous self-contradictions. The only consistencies are the passionate biases that emanate from their own personal experiences. These factors all combine to render their biographical efforts useless to the serious historian.

As alleged "victims" of Rand's "moralism," they are hardly in a position to demand that we rely only upon their credibility and judgment when it comes to that alleged "moralism." Yet, this is precisely what they do demand, and precisely what many of Rand's critics have done.

One thing is certain, Ayn Rand is not for the morally squeamish. For those of us who believe that it is distortion not to identify values along with facts—those of us who get bored with so-called "serious" academic works on philosophy and politics—Rand is a welcome relief. When Rand complains of America's having "to apologize to any naked savage anywhere on the globe," and you—like Branden—are "bothered," then Rand is not for you.

Rand herself was a woman of certainty and absolute convictions, and she was a moralist. Rand was capable of fierce denunciations and even misplaced anger. However, she cannot, from the evidence provided by her detractors, be regarded as an intellectual tyrant.

IV. The Exploiters and the Exploited

Nathaniel Branden's memoir is not, strictly speaking, a biography of Rand, and it consistently maintains a first-person narrative of events. As Mr. Branden claims, he lived them. Nevertheless, there are psychological and moral implications drawn and half-drawn about Rand throughout his book, as we have already seen.

While suggesting that his memoirs are as much an exercise in self-examination as they are an exploration of Rand herself, a confession of youthful errors and psychological confusions, Branden says that he knew the writing of his book would involve revealing many unpleasant truths about himself. Branden at one point calls his own behavior "ludicrous and unconscionable," and he admits to considerable responsibility for the sequence of events, misery and trauma leading up to the break, if not the consequence itself. (1)

However, Mr. Branden's new and overt revelations are largely confined to personal matters. For example, in contrast to Ms. Branden's portrait of her own personal victimization, Branden reveals the multiple, undisclosed affairs Ms. Branden had during the early years of their relationship. He also reveals himself to have been the aggressor in his sexual relationship with Rand.

His motive for the first correction is simple self-defense. Branden's overheated response to the publication by Leonard Peikoff of Rand's private journals—and, perhaps, a fear of what her other journals might contain—points to a potentially motivating factor in his *mea culpa* in the second instance.

Since 1968, he and Ms. Branden have steadfastly maintained that Rand's accusations of financial and intellectual exploitation were all misleading fabrications designed to hide the real cause of her falling-out with the Brandens—the end of Rand's affair with Mr. Branden. In his memoir, Branden calls Rand's statement regarding their break no less than "libelous." (2)

As will now be seen, they do not begin to address the full scope of their own manipulation and exploitation of Rand outside of their personal relationship with her. Nor do they acknowledge the grossly misleading nature of their own statements about the break from 1968 onwards. We shall, in fact, see that it was they, not Rand, who have repeatedly misrepresented the nature of the events leading up to their break.

Rand's break with the Brandens was as complicated as their relationship had been. Her interaction with Nathaniel Branden had not been exclusively romantic. According to the Brandens, it was first (and foremost) an intellectual relationship. It became a professional and business partnership, as well.

The Brandens tell us that their relationship with Rand began in 1950 with long, philosophical conversations and hours of intellectual talks on the phone. It was this intellectual affinity which fueled their later closeness.

Mr. Branden parlayed his personal and intellectual relationship with Rand—with the help of Rand's highest endorsement—into his livelihood. The Brandens' stated devotion to Rand and her ideas, in their minds, made this the natural next step.

Nathaniel Branden created a lecture organization in order to provide an explicit and systematic presentation of Rand's philosophy to her growing number of students. These students were overflowing with philosophical questions in the wake of the publication of *Atlas Shrugged* in 1957. Though seasoned businessmen had scoffed at the idea that ideas could sell, the lectures proved to be an instant success, and soon students were paying to listen to taped lectures on philosophy, psychology and economics in dozens of cities across the continent.

A couple of years later, a newsletter—to be replaced by a magazine— was founded by Branden and Rand to publish Rand's speeches and essays, as well as the essays of Rand's students, including the Brandens', applying Objectivism to the questions of the day and the Questions of the Ages.

These activities soon became the Brandens' full-time employment.

Rand's novels were really the only advertisement NBI ever needed. While the lectures at NBI—including those of Leonard Peikoff and Alan

Greenspan—provided important applications and amplifications of Rand's ideas, it was her novels which recruited the students for NBI, not vice versa.

The same must be said of *The Objectivist*, which gave Branden and other young students of Objectivism a publishing outlet which they needed far more than Rand did at the time.

Whatever the quality of the work done at NBI, it was Rand who had pulled the students through the door in the first place—every time. If, in turn, NBI contributed to the success of Rand's books, the effect was comparatively negligible.

Rand's novels, her philosophy and even her generous support turned Objectivism for them into a cottage industry which the Brandens would profit from for almost ten years.

In 1962, the Brandens' first book, *Who Is Ayn Rand?*, was published. Nathaniel Branden contributed essays on the literary, philosophical, and psychological achievements of Rand—calling them uniformly "revolutionary." Ms. Branden contributed a biographical essay on Rand.

Both have since recanted this work as one-sided and incomplete.

In order to prepare the biographical essay in *Who Is Ayn Rand?*, the Brandens taped their extensive interviews with Rand about her life. Only a portion of this material was used in that sketch, but the Brandens both tell us that they used additional material from these interviews for *Judgment Day* and *The Passion of Ayn Rand*.

As Rand's largest collection of autobiographical statements, these interviews surely represent the single best source of biographical material on Ayn Rand.

The problem is that the Brandens do not clearly distinguish the material sourced directly from these interviews and material which has its origins in their own memory or imagination or that of others. As we have seen, their tendency to suppress evidence and contradict themselves whenever it is convenient makes it nearly impossible to rely on them without the interview material itself as corroborating evidence. So their nebulous citing of these interviews as a bolstering reference is effectively worthless, and further troubling.

It is to be hoped that recordings of these interviews, now in the possession of the Ayn Rand Archive, will continue to be available for use by scholars. It would be a pity if Rand biography developed into a debate about which parts of the Branden books are reliably sourced in the Rand interviews and which are not—as New Testament scholars employ "form-criticism" and other methods in an effort to distinguish the "true" words of Jesus. As with the quest for the historical Jesus, such speculation is necessarily a fruitless enterprise. (3)

Perhaps it was the existence of this singularly glowing biography of Ayn Rand with her name on it which helped to motivate Ms. Branden to write an extensive, and much more negative, biography of her. Like Mr. Branden, she, too, has no problem literally rewriting this past while accusing Rand of doing the same. Ms. Branden does not appear to sense any irony in this, either.

For these reasons, one must acknowledge that accurate biographical material may well be contained in these books and, at the same time, that these books are historically unreliable.

If these books present a dubious account of Rand herself, they are even less likely to be accurate accounts of the events in which these authors themselves played important roles and during periods for which Rand herself cannot have been their source. This is most acutely so in their accounts of their falling out with Rand.

When Rand explained the reasons for her break with the Brandens in "To Whom It May Concern," the Brandens quickly responded with "In Answer to Ayn Rand," which they had circulated using the NBI and *The Objectivist* mailing lists.

As previously indicated, the Brandens accused Rand of manufacturing a series of false accusations in order to slander them and avoid the real issue—Rand's desire for an affair with Mr. Branden, a desire which could not be reciprocated. (4)

With the benefit of the Brandens' more recent books, however, we can now see that Rand's summary had been the accurate if discreetly incomplete one and that the Brandens' 1968 account was the dishonest version relying on direct personal slander.

The magician's trick works because the audience has been misdirected. The flash and the smoke conceal Branden's sleight of hand. This is the recurring method of operation: the accusation of dishonesty is dishonesty disguising itself as its opposite. This is the pattern to be repeated again and again by Mr. Branden. The very offense he reveals committing in his account is the same offense he simultaneously alleges against Rand. Often, the allegation *itself* commits the offense that he alleges.

Mr. Branden's dishonesty, it will be seen, has not abated in the least since his ex-wife finally told "the truth" to Rand in 1968—and it goes far beyond matters of the heart.

Although Nathaniel Branden is not an unbiased witness to the events he recounts, taking his version of them at face value can be revealing. The tale Branden weaves is highly distorted—filtered through a now-familiar pattern of self-serving omissions and exaggerations—but Branden cannot help but also reveal his systematic exploitation of Rand on every level: professional, intellectual and, finally, personal.

Such exploitation is precisely what Rand had suggested was the basis of her separation from Branden in 1968, and yet the accuracy of Rand's 1968 account of the break is still disputed by both of the Brandens.

Thus, it is to the 1968 statements that we must now turn our attention.

Rand's endorsement of the Brandens had been a high one. Their closeness to Rand had given them a status within a subculture largely of their own creation which was equally high. Rand's endorsement had made them sought-after teachers and Mr. Branden a sought-after therapist. It is clear that Rand did her utmost to remove that endorsement. She begins:

> This is to inform my readers and all those interested in Objectivism that Nathaniel Branden and Barbara Branden are no longer associated with me or with my philosophy.

> I have permanently broken all personal, professional and business association with them, and have withdrawn from them the permission to use my name in connection with their commercial, professional, intellectual and other activities.

> I hereby withdraw my endorsement of them and their
> future works and activities. I repudiate both of them,
> totally and permanently, as spokesmen for me or for
> Objectivism.

Rand explains that it involved her exploitation at their hands and
their growing departure from the principles of Objectivism. Rand tells us:

> For the past three years, I have observed a disturbing change
> in Nathaniel Branden's intellectual attitude. It seemed
> to indicate his gradual departure from the principles of
> Objectivism, a tendency toward non-intellectual concerns,
> a lessening of interest in philosophical issues and in the
> Objectivist movement as such.

Rand says that "[t]he clearest indication of this trend was Mr.
Branden's venture into the theater with his project to produce Barbara
Branden's stage adaptation of *The Fountainhead.*"

Despite Rand's alleged capacity to rewrite the virtues of former friends
out of existence following a break, Rand says that "Barbara Branden... had
written a good adaptation..."

Rand relates her concern, however, that "this project seemed to
become Mr. Branden's central concern, taking up a major portion of his
time, causing him to neglect his intellectual and business commitments.
His attitude... can best be described as authority flaunting, unserious and,
at times, undignified."

Rand noted that Mr. Branden had begun to "default" on his
responsibilities, citing as two examples, "the growing and lengthening
delays in the writing of his articles for the magazine (I have at times been
late with my own articles, but not chronically nor to such an extent) [and]
his failure to rewrite the 'Basic Principles of Objectivism' course for his
own organization, Nathaniel Branden Institute."

With regard to *The Objectivist*, we are told, "We agreed that we would
write an equal number of articles and receive an equal salary." Rand asks
readers to review recent issues and that they would find that she was writing
an ever larger share of the articles.

This disturbing trend had been observable for at least three years, Rand says.

> During the past three years, my personal relationship with Mr. Branden was deteriorating in a puzzling manner: it was turning into a series of his constant demands on my time, constant pleas for advice, for help with his writing, for long discussions of his personal, philosophical and psychological problems.

Rand depicts a troubled man whom she was doing her best to help. Until, that is, she began to detect hypocrisy and dishonesty.

> I was shocked to discover that he was consistently failing to apply to his own personal life and conduct, not only the fundamental philosophical principles of Objectivism, but also the psychological principles he himself had enunciated and had written and lectured about... he admitted that in many respects he was acting on the basis of unidentified feelings.

And then, Rand writes, Branden "presented me with a written statement" so "offensive" to Rand that she says she broke her "personal" association with Branden, if not her professional one. (In Part II, we will see, in some detail, the exact nature of the deceptions revealed by Branden in that paper.)

Nonetheless, Rand tells us that she was "about to acquiesce" in Branden's plans to resume lecturing, when Barbara Branden "suddenly confessed that Mr. Branden had been concealing from me certain ugly actions and irrational behavior in his private life, which were grossly contradictory to Objectivist morality and which she had known about for two years."

Following the "shock" of discovering him capable of "conscious deception," Rand began inquiring about the finances of *The Objectivist* and was then informed that Mr. Branden had arranged for NBI to borrow "almost the entire cash reserves" of *The Objectivist* in order to meet NBI's rent at the Empire State Building. Rand had found out about the loan after the fact; occasional loans of this sort had been taken out before, but the unprecedented amount of the loan was not revealed to her until the time of her break with Branden.

Rand writes:

> The realization that Mr. Branden was exploiting me intellectually and professionally had been bad enough; that he should also attempt to exploit me financially was grotesquely shocking.

As for Ms. Branden, her case, said Rand, was "far less complex and much more obvious." Since it was she who had exposed Mr. Branden, at first, Rand says that she "gave her credit" for her belated honesty since Ms. Branden, too, had "seemed to be a victim of Mr. Branden's policies."

Rand notes that Mr. Branden apologized to the staff of NBI at its closing, admitting to them that "Miss Rand had given him a blank check on the use of her name and he had defaulted on his responsibility."

Rand says that she then gave serious consideration to the idea of Ms. Branden running a lecture organization. Rand says that she was exceedingly reluctant because she was "not a teacher by profession and personal inclination" and that she never wanted to be the leader of "an organized movement." Despite this, she gave Ms. Branden a hearing. "The plan did not offer any relevant factual material, but a projection (by unspecified method) of future profits to be earned... a business arrangement of so questionable a nature that I rejected it at once..."

It was the very next day that Rand heard that Ms. Branden had begun "to utter veiled threats and undefined accusations against me." At her attorney's advice, Rand authorized him to invite Ms. Branden to a meeting so that they could discuss the accusations she was making. Ms. Branden never came and Rand never saw her again.

Rand noted that the change in Ms. Branden's attitude occurred immediately after the rejection of her business plan by Rand, who then asks the reader to "draw your conclusions about the cause and motive" of her behavior.

Rand concedes having made an "error of knowledge" with respect to her judgment of the Brandens, but suggested that the consequences of such an error "are never as hard to bear" as those of a breach of morality.

There is no question that Rand was not telling her readers everything. But it was also clear that this was intentional. Perhaps Rand was protecting the innocent, and much could rationally be considered not the public's business, but Rand had certainly said enough to make clear that she had felt "exploited" by them.

In response, Nathaniel Branden begins:

> The charges and accusations stated by Miss Rand are, in the overwhelming majority of cases, either false or so misleading as to be false by implication. It is very unfortunate that Miss Rand chose to make a tragic, highly personal conflict between us the occasion of a public scandal, through the publication of her article; she has left me no choice but to make my response equally public.

As an example of his reciprocating candidness, he states that the theater project "never took up more than a small portion of my time." Branden even takes issue with the suggestion "that I was obliged to justify [to her] the disposition of my time and energies..."

Branden claims that "I never committed myself to writing an article per issue, nor would I have agreed to make such a commitment." True, he had not begun the "total" rewrite of his course on Objectivism—which he planned to do "in 1969"—but he had been updating it all the time, he claims.

Branden notes what he calls Rand's "astonishing lack of grace" in accusing him of professional exploitation in view of the enormous contribution his efforts made to Rand's "career and the spread of her ideas." The idea of Rand riding on *his* coattails is too rich an irony for serious comment.

He admits that Rand had "expressed apprehension" at the size of the Empire State Building lease and that NBI "required loans from time to time" from *The Objectivist* and even concedes that the loan in question was much larger than normal. He does not dispute that Rand found out about the loan after the fact, and he does not dispute Rand's account of when she found out the exact amount of the loan. Branden merely says that he had done similar things in the past and that only part of the loan was for the rent. He says that Rand was wrong: the amount transferred was $22,500, not $25,000.

He denies that there was any "stipulation" between him and Rand (business partners in *The Objectivist*) that all decisions were to be "unanimous," presumably implying that he was authorized to act entirely on his own. Branden then notes that he voluntarily signed over his interest in *The Objectivist* to Rand for absolutely nothing in return and that he would have been "entirely within my legal rights" to have demanded that *The Objectivist* be closed. Rand's lawyers threatened him with a full investigation of his financial dealings and even a lawsuit to do so if he did not "sign immediately." This made Mr. Branden feel "moral revulsion," presumably his first pang of it thus far in his dealings with Rand.

Branden claims Rand was simply lying when she wrote that their relationship had deteriorated into "long discussions" of his "psychological problems" and "pleas for advice." (In Part II, we will see that Rand was acting in almost an official capacity as his therapist.) He tells us that it was Rand who prolonged phone calls and it was Rand who was "constantly volunteer[ing] personal advice." While it is true that Rand had been "of personal help" to him in the past, Branden says that he had helped her, too, during what he describes as Rand's two-year post-*Atlas Shrugged* depression.

As Branden describes it, he "found [him]self" in an "agonizing personal dilemma which [he] saw no way to resolve." He admits that he withheld "certain information about [his] personal life," specifically his relationship with a young woman with whom he was in love. But he gives no suggestion why this should be of any concern to Rand.

The statement to which Rand had referred as "irrational" and "offensive" had been, according to Branden, "a tortured, awkward, excruciatingly embarrassed attempt" to make clear to Rand why he felt that the age distance between them "constituted an insuperable barrier, for me, to a romantic relationship."

Notice how Branden powerfully implies that he would never, could never, have such a relationship with Rand, and recall that Branden is here in the act of detailing Rand's "astonishing lack of grace." (Branden, of course, had an affair with Rand lasting almost fourteen years of their eighteen-year relationship together.)

Branden also writes that Rand was lying when she suggests that her discovery of Mr. Branden's "falsehood" was the final cause of her break with Branden. In fact, writes Branden, the decision had actually been made a month earlier when Rand learned of Branden's "present feelings" but before she learned of any deception.

As we shall see, the Brandens' later statements contradict this and, indeed, many other of their assertions in 1968, and the comparison of the Brandens' rolling admissions indicates not only how right Rand had been at the time, but also the nature of the Brandens' continuing dishonesty on these topics.

Rand, of course, was not herself privy to Branden's memoir, nor did she make further comment on Branden after "To Whom It May Concern" was published in 1968. There, Rand tells us that she "observed a disturbing change in Nathaniel Branden's intellectual attitude," which seemed to "indicate his gradual departure from the principles of Objectivism." Rand says that this became increasingly clear to her during Branden's attempt to produce a stage version of *The Fountainhead*.

In his "Answer to Ayn Rand," Branden denied and ridiculed Rand's charge of "intellectual drift."

In retrospect, Rand appears to have been quite perceptive, for, in subsequent interviews and memoirs, Branden would himself chronicle what amounted to much more than mere "intellectual drift."

In *Judgment Day*, Branden claims that even during his earliest conversations with Rand he felt "pushed along a particular path faster than I would have moved at my own speed." (5)

Branden does not report ever expressing this feeling to Rand or ever asking for clarification from Rand. Nor does Branden specify the issues about which he felt "pushed." In his typically vague fashion, Branden just "felt pushed."

Though he never specifies the issues involved at this stage, Branden's discomfort was apparently intense. Branden reports that for "all of us" around Rand, "there was terrible violence done to our emotional life—the repression or suppression of any feeling that clashed with what an ideal Objectivist was supposed to experience, be it a sexual impulse, an artistic preference..." (6)

Branden is obviously not qualified to speak for everyone else, but taking his self-report at face value, Branden was engaged in a pretty comprehensive deception of both himself and Rand—given the "terrible violence" that he admits he was doing to his own "emotional life." His use of the word "suppression"—as opposed to "repression"—suggests that it was, at least in part, conscious deception.

Here, Branden's story confronts a certain problem: to the extent that he held views contrary to Rand's during his association with her, he was deceiving and exploiting her professionally, and such differences may partially account for his break with Rand—as Rand had said. And yet, to the extent that Branden claims to have come to these differences only after their separation, he really does look like a socially conditioned robot—the true "social metaphysician" he identified as one whose opinions will vary depending upon who his friends happen to be.

To a certain extent, Branden does his best to have it both ways.

In what looks like a naked attempt to avert the criticism of intellectual hypocrisy, Branden's version of events usually does suggest that only after his break with Rand in 1968 did he begin to have significant disagreements with her ideas, or that he was only dimly aware of these differences—perhaps psychologically repressing them—until after the break.

Branden asserts at one point that the entire situation had put him into a "trance." (7)

Branden also suggests that the very success of NBI and *The Objectivist* had contributed to an "emotional disorientation." (8)

"Increasingly," Branden tells us, "I saw to what extent my personality had become distorted through [my] association [with Rand]." And later he says, "*Today* I am convinced there are errors in [Rand's] vision, elements that need to be changed, eliminated, modified, added or amplified..." (9)

Nevertheless, before his break with Rand, intellectual differences were emerging of such scope that even Branden must relate them to us. There can be no doubt Branden's interests were straying from Objectivism. Branden reports that during one conversation with Rand she openly wondered, "hypnosis, Koestler—what next? Extrasensory perception?" (In a speech made shortly after her death, Branden would, indeed, admonish Rand for being "closed minded" on the topics of ESP and telepathy, a criticism he fails to repeat in either version of his memoir.) (10)

Although Branden was the one "excommunicated," his "dissatisfaction" with Objectivists, he told *Reason* magazine in 1971, was "a gradual thing"—a mere three years after his break with Rand. (11)

In that interview, Branden also admits that "[t]here are certain touches in her novels that bother me and *I guess always bothered me*, but in the past I did not pause to consider them, I did not think about them." (12)

For example, Branden told *Reason* that the character of Dominique in *The Fountainhead* is "completely unreal" as a "psychological portrait."

In *Atlas Shrugged*, Galt's refusal to inform Rearden that Dagny is not dead for a month, claims Branden, is "morally and psychologically... criminal."

Branden also maintained that the character of Eddie Willers—to whom he once compared his secret, new mistress—is "very neurotic and pathetic." (13)

These are hardly "touches."

As Objectivism's leading advocate outside of Rand herself at the time, it must have occurred to him that it was his professional responsibility to mention such sharp differences to Rand herself. But, of course, that would have been biting the hand that was feeding him.

Branden asks us to believe that he largely repressed his true opinion that Rand's protagonists were "unreal," "morally criminal," and "very pathetic" during all of his eighteen years with Rand, and that it all became suddenly clear to him within three years of his break with her. Improbable, at best.

If Ms. Branden deceptively smiled and nodded in discussions of her artistic preferences, Mr. Branden did so in discussions of Rand's work itself.

When the *Reason* interviewer asserts that Rand had claimed that "one must accept all of [Objectivism's] tenets or none of them," Branden agrees and calls this "pretentious" and "grandiose nonsense." (14)

As usual, the only "nonsense" here turns out to be that Rand ever said such a thing; she did not.

Of course, Branden was very familiar with what Rand had actually said, which inferred a similar but importantly different meaning.

In his lectures on epistemology at NBI, Nathaniel Branden had spoken extensively about the importance of comprehensive integration to certainty itself, the vital role of system-building in philosophy, the necessity of attending to the hierarchical structure of knowledge, and the fundamentality of philosophical knowledge.

Indeed, Branden had once proclaimed that Rand's powerful insight could, perhaps, best be seen in the manner in which she had integrated her various philosophical positions. (15)

None of this could he bring himself to mention to *Reason* in 1971.

All of this was apparently already "grandiose nonsense."

So, as early as 1971, Branden provides evidence that he had been involved in a widespread conscious deception of Rand about the state of his mind, not just his heart.

Branden suggests that—from the beginning—his relationship with Rand to a significant extent was self-denial maintained by self-deception. "In one sense," he conceded to *Reason*, "I can say I was never really happy [among Objectivists]." And about Rand herself, Branden says that it was "hard" for him to "face the fact" that he "did not really like her in important respects." (16)

In his memoirs, Branden supplies additional evidence of the very intellectual drift which Rand had observed—and that this drift involved far more than he had told *Reason*.

Branden reports in *Judgment Day* that throughout his relationship with Rand he became increasingly concerned that she seemed "closed" to certain new interests of his. He could not understand why Rand seemed nonplused by the ideas of Arthur Koestler. It bothered him that Rand did not seem more than mildly interested in hypnosis or the physiological aspects of depression. He tried to explain "non-Darwinian" theories of evolution and, again, Rand seemed insufficiently interested to him. (17)

Still more significant, Branden tells us that he was, from the first, "uncomfortable" (19) with the first sentences of Rand's "Introduction" to *The Virtue of Selfishness*, which was published in 1964 and which contains some of her most important essays. Branden suggests that Rand's alleged "moralism" was already making him "uncomfortable" in 1964.

When Rand broke with John Hospers in 1962, Branden relates that he felt "thoroughly miserable" having to "read [Hospers] the riot act"; (18) allegedly, Branden had disagreed with Rand over the severity of her reaction to Hospers' unspecified criticisms—while never breathing a word to Rand or Hospers about such disagreement until after his break with Rand.

Such differences might be regarded as marginal if they were with someone else, but to be the silently held opinions of Rand's intellectual heir suggests a widespread intellectual hypocrisy on Branden's part.

Cumulatively, these differences amounted to at least a drift—if not an active steering—away from Rand and her ideas, but the biggest indication of Branden's admittedly increasing intellectual separation from Rand rested, apparently, in his own field of psychology.

In *Who Is Ayn Rand?*, Branden credits Rand with profound insight into human psychology. Many of his essays in *The Objectivist Newsletter* and in *The Objectivist* do as well. Branden explained how Objectivism provides a means of reconciling the alleged conflict between morality and psychology, how it makes possible an objective standard of mental health, how its insights into the nature of volition, the cognitive causes of emotion and the central importance of self-esteem, productive work and romantic love are nothing short of revolutionary —and how they constitute the necessary basis of any future science of psychology.

This is strong praise, indeed, for Rand was by profession a novelist, screenwriter, and non-academic philosopher. It should be remembered that Rand had no academic or professional training in psychology. Branden himself did not suggest that Rand had presented an entire psychological theory, only that the heroes in her novels are models of certain aspects of mental health and that her philosophy provided fundamental insights into his own field.

In the *Reason* interview Branden recants his praise, saying that Rand did not offer much psychological insight at all:

> I did not realize this, or did not realize it fully, during the years of our association, but Miss Rand is *very ignorant* of human psychology. On certain occasions she admitted that to me. It was not unusual for her to declare,

"Nathan, I don't really understand anything about human psychology." But I never realized the full implications of what she was acknowledging. In *Who Is Ayn Rand?*, I compliment her psychological acumen. I was wrong to do so. That was my own naïveté or blindness. I think Miss Rand's lack of psychological understanding is a great liability to her... (20)

Although Branden claimed in 1971 that he did not "fully" realize Rand's weakness here until after the split, in *Judgment Day*, published eighteen years later, he admits that his essay on psychology in *Who Is Ayn Rand?* was "by far the briefest, since I did not regard psychology as Rand's strong point, and my compliments felt a bit stretched to me *even then*." (21)

Branden did not tell *Reason* what will become obvious in Part II, that for many years—up to the last days of his relationship with her—he quite literally used Rand as his personal psychotherapist.

Branden does not claim to have abandoned reason, volition or self-esteem as central tenets of his psychological theories. His substantive differences with Rand in 1971 appear to be over issues such as to what extent conscious and subconscious processes can be "kept separate." (22) (The invitation to psychologize shall be duly declined.)

These issues would hardly seem to a casual observer to be reasons to retract the whole of the earlier praise, which had comprehensive and fundamental philosophical gravity. What is interesting—apart from his obvious squirming over exactly when these differences became apparent to him—is the incredible contrast: In print, he goes from believing in a brilliantly insightful and revolutionary Rand in 1962 to having no intellectual disparity with Rand in 1968 to branding Rand painfully blind by 1971.

Even taking Branden's assertions at face value, his intellectual differences with Rand were widespread and growing as early as 1962, ranging from psychological theory to the characters and plots in her novels to her dealings with other intellectuals—and he never mentioned any of these things to Rand.

Nonetheless, for several more years Branden continued in his role as Objectivism's foremost champion.

Branden never mentioned to Rand that he felt his praise of her psychological insights "felt a bit stretched" to him. Nor did Branden disclose his growing "discomfort" with the "Introduction" to Rand's major book on ethics. Nor did he tell Rand that his role in Hospers' departure made him just "miserable." Nor did he say to her face that he believed that she was "closed" to new ideas—or that psychology was (at the very least) not her "strong point." When he felt "pushed" too fast along a certain path he never said "slow down."

Instead, he said, "of course, Ayn," and remained the one intellectual in her presence who seemed to her to be her most intellectually sympatico colleague.

All these conflicts, if not many more, were left to stew.

Branden cannot admit that it was ever a conscious disagreement while he was still with Rand, and, hence, he says his compliments "felt" a bit stretched, he was "miserable," he was "uncomfortable," he was "bothered," etc., about each of these issues.

It must be remembered that Branden has since written extensively about what he calls "the art of living consciously." This appears to be merely an outgrowth of Rand's principle that "man is a being of self-made soul," that each of us has the responsibility actively to introspect, honestly to identify our values, and to avoid acting on the basis of unidentified emotions. In short, to know conscientiously what we are doing when we are doing it. This was the moral and psychological doctrine he would become famous for articulating both during his years with Rand and subsequently.

At NBI, Branden would lecture students on the virtues of rationality and honesty—and on the self-destructive vice of evading them.

He advised that all aspects of our lives must be brought into the light of reason and that happiness and joy were possible to the man who thus pursued rational values. He spoke of the ongoing commitment required to apply these virtues to our actual life. The virtue of integrity was repeatedly stressed by Branden in his lectures—the need to practice what one preaches. Perhaps no psychologist in history has stressed these ideas so explicitly.

Rand's claim—the claim he angrily denied in 1968—that Branden was not living up to his own teachings and that he was acting on the basis of "unidentified emotions" is precisely what Branden now makes a central theme in his memoirs.

But these were not just personal issues and did not relate only to his private relationship with Rand. They pertained to his intellectual and professional life.

If, as a lecturer on ethics and as a psycho-therapist, he was having these kinds of emotional conflicts—for several years—and was letting them go without the benefit of any conscious thought or discussion, then Branden was—by his own admission—guilty of widespread intellectual and moral evasions. (We will see in Part II this kind of "mental drift" displayed by Mr. Branden in regard to a number of other issues as well.)

For a mind such as Branden's that dealt daily with such explicit conversation on the evil and self-destructiveness of such behavior, it seems more likely, however, that Branden was engaged in a more conscious deception of Rand regarding his positions on these issues, given not only his eloquence on the topic so soon after his break with Rand and the comprehensive nature of the unresolved "discomfort" he admits to having experienced, but also on the financial and professional dependence on Rand he had developed during this time.

In 1982, a few months after Rand's death, Mr. Branden delivered a speech entitled "The Benefits and Hazards of the Philosophy of Ayn Rand," at the University of California at San Diego.

There, he detailed a still broader range of objections to Rand's work—its subtle but pervasive encouragement of emotional repression, its lack of benevolence, its unspecified "gaps." (23)

The death of Rand in 1982 seems to account for Branden's failure to disclose these differences earlier. How much further back all of these differences go can only be guessed. In his 1999 *Liberty* interview, Branden was asked when it was that he discovered the unspecified "gaps" in Objectivism which he now contends exist. Could it have been before 1968?

> No, no, before 1968 the most I ever had was a feeling of apprehension, or something is not quite... but no. It all happened in the years after 1968 when I was out of that world and kind of took it as one of my challenges to rethink everything, and ask myself, you know, what really satisfies me intellectually, and where I feel something is not right. All of that is post-1968. I wish it had been earlier. (24)

In light of his position at the time, Branden, of course, owed it to Rand to have done so much earlier—even ignoring the other implications of this kind of intellectual—and psychological—irresponsibility to himself.

As Rand's spokesman and business partner, he had a moral obligation to Rand to think—at least once—about these things before the break.

And, of course, his self-serving account cannot be taken at face value. We are asked to believe that the "gradual thing" Branden had spoken of to *Reason* magazine in 1971 lasted less than three years.

Listening to Rand praise his essays and lectures, in which Branden himself could not yet express his true feelings, would have tipped off even the most self-deluded that his professional and intellectual life was just as much a fraud as his personal life. Branden admits in his memoir that he "felt like a fraud facing [his] own students," because of his personal hypocrisy, at least. (25)

But, it is also clear that Mr. Branden was dishonest about matters other than his love-life and to many more people than his lovers. By his own admission he was giving Rand rhapsodic praise in his first book for something he did not think was her "strong point." If he was so conscious of his growing doubts as to make the psychology chapter "by far the briefest," then Branden was also conscious enough of the potential impact of these doubts on the content of his essay, as well as its length.

Branden was lying to his *readers.* Such was the intellectual respect Branden gave his public.

Rand, of course, he treated much worse. As long as Branden continued receiving Rand's unmitigated endorsement, it was surely his ethical responsibility, according to the principles he still explicitly espoused, to be honest with Rand about even the smallest philosophical disagreement, much less the degree of "misery," "bother," "discomfort," etc., he now admits it was causing him.

And not doing so can only be characterized as professional exploitation—whether accomplished by conscious deception or by systematic evasion.

The philosophy Branden had publicly advocated, taught, and detailed holds that honesty is a virtue of fundamental importance.

In *Atlas Shrugged*, Rand tells the reader through her hero, John Galt, that any attempt to gain a value through deception, be it love, fame or money, is immoral and self-defeating.

Such were the principles that he claimed to have shared with Rand, the principles he taught others.

If Branden knew that his new beliefs would upset Rand or cause a break with her, then for that very reason he owed her the truth—whether or not her reaction would be reasonable or unreasonable. And he could not help but know this.

Rand's endorsement of him was her "spiritual property" and could not rightfully be taken from her by fraud, something Branden, of all the people on earth, knew more intimately than any other. His ongoing conduct to the contrary amounted to spiritual embezzlement.

We must also remember that Mr. Branden's relationship with Rand was not merely intellectual; it was financial. Rand had no financial interest in NBI, but she and Branden were joint owners of *The Objectivist*, the magazine devoted to the dissemination of Rand's philosophy. The magazine apparently turned a healthy profit.

Branden, it can be safely said, owed his career to Rand. It was with Rand's literary agent and Rand's publisher that he first signed contracts, presumably at Rand's recommendation. It was Rand that had the international reputation as a novelist and an individualist philosopher. It was her work and her philosophy which had given Branden a subject to discuss at NBI and the frame of reference to his own work. It was her fame which established his fame, such as it is.

Branden's own first book, *Who Is Ayn Rand?*, was the product of the generously long discussions he and his wife had tape-recorded with Rand.

The Nathaniel Branden Institute existed for the purpose of spreading Rand's ideas.

The Objectivist magazine had the same purpose.

And, before the break, Branden's reputation rested almost exclusively on the fact that Branden was Rand's chief spokesman.

In denying that his dispute with Rand involved intellectual and professional exploitation on his part, Branden contends that Rand got benefits from the relationship, as well, such as his efforts through NBI and *The Objectivist* to promote her ideas, along with the admiration and love he had expressed to her.

Without NBI, he maintains, there would have been no "Objectivist Movement," at least, the kind of "movement" that he confesses Ayn Rand never wanted. (26)

But, especially in the face of multiple deceptions, that is not his call to make.

Branden blithely claims to have come to terms with what his "own rewards were for remaining with Rand" (27), but gives scant introspection to the degree to which he was professionally exploiting her, even as he reveals the evidence for this exploitation.

As for Branden's motive in his professional deception of Rand, Branden gives several psychological justifications and excuses, but on this issue many of his statements regarding the matter are rather revealing.

Branden admits that he was afraid that the entire structure he had built at NBI on Rand's endorsement would be destroyed if he were to reveal the truth to Rand about his other affair. Recall that at this time Branden is married to Ms. Branden, having an affair with Rand which is known to their respective spouses, *and* having an affair with a third woman which both he and Ms. Branden are concealing from Rand.

He reports that during the years of his deception of Ayn Rand about his "private life," at least, he "paced the floor of [his] office for countless hours, trying to think [his] way toward an alternative that would not result in the total collapse of the life I had built." (28)

Branden relates the following extraordinary account of a conversation he had with his former wife, in which they consider telling Rand the truth:

> There was a subtle note of hard, practical calculation behind [Ms. Branden's] words, "Give up NBI?... Give up everything we've created?... How can you possibly do that? You can't. You'd never respect yourself again." I nodded in exhausted acquiescence; but my survivor-self contemplated Barbara as from a great distance, thinking: So. Well, well, well. We are all operators, it seems. (29)

In other words, business considerations significantly played into Branden's more than four-and-a-half years of deceiving Rand about his other, secret affair.

Although his income was destined to become even greater, promoting Rand's ideas had provided him with a comfortable living. Branden notes the "hard, practical calculation" involved in Ms. Branden's compact of dishonesty here, and the "countless hours" of thought and pacing which he gave these issues himself, none of which can be reconciled with his 1968 denials of financial wrongdoing.

Remarkably, Branden has long denied Rand's accusation of financial exploitation and has mocked her specific allegations to that effect, and, yet, here he provides us with the details of his (and his former wife's) very thought process as he nakedly chooses a course of exploitation.

Rand had specifically called into question both the lease at the Empire State Building, which Branden had pushed, as well as the transfer of money from *The Objectivist* to NBI in the form of "a loan" in order to pay the rent on that lease. (30)

In 1968, Branden conceded a good many of the facts Rand had alleged: that NBI "required loans from time to time" from *The Objectivist*; that Rand had expressed concern over the expense of the lease at the Empire State Building; that another, much larger than normal loan was then taken out, at least in part, to pay the rent on that lease. Nor did Branden contradict Rand's statements regarding when and how she found out about this loan, i.e., after the fact.

In attempting to dispute Rand's claim that the loan "represented the entire cash reserve of this magazine," he actually admits its truth. He does not tell us what *The Objectivist* had in the bank at the time of the loan, but as of March 31, 1968, the amount was $17,434, he says. The amount of money transferred to NBI, he alleged, had only been $22,500, not the $25,000 Rand had claimed, and, of this, only $16,500 was "borrowed."

Of course, the numbers cannot be verified by the author, but no matter how Mr. Branden slices it, the loan still required the depletion of most of the cash reserves of *The Objectivist*—as Rand had said. Rand's only detectable potential error is, perhaps, having confused 22.5 with 25 thousands, but—given Branden's own credibility issues—a "perhaps" is certainly required. Otherwise, all of Rand's basic facts are confirmed by Branden.

Mr. Branden claims that the loan was repaid at his own instigation, but he also concedes that Rand did "put in a request for repayment, not knowing that I had already given instructions to that effect." (31)

Curiously, Branden does not then explain why he initiated repayment on his own so soon—if there was no impropriety with the original transaction.

In 1968, Branden contested Rand's assertion that their "incorporation agreement" required their mutual agreement on all decisions, but in 1989—in another about face—he reveals that such was their oral agreement from the inception! (32)

Still Branden completely ignores Rand's reasonable—and, more important, legally correct—suggestion that, as co-owner of *The Objectivist*, Branden should have obtained Rand's explicit agreement to such a loan before it happened.

Even assuming that most business decisions had been the exclusive concern of Mr. Branden, the loan was of an unprecedented size, as he concedes, and, therefore, required unprecedented treatment. Any such thought, however, Branden simply brushes aside calling Rand's anger at his financial deception "controlling."

It will become increasingly evident that it was Rand's insistence on knowing the truth that the Brandens' call "controlling" and "oppressive." Whether it was a little deception—like the surprise party—or a big one—like Branden's intellectual fraud—the Brandens insist on their right to manipulate Rand with their lies. If Rand complains, they accuse *her* of being manipulative and "controlling." Projection, smoke-screen, and avoidance, all in one increasingly familiar package.

Rand tells us that she did consent to the loan when she first learned of it a few months before her break with Branden, but that the amount of the loan remained undisclosed until the summer of 1968, in the midst of the break. These facts have never been disputed by the Brandens. This partial consent probably would have made any legal action against Branden for fraud difficult, but Rand had not accused Branden of an actionable crime, only of dubious business practices—in Rand's words, "questionable policy."

Morally, of course, Branden should have obtained Rand's fully informed consent even if he was not also anticipating a break with Rand, as he now admits he was. In light of this additional fact, the loan was—morally if not legally—all the more fraudulent.

The essence of the financial exploitation involved in these transactions was not addressed by Mr. Branden in 1968. In 1989, with Rand now dead and her statement still standing as the final word on the subject, he finally gets around to it.

Less than a year before Branden's break with Rand, NBI signed a lease at the Empire State Building—"the biggest financial commitment" Branden had ever made in his life. (33) Branden was taking on such a responsibility even as he was contemplating the inevitability of a break with Rand, since this was precisely what he says he feared would happen if Rand ever found out about the various lies he had been telling her. Branden already felt, in his own words, that "his back was to the wall" because of the situation with Rand. (34)

He quotes his ex-wife as saying at the time: "Are we *crazy*? Everything can explode at any minute! It's only a matter of time until you have to tell Ayn the truth; we both know that. Wouldn't it be better to tell her *before* signing the lease?"

Branden's only response: "Eight thousand square feet in the Empire State Building to house all of our projects; I wanted that." (35) This is a strange attitude for a man who has "his back to the wall."

In this context, "financial exploitation" seems a rather mild euphemism on Rand's part. In any event, her focus on both the lease and the loan were apparently well justified.

The extent to which Branden actually verifies the facts behind Rand's denunciation of him merely heightens the hypocrisy of the ridicule he heaped on that denunciation in 1968.

During an interview with *Liberty* magazine in 1990, Ms. Branden revealed that Rand had originally intended to write the introduction for Branden's first book on psychology, *The Psychology of Self-Esteem*. Ms. Branden tells us that when she began to plead with Branden to tell Rand "the truth," Branden replied, "Just wait until she writes the introduction."

Branden's anxiety over getting that introduction from Rand has been confirmed by Joan Blumenthal, another member of Rand's circle of friends. (36)

There were, it seems, multiple layers of financial exploitation at least one of which Rand herself was wholly unaware.

In "To Whom It May Concern," Rand had said that the production of Barbara Branden's stage adaptation of *The Fountainhead* "seemed to become Mr. Branden's central concern, taking up a major part of his time, causing him to neglect his intellectual and business commitments." Rand suggests that this was chief among the reasons why Branden had become chronically late in delivering his articles for *The Objectivist* and another indication of his wavering commitments.

Branden takes issue with this, saying in 1968, of the theater project, "it never took up more than a small portion of my time." He does not dispute—in 1968, 1989 or 1999—that he was "behind schedule," or that he was becoming habitually late with his articles, or even that Rand was by then writing more than her share of articles.

Instead, Branden attacks a straw-man. "I never committed myself to writing an article per issue..." he says. (37) In her article, Rand had only asserted that their initial agreement was to write "an equal number of articles," as they received an equal salary.

Branden simply claims that Rand was "often late with her articles, too." (38) (Something, of course, Rand had never denied.) Branden says that the reason for his tardiness was actually a result of "the theoretical complexities of the issues about which I was writing." But in 1989, he adds, "I found it difficult to concentrate on my writing." (39)

Branden also now admits that "[o]f the various projects at NBI, none gave me as much pleasure" as NBI Theater, which Branden "had initiated" shortly before the break. Its first project was to be Ms. Branden's stage adaptation of *The Fountainhead*. Branden reports that his new mistress, an actress, had "reawakened" an early love of the theater in him (40).

So, however much time he was actually devoting to it, NBI Theater had become his favorite activity, and another of Rand's points against Branden appears to have been well taken—despite earlier denials.

In his 1968 "Answer," Branden actually asserts that he had no responsibility whatever "to justify... the disposition of [his] time and energies" to his coeditor on *The Objectivist*, the founder of the philosophy he had dedicated his life to spread, and whose continued endorsement buttressed his livelihood. Branden conceded Rand's point that he had not yet begun the planned "total" rewrite of his NBI course on Objectivism, though he conveniently responds that he had planned to do it "in 1969."

Rand's complaint regarding the course had included the observation that a major portion of the "Basic Principles" had by then been made available (and more affordably) in print. Even in the "updated" version which he sold on LP following the break, a substantial portion of the material appears to be (almost verbatim) what can be found in *The Virtue of Selfishness* and *Capitalism: the Unknown Ideal*. Branden's "continuous updates" consisted primarily of added quotations from Rand's newly available, *Introduction to Objectivist Epistemology*, which are also contained on these LPs. Otherwise, despite Branden's claims to the contrary, his lecture material changed very little throughout the Sixties. (41)

In 1968 Branden vigorously denied Rand's assertion that their relationship "was turning into a series of constant demands on my time, constant pleas for advice, for help with his writing, for long discussions of his personal, professional and psychological problems." (42)

Branden has never disputed that he had certain personal and psychological problems. In 1968, however, Branden insisted that Rand had not spent all that much time with him on these issues, except, perhaps, for some telephone calls which Rand herself had dragged out. Branden conceded that Rand, his coeditor on *The Objectivist*, was "a more experienced and accomplished writer" and, therefore, had "a greater number of suggestions to offer" about the writing in their magazine. But that was it.

In 1989, Branden was a bit more forthcoming. Beginning at least as early as 1964, he tells us, he began to exhibit "erratic behavior with Ayn," including an "elusiveness" and "coldness" which was "alternating, as always, with expressions of passionate devotion..." Branden admits during this period that it was he who sought out Rand's advice and help with his deteriorating marriage. Branden even admits that he knew it was wrong "to solicit Ayn's help with our marriage while withholding information" that he and his wife were both having other affairs! (43)

Although it was Mr. Branden who had solicited Rand's help, he now sees sinister motives behind the generous counseling and emotional support which Rand gave the Brandens' troubled marriage during this time. In the new edition of his memoir, he suggests that Rand had tried to manipulate the situation for her own purposes. Although Rand did make "negative observations" about their marriage "from time to time," her generous help now suggests to Branden that Rand was "keenly interested" in preserving the Brandens as a couple.

Ms. Branden was "safe," formulates Branden, and Rand never had to worry about "another woman." (44) (Of course, there *was* "another woman" at that very time.)

This theory, of course, ignores the evidence that Rand had been a warmly supportive counselor to each of them long before the affair and, indeed, before the Brandens' marriage. Both Brandens report that Rand's supportive counseling had begun in California many years earlier.

Moreover, neither of them report that Rand's attitudes towards them changed because of their legal separation in 1965.

Perhaps this is why, Branden says, "[i]t did not enter my mind" that Rand was being manipulative until decades later.

In 1999, Branden confessed to *Liberty* magazine that the thought had still not "entered his mind" when he published the first version of his memoir in 1989. (45)

It turns out this theory was the suggestion of his third wife, Devers, and that upon first hearing it, Branden responded, "Jesus, you know something? I don't know; I can't prove whether it's true or not, but it... it feels intuitively like—not that that would have been the only reason—but that would be quite like Ayn to have that as one of her considerations."

It may come as a complete surprise to readers of his book that this is not a "claim of knowledge" by Branden, or that this is only a hypothesis or "partial" explanation of Rand's behavior. In his book, Branden successfully hid all of these underlying qualifications that he admits in the interview. (46)

One can only wonder how much else of his book, which otherwise seems to be a claim of knowledge, contains such uncredited "intuition."

As his book post-dates Ms. Branden's, Nathaniel Branden's theory here is unsurprisingly one of the very few hostile to Rand which Ms. Branden does not repeat or suggest herself. It seems the thought never occurred to Ms. Branden, either.

In any event, it was Mr. Branden who solicited help from Rand as a marriage counselor, not Rand volunteering her services, as Branden has now made clear, again in contradiction to his 1968 assertions.

Branden now says that he consciously knew as early as 1964 that "the deception in the manipulation I was attempting was in conflict with my own convictions about human relationships." (47) Convictions? What is clear is that the convictions he refers to were *Rand's* convictions, the ones he was preaching if not practicing.

As a therapist, at least, Branden must have been, even then, conscious of the simple truth that deceiving one's chosen psychological counselor is inevitably self-defeating, if not self-mockery. Soliciting Ayn Rand's help with his marriage while simultaneously concealing important facts about his (and his wife's) romantic life can, therefore, only have been part of a sophisticated and deliberate effort to stall for time by deceiving Rand about the state of his mind and his relationships generally. It cannot have been part of any sincere effort by the famous psychotherapist to save his marriage. That much is certain.

Rand's generous, unwittingly futile advice is now "manipulation," according to Branden, when his own role in soliciting that help from someone he was deceiving is the only manipulation present here to an honest eye.

Branden's memoir, in some respects, continuously reflects the trickery of an expert magician, causing the very thing he pretends is caused by something else, in this case, once again covering his own manipulation of Rand by accusing *her* of manipulation. Projection, smoke-screen, avoidance.

This was by no means the only psychological counseling, as it turns out, that Branden solicited from Rand in the period during which he was deceiving her on so many levels.

Ms. Branden describes conversations between Branden and Rand in the period before the break as follows: "He spoke vaguely of problems troubling him, of physical and emotional exhaustion, of depression, of being overworked, as Ayn tried conscientiously to listen and to help." (48)

In *Judgment Day*, Branden describes his conversations with Rand in 1967 as follows: "At Ayn's, we discussed my psycho-epistemology, my mysterious emotional repression, my difficulties with the triangle of Ayn, Frank and me, the question of my real values." Branden even admits that he "had been complaining of depression a good deal" to Rand. (49)

We shall see in Rand's private journals (Part II) just how extensive this counseling had been. These confirm, however, one of Rand's chief complaints to Branden, that he had, in fact, transformed their relationship into nothing but psychotherapy. Before she had learned of his four-year romantic deception of her, Rand would write in her private journals that Branden's "worst offense of all" consisted of his allowing the relationship to "drift" into "the last two years of myself as [his] psychotherapist." She also makes quite clear in those notes that she communicated this complaint to Branden. (50) Discussions of Branden's psychology had involved more than a few prolonged phone calls, it seems.

Much of "To Whom It May Concern" was implicitly conceded by Branden in his 1968 response, "In Answer To Ayn Rand." Most of the rest had simply to wait for the publication of *Judgment Day* for confirmation. But one could never have guessed the truth of Rand's statement from Branden's original response.

Contrary to Mr. Branden's fierce denials, Rand's accusations about his intellectual, professional and personal dishonesty and manipulation of her are largely validated—by Branden himself.

Perhaps the most dishonest (and ugliest) part of Nathaniel Branden's 1968 response to Rand concerns his affair with her.

Rand's references in her statement to professional and intellectual exploitation were just cover, he tells us. The "real" cause was kept secret by her: Branden had told Rand that their age difference "constituted an insuperable barrier, for me, to a romantic relationship." (51)

No mention was made by Branden that for the previous fourteen years such an age difference had not been "an insuperable barrier" for him.

In effect, he suggested that Rand had "come on" to him and that he had been forced by his own emotional integrity to nobly refuse before any affair had begun. Preying upon the discretion of the wronged, he actually implied that Rand alone desired such a relationship, that he would have been incapable of it, and, perhaps, that he always regarded the very concept as irrational.

Rand, by contrast, had merely said that "Mr. Branden had been concealing from me certain ugly actions and irrational behavior in his private life, which were grossly contradictory to Objectivist morality..." (52)—a statement that was true and discreet while necessarily explanatory.

But by the time of his memoirs, Branden would finally concede the nature of his personal deception of Rand. His affair with Rand had been commenced only at *his* instigation and, at Rand's insistence, with the full knowledge and consent of their respective spouses. By the start of 1964 Branden had begun a new affair (with a married woman) which he kept secret from the woman's husband at first, from Branden's wife for two years, and from Rand for over four and half years.

During the course of this secret affair, his marriage with Barbara Branden now in shambles, Branden nonetheless refused to give his wife permission to have an affair of her own (with a married man), when she had the honesty to come forward with her own new interest. (This appears to have been the first instance of Ms. Branden's upfront disclosure of a desired affair, but certainly not her first affair in the course of her relationship with Branden.) Branden would continue for some time in this stance against Ms. Branden's own affair while secretly commencing his own, according to Ms. Branden.

Ms. Branden says that it was "several months" after Branden's affair with the other woman had already become sexual that Branden gave his consent, while Mr. Branden claims that it was only twelve or thirteen days. In any event, it was at least a year after his romantic feelings for the new woman were known to him, even if his account is to be credited. Today, after having been exposed by his first wife, Branden admits that such behavior was "ludicrous and unconscionable." (53)

When Branden did finally consent to Ms. Branden's affair, he still did not reveal the truth of his own affair to her, Branden admits. Apparently it was not until after their formal separation that Branden finally told Ms. Branden of his new affair sometime near the end of 1966. Even then, he told her only that he was about to begin an affair with her, not that the affair was now more than two years old.

When Branden solicited Rand's aid with his shattered marriage in 1965, he still did not disclose either his or his wife's other affairs to Ms. Branden or Rand. He failed to disclose these things to Rand during the entire duration of the counselling he got from her on this topic, that is, through most of 1967. (He would never tell Rand of his affair.)

All the while, he continued teaching courses discussing the primacy of existence, the fundamental virtue of honesty, the evil of "counterfeiting reality," the objectivity of knowledge, etc., etc.

Dishonesty had become a way of life for Branden. Ayn Rand's philosophy, the very thing he was selling, made it impossible for him to deny, every minute of every waking hour.

When Branden's ex-wife told him he should tell Rand the truth before initiating major new business commitments, Branden plunged ahead—even as he was feeling that he had his "back to the wall."

Nor was it Branden who finally told the truth to Rand. Rather, he left this dirty work to his former wife. It is not clear that Branden himself would have *ever* told the truth to Rand.

Rand's description in "To Whom It May Concern," while it certainly did not reveal the affair to which she had been a party, had been a fair summary of Mr. Branden's dishonesty in the less personal areas of their relationship. But it was also clear from Rand's statement that something was missing, that Rand was holding back certain information which, it might well be said, was no one else's business. In this sense, Rand's statement was perfectly honest.

The same cannot be said of Branden's 1968 statement, which was clearly intended to mislead the reader and to slander Rand in an exploitative way.

In his memoir, Mr. Branden says that only when his relationship with Rand had been "reduced to long, drawn-out sessions made of nothing but pity, rage, guilt, and mutually [sic] inflicted pain," and only after years of deceptively encouraging Rand's feelings, did he finally tell Rand that— despite all of his earlier protests to her concerns that she would "always be a sexual being" to him—the age difference did, indeed, matter to him. (54)

Because of Rand's understandable sense of betrayal at this prolonged deception, the Brandens both agree that Rand contemplated denouncing Branden even then and began considering whether Ms. Branden might assume Mr. Branden's professional position at the head of NBI and *The Objectivist*.

But Rand's anger, it seems, did not prevent her from continuing to have business meetings with Branden. Her private journals reveal that they even continued to discuss Branden's psychology, as we shall see.

Additionally, it is now conceded by both Brandens that Rand spoke of giving Branden another "chance." (55) Thus, the Brandens' contention in 1968 that Rand had already decided to denounce him before she learned of the deception in his personal life is—once again—something squarely contradicted in both of the Brandens' later accounts. Once again, their 1968 statement proves to be the actual series of "fabrications."

The Brandens say that it was the prospect of Ms. Branden's own financial windfall implied in Rand's deliberations which motivated Ms. Branden to tell Rand about Mr. Branden's affair. Branden probably could not have prevented this disclosure to Rand by his former wife, but he somehow still manages to give himself credit for acquiescing to Ms. Branden's decision.

If this is all true, it may say something for Ms. Branden's belated and partial honesty to Rand about Mr. Branden's four and a half year old secret affair. Mr. Branden does, however, reveal that for two years Ms. Branden had explicitly agreed to help him keep his new affair a secret from Rand. He quotes Ms. Branden as agreeing with him "because you're right, that would be the end of everything." (56) (We will also see, in Part II, the elaborate extent to which Ms. Branden would go in assisting Branden in this deception.)

Ms. Branden, possibly to her credit, could not, in the end, accept such a reward while still deceiving Rand, despite the financial motives that drove her previously. This is not something that can be said of Branden, even though it was his affair they were concealing.

Following Ms. Branden's disclosure of that affair, Rand's mind was made up—Branden was gone, the denunciation would come. Discussion of Ms. Branden's possibly running NBI suddenly became even more serious. Ms. Branden quickly drew up a business plan.

Ms. Branden reports that Rand hardly looked at it before rejecting it. She quotes Rand as saying, "I can't run a business, and I can't let anyone else run it when it carries my name!" (57)

This meant the liquidation of NBI.

The same afternoon that Ms. Branden's plan had been rejected by Rand, Ms. Branden now admits that she began to tell friends of her "growing concern at Ayn's reckless accusations and threats against Branden," her concern for Rand's "state of mind," and her concern for Branden's "professional destruction" by Rand. Even in 1968, Ms. Branden had admitted that she had openly worried that Rand's attack on Mr. Branden "would compel him, in self-defense, to reveal information which would be painful and embarrassing to Miss Rand." (58) Ms. Branden does not mention this last in her biography, but what Rand had referred to as "veiled threats and accusations against" her by Ms. Branden are again seen to be based in fact, vindicating Rand's account. (59)

In "To Whom It May Concern," Rand had observed that Ms. Branden began to take Mr. Branden's side, as it were, only after her business plan had been rejected. Rand tells readers to draw their "own conclusions regarding Ms. Branden's motives." (60)

The Brandens take issue with Rand's questioning Ms. Branden's motives. In their "Answer" to Rand, the Brandens insisted that it was Ms. Branden's despair of financial gain while still deceiving Rand that had motivated her belated honesty.

Even if this is true, it does not contradict the possibility that Ms. Branden's motivation for later siding with Mr. Branden was revenge for the loss of the windfall she had anticipated. After all, Ms. Branden had for two years deceived Rand, at least in part for financial reasons, and then suddenly signed her name to Mr. Branden's highly deceptive version of these events in 1968.

Nor can Ms. Branden deny Rand's account of the timing of Ms. Branden's sudden switch to a defense of her ex-husband.

Such facts compel one to reconsider the assertion that Ms. Branden's belated honesty was even the product of ethical considerations at all. Her revelations to Rand did have as their immediate effect the termination of any talk about "second chances" for Mr. Branden and conceivably could have put Ms. Branden in charge of her ex-husband's former businesses. There is no reason to suppose that this was not part of Ms. Branden's motive all along. It was, after all, only when Rand had put the kibosh on her own business plans that Ms. Branden turned. Ms. Branden tells us, in fact, that it was later *that same day*. And if Ms. Branden's concern for Rand's state of mind had been a sincere one, it certainly had not prevented her from proposing to make Rand her closest business associate earlier in the day.

Apparently, we can identify this day then as the day that the Brandens' need to slander Rand's psychology was born, and the day that their historical revisionism would begin.

Ms. Branden has kept insisting that her business plan had been solid and that Rand's dismissal of this plan as a mere "projection" is indicative of her growing instability. Of course, it was just a "projection," and the prospects for this projection relied as much on Ms. Branden's now-tarnished trustworthiness as on sound business judgment. And without the draw of NBI's "star" lecturer, Nathaniel Branden, Ms. Branden's projections, which as she says were based on NBI's past performance, were of little value. Nonetheless, Ms. Branden goes into some detail in her biography to justify the economic soundness of this plan. (61)

It seems that Rand's rejection of Ms. Branden's business plan *still* smarts.

Nathaniel Branden's own exploitation of Rand is far more complex and layered than Ms. Branden's. Mr. Branden, as we have seen, is compelled to concede much of this himself. Perhaps this can be associated with his newly found desire to avoid calling anyone's actions "immoral," just "harmful," as in the sentence, "I was harmful to Ayn Rand." Therefore, the obfuscation of his own wrongdoing, however artfully done, is insufficient.

"Rand wronged me, too," he spins by way of justification. Rand exploited Mr. Branden, both Brandens insist. In one of the most absurd examples of his distorted bias, Branden claims that Rand literally tried to "destroy him": "'You've got to understand,' Barbara beseeched me, '*that Ayn wants you dead!*... Ayn wants you dead! That's all that's moving her now!'... Now I asked my brain to absorb the fact that the woman who had been my idol was plotting my annihilation." (62)

To justify this operatic assertion, Branden points to Rand's published statement "To Whom It May Concern," her efforts to get both her agent and her publisher to cancel their contracts with Branden, alleged efforts by Rand's attorney to "blackmail" him when she improperly, in his view, took *The Objectivist* from him.

It probably need not be pointed out that Rand never tried to have Branden killed. Nor do the Brandens even try to substantiate this melodramatic claim. The allegation provides no insight into Rand, but, rather, it is the extent of the Brandens' own paranoia that it serves to illuminate.

The phrase "plotting annihilation," for example, in light of the actual evidence, takes Brandenian distortion to a new and intriguing level.

Rand's only written references to the Brandens after the break were the aforementioned statement and a brief "p.s." in a couple of books which still contained essays by Branden, to the effect that he was "no longer associated with" Rand or her philosophy. That's it. Then, complete silence.

While Rand also removed Mr. Branden's name from the dedication to *Atlas Shrugged*, this hardly amounts to "professional destruction."

His essays—and his name—remained in Rand's books, *The Virtue of Selfishness* and *Capitalism, the Unknown Ideal*. The "annihilation" plot apparently missed this open shot, at least, at striking Mr. Branden out of existence.

Rand had thought the Brandens to be honest people. When she discovered that they were not, it might even be argued that Rand was morally obligated to take whatever steps that were necessary to remove her public endorsement, even as Rand continued to acknowledge, in some sense, the value of their previous work. If her endorsement had secured Branden his publisher and agent, Rand had every right to withdraw her endorsement as vigorously as she could, when she no longer believed Branden to be an ethical man.

Since there are other publishers in the world, Branden was somehow able to publish *The Psychology of Self-Esteem* in 1969, the year following the break. And he was somehow able to establish a psychotherapy clientele on the West Coast. (The "somehow" was by using NBI/*The Objectivist* mailing lists.) Even if it were simply his personal deception of her, Rand certainly had every right to do her utmost to remove the endorsement to her agent and publisher which had been so valuable to Branden.

Because Branden was late in delivering the book, Rand's publisher was free to take her new recommendation, according to Branden. The agent, it seems, had no intention of dropping Branden and never did. Both were within their rights in making these decisions. (The publisher had every right to do so, if only to please one of its best-selling authors.)

Regardless of her right to withdraw her endorsement of Branden, was Rand ethically justified in doing so? In the face of Mr. Branden's prolonged dishonesty and exploitation of Rand, as well as Rand's personal responsibility for her public endorsement of him, it was not only understandable, but also, perhaps, morally necessary.

During the course of Branden's ongoing efforts to obtain professional certification, Rand had written letters of recommendation for him to agencies like the New Jersey Department of Law and Public Safety. It is true that, following their break, she wrote back with new letters simply withdrawing her previous recommendation. (63) This was the apparent extent of Rand's efforts toward Branden's professional "destruction"—the withdrawal of her previous endorsements.

Branden, however, suggests that *he* was the one who had been financially exploited. He suggests darkly that his transfer to Rand of his ownership interest in *The Objectivist* involved "blackmail" and unfair pressure, if not actual coercion.

As co-owners of *The Objectivist*, Branden and Rand each had an arguable claim to the other's copyrights to a great many substantive articles. The magazine was the chief voice of Rand's philosophy. This, according to Branden, was a focal point of their legal problems in the midst of separation. Branden signed the transfer of ownership when the documents were first presented to him by Rand's attorney. Wishing the spread of Objectivism to continue, Branden says, he was simply concerned about retaining the copyrights to all of his own articles, and via telephone Rand quickly gave him an oral agreement to the effect that Branden would be "treated fairly" with regard to his copyrights. (64)

In his 1989 memoir, however, Branden does not mention any "treated fairly" proviso and now states forthrightly that he was told that his articles were "his own property." (65) Again, it is curious that the Brandens did not mention this in 1968, when it would have seriously helped Mr. Branden's legal position, which was then supposedly still in question. It is likely that, once again, the Brandens are modifying the truth for their own ends. Branden also now adds that, despite this oral agreement, soon after the break he was claiming that Rand had "refused" to sign over the copyrights to his articles. Branden does not disclose why he started to make this accusation, but this may have simply been his way of demanding that Rand publicly acknowledge his right to his own articles.

According to Branden's memoir, when he actually inquired of Rand's attorney, Henry Mark Holzer, he was told that Rand had never refused, and Branden never makes clear from whom he got that idea in the first place. Branden says that Rand's attorney did then try to impose certain conditions, among which were: Branden must keep the affair confidential, he must not "respond" to Rand's forthcoming denunciation of Branden, and he must not accuse Rand's lawyer (who, before the break, had acted as attorney for both of them) of acting unethically. Branden does not say, but he presumably had already made this accusation against the attorney privately, as he would certainly do publicly in his 1968 "Answer" to Rand.

While it is probably the case that Mr. Holzer's joint representation of both Branden and Rand—and its sudden termination—should have disqualified him from any legal involvement in their conflict, only an attorney can be expected to be sensitive to this point in the midst of conflict, and Rand may have been poorly treated by her own attorney in this matter (assuming Branden's assertion that Holzer had previously represented him separately is true.)

In that "Answer," Branden did charge Holzer with shoddy ethics and, of course, he did respond to Rand. And, when Branden used his articles from *The Objectivist* to form the basis of his next book, *The Psychology of Self-Esteem*, published the following year, Rand took no legal action whatsoever. (66)

There is thus no circumstantial corroboration that such "conditions" were ever imposed, and Mr. Holzer is apparently the only person now in a position to confirm the truth of Branden's account on this score. Even if it is an accurate account, Mr. Holzer's interest in protecting his own license and reputation suggests that these "conditions" may have been the work of Mr. Holzer, if they are not the invention of Branden. Rand is not likely to have been the author of the attorney-ethics condition, at least. Rand may never have known of any of them, since the only "condition" in which Rand appears to have had a possible interest was Branden's discretion about the affair.

Based upon existing evidence, there is no way to tell which may be true.

If such conditions were actually ever proposed, it further suggests the truth of the "treated fairly" proviso Branden originally reported in 1968. Arguably, such a proviso would have put Rand in a legal position to negotiate the release of Branden's copyrights.

And if Rand had actually solicited Branden's discretion through her attorney, this can only have been the opening bid in an attempt to negotiate their *mutual* silence. According to his own scenario, it is probable that Branden could have avoided "To Whom It May Concern," despite his later complaints. It was Branden who necessitated the eventual exposure of his own comprehensive dishonesty.

Nor would soliciting such conditions have comprised a violation of Mr. Branden's rights, much less an effort to "destroy" him, in any event. Even assuming that these conditions were made and that Rand herself was privy to them, Rand was simply asking for Branden's agreement not to make a private matter public in the privacy interests of *everyone* concerned.

Branden refused.

The Brandens not only denied Rand's charges, they did so dishonestly. The Brandens, already comfortable deceiving their readers, would reveal in the substance of their memoirs that *everything* Rand had initially said about the break and *everything* that they had initially denied about it *was true.* Yet they simultaneously insist that *Rand's* 1968 statement, not their own, was the libel.

Mr. Branden's original description in 1968 makes quite clear that the original transfer—assuming his own copyrights were retained—reflected his own explicit, considered and voluntary wishes at the time. It was not the result of inappropriate outside pressure. Yet, in his memoirs, he now suggests it was the product of duress.

In 1968, Branden says that he would have been within his legal rights to have demanded that *The Objectivist* terminate publication. Legally, this may have been true, but to have done so, of course, would have constituted an even greater spiritual theft from Rand, whose own efforts—*sans* the intellectual dishonesty—had also built that magazine.

According to Mr. Branden, it was his devotion to the ideas of Objectivism which had already made him, in his own words, "willing" for Rand to continue publishing the magazine named for her own philosophy. (67) Scruples do not appear to have plagued the noted psychologist then or now, as he would cite this modicum of decency years later as evidence of his mistreatment.

In immediately signing over his whole interest in the magazine without financial compensation of any kind, Branden was clearly acknowledging a guilt that was obvious to all those involved at the time.

In 1968, to be sure, Branden had said that he had been threatened by Rand's lawyer to sign immediately or that Rand "would demand a full investigation" of NBI's financial dealings with *The Objectivist*—and even initiate a suit against Branden to do so. In 1968, this was the extent of the unfair pressure he was willing to allege.

"Exhausted," he tells us, and with "a last vestige of sympathy for Miss Rand's anxiety," he signed.

Ms. Branden goes so far as to call this "his gift to Ayn." (68)

Branden does not mention in 1968, 1989 or 1999, what Rand's private journals now make clear, namely that Branden had offered to sign *The Objectivist* over to Rand at least a month *before* their break, a suggestion which Rand—at the time—took as "offensive"! (69)

As has been already observed, if Branden had not relinquished his position as coeditor of *The Objectivist*, or if he had used his technical copyright on any other articles in *The Objectivist*, he would have been morally, if not legally, guilty of an enormous intellectual theft. His position at the magazine had been maintained for years by deceiving his business partner—and the originator of the philosophy he professionally espoused.

Branden's only "gift" to Rand was not to further amplify his own policy of intellectual, financial and emotional exploitation of her.

One can only imagine what Howard Roark would have done to Branden under such circumstances.

In 1989, Nathaniel Branden, for the first time, has added a much more sinister dimension to his accusations when he claimed that he was told by one of Rand's representatives, "We had to talk Ayn out of wanting to send Bob Teague up here with us to make you sign." (70) Teague, it is reported, had a "brown belt in judo."

But, if this story is true, then why did Branden fail to mention any of this in 1968? He was perfectly willing to suggest that he was being wrongly "pressured" in other ways to sign the transfer, to have an affair, etc.

Indeed, Branden was giving a rather complete list of Rand's dastardly role in the break. He certainly accuses Rand of slander and blackmail in that document. Furthermore, he was even willing to reveal Rand's part (if not his own) in wanting a romantic relationship. Why suppress just this? And why, if Branden was so willing to sign over his rights from the start, would Rand ever have felt tempted to "send Bob Teague?"

Ms. Branden, in her 1986 biography, neglected to include mention of this, as well, though it certainly would have added to the book's cinematic potential.

According to Mr. Branden, his former wife was also in the room at the time. Why did Ms. Branden not choose to include this alarming occurrence?

And, of course, there is the formulation of this double-hearsay to contend with. We are to believe that Teague never was called because Rand had already been "talked out" of it. More precisely, Rand had been "talked out of wanting to" do it. This is a very fine piece of wording, but what is it supposed to mean?

Three steps removed from Rand herself, this allegation says nothing about Rand, even if Branden's is a true report. But the prevailing evidence suggests that this is simply another of Branden's many creative and conveniently unverifiable recollections.

Unfortunately, perhaps, the story is not likely to be true. Had Branden withheld "his gift to Rand," he would have been asserting his control over Rand's valuable intellectual property. He would have been continuing in a position which he had kept up by fraud for at least five years. He would have denied Rand—who had never once consciously lied to him—control over the official voice of her ideas, and Rand—once again—would have been the one victimized by Branden's fraud.

Morally, Branden should have signed over his interest in *The Objectivist* years earlier. To have asked for monetary compensation for this, in the wake of years of systematic deception of Rand about so much, would have been the equivalent of theft, a kind of spiritual theft grievously hurtful to Rand. The transfer was perfectly voluntary and proper, Mr. Branden's subsequent objections and lies notwithstanding.

Rand had acted as best as she could to withdraw her endorsement of the Brandens.

However, it is beyond hyperbole for the Brandens to suggest that Rand was attempting to "destroy" Branden. Rand *may* have tried, unsuccessfully but perfectly legally, to prevent Branden from slandering her. Branden's subsequent lies soon vindicated this motivation in spades.

❖

The Brandens were dishonest with Rand about nearly everything a person can be dishonest about, largely in order to maintain the good thing they had going at NBI. This dishonesty lasted for years.

The Brandens not only lied to Rand, they lied to their readers about their relationship with her, and their break, in 1968—and then they lied about their lies. Ever since then, they have continued to lie in memoirs and biographies about their lies to their readers in 1968—calling Rand's 1968 statement, not their own, "libelous." This remarkably all-encompassing dishonesty is manifest even from these biographies themselves—and it is all the more apparent now that we have Rand's journal entries from this same period.

When Rand began to find out about the Brandens' dishonesty, she severed her personal and professional relationship with them. The Brandens would go on and on in their dishonest attack on Rand in the years to follow. After her 1968 statement, Rand's public silence about the Brandens continued until her death.

One thing the Brandens got right—*someone* had been exploited. But it was not them.

V. Something Between Them
He Did Not Understand

THE PERSISTENT DISHONESTY OF THE BRANDENS about their own part in Rand's life makes it impossible to rely on them as historians of events for which they are the only witnesses.

They will recollect, suppress, revise, exaggerate, and omit whenever it is convenient to their stories. Where necessary, they will pull out of their magical hats a very "private" conversation that one of them "once" had with Rand to prove what all the rest of the evidence denies. We have also seen that the Brandens' reports cannot be taken at face value because of the vast internal contradictions in their impossible portrait of Rand, even ignoring their prevailing dishonesty on these subjects.

The level of corroboration rationally required to verify their assertions makes the Brandens' own narratives virtually useless; and when such corroboration is not possible, they are entirely useless. Where the Brandens are our only source, the topic must be marked with a giant asterisk and an attached footnote reading, "Highly Dubious."

Hence, it is senseless to examine the Brandens' accounts of private conversations between Rand, O'Connor and the Brandens, leading up to the affair, or their conversations leading up to the break, or any other conversation for which there is no independent verification.

The Brandens, for some reason, did not publish detailed accounts of these things during the life-times of either Rand or O'Connor, when their self-serving claims could be challenged.

And specifically with regard to their accounts of Rand's affair with Nathaniel Branden we cannot expect any sort of corroboration, as they are the only living witnesses to these very private events. (This fact only augments the critical need for Rand's private journal entries since they represent what is probably the only real evidence of "Rand's side" of this story in existence.)

Central to the Brandens' story is their version of events surrounding Rand's affair with Nathaniel Branden, her leading follower and exponent at the time. This is the Brandens' ace-in-the-hole against Rand and by contemporary American standards it is, without doubt, an unusual story.

The "common sense" of our time and place in history is sexual monogamy. The religious, of course, believe that any sex outside of marriage is wrong, but even the more liberal generally hold that a stable, sexually exclusive relationship is best, irrespective of legal technicalities or traditional ceremonies. It follows from the conventional view that affairs— no matter how common an occurrence—must be doomed to pain and tragedy. Such affairs are usually called "cheating." The experience of a recent U.S. President has taught us that men are expected to lie to their wives (and just about everybody else) in order to conceal these shameful liaisons. After all, they can only be a source of pain for the partner who is "cheated on," if not others as well.

As they say, "this goes without saying," i.e., it is a firm conviction very few ever actually think about.

Certainly, Rand was not alone in believing dishonesty to be self-defeating, especially when the victim is someone we claim to care about. Lies to a supposed "loved one" must shatter intimacy and trust.

The manipulation and cruelty inherent in romantic deceptions are obvious. In addition, the direction of romantic energies towards anyone other than one's original partner would seem to be time and energy that could have been spent with that original partner. If such energy is directed elsewhere, it does not usually bode well for the original relationship.

At the very least, other interests have developed. Indeed, that they have been allowed to develop in the first place often indicates trouble with the original relationship.

Very often, the "cheating" spouse is acting self-destructively, satisfying some neurotic need, although sometimes the situation actually indicates that one has found a better emotional match. In either case, pain to the first partner is deemed inevitable by the common wisdom.

The pain of rejection and, of course, jealousy—whether rooted in self-esteem issues or not—are thought to be inherent in the situation.

On the other hand, it is a contemporary cliché that respectable society will often overlook the affairs of middle-aged men with younger women, even as it disapproves of them. "He's trying to recapture his past," and, if he is being financially responsible to the young woman, well...

In France, the President's youthful mistress will show up at the funeral alongside the wife and kids. Mrs. Robinson, on the other hand, must be depicted as a highly disturbed alcoholic with an impotent and equally disturbed alcoholic for a husband.

One need not be a contemporary feminist to acknowledge this venerable double standard. It reeks of stereotypes and prejudices unworthy of serious, contemporary thinkers.

These are precisely the sort of stereotypes which the Brandens rely upon in their portrayal of Rand.

In the course of human history, many societies have sanctioned polygamy and concubines for wealthy men, but it is extremely rare to find a society which has allowed women the same privilege (certain East African tribes being nearly the only ones that survive to this day). But, as in the case of the Mormons, there are many examples of polygamist families which appear, on the surface at least, to have avoided the pain and jealousy believed to be inherent in a "non-exclusive" relationship. (Whether the context of polygamy permits the maximum in personal fulfillment remains another matter.)

The bottom line is that all of this is what Rand would have called "man-made" (as opposed to "metaphysical"). Emotions and social institutions are the product of human values and, therefore, human choices.

"To love," writes Rand, "is to value." (1)

Most people take the sexual taboos of their age as given, as if they were some genetically implanted instinct; but, as history shows, even the strongest taboos are subject to reevaluation and change, being the products of human thought in the first place. Even during the course of a single lifetime, one can observe the ever-growing sophistication of one's own automatic sexual responses. These responses are plainly not immune to the effects of thought.

As many others have observed, the sexual norms of our own time—for example, a lingering moral opposition to any premarital sex—are, in part, the product of an earlier time justifiably concerned with single motherhood in an age before reliable birth control and when periodic famines were to be expected. In many respects, they are also the product of envy and a mystical hatred of life on earth.

In any event, Rand observed, they are the product of human thought and experience, not instinct, genes or conditioned reflexes.

Rand's thought, as usual, sweeps clean the past and demands a clear, rational justification for all of our emotions and social institutions.

Also typically, Rand's answers put her outside of a cultural mainstream that was, in many ways, profoundly alien to her values.

According to Rand:

> Love, friendship, respect, admiration are the emotional response of one man to the virtues of another, the spiritual payment given in exchange for the personal, selfish pleasure which one man derives from the virtues of another man's character. (2)

Rand further explains that

> Sex is a physical capacity, but its exercise is determined by man's mind—by his choice of values, held consciously or subconsciously. To a rational man, sex is an expression of self-esteem—a celebration of himself and of existence. To the man who lacks self-esteem, sex is an attempt to fake it, to acquire its momentary illusion. (3)

According to Rand, man must choose his values. While humans are not born with a guidebook to successful living, survival and happiness cannot be achieved haphazardly. Indeed, humans require a long-range perspective which can only be expressed in principles, and such success can be achieved only by a consistent adherence to such principles. (4)

Thus, Rand taught, human beings require a *science* of ethics.

With the requirements of human life as the standard, a set of objective principles—not derived from religion, social convention or rank emotionalism—is possible, and necessary, according to Objectivism. An ethics not based upon the needs of human life on earth—those derived, for example, mystically—will eventually, but inevitably, require misery, pain and even death, since it posits some value greater than life itself.

Sexual norms are no different: either the principles which we inculcate will advance success and happiness in life, or they will frustrate them. Our only guidepost is reason.

But set against fresh thought is always poised the inertial force of our unexamined emotions and prejudices, which nearly everyone takes as "given," if not biologically instinctive. Our sexual behavior, like all the rest, must be governed by an adherence to the most rational principles that we can discern. Even our sexual emotions, as deeply buried in our psyche as they may be, are in large part the product of our thinking, our evaluations, even our philosophy.

Rand believed that sexual behavior, like any other, is subject to moral evaluation. She believed that our sexual emotions are subject to psychological evaluation. Rand consequently advocated sexual standards.

Rand, therefore, did not believe in "open marriage" or "free love" in the manner of Marxists or hippies. For Rand, self-esteem was an important ethical value, and Rand believed that one's choice in a sexual partner—reflecting one's deepest values—provides a yardstick for one's self-esteem. The more discriminating and demanding a man is regarding his romantic interests, the better this surely reflects on his self-esteem.

Such self-respect, according to Rand, precludes promiscuity. Rand explained to *Playboy* magazine in the March 1964 edition:

> I say that sex is one of the most important aspects of man's life, and therefore must never be approached lightly or casually. A sexual relationship is proper only on the grounds of the highest values one can find in a human being... And that is why I consider promiscuity immoral. Not because sex is evil but because sex is too good and too important... (5)

Rand found pornography offensive but, of course, advocated its absolute right to be published. (6) Her controversial views on homosexuality are beyond the scope of the current essay, but whether she regarded it as a psychological problem or not, Rand's undeveloped and unpublished opinion here cannot be said to amount to a philosophic principle or to a part of Objectivism. (7)

Many have concluded from Rand's advocacy of "high standards," if you will, that she was a sexual conservative. Branden plays into this over-simplified view when he says that sexually Rand was "[s]urprisingly undaring," with regard to the secrecy of the affair, as if to her the affair was purely a matter of sexual adventurism. (8)

On the other hand, Rand completely rejects many of the traditional injunctions of contemporary, conservative morality, such as those against premarital sex, abortion, birth control. Her novels celebrate sex. It is also clear that Rand rejected any formalistic position about the circumstances under which a sexual relationship is appropriate. As she explained to *Playboy*:

> [Sex should] involve... a very serious relationship. Whether that relationship should or should not become a marriage is a question which depends on the circumstances and the context of the two persons' lives. I consider marriage a very important institution, but it is important when and if two people have found the person with whom they wish to spend the rest of their lives—a question of which no man or woman can be automatically certain... But this does not mean that any relationship based on less than total certainty is improper. I think the question of an affair or marriage depends upon the knowledge and the position of the two persons involved and should be left up to them. Either [marriage or an affair] is moral, provided only that both parties take the relationship seriously and that it is based on values. (9)

Rand suggests that it would be wrong to settle for anything less than the "highest value" available. However, no absolute "height" on the value-scale is ever prescribed, and Rand leaves this open to the circumstances of individual context. Nor does her position appear to exclude, in itself, the existence of two (or more) incommensurable values of similar importance, that is, different kinds of values—both of highest priority—expressed in different individuals. For this reason alone, the exclusive interest in one's "highest value" only suggests a comparison to similar values, leaving the issue of monogamy wide open in Rand's ethics.

It is also interesting to note that Rand, normally explicit and comprehensive, never directly addressed the morality of sexual exclusivity during her lifetime in any of her published writings.

Moreover, it appears that Rand's bias in favor of sex is such that she actually questions the psychology of those who do not feel the need to express their values physically (in the appropriate situation). In *Atlas Shrugged*, Rand had written that, "...just as an idea unexpressed in physical action is contemptible hypocrisy, so is platonic love—and just as physical action unguided by an idea is a fool's self-fraud, so is sex when cut off from one's code of values." (10) A suppression of sex and its unprincipled indulgence represent, for Rand, two sides of the identical coin—the failure to integrate one's thinking and values with one's life.

In her private journals, dated October 4, 1949, before ever meeting Mr. Branden, Rand had first expressed this idea as follows:

> Just as pure "spirituality," divorced from physical action,
> is evil hypocrisy—so is the materialism which attempts to
> have matter give man purpose, value and satisfaction. Just
> as "Platonic Love" is evil hypocrisy—so is purely physical
> sex, which is an evil destruction of one's values. (11)

Rand believed that happiness depends upon acting on our values, under the appropriate circumstances, and she appears to be as vigorously opposed to the concept of celibacy as to the idea of promiscuity. This still leaves the question of "appropriate circumstances" relatively wide open, while it also reveals Rand's actively "pro-sex" orientation.

Such an orientation is certainly expressed by Rand in her tribute to Marilyn Monroe, published in *The Los Angeles Times* in 1962, two weeks after the actress' death. Rand wrote:

> A woman, the only one, who was able to project that
> glowingly innocent sexuality of a being from some planet
> uncorrupted by guilt—who found herself regarded and

ballyhooed as a vulgar symbol of obscenity—and who still had the courage to declare: "We are all born sexual creatures, thank God, but it's a pity so many people despise and crush this natural gift." (12)

Even in her affair with Branden, we find that Rand—once again—had the courage to actually try to live in accordance with her abstract thinking.

Barbara Branden writes that Rand "lived in her head," not in reality, and that this was inevitably the cause of disaster in her handling of personal relationships.

> To Ayn, other people were not fully real; they were moving and breathing abstractions, they were, for good or ill, the embodiments of moral and psychological principles... It was how she saw herself; it was how she saw everyone else. (13)

Unfortunately, Ms. Branden writes, Rand's "concept of the source and meaning of sexual love" was "false to the infinite complexities and needs of the human psyche." (14) In her view, attempting to impose Rand's view of sex on real life could only lead to disaster.

Mr. Branden himself suggests much the same when he writes of "the rarefied atmosphere of philosophical abstraction" which both led to the affair and exemplified its cruelty. (15)

Today, Ayn Rand's affair with Nathaniel Branden has provided others with the conclusive *ad hominem* to end any further discussion of Rand's thought on subjects that have nothing to do with sex. Even many of Rand's most stalwart defenders question her psychology in this regard, while asserting their ability to "separate the woman from her ideas."

Because the Brandens have characterized their break with Rand as being almost exclusively the result of "a woman scorned," eyes tend to roll at the very mention of the topic, and many are simply bored by what they regard as a "bedroom drama." But, as the Brandens themselves suggest and as Rand herself had said, Objectivism, her philosophy, governed all aspects of her life—even sex—and for that reason, if no other, this topic deserves serious consideration.

❖

Rand was a married woman nearing fifty when she began an affair with a university graduate student in his mid-twenties who was also married.

In some of her best writing, Barbara Branden writes of the inevitability of "an ugly tangle of deceit and emotional savaging and pain" from the outset, and she asks, "How did Ayn... not know that course on which she was embarking could lead only to tragedy?" Rand should have known better, she could have known better, and, if Rand was "the guiltiest" of the four in this regard, then surely she "paid the highest price," Ms. Branden writes. (16)

Nonetheless, with regard to the affair, Rand's thinking was not so much reasoning as it was rationalization, say the Brandens. According to Mr. Branden, Rand could create a chain of powerful logic to justify any of her desires. In this context, Branden calls her "a sorceress of reason." (17) The Brandens can only be deliberately ignoring the fact that Rand had espoused—even before meeting Branden—precisely the ideas on sexuality that would lead her to such an affair. For the Brandens to call her later position "rationalization" is disingenuous, for, as we shall see, Rand's views on this subject were part of the logical development of her thought, views she held before considering an affair with Branden.

The Brandens' version proceeds from this premise: Rand's domineering nature led her to an affair with a much younger man whom she could "control." Rand's blindness to the context of others led her to cruelly ignore her own husband's feelings, as well as those of Barbara Branden. Rand sought the creation of a new reality, free from the pain of her actual experience, in which she was the adulated master in every way—an adulation and control which Rand "demanded."

And, of course, Rand herself is described as being completely blind to any of these psychological issues. Thus the Brandens imply that the affair represented an ill-fated experiment in Objectivist ethics and psychology— as in a sense the whole of Rand's life did—but that it was also the product of neurotic rationalizations.

Nonetheless, we read in *The Passion of Ayn Rand* that at the time, at least, Rand's motivation appeared to Ms. Branden "as crystalline in its purity and clarity as the functioning of [Ayn's] mind." (18)

The Brandens at times indicate another less neurotic reason for their own youthful receptiveness and the comparative youthfulness of many of Rand's later friends. The young, less set in their mental ways, are more open to radical new ideas. (19)

Rand's philosophy is as radical as one can imagine. Only those prepared to rethink most of the conventional opinions of our time—almost always the young—will even give such ideas a hearing. Moreover, Rand's philosophy, with its heroic sensibilities, has a unique appeal to the young. Rand says what the young need to hear—that greatness and happiness are possible. It is a sad fact that many lose this "sense of life" as they mature.

Rand did not seek out the young—including the Brandens. It was they who sought out Rand—in great numbers.

As we have seen, it was the Brandens who were the "controlling" manipulators, deceiving and exploiting Ayn Rand. And it was the Brandens, of course, who had offered her more adulation than they honestly believed Rand deserved, as they themselves now admit. Rand had never asked for such adulation—in many ways she had tried to avoid it.

Certainly, an acute awareness of the unique, almost transcendent nature of the affair existed from the beginning, as both of the Brandens concede. Ms. Branden tells us that she *wanted* to live in the kind of world about which Rand spoke. She quotes Rand as saying, "If the four of us were lesser people, it could never have happened and you could never accept it." (20)

Rand had believed that the Brandens, like herself, could transcend the conventional norms and that their emotions reflected the beliefs they claimed to share with her. Unfortunately, Rand had taken the depth of the Brandens' agreement with her at face value.

Those who cannot condone an extramarital liaison under any circumstances will never be convinced, and the defense of extramarital affairs is both irrelevant to and beyond the scope of the current focus. However, the Brandens' recurring theme is Rand's hypocrisy. And on this score, important evidence has come to light with the publication of Rand's private journals that we will examine.

By the standard of her own convictions, Rand appears to have behaved with the remarkable integrity anyone familiar with her would expect. The affair between Rand and Branden was a serious one which lasted many years. Rand had known Branden quite well for almost five years before starting the affair, which had its origins in their highly intellectual relationship. (He was not Rand's secretary or intern.) Indeed, their apparent intellectual affinity, largely due to the rather comprehensive nature of Rand's interests, seemed to encompass philosophy, psychology, art and, of course, sex.

Branden also (deceptively) conveyed an emotional affinity with Rand that encompassed everything from their esthetic preferences to the deepest aspects of their psychology.

The Brandens both suggest that, although in retrospect much too immature for such a relationship, Branden was mature beyond his years and that in many important ways Rand was unusually youthful and energetic for her years. Branden writes, "Never was our energy and enthusiasm greater than that of this woman who was twenty-five years our senior."

Branden relates that he had been bored for most of his youth, and that he always regarded himself as "too serious" for his young contemporaries. "With Ayn everything was simple, natural, easy," Branden reports, even more so than with a wife of similar age. (21)

There is no dispute that both of the involved spouses were fully informed—and that each had consented—before the affair became sexual. The Branden account suggests long and careful discussions on the subject before the affair commenced, if nothing else. No children were involved, and the situation directly involved only four consenting adults.

While the relationship was kept otherwise discreet, the mutual admiration and closeness between Rand and Branden was never a secret. Nor does it appear that Rand ever explicitly denied the affair.

We do know that she had originally dedicated *Atlas Shrugged,* "To Frank O'Connor and Nathaniel Branden."

It is, indeed, difficult to identify any dishonesty regarding the affair by Rand at any time, despite the Brandens' assertions to the contrary.

Everything short of an affair was well known, and, according to the Brandens, many guessed the affair as well. Branden reports that "one of the often asked questions" following his lectures at NBI was: "Is it possible to be in love with two people at the same time?" He reports Rand's own answer to students: "It's a project that only giants can handle." Branden even confesses that at the time he thought this was "a public announcement of our relationship." (22)

Some secret.

Rand's answer to these questions is highly revealing. She implies that a high degree of moral character is required—and, perhaps, that the intensity of the commitment required is equally high—and that such demands would probably make this a rare circumstance. The situation is not inherently evil, however, as the positive implication to the word "giants" makes plain.

In effect, Rand's position is "great—if you can handle it."

Rand, it seems, gave herself the same caution. According to Branden, the seriousness of his mutual attraction with Rand was first observed by their respective spouses. We are even told that it was Ms. Branden who declared to an utterly unconscious Branden, "You two are in love with each other!" (23)

Perhaps most revealingly, Branden also admits that Rand approached the idea of an affair with great caution from the start, carefully questioning him about his seriousness. (24) Rand's reticence, according to Branden, was repeated on several other occasions during the course of their affair.

He even attests, "I was clearly the initiator," during the period when his relationship with Rand first became sexual. (25)

Branden describes the beginning of the affair thus: "[Rand] *wanted* to be a little frightened of taking the final step, and she *wanted* me to persevere, to overcome her fears and blast through her objections. She wanted to care about Frank's feelings, and she wanted me not to care at all." (26) While he is obviously guessing at Rand's desires here, their actual behavior at the time is made abundantly clear.

Branden relates that the major hiatus in their affair—during the prolonged depression which he reports Rand suffered in the years following the publication of *Atlas Shrugged*—was of Rand's initiation.

He allows that, although it was Rand who sought its resumption, when the affair resumed, her inquiries about his continued feelings were made "almost shyly." (27)

But when their relationship began to founder, Rand became, again, the reticent one in the very months preceding their break. Branden reports that "[Rand] was *still* reticent about the resurrection of our affair" in late 1967 and early 1968. (28)

In other words, Branden was *still* making sexual advances to Rand through this period.

Branden confesses that he never once suggested to Rand that he ever found the age difference to be the slightest "barrier," or that he found Rand anything less than desirable—until the very end.

Indeed, Branden says, "[i]t was *always* important to me that [Rand] feel desirable, sexual, physically fulfilled." (29)

Branden suggests that this continued long after his libido was telling him otherwise. Yet, he can still somehow claim that he was giving Rand "non-verbal" signals to this effect which, as usual, he does not specify. What those signals were, or how Mr. Branden expected Rand to perceive them over his efforts to vanquish her reticence, his unceasing efforts to make her feel desirable, and his many explicit statements to the contrary, is not indicated.

Branden describes conversations in which Rand says, for instance, "If our romance is over, say so." (30)

Even after his secret affair with a younger woman had begun, he did not say so. Even after his legal separation from Ms. Branden, he did not say so. For *years* after it was "over," at least in Branden's head, he never said so.

Branden says that he was always somehow prevented from doing so by his fear of Rand's anger and "moralism."

Branden describes conversations in which Rand asked, "Is it my age? I could accept that." Branden reports his very private thoughts at the time: "No, you couldn't." (31) But, of course, he never gave Rand that chance; nor did he ever give himself a chance to actually know until other, much larger issues were also involved—issues like Mr. Branden's unrelenting dishonesty.

Ms. Branden even tells us that she asked Branden at the time of the break why he did not "take advantage, over the years, of the 'outs' Ayn offered you about the issue of her age?" (32)

She relates that, "over the years," Branden had repeatedly protested to Rand that age did not matter to him, informing his readers that, at the time, he could even tell himself that Rand had "no equals at any age." What Branden had told Rand, in response to the many offered "outs" *about age*, was "You will always be a sexual being," and that "The younger man is chasing you," and that "You should see yourself as a woman, *as long as you're alive*," after all, "Why should you grow old gracefully?" (33)

As we shall see, Rand's "reticence" with regard to the affair at this point, the many "outs" she offered Branden over the "age" issue, and

Branden's prolonged deception of Rand on this issue, are confirmed by Rand's own private notes.

In fairness to Rand—and taking into account the obvious efforts which she put into the relationship—she cannot be said to have "chased" a younger man, at all.

Whatever one's opinion of the Rand-Branden affair, at least Rand was honest about it to those who mattered—scrupulously, rigorously honest. Honesty is a key virtue in Rand's ethics, which, on the other hand, have no commandment against adultery.

The principal remaining ethical objection to this affair, at least from Rand's own philosophical framework, involves the apparent indifference to the feelings of their respective spouses of both Branden and Rand. If the Brandens are to be believed, this affair took a heavy toll on both Ms. Branden, who suffered at least one major anxiety attack early in the affair, and Frank O'Connor, who, we are told, slowly became an alcoholic. Their inarticulate, emotional objections, according to the Brandens, were simply swept aside with callous, reckless and, perhaps, malicious abandon by Rand and Mr. Branden.

Certainly, the average contemporary husband would find such a situation intolerable, and the Branden portrait is designed to emphasize the victim status of O'Connor and to cash in on many tired clichés. Indeed, we shall see that the Brandens are heavily invested in the notion of Rand's alleged callousness in regard to her husband's feelings. But, we shall also see that O'Connor's actual opinions and emotions about sex were given an inadequate analysis by the Brandens, and that the evidence of O'Connor's "suffering" is open to quite considerable doubt.

Their strongest basis for contending that O'Connor suffered unbearably is his alleged alcoholism.

In support of this allegation, Ms. Branden cannot claim any personal knowledge of O'Connor's excessive drinking, and she must admit that "[i]t was not until years later" that "the truth was revealed" to her.

We are told by Ms. Branden that "Frank had always enjoyed a drink or two in the evening—his powerful martinis were guaranteed to elicit gasps at the first sip by an unsuspecting guest." Despite her admitted lack of *any* other first-hand knowledge, Ms. Branden goes so far as to allege that "[O'Connor's] drinking began to be a way of life." (34)

Someone should have warned those "unsuspecting" guests that a "martini" is, by definition, straight gin with a whisper of vermouth. Whatever the strength of the drinks he served, Ms. Branden admits that she cannot report *ever* seeing O'Connor intoxicated—not once—despite their close personal association for over eighteen years. The most Ms. Branden can relate as evidence is that "Frank was always vague about what he did when Ayn and Nathaniel were together." (35)

Ms. Branden's desire to relate these two events with one another, despite her lack of evidence, is the only thing that is certain here.

Despite her closeness to the O'Connors, Ms. Branden cannot name a single member of Rand's large circle of associates, a single friend, a fellow art student of O'Connor's or a single resident of the apartment building which she shared with the O'Connors for many years who can report *ever* seeing O'Connor intoxicated. No one.

In fact, we are explicitly told that "[n]one of the friends Frank shared with Ayn were aware, during those years, that he drank to excess." In addition, "neither Ayn nor any of her friends [even] suspected" that O'Connor was an alcoholic. (36)

Those curious as to Ms. Branden's source must be satisfied that "[a] friend of Frank's," who goes unidentified and is described only as "a recovered alcoholic," is said by Ms. Branden to have "sometimes" joined O'Connor for several drinks at a Manhattan bar. Based upon this extensive evidence, then, our unnamed witness "was convinced that Frank was an alcoholic." (37)

Recovering alcoholics will almost always refer to themselves as "alcoholics" and rarely as being "recovered." But, for obvious reasons, Ms. Branden does not want to rely on an "alcoholic," even though it places the word in proximity to Frank O'Connor, albeit irrelevantly. Ms. Branden's tenuous reliance on a single, unnamed witness to establish O'Connor's drinking, a witness with credibility issues of his own, is certainly not surprising; but the internal problems with this report suggest that no such witness may even exist.

For, as indicated, even if our "recovered" alcoholic exists, his own stated base of interaction with O'Connor was quite limited, in addition to his own credibility being open to substantial doubt. Undeterred, Ms. Branden is eager to share with her readers the conclusory opinion of someone who was drunk at the time, and who only "sometimes" even saw O'Connor, at best.

Whatever Ms. Branden's motive in suppressing the name of this key witness, its effect on the credibility of the story is the same: an unnamed source, as any rookie reporter knows, is less credible than one willing to be named. It also conveniently places the witness beyond the reach of pesky follow-up interviews.

Respect for privacy is probably not Ms. Branden's motivation for failing to name another "friend" whom she quotes as inferring that O'Connor's lack of appetite in his final years was due to his "drinking all the time." (38)

We are not told whose "friend" this was—O'Connor's, Rand's or Ms. Branden's—but we are also not told that this "friend" was an alcoholic, recovered or otherwise, whose privacy might be in jeopardy from the report. The suppression of this "friend's" identity—years after the deaths of both O'Connor and Rand—can only raise further doubts about Ms. Branden's credibility on these issues. We are given no reason Ms. Branden would have to protect this perfectly safe "source" in 1986. Ms. Branden's failure to name her source in this instance has no other apparent explanation but to obfuscate her story's origins. This biographer will not always be clear as to her sources, but she rarely gives verbatim quotes to unnamed witnesses. This practice is almost exclusively confined to the subject of O'Connor's alleged alcoholism.

Still more important, Ms. Branden cannot tell us that this unnamed "friend" was relying on anything but hearsay herself—was the witness's own source Ms. Branden?

This is a conclusory opinion, as well, and, in this instance, absolutely no evidentiary foundation is provided. It is safe to believe that Ms. Branden, aware of the seriousness of her charge, would have told us if this witness did have such personal knowledge.

Ms. Branden goes so far as to actually pass on the foundationless hearsay description of O'Connor as "weaving, incoherent and smelling of alcohol" when answering the door. Her source for this? An unnamed "member of the newsletter staff" who would come to the door with papers requiring Rand's attention. Once again, the identity of her witness is inexplicably suppressed. The number of such experiences by the witness is neither estimated or even characterized as "frequently," "occasionally," "sometimes," or even "once." (39)

We can only be witnessing Ms. Branden's penchant for self-serving exaggeration, if not outright falsehood, for surely such a degree of alcoholism would have been better corroborated had Ms. Branden anything of substance to report on the matter. (40)

What is known is that O'Connor died in 1979 after a long illness and that for some time he had suffered the effects of what Ms. Branden describes as "severe arteriosclerosis." (41) Ms. Branden tells us that the effects of this disease include reduced blood-flow to the brain. Medical opinion agrees that the aging patient with this disease will often experience diminished mental functioning and even disorientation.

One might have expected Rand's "Boswell" to have indicated the potential impact of this on her own claims of O'Connor's alcoholism, since her allegation is in no way based on any personal knowledge, and Ms. Branden is forced to rely on what appear to be only two unnamed sources who cannot claim more than very limited personal knowledge themselves.

As her sole corroboration for these sources, Ms. Branden refers to the "rows of empty liquor bottles" in O'Connor's studio which Rand's housekeeper is said to have found there after O'Connor's death.

From the text, it is not clear to whom the description of "rows" can be ascribed. The most likely candidate for this description is Ms. Branden herself, since the housekeeper is said to have been indignant at Ms. Branden's allegation. She reported to Leonard Peikoff that any bottles she had found there were used by O'Connor to mix paints.

Rand's critics have remarkably ridiculed their own principal witness's position, observing that paint brushes cannot easily be used with narrow-necked bottles. But the housekeeper's assertion was to the effect that the paints had been mixed in these bottles, not that they had been used as a palette. (42)

Of course, the bottles are rather weak circumstantial evidence and are largely beside the point. Ignoring the fact that artist studios are likely to have a variety of such objects, used for paints or not, there is, in any event, no quantity given to these bottles. In addition, for all one can tell, these "rows" may have represented the entire previous thirty years of O'Connor's—and others'—consumption.

Even according to Ms. Branden's own anonymous accounts, the only two witnesses who claim to possess *any* first-hand knowledge of O'Connor's alleged alcoholism cannot also claim any kind of closeness to the O'Connors. The only identified witness, the housekeeper, rejects the opinion Ms. Branden draws from her "evidence." The principal witness admits to being a "recovered" addict himself and only claims to have "sometimes" had drinks with O'Connor at a bar. He does not report ever seeing O'Connor intoxicated. The quality and quantity of the second witness's interaction with O'Connor is not specified at all. And, for no reason, both witnesses' names are withheld.

It must be borne in mind that the Brandens are the exclusive sources for the claim of O'Connor's alcoholism, and that both have a vested interest in portraying O'Connor as a devastated man, driven to drink by Rand's callousness.

Ms. Branden's claims in this respect, if not her evidence, appear to have expanded over the years. She asserted to an interviewer in 1992, that when (again, unnamed) guests came into the O'Connors' apartment, "the first thing they smelled was alcohol..." (43) If such evidence had ever existed, Ms. Branden surely could have mentioned this six years earlier. And, again, she leaves us guessing as to who any of these unnamed people actually were, along with every other important detail. Those closest to the O'Connors in their last years together have uniformly dismissed Ms. Branden's claims.

Mr. Branden, of course, shares Ms. Branden's conviction that O'Connor drank excessively, but he does not claim to have "evidence" of any kind.

Like Ms. Branden he cannot say that he ever once saw O'Connor intoxicated during the eighteen years of their close association or that he had ever even heard of anyone who had seen him intoxicated.

Perhaps wanting to bypass the housekeeper as a witness—she does appear to be hostile to their position—Branden reports that his sister, Elayne, "told him" in the passive voice that such bottles had been "discovered." But Branden cannot tell us that his sister personally saw the infamous bottles or, as seems more likely, is herself relying on the housekeeper as her source. We are not informed as to whether Elayne ever visited the studio at all.

Branden also quotes his sister Elayne as believing that Rand had "refused to admit" her husband's alcoholism, despite the fact that we are not told that Rand (who, of course, lived with O'Connor) was aware of either of the unnamed eyewitnesses or their "evidence." (It is hard to be "in denial" of something one has never seen in the first place.) Branden cannot tell us that his sister was an actual witness to O'Connor's drinking or intoxication—*even once*—any more than she is witness to the bottles. (44)

Branden's real source for his belief in O'Connor's alcoholism is his former wife, Ms. Branden, who, she confesses, never noticed it at the time and was only introduced to the idea later, i.e., when she would need to find evidence of O'Connor's emotional devastation. Mr. Branden, as well, confirms that neither he nor his wife even "suspected" O'Connor's drinking during their years with Rand.

Perhaps feeling the ice under them cracking a bit, Mr. Branden curiously adds in the new edition of his memoir that it was Ms. Branden who first informed him of O'Connor's problem "many years later." (45) Why is Branden now inserting Ms. Branden as his ultimate source if he is not becoming less secure in his own previous assertions on the topic?

In addition to all of this, if O'Connor was an alcoholic, at least in the Sixties, he appears to have been a highly "functional" one.

Ms. Branden tells us that O'Connor not only studied at the well-known Art Students League, but that he also "served ably and conscientiously for three years" on the League's policy-making Board of Control to which he had been elected sometime around 1964. (46)

It is true that "functional alcoholics" can deceive and manipulate those around them, and that many are ingenious at hiding their addiction, but we are asked to believe that neither O'Connor's wife nor any of their closest friends nor any of the numerous people that were always around Rand, ever once noticed a sign or symptom of all this drinking through all those years.

Against this, we are provided only the summary opinions of two unnamed witnesses who had little in the way of first-hand knowledge— and one of these admittedly had a clouded head at the time.

It is also interesting to observe that immediately upon disclaiming any personal knowledge of O'Connor's excessive drinking, Ms. Branden adds that it was only "much later" that it became "a powerful and explosive source of friction" between the O'Connors. (47) As usual, absolutely no witnesses to any "friction" between the O'Connors on the issue of alcohol are suggested to exist, the O'Connors are obviously not Ms. Branden's source for this, and, in fact, she tells us that Rand herself "never suspected" her husband's drinking.

One could get whiplash from Ms. Branden's contradictions.

Curiously, Ms. Branden does not give a date to any of her unnamed witnesses' "observations" at all, and her own lack of evidence compels her to put any problems or "friction" into the period after the "break"—after any chance for Ms. Branden herself to observe anything. This, of course, would dissociate O'Connor's alleged drinking problem from his wife's affair—the suggested cause of this drinking in the first place. And yet, as previously indicated, it is those closest to the O'Connors in their *later years* who most vehemently deny this charge.

In the end, there is no reason to suppose that Ms. Branden is not the true source of this urban legend herself.

It is not surprising that we find the Brandens making bold accusations on nearly non-existent evidence, nor is it by now surprising that they manufacture and exaggerate evidence to create a common and self-serving version of history. As we have seen, they have been doing this for years. The unpleasant surprise is the new object of their attack in the quiet and unassuming O'Connor.

Unlike his famous wife, Frank O'Connor did not leave powerful words to defend himself beyond the grave. Unprepared for the impending polemic to be raised against him, O'Connor was by all accounts a man of quiet and retiring disposition.

The absence of evidence does not imply an absence of character, but the Brandens presented a void of evidence as an opportunity to proclaim that O'Connor was a void of a human being—a void into which poured alcohol and grief.

The boldness of the Brandens' claim is not matched by the quality of their evidence. Once again, this disparity casts suspicion on the whole of their self-serving assertion, rather than seeming like a painful admission of undeniable truth.

For similar reasons, the entire portrait of O'Connor's alleged anguish at his wife's affair cannot be accepted uncritically.

When the possibility of a romantic relationship between Branden and Rand was first discussed, Ms. Branden writes that "Frank and I listened, stricken, grasping only a random sentence, a disconnected thought here and there." (48)

Ms. Branden, of course, can speak only for herself. The idea that these two shared identical reactions seems highly unlikely in any event. Nonetheless, Ms. Branden will frequently lapse into the form of speech "Frank and I" in this context, arrogating the right to speak for the two of them as if they experienced the same emotions throughout. As Ms. Branden forthrightly claims, "Frank's motivation seemed to be almost identical with mine." (49) How Ms. Branden discerned this remains a mystery. "Seemed to be" seems to be a classic Brandenian formulation, and it seems also to signal a total lack of evidence for the claim being made.

If Ms. Branden is not to be believed in her descriptions of her own role in these events, as we have seen, even the report of her own alleged emotions at the time, then all the less can she be accepted as a source for O'Connor's emotions.

Contradicting his former wife's account of the events they both witnessed, Mr. Branden does not recall that Ms. Branden was ever "stricken." He writes, "[Barbara's] face disclosed no discernible emotion beyond a tinge of apprehension. It was as if she already knew everything, and no transitions, no explanations were really needed..." (50)

At least at the time, Branden reports, he "could not imagine [his wife] feeling sexual jealousy where I was concerned." (51) Ms. Branden claims in her own book that the suggestion of an affair was a shock and a crushing blow. Yet, if there was not substantial evidence to support Mr. Branden in such an unusual belief, it is hardly likely that even the most self-deluded American husband would believe something like what he professes here.

What could possibly have sustained Mr. Branden in this remarkable position if his wife had *in fact* strenuously objected to the affair?

Part of the answer lies in the fact that Ms. Branden had recently confessed to her young husband that she had had a number of secret affairs of her own.

Ms. Branden chose not to share her own sexual history with her readers—it surely would have interfered with her self-portrait of personal victimhood. But in his own self-defense, Mr. Branden does reveal this additional context. In the new edition of his memoir, Branden is quick to add that he was convinced that Ms. Branden was "not involved" with someone at the time that his affair with Rand began, but infidelity seems to have been an issue the Brandens had already dealt with repeatedly (52)

Mr. Branden does not recall O'Connor as being "stricken"—or even surprised— either. He writes, "It was clear from their exchange in the first moments of his arrival that [Frank] and Ayn had already had some preliminary discussion. He looked as if the entire situation were already known to him, as if he too had been in the living room all afternoon."

Branden even quotes Rand as saying that her husband "saw it coming before I did." The Brandens both report that Ms. Branden "saw it coming" before her husband did, as well.

Branden is nevertheless just as invested as his former wife is in painting O'Connor as a victim, so he must produce *something* to leave us with that impression. Branden reports of O'Connor that "[t]he skin of his face seemed paler than usual and drawn. I thought I saw a hint of anger in his eyes, but... only when he looked at Ayn." (53) In typical Branden style, it "seemed" and he "thought he saw a hint..."

After his wife had voiced her objections when the idea of the affair was first mentioned, Branden then claims that O'Connor shouted, "I won't put up with this, it's outrageous!" In order to leave the desired impression, Branden adds that O'Connor "then relapsed into passivity and impotence even before Ayn could complete her response." (54) The response isn't reported.

Branden's choice of a word like "impotence" is not accidental. He has taken advantage of every ragged cliché about cuckolded husbands and the alleged slights to a husband's "manhood" that this situation might suggest to the less sophisticated, in order to confirm Rand's cruel indifference to human feelings. (55)

Ms. Branden agrees that she was the first to raise an objection at the suggestion of an affair, saying, "I won't be any part of this." Ms. Branden reports that O'Connor then, "[f]or the first time... spoke. He jerked upright in his chair, and his voice was ferocious as he said, 'And *I* won't be part of it.'" (56)

Obviously, given the conflicting reports of the two surviving witnesses, what O'Connor actually said will likely never be known with certainty.

It is interesting to note that this is nearly the only comment Ms. Branden can quote from O'Connor regarding his wife's affair. She, too, notes the pallor of his face when the subject is first broached and recounts the "faint touch of relief on his face" when the affair takes its time to become sexual; but Ms. Branden can give us little else of O'Connor's response—except her own opinion.

Despite telling her readers that "Frank and I met together often" during this period, and that "[h]is *silent*, helpless suffering was terrible to see," we are told that it was "predominantly" Ms. Branden who talked "while [O'Connor] listened as I tried to make the irrational turn rational for both of us." (57) Of course, this could also be interpreted as O'Connor simply providing a sympathetic ear and shoulder for Ms. Branden.

Ms. Branden does appear to claim—unfortunately without the benefit of any quotes from O'Connor himself—that he spoke of being "tormented by the guilt of failure, the guilt of not being the hero he believed Ayn deserved..." The thought—and the language—are clearly Ms. Branden's and appear to contradict Ms. Branden's description of O'Connor's "silent agony" as well as her later statement that O'Connor had "never spoken" of his feelings to others, including herself. (58)

Ms. Branden reports the demeanor of O'Connor in these conversations as follows: "Frank listened, and sometimes he nodded—and sometimes he exploded with rage and swore he'd leave Ayn and never see her again—and sometimes his eye filled with tears and said only 'No. No. No...'" (59) It would, of course, have been helpful if Ms. Branden had provided more of O'Connor's actual words, and, as usual, the reader is left starved for more specifics on O'Connor's alleged misery and threats to leave Rand.

Extraordinarily, Ms. Branden never seems to have counseled O'Connor to express any of this agony to Rand herself.

As important as these many heart-to-heart conversations seem to have been, Ms. Branden has kept O'Connor, Rand's husband, among the least-quoted persons in her entire biography, though this surely should have provided the richest vein of support for Ms. Branden's thesis.

Mr. Branden reports that "during this period [when the affair first began] Barbara and I grew, oddly, closer..."

However, Branden also reports that this new closeness did not increase the "intensity" of their relationship to the level of "romantic love." His marriage, according to Branden, already lacked much intensity, anyway. (60)

It also seems that within a very brief (but unspecified) period of time, "[O'Connor's] *silent* agony over [Rand's] love affair with Nathaniel seemed a thing of the past..." O'Connor's newly discovered love of painting shortly after he moved to New York, according to Ms. Branden, made it "as if he had barely time to notice" his utter despair anymore. Even with Rand, it seems, "the resentments and anxieties and raw, chafed nerves" became "equally a problem of the past" for O'Connor. (61)

O'Connor's enthusiasm for painting was observed by many people during this period, so it is something the Brandens can hardly deny. But for O'Connor to retain his "victim" status, even as it seems to all the world that he is quite happy, a better explanation is required, as Ms. Branden clearly senses, especially after twice already referring to O'Connor's alleged suffering as "silent."

In a bizarre attempt to bolster her case, Ms. Branden claims that it was financial dependency on Rand which kept O'Connor in the marriage. Ms. Branden claims that this was something which O'Connor only "alluded to" years later. Despite the fact that O'Connor "revered" Rand, in Ms. Branden's words, we are told that the affair would have driven him away if he only had some financial security.

Ms. Branden's sole evidence for this is a private conversation which she claims to have had with O'Connor some twelve years after the affair had begun.

Ms. Branden reports that after an argument with his wife, O'Connor said to Ms. Branden alone, of course, "I want to leave her,"—his voice apparently "a hiss of rage and despair"—then adding, "but where would I go?... What would I do?..." (62)

The manifest absurdity of believing that the husband of a very successful author—whose crucial role in that author's own work had been publicly professed by Rand—would be left penniless from a divorce cannot be ascribed to O'Connor but to Ms. Branden. (Even in those days, husbands of high-income wives could—and did—get attractive settlements.) Surely, if such a conversation had taken place, Ms. Branden would have immediately assured him of this, and she could have used as an example the agreeable nature of her own recent separation from Mr. Branden to support her case.

After the great success of Rand's novels, there was never any reason for O'Connor to fear financially, and he is not likely to have been so dull-witted as to believe otherwise. But this completely unverifiable story does make good copy for Ms. Branden, someone whose livelihood depended upon Rand in a more precarious way.

If we are to take the Brandens' word for it, the O'Connors' marriage was an empty fraud. For Rand, it was maintained by her fantasy-like projection of O'Connor. For O'Connor, this supposed financial dependence serves to explain what is otherwise inexplicable to the Brandens—O'Connor's staying by Rand's side.

The Brandens tell us that the O'Connors' marriage was in shambles from the Forties onward. But here, as well, they cannot claim much by way of direct evidence or personal knowledge.

Branden tells us that when he first got to know the O'Connors at their ranch in California, to all appearances they were perfectly happy. "At this time I had absolutely no intimation of trouble between Ayn and Frank. Ayn told me, much later, that those years on the ranch had been very bad for them" and that they quarreled a "great deal." (63) It was one of those private conversations with Rand—"much later," as he puts it—which cannot be verified or contradicted and with which we are all too familiar.

Ms. Branden follows suit. She writes that "none of their friends suspected the extent to which the [O'Connors'] relationship was troubled. A number of years later, Ayn was to admit that during this period the friction between them and their lack of intellectual communication had come to so frustrate her that she seriously considered divorce." (64) Once again, Rand's actual words are not used, just Ms. Branden's. Even ignoring its unverifiable nature, it appears to contradict the evidence of any actual witness. And, once again, Ms. Branden strangely opts for the passive voice, Rand "was to admit." (At this point, one is tempted to call it the "passive-aggressive" voice.)

"None" of their friends—zero—ever even "suspected," yet Ms.

Branden's paraphrase of a private conversation is supposed to trump all of this. Despite her own biases, the reader is expected to swallow Ms. Branden's conclusory assertions on faith. The Brandens' pattern has become formulaic.

Ms. Branden tells us that O'Connor dreaded moving to New York, as it "tore him" away from his beloved ranch. O'Connor raised peacocks and grew crops and flowers commercially there and, we are told, found great solace in this physical activity.

This is meant as another example of Rand's callousness towards O'Connor's feelings, despite the fact that O'Connor had already turned fifty-four and the physically demanding nature of his ranch-work could not have continued much longer in any event.

O'Connor appears to have loved the ranch, and he may well have preferred California to New York City, but the question of moving to New York was clearly more complex than Ms. Branden is willing to acknowledge.

O'Connor had lived with Rand in New York on a previous occasion, and he appears to have cherished the city, if not with his wife's intensity. In addition, Mr. Branden reports that the move was then desirable to both of the O'Connors for other reasons—both "Ayn and Frank seemed so unhappy" to see the Brandens move to New York, for example. He also reports O'Connor's parting words to the Brandens, "It's only for a little while," suggesting that the O'Connors had already been planning such a move. Branden further reports that, upon their arrival in New York, O'Connor only "looked happy and pleasantly tired." (65)

Once more, the actual evidence does not align itself easily with the Brandens' assertions.

Branden admits, in his own words, "how little I really understood their marriage." He says that Rand "always seemed loving and affectionate with [Frank]," and that she "complimented him constantly." (66) All of this, it seems, was part of Rand's elaborate self-deception.

O'Connor, too, is described as being constantly and overtly affectionate towards Rand. O'Connor's motives in such continuing expressions of affection remain something of a mystery for Mr. Branden.

The Brandens both note that the O'Connors were constantly holding hands, acting "cuddly," and Ms. Branden even reports that their "private affectionate names" for one another—"Cubby-hole" (O'Connor) and "Fluff" (Rand)—were known to many of their friends. (67)

Mr. Branden theorizes that "the form of romantic love had to be maintained" even if it was "imposed on a set of facts that did not match it." (68) His principal evidence for this claim appears to be that while Rand insisted upon cooking for her husband, and even complained if he did not eat enough, Rand's writing schedule often meant that it was late at night before she could. While O'Connor could and did cook for himself, Rand "professed to feel guilty" when he did.

Rand the Callous Wife, once again, imposing her "form" of marriage on poor, hungry Frank.

Evidence and conclusions of this caliber are vintage Branden.

Rand's alleged "callous indifference" must be measured against O'Connor's actual feelings about the affair. The Brandens are no more credible as witnesses on this subject than they are on the various other topics explored so far. But, as usual, the Brandens also unwittingly provide sufficient contradictory evidence to suggest another interpretation.

Branden tells us, as still another example of her callousness, that he was sometimes disconcerted when Rand would involve him in some discussion she was having with her husband. For example, Rand wanted Frank to go shopping with her and to advise her on what to wear—as Branden did.

O'Connor is not the first husband to have had this discussion with his wife, with or without a lover, but the direct comparison of the husband to the lover makes Rand appear entirely blind to O'Connor's potential feelings. Under traditional circumstances, this would seem enormously insensitive, if not thoughtlessly cruel.

Of course, the situation would never have occurred under "traditional circumstances."

Moreover, Branden reports that "when Frank looked at me, he projected no sign of resentment; on the contrary, he had the man-to-man look of an ally, who counted on me to understand everything that could not be said and as if he saw me, too, as needing a defender."

Branden tells us that he could only respond that Ayn's shopping wish proved how much O'Connor meant to Rand. This seemed to please them both. The conversation ended with the O'Connors' being "very affectionate" with one another (69).

Among his more fascinating anecdotes in this regard, Branden relates that "[s]ome months after the affair had begun, I asked Ayn how Frank was taking it, and she smiled enigmatically and answered, 'Sometimes he finds it a sexual inspiration. He looks at it as a wonderful adventure of which he is a part.'" Branden replied, "Barbara also enjoys the situation sometimes, maybe just a little, as if our relationship makes her life more glamorous, more exciting." (70)

Since Mr. Branden is our only source for this, it must, of course, be treated with skepticism. However, it is so unusual an assertion that it requires explanation even if Branden has invented it. Moreover, standing in such sharp contrast to one of the Brandens' central and most self-serving claims it makes at least a bid to credibility.

From this exchange, Ms. Branden's enjoyment appears to have been largely a kind of "social metaphysics," for lack of a better term, while O'Connor's reaction is perfectly consistent with the "daring" and "unconventional" man of Rand's description.

Branden quotes Rand on her own first impressions of O'Connor as follows: "I could see how much alike we were in our values. He hated the conventional. He loved the daring and the heroic." (71)

O'Connor would certainly not be the first husband to report such a situation as "sexually inspiring," but such an attitude tends to detract from the tale of Rand's cruelty. (72)

In this context, it is important to remember that, as Ms. Branden had herself observed, "...no one who knew Ayn and Frank ever saw her refuse him a firmly expressed wish." (73)

Rand's husband of fifty years knew of the affair and stayed with Rand through it all, and this remarkable man certainly deserves more careful attention than Rand's critics have so far allowed.

Ayn Rand's husband, Frank O'Connor, was a sensitive and soft-spoken man with an artistic temperament and a dry wit. A film actor without much success, he held several jobs before finding a vocation which appeared to satisfy him—painting.

Leonard Peikoff has observed that O'Connor only discovered painting late in life, and, although possessed of some talent, he was never the artist he might have been had he started earlier. But it is also clear that he never possessed the driving ambition and the intellectual brilliance of his famous wife.

That O'Connor shared Rand's philosophy cannot be doubted. Before Rand was famous, she and her husband worked together in unpaid positions on the Wilkie Presidential campaign in 1940. And once, during a televised interview shortly after O'Connor's death, Rand was questioned as to whether she hoped that there might be an afterlife. She responded that if for one minute she actually thought so, she would kill herself in order to reach her husband and tell whoever sat in judgment "how good he was." But, Rand added, O'Connor was "even more of an atheist than I am, if there can be degrees..." (74)

In Mr. Branden's first meeting with the O'Connors, he recounts that Rand asked Branden if he thought man by nature was good or bad? Rand later indicated that she was trying to ascertain if Branden thought man was inherently depraved, for example, burdened with Original Sin, or if he thought that man "at least potentially" was of heroic stature. But to the initial question Branden replied that he did not think man was either, that he possesses a potential for either. Branden tells us that "Frank broke his silence to laugh at this." (75)

Students of Rand's philosophy will appreciate that laugh. Rand believed in free will, and she, like the young Branden, rejected "Original Virtue" along with "Original Sin." Rand was really after a psychological answer from Branden—the way he *prefers* to see man. But Branden had taken her words literally—another Rand virtue—and O'Connor had grasped the minor, rhetorical "gotcha" on his wife and laughed.

If this story is true, it reveals an O'Connor who understood the system of Rand's thought—and its nuances—at a very sophisticated level.

Most significant, O'Connor appears to have shared a genuine spiritual affinity with Rand, a sensitivity that is hard to explain if he had not been intelligent. Apparently, it was O'Connor and his brother who encouraged Rand to write *We the Living*, her first novel. It was O'Connor who, when Rand first unconsciously articulated the plot of *Atlas Shrugged* during a telephone conversation, said it would make a "good novel." It was O'Connor who first dubbed it "Atlas Shrugged." O'Connor's painting, "Man Also Rises," became the cover art for the paperback edition of *The*

Fountainhead. Rand believed that his work showed a "startling artistic affinity" to her own. (76)

Ms. Branden reports that O'Connor—"whose wit was wonderfully dry and unexpected"—was responsible for some of the clever dialogue in Rand's novels. (77)

And, of course, Rand dedicated her two greatest novels to O'Connor.

Ms. Branden certainly reports that Rand "did most of the talking," but O'Connor's "silence was not aloof; he seemed to be listening carefully, smiling or nodding at times..." and that "Ayn often turned to him as she spoke, as if gaining some special comfort from the fact of his presence." (78)

That they were devoted to one another cannot be doubted. They remained married for fifty years. They always spoke of one another in the highest terms, by all accounts, including the Brandens'. Photos of the couple together almost invariably show them holding hands or gazing into each other's eyes. The photographic evidence in this regard is overwhelming, and this affectionate behavior is confirmed by numerous witnesses.

Whether they were always truly happy together, especially in light of Rand's affair, can be questioned, but the Brandens' self-contradictory answers—and dubious "evidence"—cannot be trusted on the matter.

It is true that O'Connor is never said to have had any great career ambitions and that his disposition was quiet and retiring. Nonetheless, it is reported that he enjoyed nothing more than working hard on the thirteen-acre ranch he managed in California, or working at his easel after he had found painting.

Although Ms. Branden asserts—without evidence—that it was Rand who really wrote the article on film history with O'Connor's by-line published in *The Objectivist*, Rand nowhere is said to have credited her husband with any great achievement (apart from the aid he rendered to Rand herself) or major career goal. Ms. Branden says, however, that Rand exaggerated O'Connor's character in her own mind in order to give herself the illusion that he was like a character in her books.

Ms. Branden writes, "...the man [Rand] spoke of in such extravagant terms had little to do with the real human being who was Frank." Ms. Branden does not tell us what exactly those "extravagant terms" were, apart from the following, solitary example: "I could only love a hero," because "[f]emininity is hero-worship." (79)

Ms. Branden says that, while Rand's affection for her husband was sincere and even intense, O'Connor's "actual character and virtues were not visible to or appreciated by [Rand], ...she responded instead to the heroic virtues he did not possess." (80) Ms. Branden cannot quote from Rand what those virtues are supposed to have been, nor does she specify the wild claims Rand allegedly made about her husband. The only claims Rand is reported to have actually made about O'Connor are that the two of them shared a "sense of life"—a psychological affinity at the deepest level—and that O'Connor "stood by her unflinchingly" in Rand's days of struggle. (81) Hardly overblown praise—and quite easily sufficient for profound love.

Ms. Branden tells us that "Frank was a gentle, kind, sensitive man; he was not a giant of the intellect, he was not a world-mover. But for Ayn he had to be a hero..." (82) Ms. Branden mistakenly equates "giant of the intellect" and "world-mover" with "hero" in Rand's meaning—or assumes that her readers will.

Nathaniel Branden writes that he also found "incomprehensible" O'Connor's comparative lack of ambition, given that he was "Ayn Rand's husband." He admits, however, that when Rand said "I could never love anyone who was not a hero," that "literally... meant someone who excelled in moral virtue high above the average..." By all accounts, this was something O'Connor could certainly claim.

Without indicating exactly how, Branden adds, "['Hero'] also usually connoted, in the contexts in which she used the term, someone with a range of vision and ambition far beyond anything Frank suggested." (83) We are left to contemplate those Branden "connotations" again, without the benefit of any evidence.

It appears that Rand's most extreme assertion about her husband is to be found in a letter from Rand to Leonebel Jacobs, dated January 8, 1949. Rand writes that she was tempted to use a portrait of O'Connor on the jacket of her next novel. Rand explains, "All my heroes will always be reflections of Frank, anyway." (84)

A "reflection" of her heroes does not suggest anything but what it says. Rand is not asserting an identity, only a similarity, even an inspiration, but no more.

In fact, Rand's theory of romantic love does not suggest that the parties must be intellectually equal, much less equal in their accomplishments, but rather that there exist a "sense of life" affinity, a sharing of values at the deepest level. This is precisely what Rand and O'Connor seem to have shared—and one of the few assertions Rand actually made about her husband, according to the Brandens.

In other words, according to her explicit philosophy, Rand in no way needed to "exaggerate" O'Connor to satisfy some moral or psychological requirement, despite the Brandens' suggestions to the contrary.

This was not the only thing that Branden found incomprehensible. He reports that he and Ms. Branden found the O'Connors' relationship "puzzling," and Branden frankly admits that he had to "recognize that there was something between them I did not understand."

Branden admits that he "made no particular effort to get to know Frank." He later remarks that "no one knew the contents of [O'Connor's] inner life," and again Branden concedes, "Nor did we inquire." (85) (Just exactly who the "we" is meant to include strangely goes unspecified.)

What Rand actually said about O'Connor is revealing:

> I will not retell here the story of the publication of *The Fountainhead.* But it would be impossible for me to discuss *The Fountainhead* or any part of its history without mentioning the man who made it possible for me to write it: my husband, Frank O'Connor.

> In a play I wrote in my early thirties, *Ideal,* the heroine, a screen star, speaks for me when she says: "I want to see, real, living, and in the hour of my own days, that glory I create as an illusion. I want it real. I want to know that there is someone, somewhere, who wants it, too. Or else, what is the use of seeing it, and working, and burning oneself for an impossible vision? A spirit, too, needs fuel. It can run dry."

> Frank was that fuel. He gave me, in the hours of my own days, the reality of that sense of life which created *The*

> *Fountainhead*—and he helped me to maintain it over a long span of years when there was nothing around us but a gray desert of people and events that evoked nothing but contempt and revulsion. The essence of the bond between us is the fact that neither of us has ever wanted or been tempted to settle for anything less than the world presented in *The Fountainhead*. We never will....

> I did not feel discouragement very often, and when I did, it did not last longer than overnight. But there was one evening, during the writing of *The Fountainhead*, when I felt so profound an indignation at the state of "things as they are" that it seemed as if I would never regain the energy to move one step further toward "things as they ought to be." Frank talked to me for hours, that night. He convinced me of why one cannot give up the world to those one despises. By the time he finished, my discouragement was gone; it never came back in so intense a form. (86)

So, against a previous policy of not dedicating her books, she decided to dedicate the book to Frank O'Connor. This story says a great deal.

It suggests that Rand was, indeed, alienated from the culture around her, almost as if she and her husband were literally aliens on a strange and primitive planet. It confirms that Rand sometimes got depressed at the state of the world, which, from the standpoint of Rand's ideas, was quite understandable. For all of these reasons the story must be regarded as credible.

Rand's description of O'Connor evokes a true "soul mate" who must have been quite intelligent—almost everyone who knew Rand attests to how tough it was to "convince" her of anything.

Nathaniel Branden confirms Rand's account and adds that "Ayn often declared that it was Frank who sustained her through her struggle." (87)

Ms. Branden might suggest that this is an example of Rand's "fiction-like" recreation of O'Connor, but the passage, in fact, suggests otherwise. It reveals O'Connor to have been a remarkable man, intelligent, if not creatively brilliant, and a man acutely sensitive to Rand's sense of life. Sensitive enough to have never been an interruption to Rand's work, and sensitive to have used as one of his favorite sayings to Rand when she got depressed, "It's nothing a little writing won't cure." (88) Sensitive enough to be the first to appreciate Rand and to stay with her through years of controversy and struggle.

O'Connor had been the first to recognize Mr. Branden's true character, as well, it seems. Ms. Branden reports that in 1968, just before Rand was to learn the truth, O'Connor "did not speak of his feelings, as he had never spoken of them; but, once, in a sudden, contextless anger, he said [to Rand of Mr. Branden], 'That man is no damn good! Why won't you see it?'" (89) Ironic that it took Frank O'Connor to point out that Rand was projecting imaginary virtue—on Branden!

This is not the only evidence of O'Connor's perceptiveness. In a letter to her editor on *The Fountainhead*, Archibald Ogden, dated April 23, 1949, Rand wrote about her new novel in the works, *Atlas Shrugged*.

> For a long time, Frank refused to agree with me that it was bigger in scope and scale than *The Fountainhead*—and he is the first person who hears every sequence as I write it. I read it to him from my longhand before I have it typed. Well, not long ago, he was so impressed with a sequence I read that he was literally shaking and he gave in and said it was bigger than *The Fountainhead*. By the way, he is a severe critic, and getting a compliment from him is like pulling a tooth. (90)

This letter was written *before* there was any Objectivist movement and *before* there was any recognized "theory" of romantic love against which Rand would need to "justify" her romantic choices. It is private correspondence Rand can never have expected to be made public. This letter must be regarded as credible evidence.

It must be noted that this letter was written in the very period during which the Brandens claim—based upon an unverifiable, private conversation each had had with Rand "much later"—that the O'Connor marriage was in "trouble." Recall that Ms. Branden had claimed that "lack of intellectual communication" was causing "friction" between them at this very time—almost to the point of divorce, we were told.

The Brandens' credibility might even be *measurable*—if only a single item of hard evidence would line up with their hostile claims.

This letter also reveals that O'Connor was no dependent "yes-man" for Rand, but a tough critic and a sincere fan. He must have been intelligent, independent—and he must have shared a great deal of his wife's philosophy.

Certainly, this was Rand's opinion. Rand said in a letter to her sister dated August 6, 1973:

> Everything you wrote about your feelings for [your husband], I can say (and often have said) about my feelings for Frank, even using the same words. For example, "we are one, and I do not know where I end and he begins." Just like you, we think in the same fashion, and everything one of us likes or dislikes, the other always likes or dislikes as well—even music...
>
> ...It is remarkable that Frank and I resemble [your husband] and you in temperament! I am tense, aggressive and very articulate. Frank is calm, gentle and silent. But, inside, he is tougher than I am—and if we ever disagreed, I wouldn't be able to budge him, and nobody would. I call him my "Rock of Gibraltar." When I am unhappy or discouraged, which is not often, he is the only one who can give me the strength... (91)

Rand believed that "man is a being of self-made soul." By this she meant that each of us creates his own self by the thoughts and actions he chooses through the course of his life. This produces a personality, a characteristic way of emotionally approaching the world. If that is so, then perhaps the greatest of Frank O'Connor's accomplishments was the creation of a soul that could feed the creator of *The Fountainhead*.

As previously suggested, O'Connor's alleged "suffering" must be measured against what the evidence suggests were his real attitudes regarding sex. The Brandens, with a vested interest in Frank O'Connor as "Victim," never explore the possibility that Rand's behavior actually reflected the couple's shared values and beliefs on the topic of sex. To understand O'Connor's attitude towards the affair requires an understanding of his actual beliefs. However, since he was a quiet man by disposition, and considering the private nature of the topic, this question will probably never be answered with complete certainty, but, certainly, the evidence of the Brandens on this topic cannot be taken at face value.

One of the best guides to O'Connor's thinking, though obviously not a conclusive one, must surely be the thinking of his wife on the topic, for the O'Connors' stated devotion to one another provides good reason to suppose that, to a large extent, their values were at least similar.

As Ayn Rand observed, emotions are shaped by our thinking (or failure to think.) One's sexual emotions, as "instinctive" as they may feel, are no exception.

In this post-Jerry Springer age, most of us are—involuntarily—aware of not only "swinging" couples, but the enthusiastic spouses of prostitutes, bondage mistresses and sex-club patrons. However, if one has internalized the contemporary Judeo-Christian ethic regarding sex, like the majority of Americans, then anything but monogamy is imbued with guilt and horror. The difference between the former and the latter is one of values, the values that have become one's "second nature" sexual standards.

What a spouse will tolerate—what a spouse will encourage—will depend on those subconsciously held values.

Rand's alleged blindness to her husband's character notwithstanding, Rand saw her husband as sharing a "daring" and "unconventional" sense of life that was equal to her own, according to Branden.

It also seems that neither of the O'Connors was jealous. Neither ever seemed threatened by expressions of the others' values. Ms. Branden writes:

> Yet despite [Rand's] dislike for her [own] appearance, she
> took great pleasure in the beauty of other women; it was

an aesthetic delight in which there appeared to be no tinge
of envy... None of her friends ever reported seeing envy in
Ayn toward anyone. (92)

And Leonard Peikoff has said in the film biography of Rand, *Ayn
Rand: A Sense of Life*, that the same was true of O'Connor, that he had "very
little jealousy" in his make-up.

Branden *himself* repeatedly observes that O'Connor's state seemed
to him to show no sign of resentment during the entire course of the affair.
For example, when Rand first mentioned the original joint dedication of
Atlas Shrugged to him, Branden writes that both he and Rand "immediately
agreed that [O'Connor] would find the dedication entirely natural and
appropriate..." (93)

In direct contradiction to the Brandens' accounts of his "suffering,"
O'Connor is elsewhere described by Branden as possessing an almost
Roark-like Zen on the subject of the affair.

If true, then both Rand and O'Connor were living an important
Objectivist principle—that no "conflicts of interest" are possible between
rational individuals. Rand had written in *Atlas Shrugged*:

> Did it ever occur to you... that there is no conflict of
> interests among men, neither in business nor in trade nor
> in their most personal desires—if they omit the irrational
> from their view of the possible and destruction from their
> view of the practical? There is no conflict, and no call for
> sacrifice, and no man is a threat to the aims of another—if
> men understand that reality is an absolute not to be faked,
> that lies do not work, that the unearned cannot be had, that
> the undeserved cannot be given, that the destruction of a
> value which is, will not bring value to that which isn't. The
> businessman who wishes to gain a market by throttling a
> superior competitor, the worker who wants a share of his
> employer's wealth, the artist who envies a rival's higher
> talent — they are all wishing facts out of existence, and
> destruction is the only means of their wish. If they pursue
> it, they will not achieve a market, a fortune or immortal

fame—they will merely destroy production, employment and art. A wish for the irrational is not to be achieved, whether the sacrificial victims are willing or not. (94)

Nathaniel Branden himself observed the convincing nature of the respect which the heroes of Rand's novels show one another even—perhaps especially—in circumstances of romantic rivalry.

Rand implies that one cannot achieve this kind of love by wishing out of existence the very values that make your lover desired in the first place—the very values which may lead her to another and another to her.

Since your lover's experience with a rival (past or present) can never be "shared," it is senseless to envy it. It is as unique as their fingerprints, and no amount of envy, insecurity or evasion can wipe it out. As Rand has observed, such evasion simply tends to wipe out the wiper.

Therefore, the heroes in Rand's novels—all sharing similar values— can completely understand the heroine's love for another hero. And, like any fact of reality, they do not hide from it, nor do they evade it.

They submit to it.

More than this, they actually celebrate it.

The following passage represents Rand's only clear statement on sexual exclusivity published to date, and it is from Rand's private journals, dated October 6, 1949.

On the right philosophical premise about sex, on my premise, it is a great compliment to a woman if a man wants her. It is an expression of his highest values, not his contempt. In this sense, a husband would feel honored if another man wanted his wife; he would not let the other man have her—his exclusive possession is the material form of her love for him—but he would feel that the other man's desire was a natural and proper expression of the man's admiration for his wife, for the values which she represents and which he saw in her. (95)

But why must "the material form of her love" express itself in exclusive "possession"? What if—in the context of a trusting and devoted relationship—that trust and esteem were not threatened by another relationship both noble and rational? Must it, as the Brandens suggest, lead inevitably to pain, suffering, and disaster? It is obvious from her later behavior that Rand's own thinking on this issue evolved considerably; but it is also clear that Rand's later position evolved from her earlier thinking.

This also raises an additional question: could it be that O'Connor actually "took pleasure" in the thought of his wife and another man— assuming, of course, the other man to be of moral stature? It would go far in explaining Rand's comment that he found the situation a "sexual inspiration," and why he stayed with Rand throughout.

The following is from Rand's private notes written in preparation of writing *Atlas Shrugged*, dated October 4,1949:

> [Rearden] *takes pleasure in the thought of Dagny and another man*, which is an unconscious acknowledgement that sex, as such, is great and beautiful, not evil and degrading. (96)

Thus, the hero's subconscious belief that "sex is great and beautiful" includes, for Rand, the notion that the hero actually takes pleasure in the thought of his love in the arms of another hero.

Moreover, this particular account of male psychology is almost certain to be an expression of her husband's own psychology. It is not Rand's heroine feeling this, but her hero, and this passage was written before Rand *had ever met Branden*. As she said in her letter to Jacobs, Frank was "always" the model for her fictional heroes. (97)

So pleased with what she had developed in her notes, Rand was to include this idea in the final novel, only now from the heroine's perspective:

> ...[Dagny] felt Francisco's presence through Rearden's mind, she felt as if she were surrendering to both men, to that which she worshipped in both of them, that which they held in common, that essence of character which had made of her love for each an act of loyalty to both. She knew also that this was his rebellion against the world around them, against its worship of degradation... (98)

Thus, far from a "conflict of interest," the heroine's love for each is actually "an act of loyalty" to the other.

And later, John Galt even observes that, in a sense, he, Francisco and Dagny are all in mutual love. "'Dagny, all three of us are in love'—she jerked her head toward him—'with the same thing, no matter what its forms. Don't wonder why you feel no breach between us...'" (99)

The plots of Rand's three big novels all contain love-triangles centered around the heroine. As the author, Rand had every right to create characters and events that would be enjoyable to her. That enjoyment can be felt and shared by the reader—that is what makes a novel fun.

Though the topic is far beyond the scope of the current essay, and such considerations are necessarily speculative, it is distinctly possible that these stories represent a central aspect of Rand's own sexual psychology, even a characteristic sexual fantasy. (To the author, at least, a perfectly healthy one.)

If a man does not have the equivalent lusts and fantasies, there must be something wrong with him. "Two women? Who wouldn't?!" But heaven help the obviously perverse woman who would indulge that same fantasy—or the loving husband who, after twenty-five years of marriage, might love his wife enough to allow, or even encourage, her its indulgence in reality.

O'Connor almost certainly believed that his wife was an exceptional genius and a woman intensely loyal to her values. He may well have appreciated his wife's complex emotional—and intellectual—needs. Possessing such a sensitive and daring soul may well have given him the capacity to embrace his wife's quest for joy, a capacity obviously not shared by the Brandens. (And he surely could have left Rand without much fear, had he truly objected to the situation.)

Such a scenario, however probable, is something that the Brandens cannot permit their readers to entertain, even if they have to ignore weighty evidence along the way.

Whatever one thinks of the Rand-Branden affair, Rand was no hypocrite, as the Brandens contend. Rand's morality has no injunction against having affairs, and no stipulation requiring monogamy. An examination of Rand's work suggests that—even in this regard—her integrity was remarkable.

Why, then, the secrecy? If her affair was a consistent expression of Objectivism, why hide it?

The Brandens say that Rand was paranoid, obsessed with scandal, that she had "sworn them all to life-long secrecy," and that, in this, Rand was insisting on "lies and deception" (which go otherwise unspecified). It is true that Rand did not normally do things which she would not also have been proud to announce later.

But in this instance, it was not just her own feelings that had to be considered, but also her husband's and, until the break, the Brandens'. Of course, the Brandens, committed to the portrait of the Callous Rand, cannot suggest that Rand may have been acting partly to protect *them* by her discretion from a public that would not respect their private choices.

Once again, Rand's posthumously published journals are revealing. In her notes for *Atlas Shrugged*, written more than three years before she met Branden, Rand explains why the novel's heroine, Dagny Taggart—a woman also otherwise proud of all that she did—keeps her affair with Francisco d'Anconia discreet. In notes dated February 11, 1947, Rand writes:

> The complete secrecy of their affair. Nobody suspects it... Dagny's reason for the secrecy—her hatred for people's view of sex. *Furious indignation that anyone should dare to presume to lay down rules about it for her.* Contempt for those who consider it sin—no desire to fight them ([or even] grant them the right to discourse about it), only to keep away, not even to brush against them, because she senses something monstrously unclean about them. (100)

In this instance, Rand is suggesting in Dagny a Dominique-like desire not to let the world even know about something it could never understand or appreciate. And yet all the Brandens can see in Rand's silence is "hypocrisy."

We also see the *radical* nature of Rand's own thinking, and her emotional opposition to any who would "dare to lay down rules" about sex for her.

It is certainly true that the secrecy of the affair had an unfortunate effect on Rand's followers, who were not privy to the details and were compelled to make moral judgments without having all the evidence.

But to suggest that Rand's followers did not have enough evidence to make a sound judgment because of this omission is misleading. It was Mr. Branden who was compelled to an admittedly vague, but humiliatingly public, *mea culpa* in the summer of 1968, not Rand. It was Branden who felt compelled to admit publicly to (at least some of) his dishonesty.

We know that the Brandens themselves did not tell everything in 1968. They—not Rand—demanded to be taken on pure faith. And, considering their relentless dishonesty since the break, Rand's final judgment of them has been dramatically vindicated.

On issue after issue, the Branden method is consistent. The entire body of verifiable evidence (e.g., "none of our friends even suspected" and "at the time I had no intimation") is contradicted by private, unnamed, or otherwise unverifiable evidence only known to the Brandens which, gee whiz, happens to prove their point and justify the giant chips they still shoulder. All of the evidence of all the other witnesses and all outward appearances are refuted by pulling out of their hats the contradictory item that no one can contradict—or corroborate.

This is not merely the Brandens' frequent method, it is their exclusive method of providing everything required to show how "cruel" Rand had been to those around her—just as she had been so "cruel" to the Brandens.

We have seen, however, the integrity of Rand even among the rare and broken fragments of truth that can be verified in the Brandens' tale. Even, perhaps especially, with regard to the affair, Rand is seen to have had the courage to actually live up to the philosophy she taught and believed.

VI. School or Cult?

A philosopher's biography is, of course, irrelevant to the truth or falsehood of that thinker's ideas. Neither the Brandens' efforts nor this analysis can have any bearing on one's evaluation of Objectivism without committing the kind of *ad hominem* fallacy we previously observed in *The Journal of Ayn Rand Studies*.

It is clear, however, that Ayn Rand was a human being who made mistakes. She possessed a human psychology with all of the complexities which this implies. Certainly, in the course of her life, Rand suffered terrible pain. She could be angry and severe, no doubt. This much can be independently verified.

But the Brandens, as we have seen, must be entirely discounted as witnesses to the history they relate. They admit the truth only insofar as the existence of other evidence compels them. Their boldest assertions are unfailingly made where no corroboration is possible and often in contradiction to the available evidence, including their own direct observations. They have each demonstrated a level of dishonesty—both in the methodology and in the content of their works—which must be considered fatal to the reliability of anything they report. Their hostility to and joint cause against Rand is ineluctable.

Their dishonesty to their readers in 1962 and 1968 was subsequently revealed by their own writings years later, in which unverifiable claims against Rand strangely become more elaborate.

Ms. Branden's "scoop," the affair, could be expected to sell books, even if it revealed the deceptive nature of the Brandens' 1968 response to Rand in which "an insuperable barrier" seems to have prevented any affair from occurring.

In turn, Mr. Branden revealed Ms. Branden's own affairs and various other facts at variance with his former wife's account, further revealing their *mutual* dishonesty.

Rand's journals, as we will see in Part II, reveal that, for all of this "disclosure," crucial information regarding the Brandens' own conduct was systematically suppressed in their "histories" of these events.

Their books can only be seen as their final vengeance upon Rand—and each other. They continue their policy of financially exploiting their association with Rand while attempting to rehabilitate their own reputations, which, for obvious reasons, require it. In the process, they only further tarnish those reputations.

Ayn Rand's critics have been spreading falsehoods and distortions about both Rand and her philosophy for many years. Their most consistent complaint accuses the Objectivist movement of being "a cult," intentionally conjuring the image of an Eastern mystic stepping out of a limousine and being showered with garlands by chanting, brainwashed lemmings.

Predictably, Ms. Branden only gets around to considering the question of whether the Objectivist movement was a "cult" in her narrative of the events surrounding her own break with Rand. She writes that while it "had many of the trappings," such as the alleged "aggrandizement" of Rand and "the incessant moralism," the movement was not, strictly speaking, a cult.

As to those "trappings," Ms. Branden does speak with some authority.

Even after all of Ms. Branden's own confessed suppression of her "real self," all of the deceptive fawning over and flattering of Rand, and "the too ready acceptance of [Rand's] opinions on a host of subjects," she concludes Objectivism was not a cult, no matter how quasi-cult-like her description of her own dishonest behavior. (1)

But even such a comparison is slanderous insinuation.

Rand had never sought a following. She did not think of herself as a teacher or a "leader" by inclination or by disposition. She actively distrusted "organized" intellectual movements. Rand watched the hopes of Ms. Branden, and many others at the time, totally dashed, as she required the liquidation of NBI in 1968. Rand had no problem wiping out what she had been eager to keep her "distance" from in the first place. Indeed, everything Rand said merely confirms what was already clear from her behavior.

Consider what Rand taught: "Think. Think for yourself. Be selfish."

The combined emphasis Rand placed in her writings on both reason and individualism is certainly unprecedented in the history of "cults"—and for obvious reasons. Thinking for one's self—the fundamental ethical mandate of Objectivism—is cult-suicide. In fact, Objectivism teaches that "thinking for oneself" is a redundancy, that there is no *other* kind of thinking.

The image of Howard Roark standing alone against the whole world for his vision, is not the image to promote if one is seeking a blind following.

Ayn Rand, by the Brandens' own accounts, did her utmost *not* to cultivate a personal following of any kind. When it came to ideological alliances, time and again, Rand proved that she would rather be right than keep a friend. Her personality was, in many ways, simply inconsistent with managing an "organized" movement. And she knew it.

Yet, of course, Rand's circle was a bunch of crazy cult-members, Alan Greenspan and the rest, all busy getting their graduate degrees and establishing their subversive professional careers. Right.

When Rand was done alienating many of these students, and when "the Collective" went their inevitably separate ways, none of them, curiously, returned to more traditional philosophical or religious viewpoints. At most, like Branden, they attempted to "modify" at the margins the philosophy Rand had given them. Whatever their later hostility to the woman, the ideas they had learned from Rand—in some form—endured.

Rand cannot be held responsible for any of the alleged self-suppressing behavior of her legions of anonymous followers, any more than she can be held responsible for the deceptive self-suppressing behavior of the Brandens.

Remarkably, years after her death, Rand is still winning converts who have never joined any group or organization. They just read a couple of books.

Rand's was a strange "cult," indeed.

Into this context, using the very attack which for so long the Brandens resented as unfair even as they were perhaps the most cult-like followers Rand ever had, they now exploit this canard, and nearly all others of their former critics. (2) The intensity of their current accusation of "authoritarianism" is matched only by the former intensity of the deceptive sycophancy in their relationship with Rand.

Winston Churchill is credited with a pithy rationalization for government disinformation: "Some truths are so important that they need to be surrounded by a bodyguard of lies." Leaving aside the ethical cynicism that this implies outside of the (limited and temporary) context of national security, such a policy is difficult to sustain over time. As every seasoned liar knows, for it to be believed, a lie must be surrounded by a bodyguard of truths.

Many of the claims made in the Brandens' books are undoubtedly true. A good many of them are demonstrably false, misleading, one-sided and self-serving. Being unclear as to their sources—often overtly suppressing their sources—it is not generally possible to distinguish the true from the false, and therein lies the problem for the usefulness of these works to historians.

Again and again, the Brandens produce suspicious evidence from "private conversations" that contradicts the entire body of verifiable information, but which conveniently helps them grind their particular axes.

We have seen that the rest of their evidence against Rand consists of purely emotional assertion devoid of fact—precisely what Rand's philosophy terms an "arbitrary" assertion. According to Objectivism, arbitrary claims are neither true nor false. They are, in this sense, "worse" than false, *bearing no relation to reality whatever*—even a negative one. It is error even to attempt to refute them. (3)

On the surface, the Brandens' biographical efforts consist of factual claims made by people who knew their subject well. Therefore, the identification of their works as being arbitrary can only be made after (at least some) careful analysis. As we have seen, such analysis readily demonstrates that a sweeping dismissal is, indeed, warranted.

Even if one day some of the Brandens' assertions are verified by more credible sources and evidence, the Brandens will not have helped to establish their truth. Considerable independent research will be necessary to accomplish this. And it does not matter whether these discoveries cast Rand in a positive or negative light.

If one day, for example, it is somehow established, to the surprise of the author, that Rand's callous indifference drove her husband to excessive drinking, the current analysis will still stand, and the Brandens' credibility will not have been enhanced in any way. The basis of their inferences will be no more credible and no less arbitrary.

But the historical record can become clouded with the assumptions of a tradition that is largely legendary. It would be tragic if Rand's biography suffered the same fate at the hand of the Brandens' viciously crafted legend.

A movie version of *The Passion of Ayn Rand* was produced for cable television with Ms. Branden's approval. As that Emmy-winning movie depicts things, O'Connor was once found unconscious and drunk by Mr. Branden in a telephone booth in 1957. O'Connor also professes a complete ignorance of his wife's work and its meaning. Ms. Branden's own affairs, her disappointment at the rejection of her plans to run NBI, and her immediate switch following that disappointment are, of course, not shown. Rand herself is as humorless, joyless, etc., as the unsubstantiated half of Ms. Branden's many contradictions might suggest. Ms. Branden's lies to Rand on behalf of Mr. Branden are hardly mentioned. Mr. Branden's intellectual and professional exploitation of Rand is not presented at all. The extensive and deceptive counseling sessions are not depicted. The Brandens' published lies in the wake of the break go unnoticed. The philosophy of Objectivism is repeatedly misrepresented. Even Ms. Branden's already fatuous dialogue is altered once again for "dramatic" ends. Whole characters are created from whole cloth.

These are just a few of the movie's radical projections from Barbara Branden's empty claims.

Needless to say, Ms. Branden *loved* the movie. In particular, the actor who played O'Connor "was Frank." (4)

Unfortunately, evidence is not the driving force behind the current dogma about Ayn Rand. Many are willing to believe whatever is claimed without requiring much evidence. In an effort to prove that they are tolerant, open-minded and, certainly, un-cult-like even many claiming to be sympathetic to Rand do so. Such are the credentials necessary for being taken seriously in some circles if one agrees with Rand's ideas.

In their zeal to be free of any association with the "cult-mentality" of "true believers," even many of those who admire Rand trip over their own feet to proclaim their recognition of Rand's feet of clay. They accuse

Rand's defenders of being "in denial," but they have themselves adopted only dogma.

In the process, an uncritical nod has been given by an entire sub-culture to writers and books rife with lies and distortions. But the truth is just the opposite of what many are coming to accept as the real story.

One striking illustration of the contrast between the truth and the uncritically accepted dogma promulgated by the Brandens stands out as particularly eloquent.

Nathaniel Branden delights in describing Leonard Peikoff as having an "embarrassing" problem during the course of his studies at New York University. (With the famous Sidney Hook as his advisor, Peikoff earned his Ph.D. in philosophy in 1964.)

"If, for example, [Peikoff] was studying the philosophy of John Dewey he could very easily fall into Dewey's perspective without noticing it, accept the premises of Dewey that he in fact knew to be mistaken, and then proceed to panic." Rand would spend a good deal of time helping him with successive waves of confusion. This happened, it seems, with almost every philosopher Peikoff encountered, from Plato to Wittgenstein. Branden says that he was "mystified" by Peikoff's conduct and even wondered why Rand tolerated it. (5)

One might ask whether Peikoff originally "knew" those other ideas to have been "mistaken," as Branden is claiming for him, since he had so easily lost them, but for Branden, it seems, belief needs no more than a first impression. Extensive study and a detailed comparison of Objectivism to previous philosophies, Branden seems to wonder—how could these disturb anyone's "convictions?"

Branden explains that Rand would become angry and impatient with Peikoff, and that he once even came near to what Branden calls "excommunication." However, Peikoff always eventually found Rand's arguments more sound even though he was determined, no matter what the effort involved, to understand them thoroughly before declaring his level of certainty to be what it was not.

Branden himself, of course, had never dared to risk Rand's anger. He tells his readers quite explicitly that he chose years of deception over risking any of Rand's "moralism."

Why risk it anyway? He was already akin to Ayn Rand in the very structure of their souls—he had absorbed Objectivism as if by osmosis—he could glibly pronounce, in Rand's own style, the fundamental ideas of her philosophy, and recite the very lines of her heroes' dialogue, verbatim.

Sure, he spoke to his readers of Rand's revolutionary impact on psychology at a time when he did not really think the subject was her "strong point." And, of course, he was "bothered" by a great many aspects of her thought. No, he never asked Rand to clear up those doubts, nor did he give Rand the chance to explain her answers to those doubts, as Peikoff did.

Why risk a position at the top of Rand's esteem over a few niggling doubts?

Branden already had completely understood what Peikoff was still—can you believe it?—groping for.

Branden had sprung from the head of Rand fully armored with omniscience and Objectivism. Branden had practically memorized *The Fountainhead*, you see, while Peikoff came tentatively along, always vulnerable to whatever new ideas he was being taught at school.

Peikoff told the truth about what was going on in his head to Rand, to his teachers, to his chosen counselors. Peikoff gave every new philosophy he studied a fair hearing. He could still be persuaded, he was still open to new perspectives. Peikoff had to be convinced of each and every thing—every inch of the way and in competition with all other ideas—before fully adopting it.

But—Presto!—Branden's magic works its sleight of hand and Peikoff is suddenly cast as "the Randroid," the cult-leader, the intolerant "yes-man" of Objectivism, not Branden himself—in perfect form, again projecting his own identity onto his opponent.

Of course, the ultimate irony is that the essential feature of Branden's history and character is dishonesty, while the essential feature of Rand's is ruthless honesty. Her philosophy demands both a total honesty of belief to fact—and a total honesty of belief to action. Neither mindless conformity nor arbitrary contrariety, either *with* or *against* Objectivism itself, achieves the level of honesty that is a prerequisite for Objectivism.

Objectivism, the philosophy Rand articulated in her books, is, therefore, perhaps the first philosophy in history which can actually be *practiced* consistently on earth. Rand strove to practice it—often courageously and alone—in every aspect of her life. As we have seen, an analysis of the Brandens' biographical works actually demonstrates that the Brandens' central thesis—that Rand was a hypocrite who often did not live up to her stated ideals—is the precise opposite of the truth.

Indeed, it was Rand's *adherence* to her philosophy which alienated some of her former friends—including the Brandens. Actually, Rand achieved a kind of integrity between high thought and the whole of one's life that had never before been thought possible. She was willing to defy over two millennia of philosophical thought and stand alone if necessary to defend her ideas, ideas she believed could—and must—be implemented without compromise.

This unprecedented aspect of Rand's philosophy in itself suggests the importance of Rand's biography as a topic of study—a topic which still awaits an objective biographer. (6)

Few figures so deserve a complete, in-depth biography as Ayn Rand does. She survived the Russian Revolution, and worked in Hollywood during the Silent Era of the 1920s for men like Cecil B. DeMille. She struggled through the Depression, but during the 1940s she wrote the screenplays for popular films and a best-selling novel. In order to research her fiction, Rand worked in the office of a leading architect, inspected large steel mills and foundries, learned to operate the engine of a locomotive, and interviewed the inventors of the first nuclear weapon about their work. Rand testified before the House UnAmerican Activities Committee (HUAC) about life in the Soviet Union. Later, she attended the launch of Apollo 11 in person, as an invited VIP. Most of Rand's non-fiction and cultural commentary spanned the turbulent 1960s and early 1970s, just in time to dissect Woodstock, the New Left, and related cultural phenomena. In the 1970s, she attended the White House ceremonies for the swearing-in of her student, Alan Greenspan, as the President's chief economic advisor.

Ayn Rand was an extraordinary witness to the Twentieth Century, and her writing reflects not only her powerful and original thought, but her remarkable and unique life. But she was also an artist and a philosopher of vision who saw beyond the conventional wisdom of her time to a future of endless possibilities.

Besides, and as Rand herself would have appreciated, her life makes one helluva story.

In the magnificent Ridley Scott film *1492:Conquest of Paradise*, a contemporary of Christopher Columbus observes—in a moment of profound insight—that if he, a nobleman, is remembered by history it will only be because Columbus will be remembered—and only because he played a role in Columbus's life.

The Brandens, too, know this of themselves. Unlike that nobleman, it is also clearly the Brandens' design to *shape* the history of the Columbus whom they were privileged to know.

Their final act of vengeance against Ayn Rand is against honesty—and *objectivity*—itself.

Alyssa Rosenbaum, Russia, c. 1906.
Courtesy Ayn Rand Archives

Ayn Rand, Russia, 1925
Courtesy Ayn Rand Archives

Frank O'Connor, Los Angeles, 1930s
Courtesy Ayn Rand Archives

Ayn Rand with "Oscar" and "Oswald," 1943
Courtesy Ayn Rand Archives

Ayn Rand, 1940s
Courtesy Ayn Rand Archives

Frank O'Connor and Ayn Rand, 1920s
Courtesy Michael Paxton, 'Ayn Rand: A Sense of Life'
Motion picture companion book
(Ayn Rand Archives)

Barbara and Nathaniel Branden, New York City, 1952
Courtesy Ayn Rand Archives

**Nathaniel and Barbara Branden, Ayn Rand,
Frank O'Connor, and Leonard Pelikoff, 1953**
Courtesy Ayn Rand Archives

Barbara and Nathaniel Branden, 1966
Photo by Whit Hancock
(Ayn Rand Archives)

Nathaniel Branden and Ayn Rand, 1966
Photo by Whit Hancock
(Ayn Rand Archives)

New Years Eve, 1967: Alan Greenspan, Patrecia and her sister,
O'Connor, Rand, and Branden
Courtesy Ayn Rand Archives

Ayn Rand, 1964
Reproduced by special permission of Playboy *magazine.*
Copyright © 1964 by Playboy.
Photo by Jerry Yukman

PART II: *Documenting the Rape of Innocence*

W E HAVE SEEN, LARGELY FROM AN ANALYSIS OF THEIR OWN CLAIMS, that the Brandens cannot be relied upon as historians, and we have seen that other sources—such as Rand's correspondence and material from her private journals—are required to make any objective assessment of Rand's life.

The appearance of an earlier version of Part I of this analysis on the Internet in the year 2002 prompted the Estate of Ayn Rand to make available the unpublished portions of Rand's private journals, those which bear directly on Ayn Rand's break with Nathaniel Branden, for the purposes of this effort.

As indicated, this material is almost exclusively related to Rand's relationship with Branden, and, in particular, it chronicles the last several months of "psychotherapy" Rand endured with him while he was deceiving her about his marriage, his affair, and his feelings. These accounts provide an extremely detailed record of the period from the Fall of 1967 to the start of August, 1968. (Unfortunately, they provide nearly no autobiographical information about other periods in Rand's life.)

Written in Rand's distinctive script, mostly on a light blue stationery, these journals are in the form of private notes to herself, and they were obviously never intended by Rand to be published. Although remarkably clear and logically structured for "private" thoughts, they were certainly not "polished" for publication to Rand's usual standards.

These journals, therefore, cannot be taken as definitive statements of Objectivism. But, for that same reason, they must be regarded as highly credible, indeed, powerful evidence of both the facts which they imply—and of Rand's state of mind at the time.

This is by no means their only value. They also show a great mind at work. There is a good deal of valuable insight, both philosophical and psychological, including a detailed response to any who would treat Objectivism either as a "rationalist" construct or as a "religion"—precisely what Rand discovers Branden to have done.

Rand was an advocate of reason and not just "in theory." She thought in explicit, logical and *verbal* terms about just about everything in her life. As we have observed, her affair with Branden was a serious, long-term commitment. It is, therefore, hardly surprising that we find extensive notes from Rand in the period when her relationship with Branden was collapsing.

Rand *used* her notes. They are often underlined, or have check marks in the color of another pen beside them. She titles her first notes in this series, "Notes to Use." These notes represent Rand's "active" thinking on this issue. This alone shows their value, and forms a sharp contrast to the incredible drift and irresponsibility displayed by Branden throughout this period.

In her published writings, Rand was careful to define her terms, especially when she was introducing a word or phrase of her own coining, and she was sensitive not to overload her readers with too much jargon. Because these were notes made for her own private use, the reader is warned that Rand will often use concepts that may be familiar only to serious students of her philosophy. Although definitions are provided when necessary, Rand's distinctive lexicon appears frequently.

For purposes of the current analysis, this material provides only further, if rather extensive, support for our assessment of the Brandens' biographical works. While several amplifications of the original analysis were prompted by this material, the significant impact is only additive, for it exposes still more of the Brandens' bizarre lies and distortions, this time, from Rand's own perspective.

In fairness to the Brandens, it must be acknowledged that Rand's private journals do substantiate several of the claims which they have made: some confirmation of a post-*Atlas Shrugged* "crisis" period for Rand (her word for it); the extensive "psycho-epistemological" counseling Rand gave Branden in their final years together is confirmed (and then some); and that by 1968 Rand had rejected the possibility of a romantic "triangle" (more precisely, a "quadrangle") that would include Branden's new mistress—along with Rand's correspondingly negative opinion of her. And there are a few other items of lesser interest.

From February through July of 1968 the journal entries are, in effect, the "therapist's notes" for the semi-formal sessions between Rand and Branden. Thus, facts pertaining to Branden's psychology—and the deterioration of Rand's relationship with him—are, unfortunately, the limited class of topics usually amendable to such confirmation from these notes.

It should be pointed out that, of course, some of these facts—e.g., the extent of Rand's counseling of Branden—are flat contradictions of the Brandens' 1968 assertions (where Branden had overtly denied that their relationship had become little but grueling psychotherapy) and that all of their subsequent admissions are such "big" facts that the Brandens can only have known that the Estate of Ayn Rand would possess proof of them. The Estate of Ayn Rand had announced its intention to eventually release all of Rand's private journal material—before the Branden biographies appeared. They had little choice but to correct their own record on certain issues *before* Rand's journals were made public.

Moreover, there is an abundance of information that will come as a complete surprise to readers of the Brandens' works—and not because the Brandens were unaware of it.

From the analysis so far, it should come as no surprise that Rand's private journals expose several glaring, and obviously intentional, "oversights" in the Brandens' biographical efforts. The Brandens have consistently suppressed, omitted and generally downplayed several important features of the break between Rand and Branden.

The following is only a sample of such "oversights," which shall be revealed in what follows:

1. The Brandens' depictions of Rand imply that—blind to the obvious—she was "holding out" for an affair with Branden until the summer of 1968. Branden suggests that Rand would never have accepted a "Platonic" situation and the same kind of "break" as happened in the end was the only alternative—ever. He was, therefore, "compelled" to romantically placate Rand—it was a romance or nothing, all along. This is all plainly false.

Rand's private notes make quite apparent that Rand herself had come to terms with the end of the "affair" by the end of January, 1968. Her obviously intense efforts to understand and help Branden from that time forward can only have been an attempt to preserve a friendship, or, at least, a working business relationship.

Her considerable efforts will seem remarkable to an outside observer, but they were only somewhat greater than average for Rand. All sources agree that she was extraordinarily generous with her time and energy when it came to giving counsel and support to her friends. The extensive and in-depth nature of the help Rand gave them is conceded by Ms. Branden, and it is confirmed by a number of more credible sources, as well.

Of course, Branden's personal and professional relationship with Rand was unique, and he had actively solicited this help from her. There can be no doubt that Rand's efforts were especially intensive in his case.

But these efforts, by the start of 1968, cannot be seen as an attempt to renew her affair with Branden. In Rand's mind, at least, it was already over.

On January 25, 1968, she wrote the following: "...[t]he only question is: is there anything possible other than a total break? (I don't think so.) (The 'triangle,' of course, is out of the question—now.)" And later in her notes from the same date, she concludes, "...*he does not really love me.* I know I mean something important to him, but whatever it is, it is not love. Maybe it was, years ago, at the beginning, but I am not certain even of that." (1)

In early July, Rand would write of this same January period: "As far as I was concerned, this was the end. In all these years, I had never doubted his love for me, in spite of all the contradictions and the terrible greyness of our relationship. But when he said, 'I don't know,' I doubted his love then, retroactively (a little later, I tried to believe it, but never did again)." (2)

In Rand's mind, the affair was over in early 1968, several months *before* the total "break" with Branden.

2. Closely related to this, is the Brandenian myth that Rand was unrealistic about her own age. The Brandens themselves admit that Rand was sustained in her belief in Branden's love by Branden's own proclamations (for fourteen years) that his love for her was so powerful that their age-difference did not matter to him. As we have already seen,

both of the Brandens also admit that Rand had repeatedly asked if age was an issue, saying that she "could understand that." Nevertheless, and despite Branden's admissions that he explicitly and repeatedly encouraged the belief that "age" was not an issue for him, the Brandens assert that Rand's lack of self-awareness on this issue was plainly neurotic.

Branden says that, in his heart, he knew that Rand was deceiving herself whenever she offered "outs" on the issue of age. She would never have accepted being rejected because of her age, he claims. That is why, he says, he kept pleading—in the most extreme terms possible—that his love was still sexual, long after this was the reality. He *had to* keep up the pretense to feed Rand's unrealistic expectations and demands to preserve "the life I had built." (3)

Branden quotes with sympathy the assertion of his (still secret) mistress, Patrecia, that Rand was *literally insane* on the subject of himself, if not many other subjects, as well. Branden tells us that, for some years, Patrecia had repeatedly spoken of Rand's "madness." Branden says that he was not "ready to hear this" about Rand—but also implies that he agreed with this assessment. (4)

At the time of the break, Ms. Branden tells us that Rand asserted that Branden should love her—even if she were "eighty and in a wheel-chair!" (5)

Such language, however, appears to be a projection of the very language we have seen that Branden admits using throughout his affair with Rand, even into her sixties: "You will always be a sexual being," "You have no equals at any age," etc. (6) And these linguistic extremes, as we shall see, are confirmed by Rand's notes.

However, Rand's notes paint an entirely different picture from that painted by the Brandens.

Rand is clearly well aware that only the *extraordinary* man Branden had for so many years claimed to be would have been able to see past such an age-barrier. And, once Branden "reveals" to her that age actually had been a problem for him, Rand readily acknowledges this as natural and true. In her notes from July 8, 1968, she writes:

> I do believe also that he tried, for years, to "force himself"
> to feel actual love for me... which destroyed whatever part

of his feeling was authentic, and reduced his love to a purely cerebral issue, cut off almost entirely—except for brief spurts—from his actual emotions. I do believe that when he formulated his "physical alienation" notion in his own mind, then put it on paper and presented it to me, he *did* believe that he was derepressing a dark secret and that he would now be set free psychologically, even if at the price of tragic unhappiness existentially. (7)

In notes dated July 4, 1968, Rand writes that, during "this last, 5-month period,"

More than once, I had asked him to consider the possibility that my own age was now the cause of his trouble in regard to his feeling for me. I put it quite bluntly and calmly, without anger: that I was too old for him. I told him that I would not be offended by it and that we could then discuss it rationally. He answered me that this was not true. (8)

Notice that Rand was not only acutely sensitive to the fact that her age could be a "rational" obstacle, but also one which would not imply any moral shortcoming or elicit her anger.

Notice, too, that the issue is not a closed one for Rand. She is sensitive to the fact that as she continues to age, even the emotional hero of Branden's dishonest claims might reach a limit at some point. The questions are on-going, "more than once," and, well into 1968, Rand was saying that maybe "now" it matters, even if it had not before.

And, well into 1968—and at every point in their discussions through June of that year—Branden kept denying it.

In her notes from July of 1968 (*after* Branden has told Rand that, despite his prior assertions, age had mattered to him for some *years*) Rand explicitly accepted the idea "that my present age is a handicap physically" to a continued romance and that it would be so not only "to a physicalistic type of man," but also, "on purely conventional grounds, even to a better man." (9) In others words, to a perfectly moral man, it could be such an obstacle. Branden's *ethical* standing was never on the line with Rand on the "age" issue, despite the claims of the Brandens.

What Branden had claimed to possess was an *extraordinary soul,* shown by his continuing and extreme assertions that "age" did not matter to him. What Branden demanded of Rand was that *she not take him at his own word* in regard to his feelings.

Rand's realism on the "age" issue is actually impressive. Although the younger man in her life is clearly showing an interest in a much younger woman, Rand's analysis of the rationalization Branden gave this—something he called "physicalism"—is remarkably dispassionate.

By that time, Branden was claiming that the "age-issue" worked "both ways" and that as a man nearing forty, to him, the body of an eighteen-year-old woman was no longer sexually attractive to him. Rand was dubious of this claim, on its face. Again, from her July 8 entries:

> In purely physicalistic terms, I can conceive of how an aging body may be regarded as unattractive—but not an 18 year-old body. It is precisely that story of his that makes his rationalization worse, not better. If a man is sexually indifferent to an attractive 18 year-old woman, it can be *only* on spiritual grounds, i.e., on the grounds of the fact that an immature *person,* an immature *consciousness,* does not interest him; which is very rational and very proper, unless he meets an exceptional 18 year-old—but then, *and in any case,* it is an issue of *consciousness,* of his *evaluation* of the consciousness involved. (10)

Rand realizes that the "age issue" would be a rational consideration, but she also sees that Branden's *actual* considerations include something else, something not-so-rational, in order for him to have maintained this kind of sexual fraud for so long. We read the following in her "July 4" notes:

> I am convinced that the clearest and probably conscious fear in his mind was the fear of admitting to himself that I was "too much for him." He seemed to know that if he admitted that, it would tear up all his defense-mechanisms and destroy his image of himself as an Objectivist hero. (11)

And, on this score, Rand hits the mark exactly.

The Brandens' assertions regarding Rand's alleged irrationality on the subject of "age" are clearly disproved by the evidence from Rand's own private notes on the matter.

3. In contrast to the dangerously unbalanced "woman scorned" of both Brandens' claims, the notes reveal that Rand's on-going concerns—from November of 1967 through July of 1968—were not jealousy or rejection, but Branden's character, psychology, and chaotic approach to his many personal problems—his *method of thinking* began to add up to something phony to Rand. And, most distressing to her, Rand felt that their relationship had drifted into a purely (and seemingly unproductive) "therapeutic" one.

By November of 1967, Rand writes that, "[i]t is as if everything pertaining to his own emotions is that kind of vague, helpless 'I don't know'—and he lives with it for years, and acts on it..." She expresses concern that "[h]e has been willing to drift and let things drift in regard to [Barbara Branden]—and to me. No matter *what* he felt, he has lived a life which *did not* express his personal or emotional values. If one looks at the daily facts, he has lived, at best, on the premise of 'church on Sundays' [a term used by Rand to denote those who profess adherence to some ideal or creed, but confine its practice to certain specific and highly circumscribed areas of their actual lives, in her view, demonstrating a lack of integrity]..." Rand seems particularly distressed that his own awareness of these problems "did not stop him from drifting into the worst offense of all in this respect: the last two years of myself as psychotherapist"—the destruction of their friendship, much less their romance. (12)

By the end of January, 1968, Rand would write, "The first consideration that stands out in my mind at this point, is the way (the tone and content both) in the way he said he let things go by default or drift, in the past, because he '*didn't know what to do*.'"

Notice that Branden was openly admitting to Rand the irresponsibility of this "drift."

Rand writes, "I think and feel strongly that our relationship was a mistake from the start—that there was and is no way to implement it in practice... We were right to attempt it originally. But we should have broken it about 8 years ago. We might have found some form of friendship then..." (13)

In a remarkable contradiction to the Brandens' implications, Rand at one point actually suggested that Branden have an affair with someone else, if this proved to be the "solution" to his problems. Recall, in this context, that jealousy had not been an issue for Rand during Branden's marriage to Ms. Branden. This general attitude appears not to have changed. But, as always, Rand demands *an understanding*.

In her notes from July 4, she would write:

> In one of our early conversations about "Miss X," [**from the context this seems to have been sometime in late 1967, when Branden's other, secret affair was already more than three-years old**] I said that if this proved to be the only solution to his sex problem, I might conceivably accept a "Miss X," provided I understood his motives fully and rationally, and provided I did not have to meet her or associate with her. He said, with a kind of despair: "Oh, that's just the trouble: if you felt that way about her, I could not become interested in any woman!" When I asked him whether this meant that he needed my moral sanction, he assured me that it did not—but was unable to explain what it did mean. (14)

In other words, Branden did not require any "moral sanction" from Rand about his romantic decisions at all—the very idea obviously distressed her—and, with a "rational" understanding of it, she would even have "accepted" it. These are Rand's own words *long before knowing of Branden's actual affair*.

Later, with a new understanding of his psychology, she would come to believe that "...I was terribly wrong in suggesting an affair with any present Miss X"—as she believed it would only exacerbate his current problems. (15)

It is apparent that, rather than insane jealousy, it was the slow torture of Branden's vacillation that was Rand's main concern.

In July, she would write that even after it was long "over" in her own mind, Branden himself still claimed that what he felt for her was passionate love. It was merely "blocked" by other problems. She suspected—in her words, had a "stomach-feeling"—that Branden was simply being dishonest for some unknown reason, and, so,

> What followed was the total hell (for me) and the terrible torture of the last five months of "[psycho-epistemological] therapy." I could not act on my 'stomach feeling' as such, I could not prove it—and I could not break with him, so long as any hope remained. (Particularly, so long as I could not understand how anything so horrible could happen to a man of his former stature.) I broke with [Branden], one night—and he would not let me: his agony seemed so sincere (and, I think, it was) that I had to give him a last chance. (16)

Indeed, perhaps the most striking feature of these notes is the reasonable attitude Rand maintains. She wrote in January of 1968:

> I have told him, at the start of the present period, that I will accept anything which I can rationally understand— and that the only thing I dread, in his attitude, is his "I don't know." (17)

And, in July of that year, Rand would conclude that:

> ...the whole of our past and its meaning was not strong enough to make him give me the one courtesy (if nothing more) that he owed me, and owes every human being he deals with, the one value I had given him so much of in the past: *thought*—the effort of thinking and of a rational decision, even if only a rational way of parting. (18)

4. We were certainly told by the Brandens about Rand's negative opinion of Branden's new mistress, Patrecia, but we were *not* told that one of Rand's primary sources for this view was Nathaniel Branden himself!

As his feelings for his new lover were becoming ever more apparent, Branden actually speaks to Rand of "his fear of becoming attracted to an

unimportant woman, on the ground of 'What would it prove about him?'"
Rand immediately fears that this also "seems to indicate that his love for
me may have been role-playing from the start." (19)

The notes make clear that this "fear" of loving an "inferior"—which
seems ominously and intimately related to Branden's need for Rand to
"sanction" his new "Miss X"—was originally Branden's own stated fear.

We learn that it is Branden himself who had warned Rand that "he
is able to think and to judge things and people clearly, [only] so long as he
thinks of them objectively, without any relation to himself." (20)

To the idea that one should be *morally* concerned about one's
romantic choices because of what they allegedly "prove" about oneself,
Rand also gives us her insightful rebuttal:

> I told him that this was the premise of using love as a
> means to an end, rather than an end in itself—i.e., as a
> "proof" of one's own value or self-esteem, rather than its
> expression. (21)

Branden's own fears of falling for a "lesser value," however, were
apparently intense. Rand tells us:

> [Branden] realized that if he fell in love with [the] right
> woman in the future (a woman he valued seriously or
> regarded as important to him), "it would be like a *prison*."
> (This last is verbatim; the word is significant.) (22)

Branden's evolving statements about his secret mistress are highly
revealing. Rand summarizes:

> Originally, [Branden] had said that [Patrecia] represented
> his "Eddie Willers," [**a character in *Atlas Shrugged*, and
> one Branden, as we have already seen, refers to as "rather
> pathetic"**] i.e., an average person who had good premises
> although she was not at all philosophical or intellectual.
> Then, he said this estimate of her had changed: that she
> was an unusual person who, in some way, reminded him of

himself in his childhood, that she was a victim of the same irrationality as he had been, but without his intellectual weapons and that he felt very eager to help her, to "protect her from the world." Then, he began to be peculiarly defensive, when the subject of [Patrecia] came up: he told me that [Barbara Branden's] attacks on [Patrecia] were like attacks on himself—like attacks on some element in himself which was very important to him but which he had been sacrificing in (or which was being destroyed by) his marriage. I tried to help him identify that element; he was unable to do it. In all such discussions, he kept insisting that he was not in love with [Patrecia], he had no romantic interest in her of any kind, and that his feeling for her was predominantly "protective," "almost paternal." (23)

One disturbing implication of this passage involves Branden's detailed awareness of Patrecia's psychological "issues"—perhaps their origins in her childhood—along with his eagerness "to help" on this score. They suggest that Branden was—in some sense—acting as Patrecia's therapist before their romantic relationship began. (For a professional psychologist, this would be, of course, highly unethical, for obvious reasons.)

According to Rand's notes, Branden himself believed Patrecia to be "inferior" to the other women in his life. She tells us that:

[Branden's] terror was that he sensed he preferred [Patrecia] to [Barbara Branden] and me—and since he could not explain this to himself in any rational terms, he began to dread that it was a physicalistic, sexual attraction... What he could not admit to himself was the fact that she, [Patrecia], *was* the "soul-mate" of his hidden "self." (24)

During the course of 1968, Rand would ask Branden about his "fears" in regard to falling for an "inferior" woman. He explained that these were closely associated with his intense admiration for Rand, and, in an eerie echo of his "no equals at any age" line, tells Rand that "this meant that *any* woman would be inferior to [Rand]... " (25)

This can only be seen as the grandest—if not the most grandiose—of Branden's rationalizations for his behavior: Rand's very "greatness" was his fear—the "prison"—the threat to his self-esteem in a romantic relationship.

In light of his contemporaneous dishonesty to Rand, we can only conclude that Branden's sycophancy was reaching ever new lows.

5. Mr. Branden gave more than a mere impression that he had really "opened up" in his memoirs, exposing his own deepest psychology, "warts and all."

While he certainly did reveal a host of personal issues, as it turns out, Branden had not revealed the most important (i.e., the ones most relevant to his relationship and break with Rand), namely, his deep "repression," his growing "materialism," his closely related (and self-diagnosed) "autism." ("Autism" is used in these notes in its more general sense, namely, "the withdrawal from reality into a private, subjective fantasy world," as opposed to the childhood form of schizophrenia which shares the name.) We have already seen Branden's complaints regarding his neurotic "fear" of falling for a woman who did not "live up" to his alleged values.

We shall return to each of these subjects in due course.

Rand also reveals that,

> The most disturbing thing, to me, was the fact that [Branden's] growing confusion and inner despair seemed to date, approximately, from the time of his *success*, i.e., from the time when [the Nathaniel Branden Institute] became a firmly established, successful organization. If a man feels desperate at a time of existential *failure*, I do not consider it necessarily bad or significantly neurotic. But I am and always have been convinced that if a man feels desperate at a time of existential *success*, it is a sign of some ominous, major inner trouble, the sign of something bad. (26)

She writes that "[t]his was the start of [Branden's] trend toward *materialism*: his attraction to material luxury, his feeling that money is the only thing he can get out of this culture."

Rand continues:

> He said this in answer to [Barbara Branden's] observation
> that he got no pleasure out of his hectic business activities
> (what I call his "wheeling-dealing"). I asked him whether
> he had concluded, in effect, that the process of doing
> business had to give him pleasure, as his only reward... He
> said, yes. (27)

The extent to which Branden actually enjoyed his business activities,
such as the theater project—as he now readily admits in his memoirs—was
apparently another thing he wanted to keep Rand in the dark about—and
represents more evidence of his dishonesty and manipulation in all of
those "therapy" sessions. This is an aspect of his dishonesty Branden largely
ignores in his memoir.

These were not Rand's only concerns about Branden's psychology.
She writes that his "peculiar, very subtle or intangible pleasure in giving
orders to people has made me call it 'the big shot premise,' for want of a
better name: it is a combination of [the] faint shadings of an autocrat and
a show-off." (28)

Rand also shares her opinion that Branden's "too frequent and
too inappropriate use[s] of humor [have], often, the overtones and/or
implications of moral cowardice." (29)

Rand reveals Branden's stated contempt for people—and his
compulsive need for them.

> He has always admitted that he wants to like people and to be
> liked by them. So do I—in the rational, "benevolent" sense
> of the words—and that is what I thought he meant. But
> there is a very strange ambivalence in his attitude toward
> people: his bitter, "malevolent" [**attitude?**] and, today,
> almost hostile contempt for them does not fit a frustrated
> "benevolent universer." (And, [Barbara Branden] told
> me that she sensed that there was something undefinably
> wrong in his attitude toward people—as if "he wanted
> something from them," she could never discover what.)

Considering his stressed contempt for people, it is strange that he likes giving parties. (30)

By the end, Rand would see Branden, not as an independent John Galt, the hero of *Atlas Shrugged*, but as the opportunistic social climber Peter Keating from *The Fountainhead*, and a Keating who refused to admit his own flaws to himself. Rand suggests that,

> ...at 14, reading *The Fountainhead*, he might have recognized some similarity between some of his own feelings and Peter Keating's. This would have terrified him—since all of his conscious mind and better premises admired Roark and he wanted to emulate Roark. His solution was to repress the Keating element fiercely—and to make himself into a Roark by "will power"... (31)

Rand is distressed that Branden's approach is basically that of an *intrinsicist*, one who views moral and psychological questions out of context—making, in effect, "religious" demands on himself. We have already seen how Branden now claims that any religious element in his own psychology had long been purged, and that it was Rand who was afflicted by a remnant of religiosity. But to Rand he had, more or less, confessed to having a religious psychology:

> For instance, he had thought that an ideal form of love was a single, monogamous marriage—therefore, he resisted the realization that his marriage had failed, because he regarded this as his failure to lead a "stylized" life. I asked him whether he regarded Rearden's [**Hank Rearden is a hero in *Atlas Shrugged* who divorces his wife**] life as "unstylized" because of the failure of his marriage. He agreed emphatically that he had always regarded it that way. He compared Rearden's situation—the discovery that he had chosen the wrong woman—to the position of a writer who discovers that his past work is bad or wrong, and who is ashamed of it; he said that such a writer's

position was a horror. I told him that this amounted to a "Kantian stylized universe": a series of intrinsic moral absolutes to which men had to conform, regardless of context, personal choice or circumstances. He agreed very emphatically: the words "Kantian stylized universe" seemed to strike him very strongly—he said they named something important in him. (32)

While many of these psychological problems appear to have been sincerely expressed by Branden, many were clearly bogus, part of Branden's design to deceive Rand about his sex life. By February of 1968, despite his on-going affair with Patrecia, Branden was complaining to Rand of being in the grip of a "sexual freeze," the "sex problem" to which Rand will refer in these notes. His state in 1968 was that of a celibate, he tells Rand, not out of religious conviction, but because of a psychological "block" on the issue of sex. Branden analogizes himself to the "war-wounded man," for Rand's benefit, suggesting that his "problem" is much wider in scope than simply their affair.

However, despite his on-going affair with Patrecia, many of Branden's sexual complaints appear to have been sincere. One of the creepiest aspects of his psychology is revealed when Rand writes in early July of 1968,

> [Branden] said that he felt a sexual desire for me in emergencies (not exclusively then, but almost always then), such as during our violent quarrels ([he said] he felt it *even yesterday*)... (33)

So, even *after* Branden had confessed the "age issue" and ended the pretense of his romantic feelings, he was still getting hot for Rand when they quarreled, something he regards as an "emergency." Her clinical style cannot hide Rand's concern for Branden's psychology on this point.

By this time Branden knew that their physical relationship was over. Even if he was still trying flatter Rand in that way, which seems unlikely after revealing the "age issue," why specify "emergencies" or "violent quarrels"? On the other hand, such an admission can hardly have been part of any effort to extract himself from his relationship with Rand. The statement must be treated as sincere.

6. One specific revelation pertaining to all of this "psychotherapy" is particularly fascinating.

The Brandens both admitted—if not in 1968, at least in their subsequent books—that Branden was now using Rand as his therapist, and, in particular, with regard to his "psycho-epistemology." But precisely *what* Branden was having trouble thinking about is something we were *not* told in either of the Brandens' books.

Rand fills us in.

> My first very serious worry about his actual psychological state came about a year ago (Spring of 1967), when he asked me to help him with his [psycho-epistemology] in regard to [Barbara Branden]. He said that he had done something terribly wrong to his own mind, during the years of his marriage, something which he could not identify (then or since), and that his thinking on any other subject was totally clear, but broke down only on the subject of his relationship with [Barbara Branden]. The central theme of his confusion was: "I don't know what I feel toward [Barbara Branden]" (34)

The Brandens both insist that their own relationship was over and done with by 1966, if not by 1965. But, as these notes make clear, Branden was telling Rand that he still did not know what he felt for his first wife, that his marriage with Barbara was still unresolved, through most of 1967. It also appears that Ms. Branden helped maintain this impression for some time.

Rand would later write:

> That summer and fall [of 1967], I was appalled by his indecisiveness and vacillation in regard to [Barbara Branden]—and by the torture he was inflicting on her. He said that he realized it, but was helpless—and nothing changed in his behavior towards her. Finally, it was [Barbara Branden] who delivered an ultimatum to

him—and thus forced him to make a decision about their
marriage. (35)

The context makes clear that Rand has not written down the wrong
year or mistaken it for some other. The Brandens, though they themselves
know that their relationship is over (Ms. Branden even knows about the
affair with Patrecia, and has had one of her own, by now), through most
of 1967 *both* of them are still "playing out" a false hope for their marriage,
apparently for Rand's benefit—a pretense entirely unmentioned in their
own memoirs.

The evidence shows the extent to which Ms. Branden was willing
to go in order to keep Rand in the dark about Branden's new affair, and
the elaborate extent to which both of them, in concert, were willing to go
in order to deceive her. We will see Ms. Branden occasionally putting in
her own "two cents" with theories about Branden's behavior—knowing
the actual truth all along, of course—assisting Branden in his ongoing and
psychologically elaborate charade.

7. One of Branden's important rationalizations for his own behavior
in all of these events is his stated conviction that everything would have
turned out just the same with Rand—including the dissolution of the
Nathaniel Branden Institute and his business association with her—even if
he had never lied to her, even if he had never had a secret affair—his firmly
stated belief that merely rejecting Rand romantically made the outcome
inevitable.

Rand's notes, however, refute this.

In all of Rand's considerations of a "break" before August of 1968,
a "total break" always and explicitly meant *retaining their business and
professional relationship*.

Even after July of 1968, when Branden had revealed that the "age"
issue was—and had long been—a problem for him, i.e., that in this respect
he had *romantically* lied for many years—and even after Branden's feelings
for Patrecia (if not his on-going, four-year relationship with her) had been
made known to Rand—her private notes demonstrate that Rand continued
to meet with Branden on *both* professional and personal levels.

Already in November of 1967, Rand had sensed that Branden might
not be anything like the man she had once thought him to be, "[b]ut, if so,

then the only answer is to break with him entirely. That is, not to see him at all except 'functionally,' on business."

It is true that Rand also doubts whether that would "be possible to us," but, then, explains precisely "how" she could "accept this" and move on with her life. (36)

This was clearly the only kind of "break" that she was anticipating.

Instead, of course, Branden would renew all of his vehement insistence that it was still passionate romance, initiating the last, brief "Renaissance" in their relationship—and despite what Branden calls Rand's "reticence."

At the start of the year, Rand's notes indicate that her questioning of Branden resumed, and Branden was forced into more "explanations."

Based on his answers, by the end of January, 1968, after "the triangle is over"—to use her own words—Rand writes only of "a total break (*leaving only a functional relationship.*)" (37) This time, she no longer even questions the viability of such a business relationship—she simply assumes that it will continue.

For the next six months, the "therapy" resumed, and Rand would communicate frequently with Branden about their work. She was obviously working for something other than a romance by now.

Mr. Branden's hypothesis is exactly wrong. If it were not for his own repeated and wide-ranging lies to Rand, the "life he had built" would never have been "destroyed." The "outcome" was "inevitable" exclusively because of his dishonesty, and, as Rand's notes show, really had nothing to do with romantic jealousy or rejection.

8. The Brandens are particularly vague on this point, but Rand's journals make clear that it was Rand who was principally responsible for the "forced" and "rolling" disclosures of the truth—and for Branden's eventual exposure. We will see—based solely on his evasive and dishonest *mental functioning*—how Rand, objectively, came to the decision that Branden was immoral months *before* learning of his secret affair, specifically, immoral in the way he was dealing (or, rather, not dealing) with his many disturbing personal problems. Rand continued to demand explanations, and she relentlessly tried to define the "stomach-feelings" she was getting from Branden—all of which kept pointing to dishonest motives on his part, a terrible prospect considering how closely she had associated herself with him. It was Rand who pushed to get beneath Branden's ongoing rationalizations, until, in the end, the rest of the truth was forced out.

At least as early as November of 1967, Rand observes that Branden's mental drift "is inconceivable for a man of his rationality and intellectual development. *He is hiding something here. What?*" (38)

In January she is still writing that "[t]he vibrations he communicates... are fear. *Fear of what?* His inner chaos... his general [psycho-epistemological] disintegration, all are symptoms of fear." She does not yet know the full story and thinks the answer is still just in Branden's head and not in his overt behavior, i.e., his lying to her about what he had been thinking and doing and feeling and saying *for years*. She writes that "since there is no existential cause of fear, the cause must be psychological. There is something he is afraid to face. I cannot be sure of what it is..." (39)

Rand insists on answers. Every time that Branden delivers a new "explanation" for his behavior, Rand detects more rationalization, and demands more answers. This tortured cycle would last for several months— and Branden would, of course, never really come clean to Rand—but it is this series of demands which, in the end, drives the truth to the surface.

9. Objectivism certainly rejects "rationalism," as in the classical sense of the term, i.e., the philosophical approach of men like Descartes and Leibnitz. But Objectivists also use this term to mean something else, an approach not necessarily tied to the *content* of one's philosophy but to one's normal *cognitive method,* i.e., *how* one thinks. It is a "syndrome," if you will, which sometimes afflicts intellectuals, in particular; it is characterized by emotional repression and an excessive reliance on purely deductive logic— in short, the overly "cerebral" personality. More precisely, the rationalist tends to avoid the perceptual level of awareness in favor of the abstract. His values and opinions tend to be developed independently from fact and experience and, therefore, at some point invariably come into conflict with them. An ideal not based on reality will be impossible to achieve in reality. (40)

A "rationalist" is one who might, for instance, repress his genuine emotions in order to live up to what his supposed "logic" is telling him he "should" value. He might attempt to "force" himself to like, say, a certain kind of art and the facts, including his authentic values, will not be regarded as an obstacle. In other words, he will exhibit the very self-abnegating behavior which we have already seen in the Brandens. Theirs was an "Objectivism" not based on facts, but on the desire to live up to their distorted view of Rand's ideals.

Despite the Brandens' repeated suggestions to the contrary, Rand herself was not a "rationalist" about love or anything else. She never believed or suggested—much less ever demanded—that anyone love her, ever love Ms. Branden, or ever love anyone else. Rand did not believe that love could be forced, and she was explicitly deceived into believing that the Brandens' stated values on the subject were genuine.

In fact, Rand was quite distressed to discover that the Brandens' values and affections had been "forced" and "play-acting" all along.

From the evidence, it was, rather, Branden who was (among other things) the "rationalist" and emotional repressor. ("Rationalism," of course, cannot account for Branden's treatment of Rand, nor his dishonesty— which are certainly *not* necessary features of the syndrome. As we shall see, this was the least of Mr. Branden's problems.)

In January of 1968, Rand had written, "Love cannot be forced on oneself as an 'atonement,' and [Branden] cannot force it on himself." (41)

In answer to a question from Branden, she had advised the following:

> An answer to the question: "I have the power to make her happy but don't know what to do." The only possible answer is: identify clearly what would make *you* happy (in regard to her)—and this will be the right thing to do. (In practice, adapt your desire to the possible.) (42)

Rand writes the following bit of advice to Branden during this period:

> Psycho-epistemological note: re: The impossibility of acting by a purely cerebral method. The time element required to integrate and hold the full context of all the aspects of a complex issue, makes it impossible to accomplish; one needs the lightning integration provided by emotions (and by one's self-interest). When repression blocks this integrating process, one acts in a contradictory way and one is unable to preserve any continuity or

context. (Trying to hold the "interest" of another person as one's standard and one's integrating principle, will not work: nature does not permit a psycho-epistemological altruism of that kind.) (43)

In February of 1968, Rand adds:

In re: psycho-epistemology and sense of life. All sense of life issues (i.e., one's subconscious metaphysical fundamentals) have to be automatized. They are wide abstractions (integrations), involved in one's every thought, emotion, action and choice—and they cannot be handled by a conscious, conceptual process in every moment or issue of one's life. Just as the reliance on one's own rational judgment (self-esteem) is automatized and one does not wonder, in any given process of thought, whether one should accept one's own judgment or that of others or pray to God for guidance—so all fundamentals of one's sense-of-life must be automatized. (44)

As it turns out, Rand's repeated plea to Branden is for him to end the repression, the rationalistically "forced" emotion, the attempt to live up to unrealistic ideals, and the purely "cerebral" method that she sees in him. Rand was beginning to see that Branden's "fundamentals" had been forced all along, that his sense of life never matched his stated philosophy. But, she observed, "fundamentals" cannot be "forced."

We can see Rand dissecting the syndrome itself, working through its nature and manifestations, as she diagnoses Branden's troubling case.

The Brandens are simply blaming Rand for their own religious and "autistic" manner of thinking, their private and twisted view of what allegedly Objectivism "demands."

10. Despite the Brandens' repeated complaints about Rand's incessant "moralism," the reverse is actually suggested by Rand's private journal entries. Rand is hardly eager—actually extremely reluctant—to come to a negative moral judgment about Branden or anyone else.

In January of 1968, Rand's profound doubts about Branden are growing, however, and she writes:

If I know that I cannot accept his present attitude, why don't *I* break with him now? *Because I do not understand his attitude.* Because I must first understand. Because I do believe he loves me in some abstract, subjective manner of his own. And, in view of today's conversation, I think that his breach with reality is growing wider, not healing. I sense (for the first time and very dimly) the beginnings of something *immoral*—of *rationalization.* (If I am wrong I apologize for it.) (45)

Rand is actually apologizing for even considering the issue of Branden's immorality in private notes to herself.

Such a judgment of Branden was, of course, a sound one, but Rand is still being remarkably careful.

It is also apparent from these notes that the accusation that Branden was "betraying his values" must also be attributed to Branden rather than Rand. In a brief entry from February 1968, Rand, clearly trying to "buck up" Branden's spirits, writes the following advice in her "therapy" notes:

Step outside the square in re: betrayal of your values. The opposite is true. Why a social metaphysician would not have [Branden's] problem. (46)

Rand is obviously unaware of Branden's dishonesty and is here trying to get Branden *away* from thinking that he falls under that most dreaded of Brandenian classifications, a "social metaphysician," or that he has "betrayed his values." Many of the harsh moral judgments he attributes to Rand, however much Branden appears to have earned them, are clearly Branden's *own judgments of himself*—and judgments Rand only came to reluctantly.

These are not the only significant revelations, and there are many smaller insights provided in these notes, as well. For instance, we learn that Branden himself considered "suspending" pre-production of the stage version of *The Fountainhead* before the final break with Rand. We also learn that—despite the Brandens' accusations that Rand had improperly taken *The Objectivist* from Branden—Branden himself had offered to sign over his interest in the magazine to Rand—again, before the break. Rand writes in July of 1968 of Branden's previous "offer to make a present of *The Objectivist*, which was actually offensive." (47)

And, still, this does not exhaust the list of contradictions and omissions which Rand's journals expose in the Brandens' accounts.

Indeed, the bulk of Rand's "private" journal entries from November of 1967 until July of 1968 pertain in one way or another to Rand's relationship and break with the Brandens and has a direct bearing on their later accounts of this history.

Therefore, rather than simply delineate the various contradictions of the Brandens' work implied by an analysis of these journals, we are best served to simply go through the bulk of this material chronologically. Such a procedure also reveals the steps by which Rand came eventually to the conviction that Branden was a deeply disturbed and immoral man.

Not all of this material has been reproduced here. The omitted material falls into four categories: first, material which makes reference to persons other than Nathaniel Branden, Barbara Branden or Patrecia Branden, has been excluded in the interest of privacy. These passages represent Rand's very private thinking, and there is no indication that she ever meant for these opinions to be made public. There were only a handful of such references to other persons, and, in any case, most of these references are ambiguously brief. The Brandens, however, have given detailed accounts of their own version of these events, and it seems only fair to provide Rand's specific response to them, at least. In a very important sense, these journals are Rand's only surviving voice on the subject of their accusations against her.

Second, material which is wholly repetitive has been omitted. If the context makes clear that Rand had said the same thing at some earlier point, and, in fact, she had said it in much the same language, only one instance is quoted.

Many smaller notes, extremely brief and cryptic have also been omitted. For example, an item which reads simply "issue of optional choices—his apartment," with no other clues surrounding it, is not included for our analysis.

Finally, the journal entries from June 5, 1968, were given by Rand to Ms. Branden, and she later sold them. These, along with some brief entries dated from mid-July to mid-August, have not been reproduced, but all of these are highly repetitive of the material to be found here.

In no case was material left out at the request of a third party, including the Estate of Ayn Rand which made all of the material available and has accepted no royalty, charge or fee of any kind for the use of it. It can be expected that one day all of this material will be available for the use of all scholars.

In these notes, there are only five extended "essay length" pieces. Nearly the whole of these five sections has been reproduced here, and the original order of this material has been retained so that the reader can see the steps by which Rand came to her conclusions regarding Mr. Branden—and the process of her mind "at work." The lengthiest piece in this collection, and the most conclusive, dated July 4, 1968, has been reproduced in its entirety, excluding only references to persons other than those listed above.

In the text below, an effort has been made to preserve Rand's original notations as much as possible. However, when Rand has underlined something, this appears as *italics* in the text. Hence forward, no emphasis or italics are the editor's unless specifically indicated in the text. Any editorial additions and comments have been made in bold and [**within bold brackets**], and where material is omitted bold ellipses **...** are used. Light ellipses ... are all original. All of the light brackets—[and the comments within them]—are Rand's except where an abbreviation commonly used by Rand has been written out. Rand abbreviates "psycho-epistemology" in the notes as "p.-e.," and the name of Ms. Branden is always "BB," while her own is "A." For clarity, these have been substituted with "psycho-epistemology," "Barbara Branden," "Ayn," and so forth, within light brackets, since they only elaborate one of Rand's own abbreviations. Finally, Rand's own pagination of these notes is indicated as the numbers in bold brackets, thus: [**1**]. Where Rand has not left pagination, this is indicated in the editorial text as a "single-page entry."

But, before proceeding, a more detailed review of the relevant context, both biographical and philosophical, is in order.

One of Objectivism's great insights is its recognition of the comprehensive power of philosophy over human affairs. Fundamental ideas, negatively or positively, shape the individual—his mind, his emotions, his psychology, his character, his very *soul*. Fundamental ideas, for good or ill, also shape whole cultures, indeed, the course of human history—from science to art to politics to popular culture. (48)

Therefore, philosophy is not a boring or merely "theoretical" concern to an Objectivist. It is life and death. It is happiness or neurosis. It is triumph or tragedy. It is Michelangelo or Jackson Pollock. It is Jefferson or Lenin. It is America or the Soviet Union or Nazi Germany or the Mullahs' Iran.

Philosophy, in some form, is unavoidable. Whether it is a specific religious creed, or a collection of semi-consistent principles sincerely believed to be "just common sense," or a randomly associated series of vaguely defined emotional commitments, or a reality-based, logically consistent secular world-view, according to Objectivism everyone is guided by some kind of philosophy.

Philosophy provides human beings with an essential frame of reference, a context into which the sum of one's knowledge can be integrated. Successful action requires the confidence that our actions— and our goals—make sense. It is just such an integrated "world-view" that philosophy provides.

The discovery of such a world-view often necessitates the use of new language, the development of a terminology helpful to the understanding of the new insights or errors. Whether by revolution, or by a slow "trickling down" into the culture, this once-technical nomenclature is transformed into the "common sense" of succeeding generations by scientists, scholars, artists, journalists and others, each applying the new insight to their own fields. In this way, philosophers from Plato and Aristotle to Kant and Hegel and Marx, have—for good or ill—each affected *language itself* along with the basic outlook of millions: artisans, artists, writers, businessmen, clergymen and day-laborers.

As the late Jacob Bronowski put it in the context of scientific knowledge, "The commonplace of the schoolbooks of tomorrow is the adventure of today..." (49)

To take but one example, for millennia in every large society and on every continent, slavery—in one form or another—was an unquestioned institution until the moral and political thinking of brave and rational minds eventually convinced the world (or, at least, much of it) that slavery was (and is) always and inherently wrong and, conversely, that *individuals have rights*. Once upon a time, this was a controversial notion—even in the Nineteenth Century, philosopher Jeremy Bentham could call the idea of natural rights "nonsense on stilts"—today, this is simply "common sense" (at least throughout the West), just as slavery had been the "common sense" of yore.

And the concept of "rights" was added to our vocabulary.

Today, the original concept of rights is widely misunderstood and its original meaning has been grossly perverted by many contemporary academics and politicians; but, in some form, it is the idea "rights"— not "slavery"—that now holds sway in most people's minds as being "natural."

That is the power of philosophy.

Ayn Rand not only understood the power of philosophy, she was herself a philosopher and responsible for such a world-view—that system of philosophy which she called "Objectivism." Rand also developed a distinctive vocabulary—as she might have put it, she discovered new concepts that needed naming. Many of these concepts became so indispensable to her thought that they appear frequently in her notes and require some definition before we proceed. (50)

Unlike many atheists, Rand believed in moral absolutes, and she believed in heroes.

Although its ethics and politics are radically individualistic, it was, perhaps, only to be expected that Rand's school would be called "a cult," however grossly unfair the charge. The potential impact of Rand's work is comparable only to that of a great religious or philosophical system. Rand's thought—though fully secular—invades the province which had been the almost exclusive domain of religion, the field of morality, and it fully taps that field's power to inspire.

This is something Rand herself appreciated. In the "Introduction" she wrote for the Twenty-fifth Anniversary Edition of *The Fountainhead*, in order to explain the novel's unique impact, Rand complains that,

> Religion's monopoly in the field of ethics has made it extremely difficult to communicate the emotional meaning and connotations of a rational view of life. Just as religion has preempted the field of ethics, turning

morality against man, so it has usurped the highest moral concepts of our language, placing them outside this earth and beyond man's reach. "Exaltation" is usually taken to mean an emotional state evoked by contemplating the supernatural. "Worship" means the emotional experience of loyalty and dedication to something higher than man. "Reverence" means the emotion of a sacred respect, to be experienced on one's knees. "Sacred" means superior to and not-to-be-touched-by any concrete concerns of man or of this earth. Etc. (51)

For Rand, these concepts had referents here on earth. Unlike many secular philosophers, *Rand took abstract values seriously.* From Soviet tyranny to the Manhattan skyline, she saw all of the practical, "real world" consequences of philosophy too clearly to be neutral on the subject. Something *was* sacred, Rand was convinced, but it wasn't housed in Heaven, but here on earth: *the achievements of the human mind.*

Therefore, Objectivism does not consist of an arid, academic discussion of philosophy, but a call to action—a demanding, inspirational ethic. It is not only an integrated and rational way of looking at the world, but also a corresponding approach to principled *action* in that world.

Rand thought of hers as "a philosophy for living on earth."

This understanding goes to the very core of Rand's life and thought. For example, Rand became a philosopher, she says, simply because she wanted to be a novelist. Her first passion was the telling of stories and the depiction of characters that were of interest to her, in particular, heroes. But, in order to depict characters she could regard as ideal, Rand found that she first had to identify what she regarded as "ideal." She says that she was forced to do this because she soon found that she disagreed with every conception of the ideal put forward by previous philosophers. (52)

In other words, Rand had to develop *a new system of ethics* in order to properly develop *the characters in her romantic novels.* That is the kind of mind Rand possessed, and this is but one measure of the scope of her achievement.

Rand's seriousness about values—and her consequent stress on philosophical integrity—is at least one reason why Rand's art has had the "life-changing" and inspirational impact ascribed to it by so many of her readers.

This is also the necessary context to be kept in mind in any analysis of Rand's relationship with Nathaniel Branden.

Branden relates that, years before he met Rand, he had practically memorized *The Fountainhead*. He read it with the fervor and intensity of a lover and with the serious dedication of a scholar of the Talmud, he tells us. (53)

For Rand, whose impressive efforts were going largely ignored, unappreciated and intentionally misunderstood by the broader culture, Branden and his friends represented, for the first time in her life, full intellectual "visibility."

Rand and her husband shared a deep emotional, or sense of life, affinity, but O'Connor was not an intellectual and could not give Rand's mind the constant and intense intellectual "feed-back" it surely craved.

In his writings on psychology while he was still with Rand, Branden developed this idea of "psychological visibility," and came to regard this as a basic human need. Inspired by Rand's own thinking about love and friendship, the nucleus of the idea actually goes back to Aristotle's claim that a friend is a kind of "mirror."

To understand friendship, Branden would build upon the analogy of a mirror. Aristotle held that "the good man" enjoys the very contemplation of the virtues of another, that the virtuous gain an important value from the sheer contemplation of virtue. Branden argued that we have mirrors to show us our *physical* bodies objectively, but in order to see our own souls, we are greatly assisted by "the reflection" of our consciousness in that of another, i.e., another's appreciation and understanding of our character and our values, an informed appreciation of our uniqueness, our "self." To be "seen" for who and what we are—inside—is one the most profound benefits of love and close friendship, and this may be called our need to be "psychologically visible." (54)

What Rand must have starved for all of her life—what any benevolent and creative mind treading paths none had dared before would naturally starve for—is precisely such "visibility."

To discover the philosophy of Objectivism, Rand had employed a distinctive way of thinking, a cognitive method which, in itself, distinguishes her from other philosophers—what Rand would have called her distinctive "psycho-epistemology." (55)

According to Objectivism, psychology and thinking are *interactive*. Thinking (abstraction, concept-formation, logic) is volitional, it is *conscious*, and it takes effort. However, psychological factors—often completely subconscious ones—can influence the way our minds habitually operate, the *way* we tend to handle ideas—perhaps, say, a "rationalist" tendency towards deductive logic and away from inductive logic. Left undiscovered, such subconscious factors unwittingly influence everything about our personality—including the method and approach of our conscious thinking. Objectivism defines "psycho-epistemology" as the study of cognitive processes in light of this interaction between subconscious and volitional factors.

As Objectivism cautions, if you are not attentive, your thinking can be clouded by your "psycho-epistemology."

In addition, Objectivism holds that one's thinking shapes one's emotions—and that one's emotions can also shape one's thinking. While emotions themselves are not "tools of cognition" and need not impair objective thought, this "feedback" between emotions and thinking can be a positive process, beneficial to objectivity, motivating careful thought. However, to substitute emotion for thinking, to place an "I wish" over an "it is," to believe what is emotionally satisfying or convenient over the rational, is the very essence of subjective distortion.

As Objectivism cautions, if you are not attentive, your thinking can be clouded by your "psychology."

When he was still with Rand, Branden had argued that since the very function of consciousness is *to know*, cognitive efficiency is at least one objective measure of psychological health.

To put this another way, find the areas you have trouble thinking about in your life, and you will probably be able to locate your emotional problems, as well. Likewise, find your emotional problems, and you will inevitably find the very areas you need to think about more clearly. (In fact, this concept of using cognitive efficiency as a psycho-diagnostic tool is somewhat distinctive to psychologists influenced by Objectivism.)

Rand's own mind cannot be cut into parts—her extraordinarily logical cognitive method was intimately tied to her passionate "sense of life." Thus, one could say that what her relationship with Branden provided Rand—or so, at first, it seemed—was both *psycho-epistemological "visibility"* and the "visibility" of her uniquely integrated way of both thinking and feeling.

Branden reports of his first meeting with Rand on the electrifying effect of her mind in action. She was "Mrs. Logic"—and unusually feminine—and this meeting altered the course of his whole life. Branden says that he hungered for her mind and her very soul. (56) He wanted to be just like the heroes Rand had presented in her novels, a man of intellect who was also a man of action, and a man with the independent soul of a creative artist. The man who was her complete match, the ideal for which Rand forever sought.

Branden *wanted* to be Rand's ideal, her mirror, but, as he now admits, he was nothing like that ideal.

As we have already seen, Branden nevertheless ably convinced Rand that he *was* that ideal, "except for a few blemishes."

What he cared for most was *ideas*, Branden claimed, Rand's ideas, the ideas they shared. Not just her ideas themselves but all that they implied: her art, her philosophy, her sense of life, her mind and her passion, her very method of thought. *All of this*, Branden claimed, was so important to him—indeed, the perfect reflection of his own—that he "built his life around" Rand's. All of this, he claimed, he "reflected back."

It wasn't just an affair, it was intellectual admiration, moral inspiration, esthetic gratitude, and hero-worship, all wrapped up in one relationship.

Only in this context can the relationship between Rand and Branden be properly understood. Both of them (and both of their spouses) were well aware of the fact that a twenty-five year age gap stretched between them, and that both were married to people they appeared to care for quite deeply. This is what all of those careful discussions preceding the affair were about.

And they were also all aware that, despite these obstacles, these two seemed to be sharing a kind of visibility that they were not likely to find again—physical, psychological, "psycho-epistemological" and "sense of life" areas all included, and all at once, and all in the same relationship.

Rand had written that "all of love is exception-making," the highest compliment one can pay to another. And so it is.

Rand believed that our values should not be simply relegated to some Platonic World of Forms, always an ideal never to be achieved on earth. Her affair with Branden, she thought, was a noble part of two creative souls' heroic quest for happiness, a transcendent union of kindred spirits.

Branden claimed that Rand was so important to him that all obstacles could be overcome—he loved her *that* much—his commitment was *that* comprehensive.

Thus, Rand became for him much more than a lover, but also a teacher, a business partner, an inspiration, even a therapist, so completely did he pretend to reflect all of Rand's values, even long after this had become an illusion.

Rand's concept of romantic love was an exalted one. The nature of Branden's deception must be measured in this light, as well.

Rand's conception of romance is perhaps most eloquently expressed by a love letter from the heroine of Rand's screenplay for the film *Love Letters*:

> I loved you long before I met you. I've always wanted to find a man who would feel and think and write as you do. A man who would look at life not as a burden or a punishment, but a dream of beauty we can make real. It was terrible waiting for you, but finding you was such a miracle that anything I suffered seems a small payment in return. (57)

For Rand, when it came to her highest values, her attitude was "price, no object." All exceptions could be made for her supreme values. This is how Rand saw romantic love.

Rand believed in the possibility of happiness, and she was willing to take chances for it. She did not believe the world to be a "veil of tears" or innately hostile to human interests. Rand believed that—with the aid of reason and a rational code of morality—success was to be generally expected. With the appropriate effort, our dreams often *can* be made real. She called this doctrine, the "benevolent universe premise." (58)

The Brandens now regard Rand's very concept of love, exalted and beautiful though it may be, as just not being practical. The souls of John Galt and Dagny Taggart simply do not and cannot exist. Not in Rand, not in Branden. Not in anybody.

For those who think otherwise, Branden's dishonesty toward Rand was no less than spiritual fraud of the highest order, and—in at least one crucial respect—Nathaniel Branden never really understood Objectivism, despite his fervent claims to the contrary. In retrospect, his identification of the "social metaphysician" and his development of the idea of "psychological visibility," ideas already implicit in *The Fountainhead*, seem mere adjuncts to his systematic deceptions of Ayn Rand, both intellectual and personal.

Branden reports that in 1966 he took Rand to see his—still secret—new mistress, an actress, perform in a play. Rand later complimented her performance by saying that she had "applied" the philosophy of Objectivism to the art of acting. Branden reports Patrecia's response with sympathy: "What has Objectivism got to do with this?" (59)

Of course, there is no specifically "Objectivist Acting," any more than there is an Objectivist Gardening. Branden himself admits that—while he was still with Rand—he did not think of his field as "Objectivist Psychotherapy," just "psychotherapy." (60)

But, in a certain sense, philosophy, as any actual Objectivist knows, has to do with *everything*, it is "the master integration" of our knowledge. Philosophy is precisely the field of broadest abstractions which covers the most ground.

What part of existence does the term "existence" leave out? What valid knowledge do we obtain by a means other than reason? When is it ever morally right for anyone to obtain a value through intentional fraud? What is an actress projecting but values in their physical form, i.e., emotions? When related to the characterization and themes in a play, why isn't that a highly "philosophical" subject? And how on earth does this philosophical observation take away from the actress's unique achievement and contributions? Doesn't it, rather, highlight them?

According to Objectivism, it is impossible for an actress to avoid the projection of abstract values, no matter what character she is portraying, and what any skilled artist projects is an entire "sense of life," a term which Rand defines as the emotional form in which we experience our deepest philosophical convictions. (61)

Objectivism was never a description of reality for Branden, it was a "theory" disconnected from acting—except the act that he was putting on for Rand. In this fundamental way, Objectivism was entirely disconnected from everything else in Branden's life.

Branden reports that he and Ms. Branden both believed that to reveal his feelings for this actress to Rand would be a mistake. Why? Because, "it did not fit our official theories of sex and love." (62) (Of course, Rand held no such theories, even unofficially.) And later, Branden says, "If Ayn's philosophy holds that I am morally wrong to be in love with Patrecia and that I am a traitor to my values for not romantically desiring Ayn, then at least in these respects her philosophy is wrong." (63) Ms. Branden says that Nathaniel Branden's relationship with Patrecia "contradicted everything [Branden] had learned about the nature of love, everything he had taught others; and he discovered that he needed it... " (64) Of course, the precise nature of this "contradiction" is never defined. True to Branden form, just how Objectivism requires or forbids Mr. Branden's love for Patrecia is not explained.

The Brandens blame Objectivism and Rand for "making" them lie so much. Objectivism somehow says that one is "bad" for loving Patrecia. See how absurd Objectivism is? "I had *a right* to lie in the face of this absurdity," Branden seems to be saying.

Of course, Rand never thought that it was immoral for someone to love Patrecia. Branden himself reports that, at first, Rand seemed to like both Patrecia and her husband, Larry. They both seemed to be "good Objectivists." If the photographs in Branden's memoir are to be believed, Rand attended their wedding.

No, Branden is here confusing what "Objectivism demands" in the abstract with what he had been claiming about himself to Rand *in particular.* Whether Branden was ever a "traitor to his values" depends, of course, on the nature of his *actual values.*

As it turns out, Objectivism never agreed with Branden's actual values, probably from the start.

Branden seems to have always treated Objectivism like a religion, some ideal outside of his power to ever achieve on earth. But he did attempt to fake it. In his own mind, Branden *should* love Rand, and he was less of an Objectivist if his lust did not follow this "should." So, he acted the part as best as he could.

Rand, of course, never morally reproached anyone for not lusting after her, and there is not the slightest evidence that she believed that a "moral" or "rational" person necessarily should. This is absurd on its face.

Branden is here ignoring one very important fact: he had actually been wildly proclaiming to Rand for many years that age did *not* matter, that she "had no equals at any age," etc., etc., *ad nauseam*. He had *convinced* Rand that she was desirable to him, that he was like a noble Roxane to her Cyrano, that he could see past the long nose, as it were, of their age difference—because *that* was how much her soul meant to him.

But, Branden makes plain, he did *not* have the soul of Roxane, he could *not* see past the nose, and worse, he could not bring himself to admit it. He says that Rand should have automatically understood his need for a woman of "his own age," even after repeatedly insisting to Rand for many years that he did not have such a need. He claimed to have the kind of soul that the characters in Rand's novels, or Rostand's play, possessed, the soul of an emotional hero down to his core. He put on an elaborate act and then blamed Rand for not having seen through it sooner.

To be sure, Branden had, for a long time, been lying to himself about himself. Patrecia was a symptom, not the cause, of Branden's deeper fraud about his own soul.

Even the soul Branden had claimed to possess might have found at some point that the age issue mattered to him—or might have fallen in love with another woman—both of which Rand could have accepted and understood, as her notes demonstrate. Neither would have jeopardized even a *high* status in Rand's esteem, as will become clear. What Rand could not accept was Branden's continuous *lies* about it all, his faking of *her* reality.

So generous was her estimate of him, Rand could barely conceive that Branden had actually been deceiving her for several years—and so she probed ever deeper into his psychology, trying to "help" him sort out his many inexplicable confusions. But it was all simply a front, an evasion designed to forestall telling her the full truth, and Rand's mission was fruitless, as she would deduce even before learning that truth.

Branden had painted himself into a corner by professing for years that Rand was the only *kind* of woman he could desire. If his had been such a soul, it would have been devoted to its authentic passion, its natural desires, the passions and desires that Branden had always claimed as his own. Nothing could have parted him from it, not age, not anything.

This is precisely why, at first, Branden kept the new affair a secret. If his love for Patrecia was what his soul really needed, then why not come forward to Rand, just as he had been honest with his wife about his earlier relationship with Rand? Because he knew that it revealed his soul to be something other than what he had told Rand—and what he had told the world—it was.

He could not yet rationally justify his desires, to be sure, but that was infinitely less important than the fact that it revealed the lie he had been living in his affair with Rand. Patrecia may well have been a better match for Branden, but he was certainly never really Rand's soul-mate. What Branden fails to fully confront is that, for many years, he had persuaded the world and Rand that his soul *was* Rand's match.

Objectivism, as Branden knew well, takes into account the variables of personal context. It was Mr. Branden who had thoroughly lied about his own context.

He had claimed to Rand that, like her, he possessed what he called a "stylized personality" and that his was a "stylized universe." In her notes from November 27, 1967, Rand provides the following definition:

> In regard to a "stylized universe." A stylized person... is a person who *lives in reality* according to his highest values, who takes *nothing less*, accepts no substitutes, and *struggles to translate his values into reality*, no matter what the difficulties. (65)

At some point in his past, Branden may have actually *wanted* to see himself as a noble Roxane, even as John Galt, and for some time, he may well have refused to confront what his not loving Rand—while claiming that he did—said of the fraud he was perpetrating about the nature of his soul.

Blaming Objectivism is merely a *projection* by Branden of the religious way he regarded the philosophy himself. But Objectivism demands integrity first, as Branden knew well. It did *not* demand that he love Rand or that he not love Patrecia. It demanded only that Branden not lie about himself.

The soul he claimed to have, of course, would not have confronted its affection for Rand as a "should." It would have been the honest passion that Branden was only pretending it had been, a noble, transcendent romance that bridged the age gap, and was able to do so because of its natural desire for only its own highest values.

This is not something Rand or Objectivism required of Branden. This is what he had protested to Rand was the very truth of his heart for many years. This is why Rand so trusted him, endorsed him and supported him. He seemed to share her heroic soul.

For a while, Rand's love for him fed his false ego, providing the pseudo-self-esteem he was famous for insightfully dissecting.

But soon, by Branden's own admission, his protestations of love to Rand had become conscious lies. His continued affair with Patrecia made this impossible to deny even to himself. And his continued protestations of love became a double fraud, a way to turn Rand into nothing but a money-machine, a way to advance his career.

For Branden, "being himself," as Rand describes it in her notes, had become being "[a] 'self' without the strain of [the] cerebrally imposed... torture of [**attempting to maintain**] the self-image of an Objectivist hero..." (66)

Rand discovered that Branden's whole persona had become a fraud—even before learning the full truth he had been hiding.

In the first phase of their affair, in the years preceding the publication of *Atlas Shrugged*, the relationship seems to have been an intense and serious one. But, following the novel's publication, the affair was put on hold. Rand was exhausted by her efforts. And, in an important way, she had completed what had been the central goal of her life: she had completed the projection in literature of her ideal men and women. Rand is reported to have said of her life at this point, that whatever time is left, "the rest is gravy." She needed a new goal and faced what she herself called "a crisis period" in this regard.

Branden reports that at this time he experienced a bad depression himself because of the critics' largely hostile reaction to *Atlas Shrugged*, making it difficult for him to cope with Rand's state.

But, whatever the critics thought, "Atlas" was the same kind of "spectacular and enduring success" the book's jacket reports that *The Fountainhead* had become. Branden's lectures were also a dramatic success. Rand began to accept invitations to speak to packed and enthusiastic college auditoriums. All of this gave Rand and her friends a renewed optimism for what seemed a bankrupt culture all around them.

However tentative and reluctant, the Brandens report that it also inspired Rand to inquire of Branden's feelings for her.

But his new-found success and sense of hope did not inspire in Branden a renewed love for Rand, but a new passion for a young student of his, Patrecia Gullison, later Patrecia Scott, then Wynand, and, finally, Branden. She was not an intellectual but an attractive actress who had enrolled as a student at NBI. She seemed awed by Nathaniel Branden.

And Branden found her completely charming. Throughout the year 1963, he reports falling ever more deeply in love with her. She seems to have provided him with a kind of "visibility" he needed, as Rand herself would observe. Their sexual affair began, he modestly contends, in January of 1964 (more than four years before revealing this to Rand), only after Patrecia had repeatedly "begged" for Branden to make love to her. (67) However, a significant period of hugging and kissing, he admits, had preceded it.

Of course, he did not tell Rand any of this. Recall that for Branden it was "always"—repeat, "always"— "important" to him that Rand feel "desirable" and "fulfilled" in every way, even long after his romantic feelings for her had faded. (68)

Rand's endorsement of Branden now buttressed his new success, her opinion of him was now the source of his livelihood, indeed, the source of admiration he received from many others.

While Branden says that he began to exhibit a certain "coldness" toward Rand at this time, he reports that it always alternated with "expressions of passionate devotion..." (69) Whether it was because Branden wanted to believe this about himself or not, what he told Rand was that he still loved her—and loved her romantically. Branden insisted that he wanted their affair to continue. Age was not an issue for him, as it had never been an issue for him.

His heroic and transcendent passion for Rand endured, or so he claimed.

By this time, the Brandens' own marriage was rapidly collapsing. As previously indicated, Ms. Branden had become interested in someone else, but for two years Branden refused her request to begin an affair with the other man. Only after he had begun to secretly sleep with Patrecia would he consent (whether for "several months," or just a couple of weeks, is a matter of dispute between the Brandens.) But he still did not inform Ms. Branden about his new affair as she had had the honesty to do in regard to her own affair. Instead, he made her feel the enormity of *his* magnaminity, *his* generosity throughout the limited course of Ms. Branden's own affair.

But neither of the Brandens now deny that their marriage was already in shambles in 1964 and 1965, during which Branden admits to soliciting and receiving Rand's counseling in regard to his marriage. (70) Of course, he did not mention either his own or his wife's new affairs to Rand at any time during the course of this extensive counseling.

Branden says that, despite his on-going affairs with both Rand and Patrecia, the thought of separation from Ms. Branden made him both "tearful and angry." (71) Nonetheless, the Brandens formally separated in 1965. It was in the summer of that year that Ms. Branden reports that she demanded a divorce and moved out. (72)

Mr. Branden says that he soon thereafter came to terms with the failure of his marriage.

Branden also reports, however, that Barbara Branden, for a while longer, continued to hope for a reconciliation. Indeed, Branden reports on Ms. Branden's increasingly "open" jealousy of Patrecia in 1965 (73), and he reports that in May of 1966 Ms. Branden was still writing passionate letters to Branden. (74) But, by then, Branden says that he knew that the marriage was over, and, he concedes, it would not be long before Ms. Branden did, as well.

But Rand's private notes suggest that *to Rand* they were still holding out hope for their relationship until *the end of 1967*, as we shall see.

By the end of 1966, Branden would finally tell Ms. Branden, who had now accepted that her marriage was over, only that he was about to *begin* an affair with Patrecia. He did *not* tell her that his affair with Patrecia was by then already over two years old. Patrecia's own marriage dissolved shortly after the Brandens' formally separated. (75)

Somehow, Branden claims that a corner of his own mind still held out hope for his romance with Rand. Even in 1966, he claims that his "love" for Rand was, at some level, still sincere. At least, he still *wanted* to love Rand, he says, which only added to the trouble he was having in admitting the truth to himself.

Branden tells us that this was the period in which Rand completed *Introduction to Objectivist Epistemology*. The year 1966, and even the start of the next, he tells us, would mark a so-called "honeymoon" period between Rand and himself, during which Rand could even suggest, Branden tells us, that her mind was no less than an "aphrodisiac" to him. (76)

It was around this time that Branden reports telling Rand that she "would *always* be a sexual being." (77)

To be sure, Rand was, according to Barbara Branden, becoming suspicious of Branden's relationship with Patrecia by 1966, but it was during this period that he "tried to allay Ayn's uneasiness by assurances of his love, assurances that he needed and wanted her, that *she was the most important person in his life*—and he struggled to believe that it was so." And, later, "'I love Ayn,' he seemed to be telling himself." (78)

Although Rand was now sixty-one, and although his affair with Patrecia was now two years old, Branden was still proclaiming his passionate devotion to Rand, and that his transcendent and heroic love continued unaffected by time.

In the Spring of 1967, her private journals reveal that Rand began to have serious doubts about Branden's psychology and about her entire relationship with him.

After the unwittingly futile "marriage counseling," the psychotherapy did not stop, but, rather, began to intensify in 1967. His marriage, he reported to Rand, had exacerbated certain psychological problems which he needed to work through. So Rand agreed to help.

But becoming his "therapist," she knew, could only destroy their relationship.

As Rand describes this period in her July 4, 1968 notes,

> We worked on his [psycho-epistemology] for some months in formal, psycho-therapeutic sessions—and our own relationship was entirely suspended in every sense or aspect during this period. The sessions were not very good: he was not very clear on anything, he kept discussing different aspects at random, and I did not understand him

at all, in the sense that I could not tell what he grasped or not. I knew only that his [psycho-epistemology] was in *total* chaos—and I was shocked by it: I could not understand how the rational man I thought him to be had been willing to live with such a chaos and had let it go for so long. (79)

However, both of the Brandens indicate that at the end of 1967 there was another "honeymoon" period. Ms. Branden tells us that Rand spoke of Branden kissing her "in a way that's sexual" and telling Rand that he "cannot live without her," only to become yet again cold and elusive. (80)

The Brandens are notably vague on the chronology at this time, but it was clearly here that Branden began bringing his new mistress more aggressively forward into the social circle he shared with Rand.

Mr. Branden, if anything, is even more confused as to chronology than his former wife, skipping back and forth between years like a game of hopscotch rather than writing a memoir. Nonetheless, Branden, who takes issue with his former wife on many points, agrees with her as to the extreme nature of his assertions of passionate love for Rand during this time. Branden reports telling Rand nothing less than that she "had no equals at any age." He says that "Ayn did not want to pursue me; her self-concept demanded that I pursue her." In other words, *he pursued her.* He reports Rand's complaint at the end of 1967, "You act like a man in love one day, and on the next you are withdrawn." (81) Branden does not dispute the description.

By this time, however, he *does* dispute the emotion. By his own account, Branden knew quite explicitly by then that his feelings for Rand were *not* romantic. This second "honeymoon" was, by his own admission, a farce. But he continued to tell Rand otherwise in the most fervent terms conceivable. Rand's notes reveal that Branden was then telling her that he could not "live" without her.

A more vicious and cowardly manipulation of an aging woman's feelings can hardly be imagined. And the obvious motive could not be more apparent.

Branden reports that his former wife seemed astonished at his behavior, as Rand kept telling her that it was Branden who "kept pressing for a continuation of the romance," not herself. (82) Branden does not deny the reports of his former wife that he was still kissing Rand in a "sexual" way during this period or that it could seem so to Rand.

But, of course, Branden also claims that Rand—in her "insane" passion for him—would have accepted nothing less than romantic love. To maintain everything that he had built, he *had* to lie to Rand about his feelings and, he insists, about his very soul. Any "out" Rand had ever offered over the "age issue" only meant a *total* break with Rand, he claims. It could never have meant anything else. But, of course, we have already seen from Rand's own journals that a "total" break still meant only a romantic one to her.

Rand's notes do confirm that she was beginning to have serious doubts about her whole relationship with Branden by late 1967. Its devolution into essentially a psychotherapeutic one had already hurt Rand deeply by this time. Her doubts about his character and psychology go to the core of his soul and could affect even a friendship now, according to Rand. As we shall see, in Rand's mind, the romance was already over by the end of January, 1968, well before their professional break.

By then, Branden needed to invent more excuses and come up with them soon, for Rand was growing increasingly suspicious and impatient with all of the counseling that seemed to be going nowhere. His psychotherapy sessions finally began to include complaints about his relationship with Rand starting in late 1967 or early 1968.

Ms. Branden reports that, at first, Branden had complained of depression, of exhaustion, of (unspecified) problems with his psycho-epistemology, and, only later, problems with the "triangle," with always being an "outsider" in the O'Connors' relationship.

The chronological progression of these complaints is not specified by Ms. Branden, who goes into something of a vague memory-hole about such specifics between 1966 and early 1968. (83)

Branden himself suggests that his complaints centered around his own psychology and psycho-epistemology—not any problem in his relationship with Rand—until January of 1968, when he began to complain of a problem with regard to the existential conditions of maintaining the "triangle." (84)

It was at this very time that Branden reports that Rand pulled back hard. He describes Rand's attitude at the beginning of 1968, as follows,

"Although Ayn's desire for greater emotional intimacy was unrelenting, she was *still* reticent about the resurrection of our affair." (85)

That's right, it was *Branden* who was "still" pressing for sex at the start of 1968—not Rand.

In her private notes, Rand describes this period of Branden's initial complaints about "the relationship." In July of 1968, she would say of the previous January:

> I asked him what form our relationship would take now, i.e., what was his solution for our problems. I was very astonished to see that he took the question in an oddly tragic manner: he said that he did not quite know what to do, because "Platonism" was so far from his actual way of "seeing" me or "thinking about" me. In subsequent conversations he told me that he loved me so much that he could not live without me—but he did not know how to implement this in reality. He also said that I was the only relationship left on which he would "work" mentally—i.e., which he would struggle to straighten out, if there were troubles between us—and that if anyone else... made any claims that clashed with his terms, he would drop him or her instantly. (I understood this to mean that everyone else would have to adjust to him, in some unspecified way or manner, and that I was the only one with whom he would seek an understanding.) I did not like this at all, it sounded like some kind of anti-rational resignation—and I tried to make him identify or clarify this further, but he did not. (86)

It will be recalled that it was in these same January notes that Rand is declaring the romance "over" in her own mind.

And, well into 1968, Branden is still indicating that he wanted a sexual relationship with Rand to continue. She writes:

> I asked [Branden] to project what he would want, if he had a miraculous power to make anything possible, even

contradictions. (I explained that I hoped this would give us a lead to his repressed feelings.) He answered that his ideal life would be to have a secret, very private, very spiritual romance with me ("with sex five or six times a year"), a romance totally cut off from the world and from the rest of his life (as "autistic" a private universe as one could project into reality)—and, simultaneously, to have a girl of his own age, as his mistress and companion, who would "mean less" to him than I, but who would share his life in the world. I asked him what she *would* mean to him or what he would expect of her. He answered: "Oh, someone to spend money on, to share my financial success with... someone to go out with... to travel with, and such." (87)

Branden admits in his memoir that it was Rand who "felt that it was premature to [even] think about sex until the distance between us, so incomprehensible to her, was closed." (88) In other words, it was Branden who was, even at this point, the one thinking of sex.

Rand's private journals certainly also confirm that it was Rand, and her concerns for Branden's psychology and character, which terminated their sexual intimacy, and not any clear indication from Branden of *anything* on the subject of his own emotions. They also confirm that it was Rand's suspicions which brought the matter to a head—and not anyone else's honesty.

The Brandens argue—despite all of the passionate kisses and proclamations that he "could not live without" her—that Rand was painfully blind: blind, at first, in thinking that such an exalted, transcendent romance was even possible, and then blind to "the fact" that it could never last, that Branden would inevitably need a woman of his own age. Blind, as well, to his growing feelings for Patrecia.

They, therefore, both suggest that Rand was holding out for a romance with Branden until July of 1968, if not later, when he first presented Rand with his paper declaring that "age" did indeed matter to him.

In this declaration, he explained that it had mattered for some time, *for several years*, in fact.

Then, in August, came the next discovery: Branden's four-and-a-half year affair with Patrecia was revealed.

These moments do represent the *total* end for Branden—for *any* kind of relationship with Rand—and the pain that they caused her should not be minimized. The total fraud of every minute of those "therapy" sessions—not to mention the various other implications—revealed Branden to be a dishonest man—not merely a deeply troubled or even disturbed man—but one who was *habitually immoral.* And yet until then—long after the romance was over for Rand—she had still been working for *some* kind of relationship with Branden if something less than an affair.

Of course, Branden's complaints about "the triangle" were just rationalizations, as he now admits himself. Even the "age" issue was a rationalization, for it was just another strategy to avoid the real issue: the fraud he had committed regarding his true feelings for Rand. And all the rest, though some of it was based in fact, was rationalization, and he knew it.

Rand saw it as rationalization the minute it was uttered, and began to systematically take apart Branden's assertions.

Just as with the "marriage" counseling he had solicited from Rand, all of the psychotherapy sessions with her in 1966 and 1967 and 1968 were part of Branden's elaborate fraud. As a psychologist himself, he knew how to milk such a situation for all it was worth. But, the futility and manipulation of these senseless and (on Branden's part) deceptive psychotherapy sessions were unknown to Rand until the summer of 1968.

And, it is the *moral* dimension of Branden's observed behavior, long before any infidelity is discovered, which concerned Rand. She senses dishonesty in his whole approach to herself, to his problems and to his life. We shall see from these notes that Rand was already inferring much of the truth about Branden, despite the level of deception he was perpetrating.

> My over-all conclusion is that there is something horrifyingly wrong and *bad* in him—and that all the points listed above are only random symptoms, not basic causes. There is something horrible at the root, if it produced these sort of symptoms in a man of his intelligence and knowledge.

> Whatever part of it all might be subconscious and due merely to repression, I sense very strongly the presence

> of *conscious dishonesty*. The best evidence of this is his
> evasion of the question of why he let himself drift for so
> long and did not try to think about his problems. (89)

Unfortunately, the discovery of Branden's four-year deception is not recorded in Rand's journals. It appears that, at that point, there was nothing left for Rand to consider.

Branden was the consummate deceiver. He may well have, at first, been sincere, and he had certainly absorbed Rand's language and style very well. He had *memorized* her work. Branden also became an expert at "role-playing," a psychological issue that will come up in his sessions with Rand, just as acting was the profession of his new mistress. Rand later saw them both as "role-players," as her private journals reveal. Against Rand's piercing inquiries, Branden simply could not maintain the deception.

The circumstantial evidence also suggests that it was Rand's perceptiveness that proved Branden's final unmasking, for the break could not have come at a more inconvenient time for Branden. He had just signed a three-year lease at the Empire State Building in September of 1967. His first book on psychology, for which he hoped Rand would write the introduction, had not yet been finished. His stage production of *The Fountainhead,* which might greatly aid the career of his new mistress, was still in pre-production. Serious planning for the play went through the summer and fall of 1967.

The "honeymoon" period of late 1967, along with Branden's extreme proclamations of love, can only be seen as an effort by Branden to buy more time. (Patrecia's taking the stage name "Wynand" after the tragic character from *The Fountainhead* in the summer or fall of that year looks suspiciously unctuous, as well.)

Barbara Branden writes that "[l]ike her characters, Ayn, too, was damaged by her rejection of the emotional and intuitive aspects of her nature...," and speaks of Rand's psychological attempts to "avoid feeling self-contempt for her feminine instincts." (90)

However, it will be seen that the private journals show Rand to have been highly attuned to her own emotional and subconscious reactions to a situation or person (if that is what Ms. Branden means here). Among Rand's favorite phrases are "stomach-feeling" and "vibrations." It was these very feelings Rand always seeks to unpack and explain.

And, far from showing Rand to be "insane"—or even irrationally emotional—about these events, they demonstrate the degree to which Rand was able to train her powerful insight onto areas which were causing her enormous pain.

Setting the Brandens' accounts aside, at last, and turning our attention to Rand's contemporaneous journal entries, a much more focused picture emerges and the Brandenian ambiguity recedes.

Ayn Rand's notes on the topic of Nathaniel Branden commence with the date "11-27-67."

By this time, their relationship has degenerated to such a degree that Rand is already considering ending it herself. She is concerned that their "romance" has become impersonal and "grey," and she has clearly been complaining to Branden about this for some time.

Rand's own initial concern is the apparent fact that Branden's stated "symptoms" are no longer simply centered around his personal psychology (and psycho-epistemology) but also—for the first time, it seems—about his relationship with Rand, i.e., she is now among the alleged causes of his psychological problems. Above all, she is concerned by Branden's indecision and his mental "drift."

It is worth reiterating that these are private notes *to herself*.

Rand begins:

[1] 1. If I am the source of [**his**] [psycho-epistemological] trouble or emotional frustration: why or how was he willing to let the relationship drift so long into the worst, most uninspiring and *unstylized* form possible?

This question is the source of my recurring accusation about *exploitation*. I mean *emotional* exploitation, *not professional*. The emotional exploitation consists of the fact that he was getting some kind of value from our meetings—whether intellectual, or psycho-therapeutic, or the feeling of "being himself," i.e., of being understood and appreciated and "visible"—while knowing that *I* was getting *nothing* and was acquiring a dreadful feeling of depersonalization and *invisibility*.

[2] He knew (years ago) that he had hurt me in regard to visibility [**a probable reference to the "marriage counseling" he had solicited from Rand**]—yet this knowledge remained ignored or suppressed (or evaded)—it did not prompt him to any action to correct it, it was not a pressing concern of his, and it did not stop him from drifting into the worst offense of all in this respect: the last two years of myself as psychotherapist. I did it on the premise that his problem with [Barbara Branden] was the cause of his problem with me. I took him at his word, literally. I assumed that as his emotional [psycho-epistemology] improved, he would be able to clarify his attitude toward me by himself—and that this would become his first concern. *He didn't and he wasn't. That* is what I cannot understand—and nothing so far has [3] explained it.

Notice that the "psycho-epistemological" problem had originally been focused on the Brandens' marriage, even well into 1967, when in fact, to the Brandens themselves, their marriage was "over" in 1964 or 1965. The inference we must draw is that the Brandens have found, in their own defunct relationship, a way to deflect attention from Branden's *real* problems, namely, by holding out a false "hope" to Rand regarding their feelings for one another.

In Rand's own mind, at least, her relationship with Branden has already collapsed into a purely therapeutic one, bearing no resemblance to a romance, or even a friendship. Rand apparently understands that no relationship, even a friendship, is likely to survive its prolonged reduction to psychotherapy.

While the "worst" part is the decay of their relationship into one of therapist-patient, at least as disturbing to Rand is the way it has happened, this "drift"—and what it seems to imply about Branden's character and psychology.

But, as yet, it is painfully obvious that Rand hardly realizes the extent of her "exploitation" at Branden's hands.

All that Rand asks for is "clarification" from Branden concerning his "attitude" toward her.

What she realizes is that Branden—himself a psychotherapist— appears to be doing nothing about his self-admitted problems. From Rand's perspective, Branden seems to be putting her through therapeutic hell with no end in sight.

While Rand's notes indicate that the issue of "the triangle" may not have yet emerged, at least in those terms, the implication of Rand's notes is that Branden has begun to broach the subject only by saying—and for the first time—that he felt a sense of "hopelessness" with regard to the practical circumstances of their affair.

Rand—correctly—senses rationalization. (Unknown to Rand, Branden, of course, has been juggling various "triangles" for four years by this point.) It is clear that Rand has been hurt badly by this revelation about a man she thought of as a "soul mate."

It appears that Rand has also detected from Branden an "angry reluctance" to discuss their relationship. This has her greatly concerned. She writes:

> [3] 2. The two bad signs in regard to above: his [4] almost angry reluctance to "talk about us"—illustrated by two touches: 1. He did not want to see me, because I would expect him to "talk about us." (What did he want to see me for? What did he want to talk about? What would have satisfied him, if I did not insist on the "personal"?) 2. His remark in regard to the pre-Toronto period [i.e., **before their romantic feelings for one another had been expressed**]: "We didn't talk about us."
>
> It is possible that repression and the "hopelessness" of giving existential form to our relationship is causing this behavior. But I do not really believe it—that is, it is

a point on which I am "taking him on faith," against *my* own understanding of emotions, against my own way of feeling or reacting.

The bad explanation here (and the suspicion in my mind) would be as follows: subconsciously, [5] emotional relationships to him mean only the desire to be "visible"—but not to "see." Which means: to be loved, more than to love. (Although there are many signs that this is not so.) The desire to be "visible" takes the form of seeking someone with an interest in his interests: his ideas, his work, his activity, etc.—i.e., his existential interests. (This is the form he gave our relationship in reality.) His over-protectiveness, over-consideration, exaggerated "fear of hurting," selflessness or inability to decide his pleasure-principle in a relationship (inability to know what he wants), may be the conscious result of this subconscious premise: that he wants to be loved (or, rather, admired) more than he wants to love—which would mean that he senses that there is something wrong or unfair in his attitude toward the woman, and is trying to make up for it or protect her from it (which would come from [6] his better, conscious premises).

I do not fully believe that this hypothesis is true, and it does not *feel* true to me—but the fact that it can occur to me even as a possibility is a terrible doubt to carry, and is an indication of the degree of the bewildering, inconsistent and incomprehensible in his behavior.

Recall how exceedingly careful Rand was being about even hinting at a negative evaluation of Branden. We see here, again, her heartbreaking generosity to a man who has been lying about so much for so long.

But it is also clear that Rand isn't buying the explanations she is being given by Branden, although she can't make sense of them yet. At this point, even her own hypotheses don't "feel" right to her. Her suspicions are hardly unnatural: a guilty man's conscience is too often masked by an exaggerated "fear of hurting," as it is put in the notes. Rand's "instincts" are, in hindsight, precisely correct.

Rand has here stated a powerful implication of the Objectivist concept of love: that it is more important—more *selfish*—*to love*, rather than *to be loved*.

Rand held that happiness requires something more than unrequited love, but she also believed that a selfish man is primarily focused—not on someone else's values, even his lover's—but on his *own* values. It is what we claim to care about—and our existential devotion to it—that defines a virtuous man's soul, not a second-handed desire to be "admired."

Rand begins to think that Branden does not "love" women at all, that, perhaps, he does not really "love" her, however extreme his proclamations of passion. Branden wants not to value, but to be valued, to be *admired*. Indeed, it was Rand's own love which gave Branden the "sanction" he craved, and, thus, his own love was not a genuine expression of his values—buried, such as they were, under the wreckage of his repression. However painful a thought, this seems to be the only way Rand can explain the "drift."

Though Branden was specifically denying an affair with Patrecia throughout, Rand's suspicions regarding Patrecia are also already strongly present, but, interestingly, what is of most concern to Rand is simply Branden's *failure to decide*.

In the same notes from November of 1967, we read:

> [6] 3. I feel real *fear* whenever he tells me "I don't know" in regard to his feelings and desires in our relationship. It is the same tone and the same emotional vibrations as I have heard from him for years in regard to [Barbara Branden], in regard to me, and, now, in regard to [Patrecia]. It is as if everything pertaining to his own emotions is that kind of vague, [7] helpless "I don't know"—and he lives with it for years, and acts on it. *This is inconceivable* for a man of his rationality and intellectual development. *He is hiding something here. What?*

As she will later explain in her July notes, these are the "three 'I don't knows'" that will soon convince Rand that the intimacy is over between them.

Remember that we are more than eight months away from anyone telling Rand about Branden's affair with Patrecia and that Branden is actively denying it to Rand's queries, by his own admission. Despite the Brandens' portrait of a "blind" Rand, she is showing the natural suspicions that a woman would have about a partner when he begins to make another woman a subject of such interest. Rand is already—in 1967—ranking Patrecia with both Ms. Branden and herself in Mr. Branden's esteem. Rand was hardly "blind" to any of this—she was, in fact, quite sensitive to what was happening.

As Ms. Branden had done, Rand simply took Branden at his word. Could they both not rely on his devotion to Objectivism, or, simply, the truth?

Rand was, however, already beginning to sense a major conflict in Branden's actual values. She writes:

> [8] 4. In regard to the "stylized universe." A stylized person—as I see it, as I see it exclusively, without which the term is meaningless—is a person who *lives in reality* according to his highest values, who takes *nothing less,* accepts no substitutes, and *struggles to translate his values into reality,* no matter what the difficulties.
>
> *This is not what he has done.*
>
> He has been willing to drift and let things drift in regard to [Barbara Branden]—and to me. No matter *what* he felt, he has lived a life which *did not* express his personal or emotional values. If one looks at the daily facts, he has lived, at best, on the premise of "church on Sundays"— while his daily concerns have been the things he does *not* care for in any serious sense: [9] business, theatrical business, lunches (and worse).
>
> The element of *subjectivism* here is frightening. (So is the fact that he regarded subjectivism as a solution for us.)

Recall that Branden now says that the theater had become his favorite activity. What lies was Branden telling Rand about *all* of his values? Or, is this more recent claim the lie? It's difficult to say.

In any event, it is precisely this kind of split between one's stated values and one's actions in reality—a "theory-practice" dichotomy—which is abhorrent to Rand and to Objectivism. Rand had long observed that such a split renders one's actions *unprincipled*—and one's principles *irrelevant.*

Rand's focus, intellectually and emotionally, is not on moral anger, jealous rage or the pain of rejection. She is focused on what this "mental drift" suggests about the mind and character of a man she thought she loved, whose mind and character she had once highly respected, and who was her intellectual and professional partner.

However, Rand is still primarily looking for psychological explanations, not moral ones. She continues:

> [9] How can all of the above be the result of the "existential" hopelessness of his love for me? It may be true, but I can't integrate it. I vacillate between semi-belief and indignant rejection. My mind starts swimming when I try to integrate it all—and I get into some [psycho-epistemological] state that probably resembles his. This is a sign that there is some fundamental contradiction in these facts and our identification of them.

> [10] The one touch or lead to support the idea that "hopelessness" is the explanation, is what he said metaphorically about the war-wounded man. But what kind of malevolent-universe or unreality is that? I am not fully able emotionally to project that psychology—I can only sense vaguely that it is possible.

Branden may have been able to tolerate extreme cognitive dissonance in his own life, but his main problem in deceiving Rand is that she will not allow mental confusion to last in her own consciousness.

For Rand, an inability to integrate a series of facts can only mean one thing: a "sign" that our "identification" contains contradictions which must be resolved. Such a condition *motivates* Rand's mind, while it appears to generate paralysis in Branden's.

Branden's bizarre comparison of himself to a "war-wounded" man speaks for itself, but Rand fears that if such an extreme problem is involved, then this is bad news for their relationship as such, much less their affair.

Rand continues:

> [10] But, if so, then the only answer is to break with him entirely. That is, not to see him at all except "functionally," on business. (This is one more possibility—the lowest—to add to my list.)

> "I don't believe that this will be possible to us. I am indignantly convinced that it is not necessary. If he accepted it, he would never recover at all.

> "I would be able to accept it only by means of dropping my entire estimate or view of him. My estimate would then be: here is a man who, [11] for some reason unknown to me, was unable to live up to his own greatness and mine, and ran from it (particularly mine); he preferred me *not to exist*; he killed me before my time, as far as he was concerned. So I would have to forget him—as one more, and last, and worst, instance of being penalized for my virtues. This hurts dreadfully. But this is what the present situation is leading me to.

In November of 1967, a "total break" with Branden would have meant at least an attempt to preserve a "functional" relationship, so Branden's self-portrait of having his "back to the wall" must be seen as pure fantasy. Rand certainly has doubts that such a state is "possible" to them, but it is also clear that this is precisely the nature of "the break" which Rand was contemplating at this point—and that this was the type of "break" for which she is already preparing herself.

While Rand is clearly wondering about Branden's entire psychology she does not as yet question his *conscious* values. She is still speaking of his "greatness," a term Rand reserves for the moral, whatever their neuroses.

However, Rand's frustration with Branden is palpable.

Rand continues:

> [11] I can't stand any of it. I don't want any more "psychology." I don't want to wait for any "new knowledge." I don't want to live on "implications" and undefined relationships. He will have to decide on the knowledge available to him now. I have left it to drift too long. Now the choice is: total break or rationality and reality.

The subject of Patrecia, Rand already knows, is the key to Branden's unstated "problem," however "Platonic" Branden still claims his relationship with her to be. Rand senses that the torch of Branden's affections has already been passed to another.

Rand's next entry reads:

> [12] Question: he identified the "playfulness premise"— obviously in regard to [Patrecia]. What thinking has he done about our relationship? (This is why we always end up talking about others: he has something to say there— and I can't hold the conversation on me unilaterally.)

A rather poignant "P.S." is attached:

> [13] P.S. He [Branden] noticed, some years ago, my "detachment" at parties. Yet this did not give him an incentive—neither personal nor professional-psychological—to inquire about the causes or to help me.

Rand concludes her notes from this date:

> [13] I am *dead* in his mind already. I can't help this feeling. He makes me *feel dead*.

In November of 1967, Rand already felt "dead" to Branden, and she has reached this conclusion from the moment of his first complaints about "the relationship."

Rand is still unaware of Branden's true character, and the pathos of these last entries is genuine. "*Her* needs, who cares?" seems to have been Branden's implicit attitude by now. Rand is acknowledging a personal need of her own within this sea of Branden's psychological complaints, one, she fears, that might be negatively impacting her relationship with Branden. She wants to work on it. It seems to her that he never did. This is, in part, why she is beginning to "feel dead" to him—and why she is already coming to terms with the end of their affair by the end of 1967.

In light of what we all now know, Rand's innocence is heartbreaking.

As we have seen, Branden would—in the next few weeks—initiate the last of the so-called "honeymoon" periods, suggesting that Branden's answers to Rand's questions were every bit as gushing as he now concedes.

In November, Rand's "anger" was focused entirely on Branden's method—his indecisiveness and his psychological rationalizations, rather than jealousy or rejection. What Rand is demanding in November of 1967 is simply *answers* and a bit of clarity, not that Branden "love" her. If this means a break, then it means a break, however difficult an exclusively "functional" relationship might be for them.

It is apparent—from private notes to herself—that, but for Branden's overt dishonesty, it would have been at least possible for him to retain his business partnership with Rand, whatever the nature of his romantic feelings for her.

It was Branden's senseless—and, as we now know, dishonest—therapy sessions which brought Rand to the point of already considering such a break. Rand has been perceptive as to Branden's changed mental functioning, to his unaccountable "psycho-epistemology," and it is this very sensitivity which will force the rest of the matter into the open.

That it was simply from his *mental functioning* that Rand was first able to detect dishonesty within Branden's elaborate act is itself a remarkable fact.

It was this keen awareness which would drive Branden from rationalization to rationalization, each time only to be unmasked by Rand who continued demanding still more answers. *Only* such keen perceptiveness on Rand's part brought about the events which led to Branden's ultimate exposure and subsequent expulsion from Rand's circle.

There are no more notes until those dated in early January, 1968, which is consistent with the fact that December represented a so-called "honeymoon period" between them. Given the serious nature of Rand's doubts, we can now see why Branden had felt the need to go to such verbal extremes (e.g., "no equals at any age," etc.) to reassure her of his love during this period. And, by his own admission, it was Rand who was "still" the reticent one about their affair (i.e., Branden is still the one making the advances.) This, too, is confirmed by Rand's notes.

Rand's suspicions regarding Patrecia were apparently renewed following the New Year celebrations for 1968—and it is then that Rand returns to her notes.

Now she is quite explicitly asking Branden about his feelings for Patrecia. In a short note, Rand writes, somewhat cryptically:

> Notes from [Branden] 1/3/68
> 1. That the cause was not [Patrecia Scott].
> 2. That he had tried *very hard.*
> 3. Significance of New Years' Eve.

Branden admits in his memoirs that he began to bring his new mistress more aggressively forward at this very time—and Rand was on it in nothing flat. The implication of this note, is that Rand asked point-blank, "Is it Patrecia?" And here we can almost see Branden looking Rand squarely in the face and saying, "No."

Notes from this period include several short notes from "Jan. 4, 1968," regarding Barbara Branden's psychology. While not as extensive as those regarding Mr. Branden, the idea that Rand was serving as psychological counselor to both of them in this very period is something readers of the Branden biographies will find new, but one which is made abundantly clear from these entries.

The following is perhaps the clearest of these notes, also dated "Jan. 4, 1968" and titled "Questions (re: [Barbara])":

> [1] What is the status of reality in her [psycho-epistemology]? (In re: panic before "the unthinkable"— the "metaphysical impossibility" of a break—etc.) What did she do re: rationalization discovered at [the] last session?

> What is the nature and source of her guilt? (More
> specifically than "inability to deal with emotions.")...

As with many of these briefer notes, interpretation is difficult here, but Ms. Branden's mysterious "guilt" is obviously of concern to Rand, and it is Ms. Branden, rather than Rand, who seems to have been blind to the inevitability of a break with Rand at this point. On this issue, it is she who seems to have been in denial—a break is "metaphysically impossible" in her mind.

In any event, the next extended sequence is dated "*January 25, 1968*" a date which Rand has underlined in these notes.

Although we are told, without a clear explanation from the Brandens, that Rand was, once again, the one to pull back at the end of January, 1968, we are given no explanation for this by the Brandens.

Rand's journals provide some answers.

Rand's frustrated, if perceptive, inquiries about Branden's romantic feelings seem to have prompted the revelation of two new issues from Branden sometime in January. First, the "existential hopelessness" Branden claimed to be feeling is now specifically called "the triangle" issue in these notes. In addition, the issue of "Miss X" has simultaneously become explicit by now, i.e., the still, of course, "theoretical" possibility that Branden might find a new romantic interest.

From our more knowledgeable vantage, it is clear that Branden is probing Rand's potential feelings about another woman in their lives, trying to see just how "open" Rand would be to the idea, in general, without the need for him to have to sit down and give her any explanation of the past half decade of deception.

Rand, still believing his denials of an actual affair, is nonetheless aware of the implications of the arrival of "Miss X" at the same time that Branden has begun to show some kind of interest in Patrecia.

As far as Rand is concerned, this can only mean that their affair is over.

If theirs' (Rand, O'Connor, Branden) was an unworkable "triangle," Rand wants to know: into what kind of triangle is he proposing to put *her* with this "Miss X"? (As she puts it "What kind of a 'triangle' does he propose for *me* to accept in the future?") And, like any woman of self-esteem, Rand vehemently rejects the idea of "Miss X" *in the abstract*, for it already suggests that your partner is looking, and looking rather hard and actively, for a "Miss X"—that he or she is dissatisfied. For anyone who is supposed to be loved—under nearly every imaginable circumstance—it would be deeply insulting to be—even in thought—rejected for (or equated with) an entirely unknown quantity, Person "X." For Rand, this can only mean the end.

In the notes dated "Jan. 25, 1968," Rand—still unable to condemn without understanding—begins:

> [1] My trouble with [Branden] is, *most centrally and essentially*, that *I do not understand his psychology* at all— in regard to personal or romantic relationships. It is a very diffuse feeling and hard to localize and identify. But it is there now as strongly as at the beginning—and perhaps more strongly, since the situation is now less complicated existentially [**i.e., Rand, by now, has been told that the Brandens' marriage is hopeless**].
>
> Therefore, I think the most important thing to clarify is the difference in our views—before we make any decision—to clarify it as fully and *explicitly* as possible, leaving nothing to *implication*. I think the reliance on implications has been one of our disasters: I relied on them, by the logic of any given situation or discussion; he relied on them in a subjectivist way, i.e., he assumed that any decision or conclusion he reached would necessarily be reached by me also (as if it were the only possible one) and, therefore, [2] it was not necessary to tell me or let me in on it. (I would like to know the root cause of *this* type of psycho-epistemology!)
>
> So I must now start by thinking over the one indication of his psychology and of our different attitudes which he gave me in today's telephone conversation and which, to me, seems crucial.

> To state this indication clearly: *he* kept saying too often that
> the "Miss X" possibility would be a disaster because *I* would
> not accept it. It suddenly occurred to me that he might
> mean it would be a disaster primarily for *me*, not so much
> for *him*. I asked him whether he saw it as a non-disaster if *I*
> were to accept it—i.e., that only my non-acceptance would
> make it a disaster. I do not remember what he answered,
> which indicates that he did not answer with anything
> essential. I then asked him to tell me how it stood in his
> own mind, i.e., how *he* projected what *he* would do in such
> an eventuality. [3] He answered that *he* would be able to
> integrate the two relationships—and that "nothing would
> change in our relationship" (!!!), which he had told me
> before (and which I had totally misunderstood). I asked
> him what that would mean *in practice, in concrete reality.*
> He could not answer or project it.

That's right, Branden is saying in these January conversations
about "Miss X" that he cannot even "project" the eventuality of the very
real affair that he has been conducting for over four years. The context
of any discussions of "Miss X" had until now apparently been focused on
Branden's psychology, not Rand's, and the sudden switch took Rand by
surprise—and alerted her to new implications.

It is also interesting to observe that Rand's "doubts" about Branden
apparently date "from the beginning" of their relationship, and assuaging
those doubts must have required continuous effort of Branden.

We shall see in her notes from July 4 that, under certain definite
circumstances, Rand would have accepted a "Miss X"—and that this is
something which she made clear to Branden at the time. In notes dated
February 6, 1968, Rand also writes: "...I was terribly wrong in suggesting
an affair with any present Miss X," implying that, at an earlier point in
their discussions, Rand had proposed Branden should actually have such
an affair.

The Insanely Jealous Rand of the Brandens' tale is not easy to find in
such entries. In fact, these notes contradict the entire Branden portrait of
Rand at this time, and we can begin to see why Branden expressed such an
exaggerated concern over their release.

Most disturbing to Rand was the implication from Branden's remarks that there would need to be no mutual decision-making in the case of a "Miss X," as there had been in his own relationship with Rand—and that the only one who needed to do any "deciding" was Rand.

This kind of irresponsibility was anathema to Rand for whom a relationship implied a *mutual* responsibility, by definition.

The notes from "January 25" continue:

> [3] When I told him that *both* of us had to think over and reach a specific decision in regard to the "Miss X" issue, he kept saying he could not understand why and could barely hold in mind my reasons for demanding it, i.e., he kept losing the context of our conversation. Then he said: If our positions were reversed, he would not deliver an ultimatum to *me*. I asked him what this meant specifically. He said that if a "Miss X" (or a "Mr. X" in this case) appeared and he found the situation unacceptable, *he would withdraw.*

> [4] My first impression, then and now as I summarize it, is that this indicates an incredible kind of irresponsibility. This means in effect: he knows that "Miss X" would be unacceptable to me, but not to him; if she appears and he takes her, *he* does not have to drop me, *I* have to drop *him*—and the decision is mine. ... He will be free to regard it as *my* choice and to accept it as a decision or event out of his control. ... He lets it go, in effect, as: "Either she will accept it or not, *somehow*. That's her problem and choice, not mine." (All I can say to the above is: Good God!)

This is not the way Rand and Branden had faced their own affair, and Rand knew that this was not the way to approach *any* relationship. She also sees that the "Miss X" hypothetical is getting serious if Branden can ignore Rand's own context to such an extent.

Rand continues:

[5] The fact that he feels strongly that there won't be a "Miss X" is actually irrelevant. What matters here is his view of mutual responsibility in a relationship.

(He said that he could tell me in detail how he can accept a life of loneliness, rather than a "triangle." *I must not forget to ask him to tell me*; this might throw some light on the above.)

Let's try to put all of this together. Branden—engaged by now in a four year affair with "Miss X"—is telling Rand that he can accept "loneliness," but cannot even "project" the "Miss X" scenario—and, at the same time, that he "feels strongly" that there won't even be any "Miss X." In addition, Branden is saying to Rand that he can "accept" neither a continued "triangle" nor (as these journals later confirm) life "without" Rand.

We next read:

[5] In pattern, the situation between us today stands as follows: I tell him that I can accept a relationship with him [6] only on condition that there won't be any "Miss X." He tells me, in effect, "forget it, let's have the relationship anyway—and *if* 'Miss X' comes up, you can decide then." Perhaps I haven't made it clear to him why and how "Miss X" is part of the present. I think that it is I who relied on implications in this issue.

Ironically, Rand is chiding *herself* for relying upon implications, when, of course, it is Mr. Branden who has not made clear how "Miss X" is "part of the present." And, despite knowing explicitly now that Rand will need rational answers regarding any "Miss X" if their own relationship is to continue, Branden has clearly decided on a continued (and dishonest) affair with Rand.

Rand writes:

[6] The implications, in my mind, as I identify them now, are as follows: He has hurt me profoundly on the issue

of "visibility"—I want to know and experience, in *reality*, in terms of *living concretes*, not abstractions, that he loves me, and the meaning of his love, even if in Platonic terms. His answer, then, in reality, amounts to: sure I love you, but I cannot implement my feeling in any way except as a spiritual pretense, which is shrinking already (in content) and will degenerate into plain, *maternal* (on my, ["Ayn's"] part) friendship when I find the right girl.

[7] It is *this* prospect and pretense that I cannot stand. If he can, it means that his love for me isn't even Platonic love (because "Platonic" [**in this context**] still means *romantic*, not mere friendship).

Perhaps, the mistake was mine in suggesting "Platonism" in the first place. But this might have been tenable so long as he was married to Barbara. It is a grotesque pretense now—in the light of "Miss X."

We learn here that it was Rand who had previously suggested a "Platonic" relationship because of the practical situation. It was Branden who, by his own admission and the context of these notes, was still pressing for a *sexual* relationship with Rand at this time—even as he wishes to leave the future "undecided." And, Rand will write later in these same January notes:

[16] I must ask him: he said once that "Platonism" is so much what he cannot associate with me, that it is so contrary to his view of me. (91)

As we have already seen, at this time Branden is telling Rand that he "cannot live" without her, that she has "no equals at any age," etc., *ad nauseam.*

But it is clear that by at least the end of January of 1968, Rand has reconsidered her previously "open" indications regarding a hypothetical "Miss X." Branden's inconsistent protestations of passionate love will no longer suffice. After months, even years, of "drift," Rand is now going to *force* the issue.

Specifically, Rand is forcing a *decision*: Branden must decide whether he really loves her or will leave her for the hypothetical "Miss X." Branden's plan for Rand to just step aside, to become a benevolent "Mother Figure," is understandably intolerable to Rand while Branden is still "kissing her in a way that's sexual," and pressing for a sexual relationship. Rand will not permit him to have his cake after he has thoroughly ingested it, leaving Rand alone with the sole responsibility of eventually ending it.

Rand has called for "a moment of truth."

And, once more, Branden decides to punt.

Her notes from January 25 make extremely clear that Rand has already come to terms with the end of their romance:

> [7] I think and feel strongly that our relationship was a mistake from the start—that there was and is no way to implement it in practice. But I do not know any solution other than a total break (leaving only a functional relationship.) We were right to attempt it originally. But we should have broken it about 8 years ago. We might have found some form of friendship then (though I am inclined to doubt it.) [8] Today, it is impossible—and it is these last 8 years that have made it impossible.

> The first consideration that stands out in my mind at this point, is the way (the tone and content both) in the way he said he let things go by default or drift, in the past, because he "*didn't know what to do.*" This implies that a lack of knowledge absolves one of all responsibility; or, that only moral errors have to be considered, but errors of knowledge do not—so that if *I* suffered because of *his* error of knowledge, he need not be concerned about it now nor even try to think if he *can* make up for it or not.

> (There is, of course, no way to make up for it. Love cannot be forced on oneself as an "atonement," and he cannot

force it on himself. But the horrifying [9] thing is that *he was willing to hurt me some more and deeper*— that he has projected his "I don't know" into the future, and is willing to let it be my responsibility or choice. This amounts, in effect, to saying: I know that I will cause her unspeakable agony in the future, but I don't know how to avoid it, so I'll leave the agony and the situation to her.)

If I know that I cannot accept his present attitude, why don't *I* break with him now? *Because I do not understand his attitude.* Because I must first understand. Because I do believe he loves me in some abstract, subjective manner of his own. And, in view of today's conversation, I think that his breach with reality is growing wider, not healing. I sense (for the first time and very dimly) the beginnings of something *immoral*—of *rationalization*. (If I am wrong I apologize for it.)

Notice Rand's *reluctance* to come to a negative moral judgment, not the reverse. For Rand, moral judgment requires, above all, *understanding*. Apart from a morally obvious case of virtue or vice, such as murder, for Rand confidence in her moral judgment required *a knowledge of the personal context involved*.

Rand's ignorance of the wide array of lies, however, could not survive the careful moral thinking which Rand was bringing to the matter.

Moreover, though Rand doubts that any kind of relationship is possible now, any further efforts put into this relationship by Rand must be seen as a desperate effort to find something less than romantic—but more than a merely "functional" relationship of which she grimly speaks here—i.e., to find a friendship.

That is all that her efforts in the next six months, all of the continued therapy and advice, can have sought, for that is what a "total break" *still* means to Rand. Even the end of their "friendship" means an attempt to make the "functional" work, and for that no counseling or note-writing would have been necessary.

In any event, that was the sort of "break" for which she is preparing, however difficult this prospect seemed to her.

So much for Branden's "inevitable" ending and his fears of destroying his career by cutting off a romance with Rand.

Notice, too, that Rand does not regret *in principle* her affair, nor does she ever appear to have done so. But—*before* learning of the nature and extent of Branden's dishonesty—she has already come to grips with the fact that, under the current circumstances—including Branden's psychological condition—there was no way to "implement" it.

In this passage, we find Branden himself admitting that he "let things go by drift" in the past. We also see Rand's understanding that love cannot be "forced" on someone. The minute, it seems, that she sensed that Branden's love was in some way "forced," the affair was over for Rand—in her words, "out of the question—now."

Rand's ignorance of Branden's duplicity has been enlightened somewhat since November—we see in these notes that Rand has begun to detect that Branden is operating on "undefined emotions." And other suspicions are obviously mounting—just as Branden's rationalizations are growing more complex. The entries from January 25 continue:

> [10] These beginnings [of "**something immoral**"] are in the form of what he calls his "de-repression." [Branden's] sole standard, today, is "what is right for me (himself)" or not—but this right is experienced by him in "sense of life" terms, which are not conceptualized, i.e., purely in the form of an undefined and unidentified emotion. This is terrible *per se*—but still worse, if he regards it as proper and rational.

> What standard or what "sense of life" issue seems to motivate him today? Only one: *his "visibility."* Out of all context, out of any relation to other even "sense of life" issues. In "sense of life" terms, this may be true—that proper "visibility" is his motive—but if he does [11] not translate his feelings, desires, motivations and actions into *conceptual terms*, then, in reality, in practice, there is no difference between holding "visibility" as a primary, [or] a motivation by vanity, flattery-seeking and, ultimately,

glamorizing and reality-faking. The desire for visibility is not a primary: it depends on *what* is being perceived and by *whom*...

It is on the ground of his "being himself" that he rejects the question of the triangle. What kind of "triangle" does he propose for me to accept in the future?

And: if he could not properly integrate and make the [12] two relationships work in reality, when it was me and Barbara—what does he imagine in the future? Since I cannot project or concretize it even in general terms, and neither can he, this indicates that he *has*, consciously or subconsciously, relegated this problem to me—as my future burden and choice, not his.

It takes only simple logic to find the latent contradictions in Branden's rolling disclosures, and Rand has no trouble here. Branden may still be pressing for sex and proclaiming his devotion, but asking Rand to accept "Miss X" while also saying that the "triangle" for him is no longer acceptable, is more than a slight contradiction.

All Rand wants is consideration for her personal context, a context that now precludes a "Miss X." Indeed, it is her *selfishness* that also proved crucial to her ability to unmask Branden, i.e., her refusal to be compared to an unknown quantity, and her refusal to accept the continued torment that Branden seems comfortable with dishing out.

The notes from January 25 continue:

[12] He knows and deeply appreciates the kind of visibility implied when someone is aware of his problem and his context, in dealing with him. How can he fail to see that this kind of understanding and concern is mandatory in any romantic relationship? Yet he is not aware of it. The issue here is: in any relationship (even business), one must always know that what one seeks or asks from another is

possible to him—and one does not seek that which one knows is impossible or harmful to the other person. Yet, he did it to me in the past—and is willing to do it again.

[13] He has been evasive on the issue of "Miss X." (Such statements as "Don't worry.") I thought he knew it had to be discussed. Yet he resented my attempt (recently) to discuss his projection of his future.

He resented the question about sex-psychology applying to him—when we discussed the abstract theories of other psychologists. *What is going on in his mind?* Does he really think that his [psycho-epistemology] is now normal in this respect?

Here we see that it was Rand pressing the "Miss X" issue against Branden's refrains of "don't worry." But Rand already knows one final answer, and we almost read the moment when she came to her final decision:

[13] The more I write this down, the more I know that the romance is finished (or never existed.) The only question is: is there anything possible other than a total break? (I don't think so.)

(The "triangle," [**i.e., Rand's affair with Branden**] of course, is out of the question—now.)

And, here, there is a break in the notes.

Remember that this was the period of Branden's first complaints about the "triangle," but not yet the "age" issue. It is a period in which he and his former wife have depicted Rand as being in almost complete denial about her status with Branden. It was during this period that Branden's problems became "problems with the relationship" in his discussions with Rand for the first time. And, it is precisely there and then that Rand, in her own mind, saw the end of their "romance."

Recall that Branden reports that, during this same period, he was telling Rand that she had "no equals at any age." He was telling Rand that his feelings were still romantic ones. Even in the weeks to come, he will confess to Rand that his "ideal scenario" still involves approximately six sex acts *per annum* with Rand.

But, in January, Rand senses the distance and the coldness and has reacted to these "vibrations" and "stomach feelings." For the first time, Branden doesn't want to talk about sex or "about us." For Rand, that is enough evidence to demand more answers.

At some level, Rand already knows what is going on, whether Branden is admitting it to her (or to himself) or not. She resumes her notes on January 25, as follows:

> [14] I want to add one more very important point: when he said yesterday, that he is perfectly happy to see me there, but the feeling vanishes when we talk about sex (or, I'm not sure which, when we talk about any possibility of a "triangle")—I shuddered, because the parallel to his attitude toward [Barbara Branden] is too obvious. He said many times that he enjoys seeing [Barbara Branden] and talking to her—until the conversation touches on their personal relationship; then his enjoyment vanishes.

> [15] In my case, this is an indication of what his *subconscious* is planning for the future: *an impersonal, intellectual friendship with me—when "Miss X" comes along—*a friendship in which the fact that I love him will simply vanish, by gradual suppression or attrition, and will become *my* problem, not his, and will not matter to him, just as the fact that Barbara loves him does not matter to him. This, if true, is unspeakable.

> I cannot be sure that this is true. But he must convince me of what it does mean, if not the above. *This is one of the first things to clarify.*

Also, I must ask him: he said once that Platonism is so much what he cannot associate with me, that it [16] is so contrary to his view of me. What happened to that view of me? Is he in the process of repressing it into something monstrous?

Whatever Branden is urging, it is clear that Rand will not continue to sleep with a man who will not discuss their future and who is, to her eyes at least, subconsciously preparing to displace her for a "Miss X."

In these same notes from January 25, Rand writes:

[16] [T]he minimum he owes me is to *think* about *my* part of the situation, about *my* context and to take the responsibility of a decision. If he "does not know what to do," [then] he has to act on such knowledge as he has. Non-omniscience is not an escape from taking the responsibility for the consequences of his own actions.

[17] I have told him, at the start of the present period, that I will accept anything which I can rationally understand— and that the only thing I dread, in his attitude, is his "I don't know." Yet I have been confronted with an "I don't know" over and over again. I have told him: "Let me in on what you think about our relationship." He hasn't. What's worse, I feel something closed in his manner towards me, as if, even in his best or happy moments, there is still a wall between us: something in him is closed, private, not to be reached. [Barbara Branden] spoke of feeling this, in the past. I had never seen it before, even in our worst times; it is there now.

As far as I can judge from the little [18] I grasp about his [psycho-epistemology] from our formal psycho-epistemological sessions, his symptoms seem to indicate the following: he "does not know what to do" or he cannot "be himself" when he is repressing some issue which he does not permit himself to consider or, more exactly, does not want to know. In our case, the only such issue that I can think of (judging by his actions) is that *he does not really love me*. I know I mean something important to him, but whatever it is, it is not love. Maybe it was, years ago, at the beginning, but I am not certain even of that.

I do not believe that there is such a problem as being in love, but not knowing what to do. The conceivable variants of such a repression are not applicable to him: a person [19] may be inarticulate, but then he communicates his feeling indirectly; or, a person may lack self-esteem to such an extent that he does not believe that he can be loved, but that is hardly his problem. The vibrations he communicates, in this issue, are fear. *Fear of what?* His inner chaos, his inability to keep context or to grasp the other person's context, his general [psycho-epistemological] disintegration, all are symptoms of fear. Since there is no existential cause of fear [**that Rand yet knows of, at least**], the cause must be psychological. There is something he is afraid to face. I cannot be sure of what it is. But, as things stand, the only thing I can suspect is that his feeling for me is not love and he is afraid to face this, because it would be a blow to his self-esteem (and it would be, with justice, in fact). (I hope I am wrong about this.)

We see here the real "pressure" on Branden: Rand's high self-esteem. Rand has the confidence that Branden's love for her would have been objective—that she was "worthy of love"—and that if Branden does not really love her—as he had claimed—it will, in fact and in "justice," be a "blow to his [own] self-esteem."

This in no way implies that Rand believed that she should be the objectively top romantic value of every man, as Branden suggests. *He* presented himself as *just that man*—spiritually identical to Rand in all ways and a romantic hero who could look past the age-gap. If he is *not* that man, the man he had *wanted* to be, the difference between his fantasy and the reality would be a crushing blow to his confidence.

The "justice" of the "blow" depends upon *Branden's* values. If he never believed in the nobility of his stated love for Rand, then, of course, there would be no threat to his self-esteem. Under that circumstance, he would not be a traitor, merely a comprehensive fraud from Day One.

Rand was a proud woman, and *not* loving her as he had claimed to *does* mean that Branden will be diminished in her eyes, one of Branden's great personal fears, but it clearly will *not* necessarily mean the liquidation of the Nathaniel Branden Institute and the end of Branden's "life," as Branden has publicly alleged. A fair reading of Rand's notes suggests that this kind of disillusionment on her part could not have led to this.

Branden *was*, by his own admission, paralyzed by his *intellectual* belief that Rand *did* represent everything he cherished, and the growing conflict between this belief and his actual emotions. A woman of lower self-esteem than Rand would never have seen this basic truth. He did "betray his values" in the worst way possible—but only if these had ever truly been his values.

At this stage, Rand still thinks that they are his values, for her January 25 entry continues:

> [20] To sum up: nothing in his attitude, from the beginning, and particularly now, is my idea of love. I do not believe ideas of love can be that radically different—particularly in two persons whose basic premises and "sense of life" and abstract views of romantic love are as identical as his and mine.
>
> I do not know whether repression can cause a distortion of this kind. But I must conclude that he not merely hasn't de-repressed in regard to me, but that his repression is now deepening.

Rand is still laboring under the assumption that Branden's "abstract views" are as stated, that his emotions are as stated, and that his "sense of life" is what he pretends it to be. This means that his pretended ideas and values and sense of life are not just similar to Rand's—*they are identical.* This was Branden's claim, and this was Rand's original belief.

In any case, however, Branden's indecision is a remarkable display of moral cowardice, and Rand is reluctantly coming to this conclusion even without being told the full truth.

We read further in her notes from January 25:

> **[20]** *What is he repressing?* And how is it possible that **[21]** he has not thought about and clarified to himself his attitude toward me in *all these years?* It cannot be so complicated that he thought and thought and gave up in helplessness. Has he discovered that he is through with me, but does not dare face the issue of telling me? If so, he is a coward of the worst kind—a moral coward who prefers to torture me into making the decision to break with him, rather than take the responsibility himself? (I cannot believe this last.)

> He said once that I should have enough faith in him, on the basis of what I do know about him, to believe that the basic explanation of his behavior is good, even though neither I nor he can understand it at present. This, of course, is wrong *per se*. But, in the present context: it is precisely what I do know about him **[22]** that clashes with his actions; my view of his character makes his actions impossible—none of it is like him—and the contradiction is unbearable, and if I think of bad motivations, it is because *I do not know what to think at all.*

> I cannot make any decision until he has answered *and explained* all the things I wrote here.

In these January notes, Rand is still assuming that Branden's values are what he had claimed them to be, and that his vacillating and evasive behavior is an aberration for him. She still thinks that she can somehow motivate him into responsible behavior, and that they can still preserve *something*, if no longer a romance.

Branden's request that Rand have "faith" in his motives is the line of a con-artist in this context. If these are the things for which Rand is

demanding an explanation, then—four years into his affair with Patrecia—
Branden's failure to "end it" with Rand immediately—if not also to inform
her about that affair—and at last show some respect for Patrecia—can
only be seen as sadistic torture of both women for his own financial and
professional ends, if not worse.

Rand concludes her notes from January 25:

> [22] (Maybe he wants me to "be happy"—hence all
> his compliments, his encouragement of my "glamour-
> oriented" attitude, etc. Hence his desire to have me take an
> active interest in [Nathaniel Branden Institute] "socials,"
> in his theater projects, etc. Either he wants me to be
> happy, in order to reassure himself that he has not hurt
> me permanently, and/or he wants me to continue as his
> friend and impersonal admirer—but there is no personal
> meaning [23] or place for me in his life. If so, then I must
> tell him that he has hurt me dreadfully, more than anyone
> else ever has—dreadfully and permanently—and that
> there is no way out of this fact, and no "benevolent" ending
> a la Barbara, that we are long since past the point of no
> return in this issue, and that there is no way to save his
> self-esteem from this—*that there is no way out now* except
> in the form of a monstrous betrayal of all his values on his
> part, and that *he has to* acknowledge this. Anything else is
> faking reality—and I will not help him to fake.)

There is no suggestion, yet, that this lack of a "benevolent" ending
means the kind of permanent break that is to come, including an end to
"the functional" aspects of their relationship—only that it must now take
into account the profound damage Branden has already inflicted on their
relationship; otherwise, even the mutual respect required of a friendship
would be impossible. It is Branden's *self-destruction* that Rand regards
as the significant problem, and if the romance has reached its terminal
crisis in Rand's own mind, as we have seen, we now are witnessing Rand's
intention to tell Branden just that.

Given Branden's response to Rand, we must conclude that Branden does not simply want to "preserve" his "functional" relationship with Rand, he needs her *enthusiastic endorsement* for his new projects, such as the theater venture, and the introduction to his new book.

So Branden will go on proclaiming his passionate love for Rand for several more months to come. And he would go on putting her through the hell of his indecision about this.

Despite the degree to which this subject impacted her personally, Rand is neither "insane" nor "irrational," as has been alleged, but impressively reasonable, even amazingly perceptive about these matters. Acutely in touch with the emotional subtext, the "vibrations," her suspicions are natural and understandable, and her insight even catches a glimpse of the much deeper dishonesty that is at work in Branden's mind.

Indeed, given how much of Branden's dishonesty of which Rand was still unaware—and given his literally professional skills as a deceiver—it is something of a tribute to Objectivism that Rand was able to notice the tip of such a mighty ice-berg of dishonesty simply from Branden's method of *mental functioning*, that is, his "psycho-epistemology."

The emotional cues—exaggerated guilt, increasing coldness and "not wanting to talk about us"—that signal the end for Rand are less exotic and are easily understood—they are precisely the "vibrations" which "women's intuition" would alert on—the very "instincts" which the Brandens strangely claim that Rand lacked. But Rand's perceptiveness, as usual, goes a step deeper: she concludes that Branden's mind is not functioning in a reality-based way.

Branden's "non-answers" and continued assertions of love apparently prompt more "therapy" and the notes now take on a more "clinical" aspect. This was undoubtedly additional torture for Rand, but for the student of Objectivism, these notes are full of insight into the syndrome Rand called "rationalism."

According to standard psychology texts, psychological "defense mechanisms" are subconscious, automatized "strategies" for avoiding emotional pain, and the facts and the experiences inspiring that pain. "Repression" is among the most common of these. According to many psychologists, the habitual (or traumatic) suppression of emotions can cause this suppression to become automatic, a "mechanism"—one that is often difficult to shut off. There are many such defense mechanisms, as the briefest glance at the standard texts reveals. Such "mechanisms" are about as common as the human race itself.

"Rationalism," as Rand used the term, is not to be found in the standard texts—being first identified by Objectivism—and it is a relatively rare phenomenon, most common among intellectuals. Hence, the "rationalist-repressor" is a relatively rare species of repressor.

At root, rationalism is not a psychological but a *psycho-epistemological* syndrome; specifically, the rationalist *eschews the perceptual level of awareness in favor of abstraction*. The rationalist tendency is to favor purely deductive logic and to focus on the highly abstract. The "concrete," the perceptual, is avoided. Therefore, the rationalist is one whose abstractions are frequently detached from reality. As a consequence, another rationalist tendency is to become an "intrinsicist," one whose ideas and values are divorced from the factual context of his own life, and, thereby, objective thought.

In contrast, the psycho-epistemological "empiricist" is the "concrete-bound" mentality, one which eschews abstraction in favor of the perceptual and sensate.

Objectivism rejects both methodological approaches, of course, as two sides of the same dichotomized coin, while it recognizes that one's psycho-epistemology can be as deeply ingrained as one's "psychology."

Closely connected to this rationalist tendency to avoid the perceptual is a tendency toward emotional repression. There are certainly many developmental reasons behind the various types of repression, but the psycho-epistemology of rationalism itself will often lead the rationalist to become an emotional repressor.

The rationalist's ideas are often detached from the facts—his abstractions are "floating," if you will, disconnected from any foundation in reality. Inevitably, the facts, including the rationalist's emotions, will at some point come into conflict with these abstractions—and may present an actual *threat* to those abstractions. The committed rationalist clings to his floating abstractions, even if this means repressing his emotions. Among the material a rationalist will habitually disregard are the physical aspects of his emotions, and these are experienced just like sensations, automatically and immediately. To be effective, the strategy to avoid them must also be automatized: repression.

But, of course, the rationalist, like any repressor, will only end up impairing his entire consciousness, for his subconscious values won't just go away—repression will merely deaden the entire emotional mechanism, a mechanism vital to our well-being. In addition, even his conscious values—whatever their merit—will never be properly integrated into his emotional mechanism, and an inner "self" will inevitably begin to scream to be set free.

Here, the rationalist comes to a cross-roads. To end the tormented conflict, in the extreme case, he must either uproot the repression—going deep to get at those latent values—or he must abandon his conscious values. He can either begin the (often difficult) work of introspection, uncovering his repressed emotions, discovering their origins and nature—or he can simply abandon his conscious thought and values, what were only "floating" abstractions in any event, and surrender to his undefined emotions. If he decides on the latter course, he will probably end up blaming the "abstract" values for having been his "prison," as having prevented him from "being himself," as having "repressed his true self"—that is, all the things that Branden has said about himself.

A "burned" rationalist will often flee to the seemingly opposite direction: empiricism, replacing his intrinsicism with subjectivism, his idealism with materialism, never discovering *reason* along the way, the integration of experience and abstraction, fact and value, life and thought.

Rationalism alone cannot account for Branden's psychology and behavior. His self-reported autism, his autocratic bluster, and, above all, his dishonesty cannot be blamed on rationalism. For Rand rationalism was simply one way to integrate a number of Branden's symptoms. It was a diagnosis she came to slowly and, curiously, only after Branden himself suggested it, or, rather, revealed it as something he "feared." But rationalism was only a small item among Branden's issues—and a good distraction from some of the bigger ones.

Even on this score, though, Branden is plainly suffering from a particularly extreme form of "rationalism." Desperately needing to live up to his consciously imposed "self," Branden tried to "force" himself to love Rand in every way. And yet, as we have seen, Branden will actually end up blaming Rand and her philosophy for "demanding" that he love her.

Rand certainly possessed a healthy self-esteem—she believed that it was objective for a man who professed to share her spirit to love her. But Rand also made allowance for a whole range of other values and options just as objective as passionately loving her. (She certainly did not require romantic love from any of her other admirers and students.) We see in these notes Rand patiently and without "moralism" simply urging Branden to honestly identify his true emotions, whatever they turn out to be.

We see Branden refusing. Repression, however accurate the diagnosis, was also a convenient excuse for not identifying for Rand (or himself) the nature of his authentic emotions, his true self. As a psychologist, Branden knew precisely how to duck that question.

In brief notes dated "January 28, 1968," three days after she had written these last entries, Rand writes on a single page,

> Questions:
> 1. What inspires him?
> 2. The distinction between emotions and sensations. How does he know what he feels—what is a value or disvalue—what he wants or not?
> 3. What was his former "abstract reaction" to attractive women?
> 4. What is the influence of this repression on the objectivity of his mind?
> 5. "The relationship." (What was the actual story of the past 8 or 10 years: Particularly of the "Platonism" decision?) (Here it is terribly important to discover what he actually and selfishly wants.)

For Rand, what is "terribly important" is Branden's seeming inability "to discover what he actually and selfishly wants," the very plight of a rationalist-repressor.

In notes dated "January 28, 1968," the next day, she writes,

[1] An answer to the question: "I have the power to make her happy but don't know what to do." The only possible answer is: identify clearly what would make *you* happy (in regard to her)—and this will be the right thing to do. (In practice, adapt your desire to the possible.)

Rand does not believe that Branden *should* love her or anybody else; indeed, Rand is simply trying to get Branden to be *selfish*, i.e., to identify what *would* "make him happy"—"what inspires him"—and do it. She is accused by the Brandens of employing an emotionally repressed, over-intellectualized, rationalistic approach to human psychology when the opposite appears to have been the case. We see Rand trying to help Branden uproot his *own* repression and rationalist leanings. Notice, for example, Rand's concern over Branden's self-professed "abstract" reaction to attractive women, his emotional repression and its effect on objective thought, and the great concern over getting at what "he really wants." One thing becomes powerfully clear: Rand never wanted to impose duties, "shoulds," or forced love of any kind—on anyone—and the exact reverse of the Brandens' accusations is the truth.

Along these same lines, in another single-page note, dated that same day, Rand writes:

Psycho-epistemological note: re: The impossibility of acting by a purely cerebral method [**in this context, as a lifestyle; Rand did believe that, when it came to a conflict between the two, we must act on our rational judgment, whatever our emotions may be**]. The time element required to integrate and hold the full context of all the aspects of a complex issue, makes it impossible to accomplish; one needs the lightning integration provided by emotions (and by one's self-interest). When repression blocks this integrating process, one acts in a contradictory way and one is unable to preserve any continuity or context. (Trying to hold the "interest" of another person as one's standard and one's integrating principle, will not work: nature does not permit a psycho-epistemological altruism of that kind.)

Emotions are not a means of logic or thinking—as Rand would have said, they are not "tools of cognition." But they are vital evidence about one's self, and objective *introspective* thought requires them. In most situations, we should be able to rely upon our emotions as familiar quantities, their causes and natures understood if not simply taken for granted.

One could never decide what to have for lunch, for example, by starting with a check on one's basic metaphysics, making a quick review of epistemological principles needed to make a proper decision, a full consideration of one's entire hierarchy of values and producing a summary of the various implications and ramifications of ordering each item on the menu. One would starve first. When our emotions are allowed to surface, we allow ourselves to directly experience our values without having to establish their desirability and rank all over again. In effect, we can "be ourselves."

By implication, we see that Rand perceived in Branden an emotionally repressed psychology and an overly "cerebral" approach to dealing with his own psychology, one which Rand sees as dangerous to happiness and to objective thought itself.

Rand is also trying to get Branden to hold his focus on the subject, from which he seems to have persistently strayed, giving him "tips" for doing so, whatever the enormity of his problem may be. She continues:

> Remember to associate "fear of hurting [Ayn]" with the fact that you are hurting [Ayn] in that very moment, by that very thought. [**Here, as elsewhere, Rand is referring to herself as "A." which has been spelled out as "Ayn" in the brackets.**]

> Establish for yourself the inner signs of when you are off, psycho-epistemologically, and the standing order to stop and regain perspective—whether in talking or in your own thinking.

Then, in another single-page entry dated January 31, 1968, Rand writes in a hurried script:

> For issue of repression by means of the premise "I want (or do not want) to be a certain kind of man": I have never thought of "what kind of a woman" I want to be; I always think only: "I want to accept the truth—I want to accept the ideas which are true." (This is the basic principle in re: "man is a being of self-made soul.")

A rationalist, in a sense, has first determined what *kind* of person he wanted to be and then tried to squeeze into that ideal as into a pair of undersized Levis. Rand is suggesting that the button will eventually pop and that you'll be miserable in the meantime, anyway. She is suggesting that we should start by thinking and work out from the truth. That's how we should *determine* our values. That is how we *become* the person "we want to be." We see again Rand working to undo Branden's artificially imposed "self," the one he would later blame her for creating in him.

And, perhaps, most fascinating, on this same date, further down the page, she writes:

> Question: What did he mean when he said; "I do not feel guilty—and that's the trouble."

One wants to cry out to Rand and tell her the truth, despite the logical paradoxes involved in time-travel. Rand does not want Branden to sacrifice *either* his emotions *or* his mind. It seems to her that he is doing both. She wants him to be selfish—and to start by defining what "selfishness" is in his case, i.e., what he really *wants*. It is on this very topic that Branden goes fuzzy on her.

Ayn Rand was not preventing Branden from "being himself." She was encouraging it. She saw Branden literally heading for *self*-destruction.

Rand's eloquence against Branden's extreme form of rationalism is impressive in these private, unedited entries. By repressing and ignoring his emotions, Rand is suggesting that Branden has engaged in *self-sacrifice* and a kind of *altruism*, the sacrifice of his values to those of another—i.e., those abstract values his conscious mind is trying to impose on his entire being. Whoever those values "belong" to, it is not Branden—at least not *subconsciously*.

Rand believed that even *good* values can be perverted into a source of pain by this process. Rand is implicitly urging Branden to stop "suppressing his real self"—even in the name of Objectivism.

As we have previously seen, Rand was a philosophical *egoist*. Her ethics teaches that an individual should be the beneficiary of his own efforts. Closely related to this, Rand held *self-esteem* to be a primary value and pride to be a fundamental virtue. According to Branden's psychological theories, self-esteem is the hallmark of psychological health.

On the level of physical sensations, a kind of selfishness is "built in" to our bodies, namely, the pleasure-pain mechanism, which is automatically calibrated to inform us of key aspects of our physical well-being. The frustration or fulfillment of more abstract values is also experienced as a kind of pleasure or pain, as well, but here the mechanism is, in a sense, "programmed" by the thinking (or evasion) of the conscious mind.

Objectivism holds that, while selfishness is as natural and healthy as eating or breathing (although it takes greater effort), many people, unfortunately, act self-destructively. Often, this is simply a question of ignorance, i.e., of *not knowing* what is in one's actual, long-term interests. Also frequently, however, it is because the actor does not hold his own interests to be a sufficient motive—i.e., because he lacks *self-esteem*.

The subconscious belief that one is either unable or unworthy of achieving one's goals is usually experienced, emotionally, as *anxiety*—not a fear directed at some external threat, such as a gun pointed at your head, but that diffuse sense that one brings to every situation, one's *self-evaluation*.

The junkie may well know that the needle poised at his vein is responsible for the loss of his job, the end of his marriage, and his current life of criminal activities. He knows that his addiction is suicide on the installment plan. He knows the short-range has trumped the long-range.

But *his* "long-range" is not a sufficient incentive to prevent the injection. The momentary relief from his chronic anxiety is a stronger incentive than any goals he could achieve while sober.

As a criminal prosecutor with some experience in this area, I can report that, when queried about these other goals and values, the drug addict will usually respond with some variant of the following: "That kind of thing's not for *me*!" or "Why should *I* have that?" or "Oh, I couldn't do that, anyway!" or "What's the use, I'd just screw that up, too!"

In Objectivist terms, he lacks the *self-esteem* that would make the difference and significantly improve his life.

Indeed, his lack of self-esteem has *generated* this chronic anxiety, the very symptom he seeks to avoid by heavy sedation. Such low self-esteem—with a destructive impact this clear—is *pathological*.

The opposite, a sense of self-worth and efficacy, can have the opposite results. It can give one the extra confidence needed to leave that dead-end job for a more fulfilling one, or to keep the needle away from your addict's arm, or to take that creative step in your work, or to make that investment, or to leave that controlling husband, or to take the calculated risk involved in space exploration, etc. High self-esteem is *life-enhancing*.

This fundamental "sense of worthiness" does not pertain to any particular goal or value, but to the way one values *oneself*. It is one's subconscious self-estimate that matters here, not necessarily the conscious one—which is often just gloss. This subconscious self-estimate is experienced in the form of eager confidence or inhibiting anxiety or somewhere along the continuum in between.

Only a healthy self-esteem can make possible a proper hierarchy of values, according to Objectivism, resolving unnecessary doubts and conflicts. (92) In other words, without some self-esteem, you will have trouble even identifying *what is in your self-interest*.

For example, you are offered a job. Should you take it? In order to answer that question, you first have to answer a deeper one: what are you *really after* in your career: a certain kind of achievement, the satisfaction of performing a certain skill well, expression of your esthetic values, money, fame—or what? Does that goal make sense? Will this job serve this "higher" goal and, ultimately, your *actual* "self-interest"?

Often, such "higher" motives for our actions are unclear to our conscious mind. We are moving to gain some value *subconsciously*—because it "feels" right or it "feels" wrong—and the task of psychotherapy is often simply the determination of what the patient is "really after" through his behavior.

This "higher selfishness" Rand called one's "meta-selfishness"—not the particular job or even career, but the ultimate goal of your career. In common parlance, *what's really in it for you*.

In this task, the enemy is *repression*. Being out of touch with your desires, your preferences, your emotions, will leave you out of touch with this very issue—you miss some of the best evidence of the nature of your deepest, authentic values. The rationalist-repressor is ultimately being *psychologically* unselfish.

To continue our career example, an intelligent young man loves sculpture more than anything else in the world and, in sculpting finds greater satisfaction than doing anything else. Loving it so, he spends a great deal of time sculpting and gets good at it.

Formal logic, debate, politics, rhetoric, negotiation all leave him cold.

But, his mother believes that artists are destined to suffer and struggle, and she wants the young sculptor to get a "practical" job, say, as a lawyer. She spends hours telling her son about how the proudest members of their family were all lawyers, serving the oppressed and downtrodden, earning a "good living," and becoming pillars of the community. "Why, two of them even became judges!"

If the young man, like Peter Keating in *The Fountainhead,* succumbs to this kind of pressure, perhaps even with his own "logical" mind telling him that law school is "just more practical," his love of sculpture will become an actual *threat*—something he may end up *repressing in the name of his "conscious" values.*

Our fledgling sculptor's repression will progressively deaden his emotional responses, especially in his career, and, perforce, his hierarchy of values will be thrown into chaos as the evidence of his "meta-selfishness" becomes ever more alien to him. Paralysis and indecision are to be expected.

One who represses his emotions for the sake of some allegedly "logical" set of values he has learned from another has also become, in practice, *an altruist*—he has sacrificed his real self-interests for something else, he has given something—and someone—other than his own selfishness a higher priority and a first claim on his conduct. That "someone" is the author of those "abstract" values. In the sculptor's case, it is his controlling mother.

The same reasoning can be applied to human relationships as to jobs. Here at least, Rand recognized, Branden was having trouble identifying his "meta-selfishness," and, as a result of his rationalism, was acting *altruistically*, i.e., he was sacrificing his true values to somebody else's values—*whatever* those values may have been. This self-alienation has resulted in his indecision and paralysis. This process has blinded Branden to his own romantic self-interest, inevitably causing a conflict in his values and his senseless misery.

On a deeper level, Rand's obvious concern is that Branden has literally sacrificed his *self* to a mistaken idealism. She still hopes that it is a *noble* idealism, something like the sculpture in our example. But in any event, Rand does *not* want to be like the controlling mother in our example, or to be any kind of Deity worshipped in such a sacrifice. She is concerned for the consequences both to Branden and to herself.

Again and again we see that Rand was urging Branden to end this self-abnegating behavior long before Branden would blame Rand for it.

On January 30, 1968, Rand writes:

[1] *Notes re: consequences of psychological altruism.* Since man's emotional mechanism, by nature integrates things by the standard of "What is for me or against me"—a man who attempts to use a different standard, to take the good of another person as a primary, suffers the following consequences. His emotional mechanism still continues to function by a selfish standard and to sum up his experiences according to *his* pleasure and pain. But now his experiences with the other person (the woman he loves) add up predominantly to negatives—pain, frustration, failure—both by reason of the existential trouble caused by [2] his unnatural attempt (which requires repression and *impersonality* whenever he sees a real or imagined clash of interests), and, *more importantly,* by reason of the psychological disaster imposed on himself: a sense of selflessness, self-invisibility, a forced breach of self-esteem, the loss of "meta-selfishness" (since his own happiness is no longer a primary in that relationship).

After a while, this leads him to a reason-emotion breach. His reason tells him that the woman is his top value (in the right sense of the word), but his emotions tell him that the relationship has brought him nothing but pain. [3] If he does not repeal the "altruistic" premise, the consequences go as follows: The more he tries to hold on to his rational evaluation (by old-fashioned will power, motivated by unearned guilt and damaged self-esteem, on the formula of: "What's wrong with me, I don't want to be the kind of man who betrays his conscious values!"), the greater the breach between his mind and his emotions.

Then his emotions will lead him to seek pleasure elsewhere—and, since his mind is forbidden to face the issue consciously, his emotions will force him to *rationalize* his new pleasure, in [4] order to convince himself that it fits his values, that he is *not* betraying his values, while, in fact, *he is.* Thus his mind (and his reasoning, and his proper grasp of reality) grows incapacitated further and further.

The new pleasure (or new woman) has to be *inferior* to his values—because (1) if it (she) were not, the same "altruistic" pattern would set in; he can feel free to "be himself" and enjoy it only so long as it (or she) is regarded by him as "unimportant" or dispensable; (2) if the new were not inferior, it could not be isolated from his hierarchy of values and he could [5] not attempt to enjoy it out of context; he would have to face the problem of integrating it with his former great value and attempt to explain to himself his giving up the former value.

In [Branden's] specific case, the pattern seems to have been as follows:

1. In the case of [Barbara Branden], the standard he introduced into his emotional mechanism, superseding his own interests, was, in fact, an "I wish" over an "It is" [**an Objectivist term for evading some aspect of reality on the basis of one's emotional preferences**]: he would not permit himself and he repressed the thought of the possibility that she was not the right or ideal woman for him; [6] on the one hand, he had to maintain (for himself)

the idea that his sex life was an expression of his highest values (a proper premise, but not to be implemented by repression, i.e., by faking reality); on the other hand, the "altruistic" premise entered also, on the mistaken premise that where his high values are concerned, price no object, including his own suffering as part of the price (which, again, is a proper premise, but not at the price of his fundamentals: of his self-esteem, his pleasure-principle, his meta-selfishness).

The pattern here was as follows: I want to be happy—sex is one of two [7] most important elements of happiness in man's life—I cannot have sex in my life, except as an expression of my highest values, therefore only with an ideal woman—I want this particular woman, therefore, she must be ideal (this became a metaphysical absolute)—therefore, I will bear anything (including selflessness), since it is suffering borne for the sake of my own happiness and my highest values.

2. In the case of [Ayn] his mind evaluated her as the right woman for him (or the ideal woman). Outside circumstances (including the age difference) made him approach the relationship with a great deal of uncertainty [8] and, therefore, fear. The rational part of this could have been corrected. But he came to the relationship with two dangerous frozen absolutes: (1.) repression in general, plus the particular repression of the fear [unstated] that he does not know how to have a relationship with a woman, and this time, he must succeed, or his self-esteem will be destroyed in the realm of romance; and, (2.) the "altruistic" premise in full force (due to his own uncertainty about himself in this realm, on the one hand, and his rational admiration for the woman, on the other.)

[9] The case of [Barbara Branden] ended in disaster—i.e., the consciously initiated policy of sexual repression.

For a while, [Ayn] was a precarious antidote; but the troubles of that relationship (plus [Ayn's] withdrawal during the personal crisis years [**i.e., the two years following the publication of *Atlas Shrugged* in 1957**]) led to [**his**] subconscious *total renunciation* of sex (and of romantic happiness) [**notice the conclusions Branden has persuaded Rand to reach about his alleged current celibacy**]—as the result to the threat to his self-esteem. (The conflict became: sex or self-esteem, both held as absolutes in his mind, and one set against the other by reason of repression and the consequent incapacitation of his mind, and the consequent faking of reality.)

[**10**] 3. The case of [Patrecia]. He came to this relationship with his emotional-sexual capacity cut off. As he began to find personal pleasure in it (particularly the pleasure of sexual visibility, real or imagined), the conscious base of his friendship began to switch. His emotions began to add up the sum of his experience as pleasure—the exact opposite emotional sum he got from the two former cases. He came to this relationship without frozen absolutes: no "duty" to feel anything, no "altruism," no concept of an ideal woman. The [**11**] new and unusual experience, for him, was the experience of proper 'meta-selfishness' and, consequently, proper emotional freedom. (The obvious inferiority of the woman to himself permitted him the freedom of selfishness, the conviction that *his* terms and standards were *right* and should be given supremacy— so long as the mind classified the relationship as mere friendship and, therefore, not of primary importance and not a threat to his self-esteem.)

But since this was the only relationship in which he could experience the proper [**12**] rewards and consequences of romantic love (meta-selfishness, emotional freedom, the sense of "being himself"), his subconscious grasped the approach of a new and deadly conflict: the impossibility [of] reconcil[ing] this relationship with his conscious values (which were in a dreadful state of confusion, repression, chaos, wounded self-esteem and, above all, of solid pain—an unidentified, unanalyzed pain, made worse by the feeling of having struggled to untangle it "rationally" [which is impossible in the presence of repression] and having failed, and carrying the unadmitted [13] conviction that the struggle is hopeless and the chaos is never to be grasped or resolved.)

Therefore, his subconscious moved into the only direction left open to it: *rationalization*—the faking of reality, *the same faking* that brought him to disaster in the case of [Barbara Branden]. He began to glamorize the character of [Patrecia], in order to convince himself that she represented his values (at least, in part). He minimizes the extent, nature and seriousness of her flaws—and exaggerates the extent and meaning of her (potential) [14] virtues. His proof of her virtues does not consist, *primarily* (basically), of observed facts, but of an undefined "sense of life" feeling or "hunch." (He should compare this to the way in which he established the virtues of [Ayn]. The [psycho-epistemological] difference is shocking.)

The repetition of his tragedy with [Barbara Branden] is an obvious danger here, but with certain even more dangerous elements (more dangerous to his psycho-epistemology, his happiness, and his mind): in the case of [Barbara Branden], he had reason to think that she was, potentially, his ideal woman, and it was only his [15] "sense-of-life" emotions that gave him, at times, a warning to the contrary; he was much younger and knew much less about psychology and about how to judge human character or a woman's potential; he was, in effect, sacrificing (repressing) his emotions in name of his (mistaken) rational judgment.

Today, in the case of [Patrecia], it is his rational judgment, *his mind,* that he is sacrificing to his emotions. His emotions are not a response to the woman (or to her character), but to his own state: his starved, frustrated (and, in this case, blind and twisted) [16] desire for meta-selfishness, masculine visibility and full self-confidence (which means: an unclouded, unquestioned self-esteem). In the case of [Barbara Branden] the [psycho-epistemological] pattern was: I want her to be ideal, I must believe that she is ideal and repress my doubts. In the case of [Patrecia], the [psycho-epistemological] pattern is much worse: I like (or, possibly, love) her, therefore, she is ideal—and if my mind doesn't agree, to hell with my mind—it (the mind) misled me once before, now I have the right to feel, without thinking. (It is this *righteous* attitude here that is the deepest sign of danger; [17] it is being combined with the following [subconscious] rationalization: I have demonstrated to myself that I am rational, by the great amount of brilliant thinking and professional success which I have accomplished; therefore, I can trust my emotions to be automatically right—even though I cannot fully understand them nor justify them rationally and *objectively.* Which means: I have done enough thinking— now I can permit myself to feel.)

The horror of such a [psycho-epistemological] trend is obvious. The central, crucial, [18] cardinal, overwhelming error here is his disregard of repression—of the fact that a repressor cannot trust his feelings, and more: cannot even fully trust his mind, until the repression is removed. (If it is not removed, then it is precisely his mind that will now be progressively disintegrating.)

The danger in his relationship with [Patrecia], if he makes it romantic, is as follows: it will become a permanent threat to his self-esteem, he will be forced to repress [19] deeper and deeper the fact that his motivation for the romance was irrational, and came from a weakness, from pain, fear and a breached self-esteem that led him to fake reality; he will not take the blame on himself (because this would force him to see her true character and would blast his self-esteem); thus he would be in another impossible conflict, another unresolved dichotomy—and the result would probably be a permanent renunciation of the romantic-sexual realm, [20] a crippled and twisted and pain-exhausted mind, and the loss of any capacity for enjoyment or happiness. [**Such as the "sex problem" he had begun to complain of during these 1968 sessions.**]

There is no way out for him and no way to solve anything or take any action or make any choice until he has fully derepressed.

Since [Ayn] seems to be the issue most involved in repression at present, this is what we must de-repress. (I do not know whether his obsession with "the relationship" is the result of a repressed love or of his last emotional tie to reason, i.e., to his mind—or both. It is probably both.)

[21] On rereading the above, my likeliest hypothesis is that his intelligence and all his rational premises and sense of life will not actually permit him to take [Patrecia] seriously as a romance. But anything is possible so long as he is repressed, i.e., out of control. So, again, derepression is the first absolute now.

I cannot believe that such a magnificent mind and person can come to so ignominious and small an end. I do not believe that a life worthy of him—a rational life, on his own rational terms—is impossible to him.

> I think that "altruism" and repression, [22] in a mind like his, are sufficient causes to explain all the dreadful contradictions of his present state—and are the two deadly enemies which he must fight and eliminate.

Whatever Rand's despair at Branden's conduct, she still regards it as possible for Branden to live up to his rational, stated values. She is still laboring under the impression that these really *are* his values. This impression will not last.

Rand has noted the ominous "faking of reality" that appears to be the consequence of his repression and altruism.

The psychological counseling sessions, though obviously futile due to Branden's dishonesty, have caused Rand to write down keen and valuable insights into human psychology generally, and are worth studying for this reason alone.

But these sessions were a grueling torture for Rand and one of the worst aspects of Branden's behavior. Rand's advice is sincere and, obviously, a powerful, if incomplete diagnosis of Branden's psychology. She may not know all of the facts, but this makes her analysis is all the more remarkable.

Branden has, one way or another, completely sublimated his true values, whatever those may have been. He has cut himself into "shoulds" versus "wants" and has excavated a chasm between his "intellectual" values and his emotions. This self-destructive behavior can only have cut a swath of agony through the women he claimed to have cared about, not to mention his own mental functioning.

Bullseye, Miss Rand.

It is pure projection—and overt dishonesty—on the part of the Brandens to suggest that Rand was imposing rationalistic "shoulds" on anyone. The Brandens did it to themselves, and, from the new evidence, they did it against Rand's strenuous and specific advice.

Rand does add the following "Note to page 21 of 'Notes' of 1/30/68":

> [2] (As to [Patrecia's] character: I do not know or understand her at all, which, *per se*, is a bad sign under

the circumstances (4 or five years of acquaintance). My "stomach-feeling" is: I do not trust her—I do not think that she is honest—in an inner, fundamental way—I think that she is role-playing (the "actress premise")—I think that she is self-centered in a bad sense of the word—I think that she is shallow, superficial and presumptuous, the presumptuousness consisting of her "idealism," which is unearned and unsupported conceptually or intellectually—I think that her "understanding" of [Branden] is done by [social metaphysics] so far—I think the continuation of her [3] alleged belief in openness, and of her social "act" is a bad, and probably evil, symptom— and, perhaps above all, I cannot stand people with "acts," *particularly women* with "acts": it is too clear to me that such acts come from dreadful premises.)

Rand's critics will read only jealousy here. But, in light of Rand's proven lack of jealousy in the case of Ms. Branden and the facts which demonstrate the truth behind Rand's "stomach-feelings," a different explanation is suggested.

As Branden's secret mistress for the previous four years, Patrecia is, in fact, hiding something from Rand, implicitly lying every time they meet. According to Branden's memoir, Patrecia knows about Branden's affair with Rand from the start of her own affair with Branden. (93) Rand, of course, does not enjoy the same respect from Branden.

Moreover, it is Branden's claim that Patrecia had been telling him for some time that she *literally* thought Rand to be insane. (94) This did not, of course, prevent Patrecia from continuing to actively socialize with Rand and her friends, the leaders of an intellectual movement created by someone who was "mad," nor did it prevent her from taking her professional name from one of the characters in Rand's novel, *The Fountainhead.* Apparently, these seemed to be good career-moves.

In a letter to Rand, now in the possession of the Ayn Rand Archive, dated July 22, 1967, Patrecia praises Rand for the personal advice she had provided her and asks for more "sessions" with Rand to discuss her psycho-epistemology. In another letter, dated November 22, 1967, Patrecia wrote

Rand to apologize for her behavior during a discussion of art at their last meeting, and to express her concern that Rand would justly be left with a negative impression of her.

Patrecia *was* a fraud with Rand, along the same lines as Branden. Rand's "stomach-feelings" were rather impressively accurate.

Just as Branden's skills as a psychologist served him well in maintaining his four-year deception of Rand, so Patrecia's skills as an actress must have been a similar advantage to her. Even this is something to which Rand's perceptiveness is alert.

Once more, let's try to put all of this together: at this time, Branden was still insisting to Rand that his feelings for her are romantic and those for Patrecia are definitely *not* romantic despite his secret, four-year affair with her. At the same time, he was agreeing with Patrecia about Rand's "insanity" and assuring *her* that he was trying to get out of the situation with Rand. And, meanwhile, Branden was using his former wife—including assertions of his alleged continued feelings for her—to run interference in his on-going deception of Rand.

Branden certainly used the women in his life, putting them each in a completely untenable relationship to one another, although with the willing complicity of two of them. Patrecia *had* to be a fraud in Rand's eyes. Rand could only ever perceive her as such. Barbara Branden, a trusted friend of Rand's, was asked to lie to Rand, as well.

Branden had sabotaged any possibility of a "happy ending," but he can still wonder why they all couldn't just "work things out," and blames Rand for the painful end!

Whatever her opinion of Patrecia, Rand is not asking Branden to love or not to love anyone, she is pleading with him to identify what he really wants, emotionally and intellectually. And, by now, Branden is compelled to admit his fear of being a full-fledged rationalist, a suggestion Rand initially treats with some caution.

In a note dated February 6, 1968, Rand writes:

> [1] Elaborate the element of surrender. ("All heroism is psycho-epistemological.") If you do not speak about your deepest (most personal or "subjective") emotions, you make yourself invisible and suffer from a feeling of self-suppression.

If you continue on [the] road of withdrawal, you will feel an ebbing of self-esteem, without being able to identify the cause; (then your subjective choices will fall lower and lower).

The fear of his mind (of... "rationalism") is one proof of [Branden's] mind- [2] emotion split. (Review explicitly the conscious thoughts that made him bear the [Barbara Branden] situation so long.)

In re: me. If his mistake was: "Nothing matters but one's goal," then his [psycho-epistemological] state made him, in fact, incapable of achieving a goal he really wanted—our relationship. [**Rand is still believing Branden about the things he claimed to have "wanted."**] By seeking efficacy in the wrong way, he, in fact, destroyed his efficacy. (This feeling of "If I failed in the most important relationship, lesser ones cannot matter," has a psychological base or cause, but not in the way he thinks.)

The danger sign is his indifference [3] to theory: since his problem is emotional (involving the deepest, personal, sense-of-life emotions), he is waiting for an emotional cure. This cannot be done. The problem is really intellectual—and can be solved only by intellectual means, i.e., by correcting his way of identifying his emotions and his "rational" decisions.

Objectivism holds that "free will" lies in our capacity to regulate the functions of our consciousness, that we are beings of *volitional consciousness*. For Rand, therefore, our principle *ethical* choice is "to think or not to think." In a fundamental sense, "all heroism is psycho-epistemological," according to Objectivism.

By this measure, Branden's behavior was certainly anything but "heroic." Branden seems to have realized this and expressed to Rand his own "fears" of being a "rationalist." (The "surrender" reference is, perhaps, too cryptic to interpret with confidence, but Rand appears to be suggesting that Branden "surrender" to his "deepest emotions," in this context, to *experience* them, rather than *repress* them. She is not likely to be advising Branden to *act* on undefined emotions—a policy anathema to Rand—but, she realizes, Branden first needs to *experience and identify* his emotions. Nor is it likely that Rand would ever have suggested "surrendering" reason as the only means of cognition. Rand may simply be suggesting that allowing himself to experience emotion—not a stoic fight *against* emotion—would be Branden's "heroic" choice, the one rejecting evasion.)

In the last paragraph, Rand is obviously not prescribing "rationalism," just plain, old-fashioned *rationality*.

In an entry dated, February 10, 1968, Ms. Branden can be seen giving some advice to Branden on maintaining self-esteem:

> [3] ([Barbara Branden's] theory re: [Patrecia]):
>
> [4] [**Barbara Branden's comments apparently addressed to Nathaniel Branden**] Over-all premise for therapy: regard it as a challenge (as you regard difficulties in business). This requires a firm (and objective) sense of self-esteem (start from inner feeling of innocence) [**something Branden can hardly do**].

That Ms. Branden, fully aware of Branden's relationship with Patrecia, can be floating "theories" about the situation to an ignorant Rand speaks volumes to Ms. Branden's own dishonesty in these events. Her advice to Branden (in the presence of Rand): "more will-power, Nathan!"

One must remind oneself that this advice was being addressed to a professional *psychotherapist* who should, of course, not have needed this sort of reminder. One can only stand in awe of the degree of "drift" which Branden permitted himself.

In a single-page entry dated February 6, Rand wields her pen against Branden's rationalism once more:

> In re: psycho-epistemology and sense of life. All sense of life issues (i.e., one's subconscious metaphysical fundamentals) have to be automatized. They are wide

abstractions (integrations), involved in one's every thought, emotion, action and choice—and they cannot be handled by a conscious, conceptual process in every moment or issue of one's life. Just as the reliance on one's own rational judgment (self-esteem) is automatized and one does not wonder, in any given process of thought, whether one should accept one's own judgment or that of others or pray to God for guidance—so all fundamentals of one's sense-of-life must be automatized, particularly meta-selfishness and benevolent universe (which correspond, on the conscious level, to "worthy" and "able.") (The verbal equivalent of this automatized absolute is: "I must pursue my own happiness and I am able to do it.")

It is the repression of meta-selfishness that prevents the use of one's reason in the service of one's happiness—and leads to an out-of-context, duty-oriented, anti-self [**and**] arid... "rationalism."

In this connection: the desire "to be oneself" is the desire to rely on the automatized processes of one's mind (on one's present knowledge, as against the work of seeking new knowledge.)

By now, Rand has explicitly identified one of Branden's problems as "rationalism" and, in the process, given us an elegant definition of the desire "to be oneself."

Rand's mind is the equivalent of a Magnetic Resonance Imaging device in psychological diagnosis. Even the religious nature of Branden's psychology is becoming ever more clear to Rand. In notes dated February 14, 1968, ironically, St. Valentine's Day, Rand writes:

[1] [Branden's] universe is split into three realities: 1. the "practical" world (his work)—2. the (spiritual) "intellectual" world (me)—3. The "consumption" (or "pleasure") "emotional" world (autism).

This is the Christian trichotomy: mind-body-spirit. (By "spirit" here they mean "values," i.e., emotions. They consign emotions [personal rewards] to God or the supernatural; he consigns it to his own consciousness, autistically, cut off from reality.)

(The Christian idea of "taking upon yourself the sins of others" has a frightening application to him and me: to save him from selflessness, I have to sacrifice my meta-selfishness. I hope temporarily [?])

Such "compartmentalization" is the inevitable result of rationalism and the division of the soul into emotional "wants" versus logical "shoulds." In Branden's case, Rand senses that she and Objectivism are autistically "cut off" from reality in his mind. Branden is unable to integrate his work, his intellectual values and his "pleasures" as a consequence, rendering Branden's personality similar to the classical Christian division of man into material body, "practical" reason, and abstract values.

The final comment from the above passage appears to have been the last expression for any hope for a "personal" relationship with Branden of any kind. Her concern is that this Christian-like compartmentalization has affected Branden's *ability* to make judgments—that, therefore, "his hierarchy of values" is in deep confusion. Rand continues the entry from February 14:

[2] The psychological meaning or mechanism of the "multi-universe" idea is: blocked integration. A rational mind integrates everything into one context and preserves a single hierarchy of values at all times, in all aspects of one's existence. A blocked or repressed mind cannot integrate; and, since a man cannot repress fundamental needs out of existence, he begins to integrate different aspects into different, separate contexts. (Repression prevents him from realizing that that's what he's doing; the only symptom would be inner uneasiness and unhappiness.)

That is what makes it so dreadful for me: I cannot integrate the various aspects of [Branden] with the total of my view of him; but the [3] fact is that they are not integrated in him and not integratable. Therefore, I have to regard him as still in process, and help him remove the contradictions by removing the barriers to integration. (This may be the reason why he feels he is still "in process" in regard to me: I am the symbol [or ally or "mirror"] of his mind. He senses that his mind is not fully integrated or fully in control.)

The integrating principle is, of course, meta-selfishness (since the purpose of all man's actions and goals is the achievement of his own happiness).

("Without meta-selfishness, no value-calculations are possible"—and without value-calculations [4] there can be no hierarchy of values and no integration. If a man cannot hold his values and interests hierarchically, he is at the mercy of the range of the moment, without context, and he builds up impossible inner and outer contradictions.)

(This process in [Branden] may be why he projects, out of context, such notions as "keeping me and Miss X" in his life *somehow.* He has to be brought to the realization that the choice is: me *or* Miss X., with everything it implies in the *full context* of reality [of *one* reality], then see how his emotions react to such a choice [i.e., how would he like to live without intellectual visibility].) (The mixed up sentence [5] in his draft of Part II of his article [**the specific "sentence" referred to is unknown, but Part II of Branden's article "Self-Esteem and Romantic Love" appeared in the January, 1968, edition of *The Objectivist,* an article in which the implications of the physical differences between the sexes are discussed**] may be enormously significant here—i.e., he may be moving subconsciously toward the notion that "masculine visibility" is a separate issue or faculty, [**later, he will indicate to Rand that this faculty is "physicalism"**] that one may be "visible as a man" without being fully "visible as a person"—which is the road to the opposite of his conscious sex-premises: instead of being the "highest celebration of one's own person and highest values," sex becomes a celebration of one's "sexuality," which is the lowest, physicalistic view of sex, which is sex as seen by "women chasers" and "femme fatales," sex divorced from any spiritual or intellectual values, with "sex appeal" as a separate quality or faculty.)

[**6**] (In this connection I was terribly wrong in suggesting an affair with any present "Miss X." If he succeeded in it, that would destroy his mind, in the sense of making any integration all but impossible; that would be the destruction of his rationality—and the institutionalization of a split-universe supported by growing rationalization.)...

(The danger sign here is the defiance of his own mind in the matter of: "I do not want to work on the problem.")

An automated "benevolent universe" premise would not permit a man ever to feel that reason and reality (therefore, thinking) can ever be set against his [**7**] meta-selfishness. I could (and do) feel that kind of rebellion against the demand for more thinking in regard to others; I would not feel it if I realized that the fault or trouble is primarily mine, not theirs. He must realize this fully. I did experience that "self-protective withdrawal"—and I realized that it is a state without a long-range view, i.e., without any use for one's mind or rational faculty. He has been living in that state alone for many years; hence the depression when he is alone.

If nothing else, Rand's admission about her own psychology in these notes confirm their authenticity and power as evidence.

Branden's own complaints of depression "when he is alone" are also of interest. Branden himself had long observed that being miserable when one is alone is a sure indicator of low self-esteem—it suggests that you do not like or respect the company you are keeping, i.e., *yourself.*

Rand continues to inquire whether Branden's true feelings for Patrecia are sexual in nature—as she obviously still suspects—but she is now inquiring in as "non-judgmental" and clinical a manner as one can imagine. The February 14 notes continue:

> [7] (For me)
> (In what sense does [Patrecia] "draw him to me [**i.e., Rand herself**]?" By helping [him to objectify] his masculine self-esteem—or his split universe? [To check this, ask him the nature of his feeling: sexual or emotional?] If it is the first, then it is clear why [Barbara] would have had an opposite effect.
>
> **[the following paragraph was crossed-out with a single diagonal line]**
> But if it is the second, here is a horrifying hypothesis: he gave up sex when he gave up the possibility of the ideal of full intellectual-sexual visibility, integration and happiness; [Patrecia] gave him the illusion of having a sexually-right attitude, without any intellectual base or content; his subconscious began to adopt that possibility for himself—but then, he would desperately need, as a kind of balance or counterpart or emptiness-feeling compensation, an intellectual-spiritual relationship with me, in order that he may live in two separate realities. This, of course, is impossible—and would be disaster for all three. As far as I am concerned I will not be Cyrano to a brainless Christian.)

Again, one must be impressed both by the honesty of Rand's sentiments and the power of her insight. Crossed out as inapplicable when she discovers that this doesn't name Branden's problem—perhaps when she discovered that Branden's "sexual freeze" was a fraud—she is nonetheless on the right track. Only, such impotence is actually a more benign view of Branden's character than will turn out to be the actual case.

The comparison of her own situation to that in *Cyrano de Bergerac* is, of course, apt as well, and in itself shows Rand's realism and sensitivity to the actual circumstances, including her age.

In a fascinating but brief note on small white square of paper, dated "February 15, 1968" Rand writes the following:

> (Also: remove fear of impossible contradictions and "traps"—of ultimatums to reality or from reality.)

It seems that Rand was trying her best to make it *easier* for Branden to accept *whatever* it was that he was having trouble confronting. She set out to "remove" his "fears" of "the impossible" and "ultimatums." Branden has apparently sensed a "trap" laid by Rand's demand that he choose between her and "Miss X."

Branden, once again, punted.

Rand's reaction was not moralistic, but sympathetic and sensitive. She was trying to "ease up." But no attitude from Rand, neither decisive ultimatums nor patient understanding, can inspire honesty from Branden. It was this very patience, sympathy, and sensitivity that Branden was relying upon, in fact—and abusing.

In a similarly sketchy note, dated "February 17, 1968" appears the following:

> (Step outside the square in re: betrayal of your values. The opposite is true. Why a social metaphysician would not have [Branden's] problem.)

At this point, Rand was telling Branden that he was *not* "betraying his values." While Rand had previously suggested this in her earlier notes, it is clear that this was *something Branden was confessing to Rand*. Branden, it seems, was the first to mention this fear. Branden also appears to be the first to mention his fear of being a "social metaphysician"—another concern which Rand, at this point, was *actively discouraging*.

Rand's sympathy for Branden during this very period is remarkably generous. She would give Branden the following advice, advice she gave herself. In notes also dated "February 17," Rand says:

> [3] Accepting a view of yourself as seen by others (as maltreated by others—i.e., self-pity) is a form of surrendering the world to others, i.e., surrendering the most important part, the center of the world, yourself (your self-image). It means: granting metaphysical rightness or potency to others.

Since both of the Brandens were complaining of "romantic rejection" (from each other) at this time, it is unclear for whom the following single-page note dated "February 17," was intended, or if it was a note for her own, more personal reflection:

> Romantic rejection is painful because it contradicts and violates "visibility," one's view of the objectivity of one's own value, it projects the wrong "feedback." But romantic self-assertiveness must come from happiness [from self-enjoyment], never from suffering [i.e., bitterness].)

It is on this basis alone that Rand will not accept any kind of "forced" affection from Branden, love must never "come from suffering" or "bitterness," only joy.

In notes titled, "Session of Wed., March 6, 1968: Key Points," we find the following:

> [4] Issue of identifying [Branden's] needs in past emotional situations: he finds his mind stopped, unable to get anywhere with this assignment. We identified only that he does not think in terms of "his idea of love," but in terms of "what viewpoint is rationally possible." This needs further discussion.

Branden senses that Rand is on the right track: she is simply applying Branden's own previously stated desire to be a certain "kind of man" to the issue of love. Branden recoils and denies this as convincingly as he can. But Rand seems not to have been distracted by such denials.

Branden appears to have been aware of the fact that his own uses of humor were often inappropriate—even a tool for evasion. Rand continues:

> [4] Issue of "seriousness." [Branden] has to remind himself that he "is here, now and in reality." Humor or forced cheerfulness as opposite of "seriousness." (I told him: "Courage does not consist of evading the existence of danger.")

> [5] Issue of reality (connected with above). He identified that his form of repression (ignoring the reality of negative emotions) is, in essence, as bad as any other form of escape from reality. "It is weakness." (I said that it may not have started as weakness, but it becomes that once he identifies it, if he continues it.) He made the mistake, in childhood, of regarding the evaluatively unimportant as the unreal.

Rand is constantly having to combat what she has begun to concede are Branden's "rationalist" tendencies. She writes:

> [5] [Branden] asked whether it was wrong to identify various issues at random, somewhat chaotically; I said it was all right—so long as it does not become a means of escaping integration.

Ever since the psychotherapeutic technique of "word association" became a household word, psychotherapists have used a variety of "random association" or other "stream of consciousness" techniques to bypass repression and other defense mechanisms erected to "protect" the mind from facing some painful truth. That Branden has never queried Rand about its propriety until now is somewhat surprising. It appears to reveal a Branden unable to think outside of a rigid box—that "square" outside of which Rand is urging Branden to think.

Or, as Rand implies, Branden could simply have been trying to avoid the task of integration for himself and present a moving target to Rand's mind.

By mid-March, Rand was clearly no longer harboring even a remote illusion about the possibility of a continued romance. Nor does Rand assume that she and Branden share "identical" views on the subject of romantic love as she once did. She is now reconsidering their entire personal relationship.

In an entry dated "3/18/68" Rand jots down the following:

> [2] What is the [psycho-epistemological] mechanism that made him drop context in a matter which was so important to him? (Ask: what was the status of our relationship in his mind during the past 8 or 10 years?)

Rand now begins to wonder: what are Branden's actual views on the subject of love? In a separate, single-page note—ambiguous and brief, reading like a thought in mid-stream—also dated "3/18/68", we read as follows:

> But "spiritual closeness" was exactly what we never had. If it was not romantic love, what was missing? And: what *is* his idea of romantic love and *of* [the] *proper woman*? What is he afraid of?

> He does not want me as part of his life (as "a way of life.") Why?

By late March, Branden's mask is clearly slipping some more. In notes dated "March 20, 1968," Rand elaborates significantly on the issue of Branden's role-playing:

> [1] Role-playing. We assumed that role-playing applied only to unhappy emotions, as "a last resort against suffering." I think that it might apply to everything, across the board—to the whole emotional realm. I think [Branden] might have been role-playing the part of philosopher-psychologist and the relationship with me.

Rand now no longer doubts that Branden's values differ significantly from what he had always claimed, not only in the romantic realm, but also in his career and "across the board." The original motives for his love were never real—it really was "role-playing." Rand has turned another significant corner in her understanding of Mr. Branden.

And Rand has long stopped believing Branden's denials—at least on the subject of his psychology.

Directly beneath this entry, we find the following:

> [1] (The above was discussed over the phone, 3-20-68. Further elaborations: only action has personal meaning and pleasure for him. [Branden] reverses cause and effect: the goal is only an excuse to undertake the action, i.e., the end is the means to the process of enacting the means which are the end, for him. In this context, I would be the symbol of that which gives meaning to his action, the psychology-philosophy goal which is not his actual goal (since he does not apply it to himself), but is only the excuse for his action.) (Action both mentally, as theoretician and, existentially, as entrepreneur.)

> (He denies this. It does not "ring true" to him.)

Rand is beginning to identify that Branden's "actions" are *all* "role-playing" and that she and Objectivism are just symbols for his motives, not the real motives themselves, i.e., he *is* a fraud in his professional as well as his personal life.

Rand dispassionately notes his denial without comment; this doesn't "ring true" to Branden. Of course, if his memoir is any indication, *he actually knows that Rand is spot-on.*

Score another for the hopelessly blind Rand.

For Rand, a pattern is starting to develop involving several of Branden's character traits.

The notes from March 20 continue as follows:

> [2] *Other hypotheses made by me yesterday. The "materialism" issue.* He hates his practical activities (i.e., having to deal

with people) more than he admits to himself; this is made possible by repression. But since all of the concretes of his life are in that realm, he was forced eventually to seek pleasures in that realm. (His pursuit of luxury as the "only reward" he can get from the world—the issue of his apartment—his projection of the activities he would share with a "Miss X" of his own age, such as nightclubs and trips, which he does not actually enjoy.) In this case, I would be the only remnant of the ideal, of the world he [3] had wanted to exist, but now regarded as impossible; therefore, our relationship would be consigned to unreality. (This sort of development would be connected with "perceptual deprivation," i.e., the absence of concretes representing one's value-abstractions.) (Example: man who would take pleasure in training a parrot (conventional pleasures)—in a concentration camp, where it would be the only type of pleasure available.)

This "materialism" issue is not merely Rand's theory. In the notes from July, we will see that Branden not only admitted to this, he was providing psychological *explanations* for this "materialism."

In the above passage, the "age-issue" has even been broached by this time, in form of the "Miss X" issue, for she is now a "Miss X" of "his own age." Rand has not "exploded" with rage but has accepted the issue as a natural one. In this passage, the rationality of the point is simply assumed.

Rand's "March 20" notes continue:

[3] The "self-protection" premise. If, in his selfless period, his attitude was that his emotions do not matter—then now, his rebellion consists of feeling that only his emotions matter (which is only the other side of the same error). If before, he did not consider the facts which caused his negative emotions, and dealt with them by repressing the emotions—so now, he does not consider the facts which cause his emotions, but proposes to seek or accept only that which arouses "acceptable" emotions in him. In both cases, reality has to adjust to his emotions.

Rand was just one of those bits of reality that wouldn't "adjust."

In a very brief, single-page note dated "May 14, 1968" Rand jots down the following comment of Branden's: "I should look at this as his post-"Atlas" period."

Branden was then confronted with a measure of real-world success, and this comparison by itself indicates the remarkable extremes to which Branden was willing to go in order to avoid telling Rand the truth. Notice how frequently these notes speak of "concentration camp" victims and "war-wounded" men. Branden appears to have been complaining of very serious neuroses—especially given the actual circumstances of his life.

The religious and rationalistic nature of Branden's psychology was becoming ever more obvious to Rand, for on the same date she tantalizes us with this brief, single-page entry:

> ([Branden's] two views, "woman who needs him" and "goddess," are views of himself. Let's be atheists.)

These two phrases are in quotes, and they are called "his views." It is safe to credit Branden with this self-identification of his "two views" of women. Applied to his real circumstances, Rand is the "goddess" in his mind and "Patrecia" is the "woman who needs him." These are *Branden's* terms. Whatever Branden was neurotically getting from women, it was not the love of a spiritual equal.

Rand was a religious figure to Branden, by his own statement, "a goddess," unreal and disconnected from everything of this earth. So were the intellectual values she represented.

In notes dated "May 15, 1968" Rand again reveals to us what Branden was telling her at the time:

> [1] The crucial (to me) points of [Branden's] identifications (discussed on ride to country): Immediately after [the] Toronto car ride [**when their romantic feelings for one another were first identified**], he repressed the intensity of his feelings for me.

Can you believe this guy? His attempt to placate Rand has Branden actually saying that his feelings for Rand are "*so intense*" that he was compelled to repress them! In an important sense, no doubt, Rand was "too much" for him, but Branden's excessive toadying apparently knows no bounds.

Rand continues:

> [1] The repression caused "psycho-epistemological helplessness"—and he threw the [psycho-epistemological] burden on me.

> His love for me undercut his self-esteem.

Branden is suggesting that Rand is the cause not only of his repression and lack of self-esteem, but also of his *irresponsibility*. We also hear, for the first time, the complaint against Rand's "moralism." Pushed against the reality of his own lies and evasions, Branden says that his fear of Rand's moral anger and condemnation has worsened his problem.

Nonetheless, he complains to Rand that:

> [2] His fear of my moral condemnation or suspiciousness augmented his problem. I was "unpredictable" to [Branden] because, by his [psycho-epistemology], he could not tell when I would explode at him. (I.e., he understood what I complained about or blamed him for, but was unable to correct his behavior.)

Of course, Rand has every right to be angry and suspicious—she is, after all, being lied to and manipulated—and there is nothing "unpredictable" about her potential reaction. Even Branden tells Rand that he "understood" Rand's specific "complaints," every time.

Ms. Branden now chimes in with her agreement: it was a kind of "Goddess" issue that had affected her, too. Branden was her own "Kantian God." Rand writes the following in her notes from May 15:

> [2] "The Kantian Goddess" issue, applying also to Barbara.
> (*I* told her "she must love Nathaniel.")

In this short but fascinating note, Rand has faithfully recorded Ms. Branden's own version of Branden's latest complaint—Rand had "told her" who she "must" love—Branden. In effect, it was her "duty," an ethical concept Rand rejected (95) and which is closely associated with the teachings of Immanuel Kant (1724-1804), the philosopher whose ideas Rand most vehemently rejected.

Kant was a philosophical "subjectivist," for he had proposed a "revolution" in our understanding of human knowledge. Rather than our knowledge conforming to the external objects of our awareness, Kant proposed that we look at the objects as having "to conform" to our means of knowledge. The "categories," the forms in which our consciousness must perceive things, in effect, *create* the objects we perceive—not any external world. Thus, reality *in itself* is perpetually beyond the reach of empirical science, according to Kant.

Kant said that his goal was to demonstrate the limitations of *reason* in order to "make room" for *faith*—which he (correctly) felt was under attack from Enlightenment secularism and science.

In ethics, Kant held that the consequences of our actions—their "performance or effects"—are irrelevant to questions of good and evil. The "good" is good *in itself*, and definitely *not* because it accomplishes anything—or, as Rand would say, Kant believed that the "good" is "intrinsic." For Kant, that intrinsic "good" consists of one's noble intention to do one's duty regardless of personal interests or any other consequences. (96)

In short, Kant's philosophy puts reality-in-itself outside of human perception and science and makes the "good" independent of human needs and goals. Across the board, this is the very opposite of Rand's "philosophy for living on earth."

We have already seen how Branden viewed any divorce—and, by implication, any mistake in knowledge or judgment, or even any process of discovery—as being "unstylized." For Branden, as for Kant, context is irrelevant, and hence, Rand's previous term "Kantian stylized universe," to which Branden eagerly identified himself, has now been identified as the "Kantian Goddess" issue.

Thus, the "Kantian Goddess" issue must somehow mean a view that places one's values—especially romantic values—outside of the context of individual needs and circumstances. It suggests that "love" is being treated as an "intrinsic absolute," not to be sullied with practical or personal considerations, and, perhaps, not to be given earthly expression. In effect, a love *worse* than Plato's famous "Platonic" kind of other-worldly love—at least Plato nominally took human goals and interests into account, however much he disparaged the material world.

Dispassionately, Rand notes the Brandenian accusation against her: Rand allegedly "told" Ms. Branden that she "must" love Branden, just as, it is now alleged, she implicitly told Branden that he "must" love Rand. Such a "must" in the love department, of course, ignores the individual's actual context and whether the "intellectual" values behind that "must" are the operative values in a person's soul or not. Such a "Kantian" kind of love would indeed be an "intrinsic absolute," one which ignores the Brandens' actual contexts.

Neither of the Brandens means that Rand had literally "told" them to love anyone. It was Rand's *philosophy* and Rand's o*wn passionately held values* doing all the "telling." But, of course, such a "Kantian" view of love was the very opposite of Rand's *philosophy* and *passionately held values.*

In light of Rand's repeated efforts to get Branden simply to *name* his emotions and values—and in the context of both Brandens having lied about, faked and aped their values, including their esthetic tastes—fully suppressing their "real selves" in order to be "good" Objectivists—this accusation is grossly unfair. *They* were the Kantians, as they admitted to Rand, imposing on themselves intrinsic absolutes.

From the evidence of the journals, it is clear that Rand was forever attempting to get Branden to *stop* acting in an overly "cerebral" way, to *stop* "repressing" his true emotions, to *stop* treating Objectivism "autistically," to find out "what he really wants" and "what inspires him," so that he can end all of this "psychological altruism." Rand was perfectly accepting of individual context, and it was the Brandens who had systematically deceived Rand as to their true values, their own contexts.

"Let's be atheists," Rand insists, meaning that such "worship" and "other-worldly" affection had no appeal for Rand. To Ms. Branden it means: if you love him, love *him*, not some idealized "abstraction"—not some "God." The rationalism here is not Rand's, but a feeble projection of the Brandens' own distorted approach to Objectivism.

But by now, Rand is not buying any of these allegations. Once

Branden knows that he cannot think straight—and even *why* he cannot think straight—why does it go on and on? Branden appears to be evading—again.

We read in these same notes from May 15:

> [3] My own question re: "psycho-epistemological helplessness"—he is repeating the same wrong at present, by throwing the [psycho-epistemological] burden on me, in regard to how I am to act toward him.
>
> He escaped from me to business, because he could not stand his own [psycho-epistemological] state. How does this differ, in principle, from men who avoid [4] fear-producing situations for the same reason?

Between February and May another change has occurred: Rand is now willing to accept Branden's complaint that he has "betrayed his values." She is no longer reluctant to agree with Branden on this point. Of course, this still dubiously credits Branden with actually sharing Rand's values. She continues:

> [4] (I think what made his betrayal of values possible was the conviction that he was doing it in the name of the highest values: creativeness and [the] battle against evil. This element of moral idealism was absent in men of similar problems, but lower stature. Yet, the problem is the same.)

Rand has been deeply hurt by the charge of being "moralistic." Again, it is Rand's self-esteem that sees through this rationalization at once. They do not question the truth of Rand's specific moral judgments, but, rather, complain of her "moralism" *as such*. Their assertion can only mean one of two things: a confession of guilt or an expression of *moral envy*, the resentment against Rand's own moral character.

Rand, still unwilling to attribute an existential guilt to the Brandens opts for the latter view. In these same notes from May 15, she writes:

[5] The most awful issue to me is [**the accusation of being**] "moralistic": he (and perhaps [Barbara Branden]) blame me for being blameless, i.e., moral and rational. This, to me, is penalizing me for my virtues because they are my virtues. (Had I been less, he wouldn't have been afraid of me. Even the present fear is an escape from his actual guilt: the [psycho-epistemological] betrayal of his values.)

This is the charge that stings the most—the one the Brandens saved up for such a special occasion as the obfuscation of their own dishonesty. The fact that this charge is "the most awful" to Rand is itself at odds with the Brandens' accounts.

The end is near.

Unfortunately not reproduced here are the short notes on Mr. Branden's psychology dated June 5, 1968. However, they largely repeat the opinions we have already seen expressed in these notes. (The notes were given by Rand to Ms. Branden, and they were later auctioned, although copies of them are now also kept at the Ayn Rand Archive.)

There do not appear to be journal entries during the rest of June and the notes only pick up again in early July. Fragmentary entries from the month of July suggest that there were several disturbing events in the previous month: Branden's continued "inappropriate humor," his continued emotional "disappearance," his "bad mood," and an unknown "remark about [Rand's] preferences which hurt [**her**] badly."

It also appears from such snippets that in early July, Rand had telephone conversations with Branden which were so disturbing to her that she once again took up her powerful pen. Branden is blaming his "mood" on his (bogus) "sex problem" and has vigorously returned to the belief in his self-diagnosed "autism."

But Rand has crossed the Rubicon. She no longer assumes that Branden is being honest about his values, beliefs and motives. Branden is now definitely *not* the man she had once thought him to be.

She is now convinced that he is *immoral.*

In the entries dated "July 1, 1968," we read:

> [1] Today's Telephone Conversation
> [Branden] cannot work on his personal-realm [psycho-epistemology] [**as opposed to his "work realm" psycho-epistemology recalling the "Christian trichotomy" suggested in the February 14 notes**] because his anguish over the sex problem keeps pulling his mind to this problem—and cannot get rid of the feeling that he has to discover some one specific "conflict" or premise which underlies it and caused it.

Branden continues to complain of a "sex problem," the unending headache of 1968, which is "blocking" his still passionate love for Rand. He appears to Rand to be waiting for the mystical insight that will move him from his passive—if not catatonic—indecision. But Rand is no longer sympathetic to his plight.

Rand continues in these July 1 notes:

> [1] By "work," he meant fully and properly; he said it requires an enormous effort every day to force his mind to work on [psycho-epistemology]. Which means that he is not sold on it and is not motivated.
>
> Which means that even so horrible a discovery as his "autism" does not motivate him to correct it. (What, then, is the status of his mind, of reason, in regard to his personal-realm [psycho-epistemology]?)
>
> [2] In spite of the urgency of the problem, he keeps busy with other, lesser issues, any issue, rather than work on the problem. ...
>
> (*My problem re: all of the above.* I do not understand how a mind can simultaneously regard a problem as urgently important—and keep off it, and engage in trivial activities.

Existentially, it is a totally *unstylized* way of living.)

[3] *In regard to me*:
He claims to know what suffering he is causing me—*yet it does not motivate him to keep context in his mind in relation to me.* (Neither does his love motivate him to keep context.) Therefore, all these years and no matter what importance I have for him, intellectually, neither my value nor my pain, neither positive incentives nor negative, can make him be concerned with me enough to preserve context. (To the best of my knowledge, one preserves context in any issue one regards as important. Assuming even that he does, but is blocked—it still means that in reality, in fact, his [psycho-epistemology] is such that I am of no importance to him. And he has no real desire, no motivation, to correct his [psycho-epistemology].)

[4] He knew that he had broken our agreement about the definition of our *provisional* relationship [**reference unknown**]—yet he said and did nothing about it. He knew that trouble was coming sooner or later—but he let it go, counting only on my enduring the torture or breaking down. This is decision making by "attrition." (He did the same in regard to [Barbara Branden].) Yet this did not motivate him to work on his psycho-epistemology.

Whatever else is innocent, *this* is *immoral.*

Unfortunately, but not unexpectedly, Mr. Branden has not informed the readers of his memoir about any "provisional relationship" Rand had apparently worked out with Branden in 1968. To have revealed this would probably have required that he also reveal to us precisely how he "violated" it, as Rand here suggests that he had confessed to doing.

Remember that Branden has a vested interest in the notion that it was "romance or nothing" with Rand, that he had no choice, that things would have ended the same way no matter what, etc., etc. Any acceptance by Rand of a "provisional" relationship tends to contradict this portrait of the situation.

Another curiously new item of information comes in the very next entry:

> [4] (Also, he is thinking of suspending "The F." [**This is certainly a reference to the planned stage production of *The Fountainhead*.**] It may have a good motive—or a very bad one. My stomach-feeling is this last. In one form or another, it is [a] retreat from his problem—and resignation. I don't like the tone in which he said that the problem interferes with the function of his mind. It was "the achiever" speaking.)

Notice that Rand is now no longer doubting—or apologizing for—her negative guesses about Branden. Observe, also, Branden's own *continued* complaints about "the functioning of his mind," i.e., his psycho-epistemology.

But, this time, Rand's insistence on answers has finally caused Branden to come to some decision, it seems. Branden is now assuming a new role, "the achiever," perhaps evidenced by something decisive in his attitude—for the first time.

And we can easily see why. Rand is convinced that she is dealing with *dishonesty* by now—and she is making this clear to him. Most of the former sympathy with his assumed motives is now gone. Rand's foot has been—squarely and unmistakably—put down.

In these same "July 1" notes, she writes:

> [5] *My Conclusion:*
>
> I would have believed him about his inner state and the sincerity of his efforts to solve the problem *only if he devoted all of his time to it, except time for his writing*—and suspended *all* other concerns and activities, except lectures (i.e., earning a living).

This is my view of how a man who shares my philosophy and my sense of life, would act if he had so serious a problem. It would mean that the problem does not involve and incapacitate his total mind and person.

But a man who would live and act as he does, in the presence of that problem, is [6] outside of anything I can conceive of as possible to a *basically rational* man.

Intentions do not alter facts. Inner premises unexpressed in or contradicted by actions are worse than nonexistent. A man who knows that he is torturing the one person he regards as ideal (according to his own values, judgment and sense of life)—yet is able to ignore it mentally and to go swimming, shooting or keeping trivial social appointments (out of "politeness" (!)), is *not* stylized and *not* my kind of man.

If he acts, *in reality*, as a vulgar, unthinking "materialist"— of what [7] importance are his "spiritual" values? It is worse than if he had no values—because, if he has, his actions are treason.

It is his form of "consolation" and escape—daily escape—that I find horrifying. It is the conflict between his intellectual values and his actual, daily concerns that is becoming unspeakable. How can a hero sell out for trivia?

If he literally did nothing and was paralyzed...—it would have been better; more understandable, more consistent. But this, his way, is a descent into crass materialism, made possible by rationalizations—therefore, a gradual destruction of his mind and values.

[8] I have a stomach-feeling that I *know* the sort of person he is becoming—but I cannot describe it. I have the feeling

that the secret lies in what he feels in regard to the theater: at auditions, etc. If he focused on his inner state and identified it, he would know it, too. (As part, but not all of it, the theater is an institutionalized form of autism.)

Branden's new more "social" attitude *was* focused on his new "favorite" activity, the theater project. Branden tells us that it was his new mistress Patrecia, an actress, who had "reawakened" his love of the theater. That Branden, role-playing his life with Rand, should find such comfort in the theater is, indeed, worthy of note. Rand's "stomach-feelings" are right on target, as usual.

All of the "role-playing," all of the "wheeling-dealing," and even his friendship with Patrecia, are now centered around this project. Rand, the novelist, sees the eloquent symbolism: the theater is itself a form of "institutionalized autism."

The fabric of Branden's deceptions has worn so thin that it simply will not take another washing through the Rand spin-cycle.

On "July 2, 1968," this is Rand's only entry:

> [1] Today's ([**tele**]phone) conversation infinitely better in general tone and manner.
>
> [Branden] made two very important [psycho-epistemological] identifications: 1. He was somewhat off (or out of control) in yesterday's conversation, because he was torn between concern over our relationship and the need to understand the intellectual aspects of the conversation. He said this was an instance of a state where he feels that "too much is coming at him." 2. He identified the [psycho-epistemology] of the... incident [**an unidentifiable incident involving the stage production of *The Fountainhead***]: he was thinking about our problem on his way down; since I was not alone and we could not discuss it, he decided, in effect, that "this period of time does not matter"; therefore, it was actually chance that determined what he would talk about. [**This "incident"**

appears to have been one during which Rand took exception to the content and/or the method of Branden's conversation. In her later essay dated July 4, she will refer to this incident as the one which "broke her back."]

[2] This is a very important [psycho-epistemological] lead. I pointed out to him that this is a form of the "drunken driving" [**premise, defined below**]. But there is more to it: I must think out the matter of impatience, which, I have sensed before, is a crucial issue in the [psycho-epistemological] errors of good repressors.

This fascinating reference to impatience as a "defense mechanism" employed by "good repressors" is the most sympathy for Branden Rand can muster at this point. She is still unaware of the degree of his conscious dishonesty.

On the next day, July 3, Branden would present to Rand a "paper" admitting to Rand that the age-difference did matter to him, in fact, that it had been bothering him—in contradiction to his elaborate protests to the contrary—for some time, that he had lied to Rand—in a most manipulative way—about his feelings for the last *several years*. In that paper, Branden apparently attributed the "age" issue to something he called "physicalism." It is unclear from either Rand's notes, or Branden's memoir, whether he ever provided an explanation for his multi-year dishonesty on this issue in that paper, though it seems unlikely.

The journal entries for July 3 appear to have been written *before* Rand had received this paper from Branden. In an entry dated "July 3, 1968," and titled "Additional thoughts on above," Rand only seems to have some new thoughts upon reviewing her notes from July 1 and 2 (above).

We read:

[2] In re: "drunken driver." [Branden] coined the expression to mean "a man who acts on his emotions." [**This recalls his later expression, "the art of living consciously."**] In his own case, he was a man who *repressed* his emotions, so he might think [3] that this

represents the opposite. Actually, it is merely the other side of the same [psycho-epistemological] method: when he represses emotions, he represses values, i.e., his mind's value-premises and judgments, and, therefore, he cannot keep context. The dreadful thing is that he becomes worse than an "emotionalist": if his actions are determined by sheer chance, he is, technically, a whim-worshipper, who has nothing to gain from his momentary whims and who achieves nothing but destruction. Whatever the reason of that state, the wider meaning of a "drunken driver" is: a man who acts without knowing what he is doing.

(An "emotionalist" is better, i.e., closer to reality, in the sense that he runs blindly after what he believes are his values, whatever they might be, rational or irrational. But [Branden] runs blindly away from his [4] values, since his state is caused by repressing, i.e., suspending and negating the existence of his values; therefore, it is those he values most that will necessarily be the ones he hurts or destroys.)

July 3 was also a day of "discussion," as we will see, and on July 4, Rand returned to her journal to write the single longest piece in this collection of notes, a clear response to his "paper" so extensive that Rand first separately outlined her thoughts. This outline is so perfectly recapitulated within the text that it is not reproduced here.

It was written with unusual care and depth in comparison to the other entries, and, it seems, Rand intended this to be read by others, such as the Brandens and, perhaps, Allan Blumenthal, the psychiatrist and friend whom the notes confirm Rand had brought into the situation at this time.

This essay is also the most detailed statement of Rand's revised position on Nathaniel Branden. It must be borne in mind that this was written *before* Rand had learned of Branden's four-and-a-half year-old affair with Patrecia. However, its diagnoses and insights are still largely valid despite this fact. This, too, is something of a tribute to Objectivism and to Rand's powerful mind.

Among the important changes still to take place in Rand's mind involve her opinion of Ms. Branden, for whom Rand was still (unwittingly) exhibiting an overly generous sympathy.

Rand's anger at Branden, however, is evident in these pages, and although she has long abandoned any hope for a romance with Branden, this wound has been painfully reopened by the discovery that *for several years* their relationship had been a prolonged fraud. Rand's anger is also, in part, intellectual: Branden is resorting to rationalizations *completely inconsistent and outside the context of Branden's own psychological theories.* He had committed this rationalization to paper, but, unfortunately, no copy of this is known by Rand's estate to have survived. (She may have returned her own copy, perhaps annotated, to Branden.)

Rand's extensive reaction to Branden's "paper" is here presented, without significant interruption:

[1] *July 4, 1968*
Yesterday's discussion

1. *His basic premise.* He said (for the first time) *that in his early childhood he blamed himself for his inability to understand the irrationality of the people around him—and he wondered what was wrong with him.* This is the same kind of pattern as the example, in his article, of the fear of dogs in children. [**A reference to an example used in Branden's article, "Self-Esteem," Part II,** *The Objectivist*, **April, 1967, to illustrate a child's early response to fear.**]

Apparently, what he feared was the state of mind which his self-blame induced in him, the sense of a lack of efficacy, i.e., a loss of self-esteem. Thereafter, he did not face the fear and correct it, but spent his life repressing it and avoiding the necessity of thinking about people. By now, this is an in-built part of his sense of life. It is probably the cause of his "invisibility" premise.

(I have *underlined in red* his statements; the rest is my conclusions, which I told him.) [**The red underlines**

are represented in the italics following the number 1, above.]

[2] 2. *Personal relationships.* He said that his protracted refusal to think about his problems in personal relationships (both in re: to [Barbara Branden] and to me) was caused by the fact that he felt dimly that if he thought of it all the way down, he would lose the relationship—because *he* would break it off. He *did not* state why. This seemed to be a consequence of point 1.

3. The post-"Atlas" period (post 1957). He said that before the publication of *Atlas Shrugged*, he had believed that he was doomed to invisibility in the personal realm; after the publication, he began to believe that he was also doomed to invisibility in the intellectual realm. This meant that he could expect no pleasure or rewards in his career, and that the only pleasure he could have was the pleasure of the process of writing, which, he said, was intensified during this period. Also, this made him believe that the only pleasure possible in today's culture was the immediate, the now, the range-of-the-moment. This [3] was the start of his trend toward *materialism*: his attraction to material luxury, his feeling that money is the only thing he can get out of this culture. He said this in answer to [Barbara Branden's] observation that he got no pleasure out of his hectic business activities (what I call his "wheeling-dealing"). I asked him whether he had concluded, in effect, that the process of doing business had to give him pleasure, as his only reward—on the same premise as the process of writing. He said, yes.

4. *Issue of me.* I told him that perhaps I was not too much for him in a vacuum (in the abstract, as two personalities regarded by themselves, outside existence), but I *was* too much for him existentially, in reality—because he did not

know how to integrate or apply his values to reality or how to live by his values. *He seemed to agree.* (I did not tell him then, but realized later, that *this* is the exact opposite of his "stylized universe" premise. Also, this means that the degree of his love or the intensity [4] of his valuing would be the degree of danger to the relationship in reality; which means that *he was penalizing me for my virtues.* Also, this point raises the frightening question: if a man consigns his values to an autistic private world, *by what is he guided in actual reality?*)

5. The "stylized universe." [Branden] had identified some time ago that what he meant by the "stylized universe" was a life lived exclusively according to one's own values and in one's full control. Yesterday, he indicated how he actually thought of this premise in practice: he thought, in effect, that one determines in advance, as an out-of-context absolute, what is "desirable" in life or "stylized"—a kind of disconnected series of "intrinsic" absolutes, which one is then to achieve, regardless of what one feels or wants, regardless of whether it is in one's exclusive power or not. For instance, he had thought that an ideal [5] form of love was a single, monogamous marriage—therefore, he resisted the realization that his marriage had failed, because he regarded this as his failure to lead a "stylized" life. I asked him whether he regarded Rearden's life [**Hank Rearden is a hero in** *Atlas Shrugged* **who divorces his wife**] as "unstylized" because of the failure of his marriage. He agreed emphatically that he had always regarded it that way. He compared Rearden's situation—the discovery that he had chosen the wrong woman—to the position of a writer who discovers that his past work is bad or wrong, and who is ashamed of it; he said that such a writer's position was a horror. I told him that this amounted to a "Kantian stylized universe": a series of intrinsic moral absolutes to which men had to conform, regardless of context, personal

choice or circumstances. He agreed very emphatically: the words "Kantian stylized universe" seemed to strike him very strongly—he said they named something important in him. (I did not have time to discuss it [6] further, and did not tell him that this could be the cause of his forced 'role-playing' in regard to his actual life and his personal values.) (But "role playing" was mentioned, in another context, and he said that this may be true of him, but then it means a different category of role-playing than what he had originally meant by that term.)

6. *His attitude toward women in general.* He said that he felt fear of becoming attracted to some woman who had no great stature or value, because of what this would "prove" about him (about his own character). This fear had been in his mind for some years past, in connection with me, and was very intensified in the last 5 months, causing a worsening of his sexual freeze. [**Notice that Rand still believes him to have been "sexually frozen" and celibate during this period.**](This is very significant in connection with preceding point 5. Also, it seems to indicate that his love for [7] me may have been "role-playing" from the start. I told him that his was the premise of using love as a means to an end, rather than an end in itself—i.e., as a "proof" of one's own value or self-esteem, rather than its expression.)

7. *His view of love.* In connection with preceding point 6. He realized that if he fell in love with a right woman in the future (a woman he valued seriously or regarded as important to him), "it would be like a *prison*." (This last is verbatim; the word is significant.) (I do not know whether this is the right view of love perverted by the Kantian "metaphysical necessity" premise into a "duty" and, therefore, self-destroying, by becoming a duty instead of a free, personal choice—or whether the "Kantian duty"

premise is a screen to hide from himself a repressed desire for a purely physicalistic, value-less, mindless sex. [Barbara Branden] must check on this: it is dreadfully important.)

[8] 8. *His reaction to emergencies.* He said that he felt a sexual desire for me in emergencies (not exclusively then, but almost always then), such as during our violent quarrels (he felt it *even yesterday*), but he could not maintain it consistently in normal or or daily life. I said that this might mean that he feels at home in a "malevolent universe," but not in happier times. (I am not at all certain of what it actually means—but I think that this has some connection with point 4, and again raises the question of what happens to his values in actual, daily life.)

[9] My conclusions:
My over-all conclusion is that there is something horrifyingly wrong and bad in him—and that all the points listed above are only random symptoms, not basic causes. There is something horrible at the root, if it produced these sort of symptoms in a man of his intelligence and knowledge.

Whatever part of it all might be subconscious and due merely to repression, I sense very strongly the presence of *conscious dishonesty.* The best evidence of this is his evasion of the question of why he let himself drift for so long and did not try to think about his problems. He answered that he felt that discussions of his problems were useless and beside the point, because he felt that there was some crucial element in his mind which was repressed and which made thinking futile or extremely difficult. [Barbara Branden] said that, as a psychologist, [**Nathaniel Branden**] knew that this was knowledge—that the presence of such a repression should be the beginning of thinking, not the end. [10] He did not answer.

The horrifying and incomprehensible thing to me is the fact that whenever we identified (now or in the past) some actual or suspected premise in him which was a total contradiction or opposite of his conscious convictions, some evil which he consciously professed to despise—it left him completely indifferent. He did not pursue it, he simply dropped it, it did not arouse him or motivate him to work on his problems and to prove or disprove the suspicion. *This cannot be unconscious. This is conscious evasion and conscious immorality.*

This indicates an overwhelming inner indifference to his own conscious, rational convictions—it undercuts *the total of his philosophy*, the total of the *intellectual* content of his mind. The complete split between his conscious knowledge and his emotions or inner self, his [11] inability or unwillingness to apply his knowledge to himself, are [**appalling?**] I have observed this type of inability in my "clients," [**an apparent reference to the friends whom Rand had counseled informally over the years**] when they regarded some problem as hopeless and were psycho-epistemologically unable to apply their knowledge. But they did not ignore their problems: they admitted that the problems undercut their self-esteem, and they were pathetically eager to grasp at any lead that might help them to solve their problems; even when they were mentally passive, their problems were a constant, live, painful presence in their minds. [Branden] is different: with an incomparably greater knowledge and mental power than theirs, he refused to acknowledge his problems even to himself, to take them seriously or to pursue leads to their solution, even when the leads were suspicions of some immoral premise which should have been intolerable to his self-esteem. He maintained [12] a stubbornly closed wall between his mind and any discussion of his problems; he maintained the appearance and the verbal claim of an unbreached self-esteem—which is rationally impossible to a fully honest mind in this state.

This makes me certain that his self-esteem is not merely breached, but is so undercut as to be on the way to complete destruction (unless he changes drastically, fundamentally and right now, if it is not too late). I think that the rational, "productive," intellectual aspect of his self-esteem was authentic at one time, but that in the personal, repressed aspect of his consciousness he had no self-esteem at all and that this was the secret he was repressing. But since one cannot repress a bad premise forever, since it will grow, unless it is corrected, this secret has grown until it has reduced him—in the realm of his authentic self-esteem, of his conscious [13] values—to a progressively less and less convincing "role-playing."

His conscious immorality is his refusal—*his fear*—of checking his premises or of doubting his own psychology, policies and actions. The growing symptoms of his psychological disintegration is that he had acquired *defense mechanisms* to avoid facing an inner truth which he is hiding. For instance, he has often given the appearance of doubting himself, by assuming some unearned guilt (in regard to me or [Barbara Branden])—which masked the necessity to identify the real guilt.

He gave the appearance of an excessive fear of hurting me or [Barbara Branden]—while ignoring (or evading) the actual, existential torture which he was inflicting on both women and which was available to his conscious mind (and he has done this for years). He gave the appearance of an excessive generosity—in things which did not matter (such as his offer to make me a present of *The Objectivist*, which was [14] actually offensive), while acting like a badly "selfish" (in the conventional sense), self-centered monster in all the things that mattered. He was guilty of projection—for instance, accusing [Barbara Branden] of all the things which he himself had practiced, in their marriage (and, even if, as repressors, they were both guilty, her guilt was emotionally real to him and he projected enormous bitterness, but he never worked seriously on identifying and correcting the causes of his guilt). Wors[t] of all, he is now practicing rationalization openly. (His "paper" on the "secret" of his trouble with me is an arch-example of rationalization; about this, in detail, later.) Rationalization was part of his psychology in all of his bad premises, listed here (those discussed yesterday) and earlier—but it was subtler and it was kept subjectively in his own mind. Now, it is coming into the open—where it is available to his conscious mind, yet he does not see it. This is why I fear for his conscious mind—i.e., I fear that he will betray [15] Objectivism intellectually, in practice and in reality, as he has already betrayed it emotionally, in regard to the personal realm, and that his *defense mechanisms* will hide from him the nature of what he is doing. If his conscious mind was impotent to see and to stop the complete betrayal of his professed values *in action, in reality*, in the personal realm—what ground has he to trust the reliability of his conscious mind in the "work realm" (the intellectual realm), so long as so enormous an inner problem remains uncorrected?

He has told me very recently that he is able to think and to judge things and people clearly, so long as he thinks of them objectively, without any relation to himself. He said that he can judge me and see my character, my context or my needs clearly, when he thinks of me in a vacuum—but *all of it vanishes when he tries to relate it to himself.* He said the same is true when he tries to think of [16] anyone in relation to himself. [**Nathaniel Branden**] said that if the ability to think of people in relation to himself was a special sense, it feels to him as if he were born without that sense. (And yet, knowing [**of**] this kind of thinking disability, he wrote and offered the ugly superficiality of his "paper" as a "basic" explanation of the trouble between us! This is how little importance our relationship now had for him—and how casually he threw it away. If I ever had any importance to him, even intellectually, he would not be able to do it that lightly, he would be motivated to think about it. Since he would *not* think, this means that the secret he is protecting is truly dreadful.)

I think that in answer to the question on the preceding page (p.15), he will hide behind the rationalization involved in the split between his impersonal (objective) and his personal (frozen) method of thinking. But he [**17**] knows that such a split is impossible to maintain for any length of time, that it is too irrational, that no man can pursue a career (*in the humanities!*) without [**being able to think about people in**] any relation to himself. (Note to [Barbara Branden]: don't let him try to get away with this.)

I have not pointed out to him (nor did I realize fully) at the time the full and horrible significance of his statement about his inability to think of people in relation to himself. I supposed that this was a consequence of his "invisibility" premise which, of course, he had to correct. Now, in the light of his break with me [**Rand already regards her current situation with Branden as a "break" despite their continuing communication**] and of his "paper," I see a much deeper and much more evil aspect: that inability means that *he has exempted himself from all of his conscious value-premises, from all his conscious moral standards*— and, therefore, he cannot relate the incommensurable, i.e., two realms [**the "dichotomized" aspects of Branden's consciousness**] (or two persons) which have nothing in common.

[**18**] I think that his 'invisibility' premise is part-rationalization. On his conscious level, he may have thought that an irrational, evil world would never see his good, rational values; but, subconsciously, he was afraid of visibility—afraid that his hidden, repressed, emotional self would be seen, since he dared not see it himself.

Consequently, his "meta-selfishness" premise was also a rationalization. The fact that he was unable to identify his own proper "meta-selfishness" in relation to [Barbara Branden] or me—to know what he wanted in the relationship, what made him happy or unhappy—cannot be explained by such superficialities as excessive consideration or excessive admiration. *The horrible truth is that he had no self to assert*—that his hidden, repressed self had no connection with his conscious values or with the two women who represented those values and whom he loved (or professed to love).

[**19**] Now, as to his emotional emptiness. He told me, in the past 5 months, that at the time of the "car ride," [**when they first realized their romantic feelings for each other almost fourteen years earlier**] his attitude, in effect, was that he felt at home and in control of the intellectual realm and the sexual realm, but was "repressed" or frozen in the emotional realm. He said something like: "I felt, give me the intellect and sex—and to hell with emotions, leave them to others!" Through all the years, this seems to have been his attitude, which never changed. Yet emotions are the form in which one experiences one's values. Therefore, this means that he expected to have a sex-life divorced from values. More precisely, he thought that his values were chosen by his intellect and that his sex-responses would proceed directly from his intellect, by-passing his emotions. But what he meant by "the choice of his intellect" was not the *rational* process of forming abstract value-judgments and

applying them to oneself and to one's choice of concrete values, with one's emotions following automatically; he meant the "Kantian-Christophian" [**the second reference is to *Jean-Christophe*, the most famous novel of Romain Rolland, the socialist writer who Branden reports was a major influence on him in his youth**] method of "willing" himself to feel whatever [**20**] he thought he should feel and repressing anything he did not want to feel. Some of his emotions did correspond to his conscious values and were authentic, at first, in his youth (roughly up to his thirties); but this kind of "forced" emotions and repressions, automatized into a whole psycho-epistemological system, had to be corrected or had to grow; they grew—until they choked off his authentic value-responses or emotions and turned him—in the realm of his intellect and his conscious, rational values—into all but solid role-playing.

His defense-mechanism against the need of identifying this became: *autism*. (He may have had traces of autism earlier; but now it became a semi-conscious ego-value [**in this context, a psychological defense-mechanism "protective" of one's self-esteem**].) He began to switch his rational values away from reality and into an autistic world—in order to preserve, in his own eyes, the illusion that he was a "valuer," a rational "idealist," a "stylized universer," and thus protect his self-esteem. (His main protection was the stubborn belief that [**21**] self-esteem consists primarily, and exclusively, of "achievement" and that so long as he was an "achiever" nothing could be seriously wrong with him psychologically.) It should have been obvious to him as a psychologist—and on the ground of his own psychological theories—that such a (psycho-epistemological) method as "intellect to sex, bypassing emotions" was a sufficient (if not exclusive) cause of his sexual paralysis. But he did not see it—even though he had 8 to 10 years to think about it. He refused to see it or to think about it, when I raised the question repeatedly in the past 5 months. In spite of overwhelming evidence of the fact that his entire emotional realm and emotional [psycho-epistemology] were in a frightening state of chaos and contradictions—he refused to accept, even as a hypothesis, that he had to straighten out his emotional realm before he could solve his sexual problem. He now claims that his sexual problem caused his emotional chaos—in the face of the fact that his [22] emotional problem existed when he first met [Barbara Branden] in Winnipeg. If even so dreadful a problem as his sexual paralysis does not motivate him to think and to face the truth abut his subconscious—how dreadful is the secret he is repressing?

Now, to his relationship with me. I was—in the proper, rational sense of the words—the symbol of his intellectual-philosophical realm, and the embodiment of all his consciously chosen values. Both he and I had felt, from the beginning, an unusual affinity and similarity in our sense of life and in our intellectual [psycho-epistemology]. I think some of this was authentic in him and that he really loved me, at first (at least to the extent to which any love is possible to a man in his psychological predicament). It is significant (in the light of his present "paper") that his feeling for me started as a sexual desire [23] without any conscious identification of the emotion of love (i.e., it was the sexual desire that made him realize that he loved me). This seems to indicate that his [psycho-epistemological] method worked as he later described it: from his intellectual value-judgment to his sexual response, bypassing the realm of emotions (or as near to that as so irrational a method can work). (It cannot, of course, work fully: some of his emotions must have been sincere and authentic.) But it is precisely his feeling for me that was disastrous to him (in his uncorrected psychological state).

He could not project or express any emotions toward me; our relationship was, emotionally, empty and *arid*. His "disappearing professor" states caused quarrels between us, followed by psychological sessions which raised in him more self-doubts than they cured; his sexual desire began to grow dim in about a year.

[24] From the post-"Atlas" period [**after 1957**] on, our relationship became a quiet nightmare: impersonality, the "disappearing professor," my total "invisibility" to him, his lack of interest even in intellectual matters, the constant one-sided *exploitation* of me by him—intellectually, emotionally (i.e., I suppose artistically), psychologically (i.e., in the role of his psycho-therapist) and professionally (i.e., in regard to constant business conversations)—all of this interspersed with occasional protestations of love, assurances that he knew there was something wrong with our relationship, and promises to correct it some day (after he had corrected one emergency disaster after another, the chronic one being his relationship with [Barbara Branden]). This went on for ten years—yet he let it go on and gave it no thought.

I am convinced that the clearest and probably conscious fear in his mind was the fear of admitting to himself that I was "too much for him." He seemed to know that if he admitted that, it would tear up all his defense-mechanisms and destroy his image of himself as an Objectivist hero. This particular fear was not the [25] fundamental cause of his trouble and it was not the real secret which he was repressing, but it was an important symptom, which he feared. I was too much for him—in every sense of that phrase and in a deeper sense than would apply to the type of men he despises. *I want to stress this: I was and am too much for him.* This is my full conviction, reached with the full power, logic, clarity and context of my mind—

the mind he professed to admire. And if I gave him the impression of softening this verdict when I told him that perhaps I was not too much for him "in a vacuum," I retract that softening now, after I have had time to consider and integrate the evidence. Or put it this way: perhaps, I would not have been too much for the kind of man he had the potentiality of becoming: a real Objectivist hero and creative genius. But I am too much for the role-playing imitation of that hero, which he chose to become, instead.

[26] Now, examine his "paper." The worst thing about it is its glaring, ugly, unthinking superficiality. If he claims that I am the kind of conscious value to him that he professes to see (he said that I was "Mrs. Objectivism" to him—which is rationally true, but which, he claims, paralyzed him emotionally)—what destroyed our relationship? Some undefined anti-concept which he calls "physical alienation." If this were true, in any sense, it should have jolted him at least into defining what such a concept is—since it appears to be some form of physical determinism (age) powerful enough to destroy all of a man's conscious, intellectual, philosophical and emotional values (or to negate them and consign them to an autistic world, entirely cut off from reality or from any expression in reality, even a Platonic expression at which he failed miserably). Yet he did not feel the need, for his own sake and mine, to define that concept explicitly or to integrate it into [27] our total sum of philosophical and psychological knowledge, and thus to make himself intelligible. His mind did not *see* the shameful unintelligibility of that "paper." I *do* believe that that "paper" represents something which he is trying to make himself believe. But it is a *rationalization*.

It is an unworthy attempt to escape from the need to think about his sex problem—by blaming his problem on two concretes, one of which, he claims was wrong for him in spirit ([Barbara Branden's] undefinably "alien sense of life"), the other in body ("physical alienation"); thus, he can claim that there is nothing seriously wrong in him—it is only a matter of accidental "bad luck" in his personal history.

Intellectually, that paper is the most contemptible thing I have ever read in my whole life. *What* is he giving up—and for the sake of *what?*

[**28**] Now, consider his state in the past four or five years, ever since the so-called "[Patrecia]-break." [**Rand, still not informed of Branden's four-year affair, or even the intensity of his feelings for Patrecia, still appears to regard Branden's meeting with Patrecia some five years earlier as a kind of "break" between herself and Branden.**] He claims that this was a period of progressive derepression. (And, today, I believe that it actually was, but not in a good sense of the word.) Outwardly, he seemed to become more open and more cheerful, both with me and with [Barbara Branden.] But, in regard to making me visible, he became less able to do it, i.e., he became more and more impersonal, under a cover of what appeared like authentic cheerfulness. At the same time he became more "social"—i.e., he became progressively more engaged in what I call "wheeling-dealing," i.e., in business activities that required constant dealing with people. I had been astonished, at the time of the first [Nathaniel Branden Institute] ball, at why a man who claimed to feel such a hopeless "malevolent universe" feeling in regard to people, would want to be (and in some way enjoy it) the host at a ball given for the people he *professed* to despise. I was astonished, in the same way, in these past years of his alleged derepression, by his growing social life—in the sense of business dealings always [**29**] with and among people, culminating in his theater project.

A disturbing and incomprehensible sign was his friendship with [Patrecia]—which contradicted everything I had known about him in the past, particularly his passion for intelligence and intellectuality. What was worse, he began to claim that [Patrecia] reminded him of me or had some of my characteristics or some part of my sense of life: a "sexual view of the universe," a "stylized universe," "man-worship," "self-assertiveness," the "constant expression of value-judgments," etc. I tried to get acquainted with her myself—and observed nothing of the above, but only a faintly pretentious emptiness and fear. But [Patrecia] had declared openly that she was in love with him [**this is something which Rand had apparently learned only recently and is referring to it here only in retrospect**] and, apparently, projected open worship toward him—which seemed to please him and meant a great deal to him.

Originally, he had said that [Patrecia] represented his "Eddie Willers," [**a character in** *Atlas Shrugged,* **and a character Branden, as we have already seen, refers to as "rather pathetic"**] i.e., an average person who had good premises although she was not at all philosophical or intellectual. Then, he said [**30**] this estimate of her had changed: that she was an unusual person who, in some way, reminded him of himself in his childhood, that she was a victim of the same irrationality as he had been, but without his intellectual weapons and that he felt very eager to help her, to "protect her from the world." Then, he began to be peculiarly defensive, when the subject of [Patrecia] came up: he told me that [Barbara Branden's] attacks on [Patrecia] were like attacks on himself—like attacks on some element in himself which was very important to him but which he had been sacrificing in (or which was being destroyed by) his marriage. I tried to help him identify that element; he was unable to do it. In all such discussions, he kept insisting that he was not in love with [Patrecia], he had no romantic interest in her of any kind, and that his feeling for her was predominantly "protective," almost paternal.

My first very serious worry about his actual psychological state came about a year ago (Spring of 1967), [31] when he asked me to help him with his psycho-epistemology in regard to [Barbara Branden]. He said that he had done something terribly wrong to his own mind, during the years of his marriage, something which he could not identify (then or since), and that his thinking on any other subject was totally clear, but broke down only on the subject of his relationship with [Barbara Branden]. The central theme of his confusion was: "I don't know what I feel toward [Barbara Branden]" and his central identification was that [Barbara Branden's] sexual rejection of him had damaged his sense of himself as a man more profoundly than he was able to identify. We worked on his [psycho-epistemology] for some months in formal, psycho-therapeutic sessions—and our own relationship was entirely suspended in every sense or aspect during this period. The sessions were not very good: he was not very clear on anything, he kept discussing different aspects at random, and I did not understand him at all, in the sense that I could not tell what he grasped or not. I knew only [32] that his [psycho-epistemology] was in *total* chaos— and I was shocked by it: I could not understand how the rational man I thought him to be had been willing to live with such a chaos and had let it go for so long. But, finally, he declared that his [psycho-epistemological] problem was solved, and that his mind was now able to think about his relationship with [Barbara Branden] clearly. I did not know what exactly had helped him. Today, in retrospect, I believe that all he wanted from me was my sanction on a decision he had already made: my agreement with the premise that he had a right not to suffer indefinitely and to dissolve his marriage, if the situation was unbearable to him, after years of his alleged struggle to identify the reasons of the break-up, *even though he was still unable fully to identify them.*

That summer and fall [**of 1967**], I was appalled by his indecisiveness and vacillation in regard to [Barbara Branden]—and by the torture he was inflicting on her. He said that he realized it, [**33**] but was helpless—and nothing changed in his behavior towards her. Finally, it was [Barbara Branden] who delivered an ultimatum to him—and thus forced him to make a decision about their marriage. This was the first time that I observed his policy of solving a problem "*by attrition*"—by bringing his victim to a state where she could not bear it any longer and had to take the decisive step.

Today, I think that he was doing this because (subconsciously?) he felt that it absolved him of moral responsibility—and yet permitted him to continue his repression, without having to face the *root* of his own indecisiveness.

[**34**] The next danger sign was in regard to [Patrecia]. I was holding angry and somewhat indignant discussions with him on that subject, because he was getting vaguer and vaguer about it. The three shocking things were: 1. When I asked him what he did feel for [Patrecia], he answered "I don't know"—which, for a rational man, was more than odd in regard to so unimportant a person in fact, and, in his mind, in regard to so unimportant a relationship as he claimed it to be. 2. He said that only three persons meant anything to him, in the whole world: I, [Barbara Branden] and [Patrecia]. This was an equation like: "Philosopher, novelist and notary public (or advertising model)." When I asked him what [Patrecia] meant to him, he said he did not know. 3. He said that if he dropped his friendship

with [Patrecia], he would miss her and he would feel "*like a thinking machine.*" This was the real shocker. I asked him whether his relationship with me made him feel like a thinking machine. He assured me that of course not, but he was completely incoherent and unconvincing in his explanations. I do not believe that a slip of this kind can be made innocently.

During this same period, I noticed the peculiarly unattractive new traits in him, the results of his alleged de-repression: defensiveness, when he was being questioned about any aspect of his inner state—a kind of defiance (it was hard to tell against whom or what, it seemed directed at reality at large)—bitterness— [35] and, particularly, *self-pity*, which I had never seen in him before and which contradicted everything about his former character. The most disturbing thing, to me, was the fact that his growing confusion and inner despair seemed to date, approximately, from the time of his *success*, i.e., from the time when [the Nathaniel Branden Institute] became a firmly established, successful organization. If a man feels desperate at a time of existential *failure*, I do not consider it necessarily bad or significantly neurotic. But I am and always have been convinced that if a man feels desperate at a time of existential *success*, it is a sign of some ominous, major inner trouble, the sign of something bad.

After he had finally decided that he would end his marriage, he told me that his [psycho-epistemology] was now in order, and then I asked him what form our relationship would take now, i.e., what was his solution for our problems. I was very astonished to see that he took the question in an oddly tragic manner: he said that he did not quite [36] know what to do, because "Platonism" was so far from his actual way of "seeing" me or "thinking about" me. In subsequent conversations he told me that

he loved me so much that he could not live without me—
but he did not know how to implement this in reality. He
also said that I was the only relationship left on which he
would 'work' mentally—i.e., which he would struggle to
straighten out, if there were troubles between us—and
that if anyone else (including [Patrecia]) made any claims
that clashed with his terms, he would drop him or her
instantly. (I understood this to mean that everyone else
would have to adjust to him, in some unspecified way or
manner, and that I was the only one with whom he would
seek an understanding.) I did not like this at all, it sounded
like some kind of anti-rational resignation—and I tried to
make him identify or clarify this further, but he did not.

The next shock to me was the issue of "Miss X"—his
statement that he had thought, years ago, before his
separation, [37] that if he ever broke with [Barbara
Branden] there could never be another woman in his life
(whom he called "Miss X") because I would not accept it.
At first, I was delighted by this: I took it as a sign that I was
really "visible" to him and important in his life—a feeling
I had lost almost completely. I had never thought of any
"Miss X" (I had hoped to the last moment that he and
[Barbara Branden] would be reconciled), but I had told
him that he was right, I would never accept any "Miss X,"
and that we would have to discuss this question seriously
later, after he had recovered fully (he told me he was still
so traumatized by the failure of his marriage that he was
unable to think of his future).

The period that followed was our so-called "Renaissance"
(November 1967 to January 1968, approximately two
months). He became more openly, romantically expressive
toward me than he had been, at any time, in any period of
our relationship since the beginning. He seemed to be [38]
openly emotional and derepressed and actually happy,

without any forced cheerfulness. Only it was completely out of context. He would not discuss the past, or any of the problems between us that puzzled me, or the future, or "Miss X." (His only answer, when I asked him about this last, was "Don't worry.") Also, I noticed a thing which [Barbara Branden] had described to me, but which I had never seen in him before: when he talked openly and romantically, I looked at his eyes and felt the presence of some undefinable wall, as if something in him was closed or withdrawn or not there, not present in that moment.

The "explosion" came when [**sometime in January, 1968**] he finally had to confess to me that he had a sex problem (and had had it for about ten years). In that context, I asked him what was his feeling for me and he answered: "*I don't know.*"

As far as I was concerned, this was *the end.* In all these years, I had never doubted his love for [**39**] me, in spite of all the contradictions and the terrible *greyness* of our relationship. But when he said, "I don't know," I doubted his love then, retroactively (a little later, I tried to believe it, but never did again). The three "I don't know's" (in regard to [Barbara Branden], [Patrecia] and now myself) formed a pattern: I had a very, very strong *conviction* (it was only a "stomach-feeling," but I felt certain of it) that I knew what was going on in his subconscious and what was going to happen. As follows: his subconscious had decided that he must get rid of [Barbara Branden], then of me—in favor of [Patrecia]. (Strangely enough, I did not feel sure that it was necessarily [Patrecia] as a person, but I felt sure it was [Patrecia] as a symbol of a certain category of women, i.e., [Patrecia] or an equivalent.) It was, I felt, a subconscious, semi-repressed decision—and the rest would be only a process of rationalization to make it acceptable to the remnants of his conscious mind and his [**40**] former, rational self.

The rationalization (and "glamorization") in regard to [Patrecia's] character was obvious: he still needed the pretense, the illusion in his own eyes, that he was loyal to his conscious values, to his "stylized universe"; he was still struggling (badly and ineptly) to preserve his crumbling self-image as an Objectivist hero (in the good sense of that word).

What followed was the total hell (for me) and the terrible torture of the last five months of "psycho-epistemological therapy." I could not act on my "stomach feeling" as such, I could not prove it—and I could not break with him, so long as any hope remained. (Particularly, so long as I could not understand how anything so horrible could happen to a man of his former stature.) I broke with him, one night—and he would not let me: his agony seemed so sincere (and, I think, it was) that I had to give him a last chance.

Nothing in this last period made any sense, nothing [41] lasted and nothing worked. He did not take seriously any issue that we had identified about him—and some of these newly discovered premises were dreadful: the "Christophe" premise [**a major theme of *Jean-Christophe* is Rolland's belief in the semi-tragic and "selfless" perseverance required of an artist, what Rand would call a "malevolent universe" premise**] and the consequent role-playing and faking of reality—the automatized withdrawal from reality whenever he was unhappy, or under pressure, or had to do some unenjoyable duty—the automatized negation or repression of his values, when under pressure (which, he said, was the cause of his "disappearing professor" attitude) etc.—leading finally to his own identification of "*autism*," in a vague, undefined form, which he never specified or explained any further. None of it could be believed in regard to the kind of man he had been. Yet none of it aroused him to any mental fire, any thought or effort: it looked as if he were agreeing to anything or accepting anything as a temporary rationalization, a smoke-screen for something he had to hide. All of it had the unreality of a nightmare.

But here was the only consistent line running through [42] that unspeakable, shifting chaos: his search for some rationalization of his present feeling for me. First, he said that he loved me, but that "the triangle" was the obstacle to his love, for some reason which he could not identify; he said that it was [now] an issue of "exclusiveness" and that "exclusiveness" had some special importance for him, he did not know why. Then, he accepted my hypothesis that I was some sort of ideal to him, which was too much for him in reality (but [Barbara Branden] told him that this did not sound like him, and he agreed that this was not true). Then, he declared that he loved me, but not romantically— and when I asked him to define it, he withdrew it. Then, he accepted [Barbara Branden's] hypothesis about "the goddess" premise—and (after a week of rest and going to the movies with me) told me that he still found it a problem to get rid of "the goddess" premise. When I exploded, he dropped "the goddess" hypothesis. Then, he said that after all of his soul-searching, he became convinced that *he really loved me*, in the full sense of the word. (I asked him how he could be certain of it, in his present state—but he said that he was.) Then, he said that in the past, at the time of the "car ride" or shortly thereafter (about a year later), he discovered that his love for me was "a threat to his self-esteem," but that he did not know it consciously at the time. He also said that my "moralizing" anger, in our past and present quarrels, had a traumatizing effect on his love for me. Then, recently, he said that the trouble with our relationship was that he regarded me, in some undefined way, as a "*moral authority*." I made notes on what this could mean, which he was to study and think over, but he never did. Then he discovered "autism." (This was, I believe, on the weekend of June 15, when he was in Atlantic City.) There followed two weeks during which he did not pursue the discussion of "autism" any further. On Saturday, June 29,... there came his worry about [**an acquaintance involved in the theatrical production of *The Fountainhead***], which was the straw that broke my back: it convinced me that neither his own problem, nor I, nor his torture of me had any importance to him or any reality. On Monday, July 1, in a telephone conversation, I learned that he had spent the [**44**] previous day, Sunday, in the country—not thinking about his problem, as I had thought he intended to, but "swimming, sailing and shooting" with a student of his. That was that. I told him that this could not go on. He said that he would reach some rational decision or clarification by Wednesday, June [**actually, July**] 3, he gave me his "paper" about "physical alienation."

Does this long progression sound like a struggle to think—or a struggle to find a rationalization? The answer is obvious.

Two things are significant during this last, 5-month period of "[psycho-epistemological] therapy." 1. More than once, I had asked him to consider the possibility that my own age was now the cause of his trouble in regard to his feeling for me. I put it quite bluntly and calmly, without anger: that I was too old for him. I told him that I would not be offended by it and that we could then discuss it rationally. He answered me that this was not true. (He had said, a few years ago, that age had been a kind of spiritual barrier to him at the beginning, in the pre-"Atlas" [**45**] period [**before October of 1957**], because he had been unable to be sure of himself in regard to me, but that this

was not so any longer.) If the age-barrier was the thing
he had been repressing so painfully, I think that he would
have seized the opportunity to admit it when he heard me
naming it, but he didn't. I do believe that he believes this
now—but it is only a rationalization for something deeper
and much worse about himself, which he has to repress,
to hide from himself at any price—even at the price of
losing me and everything I represent to him, which he had
desperately tried to preserve, in some impossible way, by
some impossible contradiction. He had to break with me
when his subconscious began to sense that it was either-
or—either I or the repression of his basic secret.

2. In one of our early conversations about "Miss X," I
said that if this proved to be the only solution to his sex
problem, I might conceivably accept a "Miss X," provided I
understood his motives fully and rationally, and provided
I did not have to meet her or associate with her. He said,
with a kind of despair: "Oh, that's just the trouble: if you
[46] felt that way about her, I could not become interested
in any woman!" When I asked him whether this meant
that he needed my moral sanction, he assured me that it
did not—but was unable to explain what it did mean. This
gave me the strong "stomach feeling" that he wanted me to
be a kind of spiritual "Mother-figure" in his life.

Later, in a somewhat similar conversation, I asked him
to project what he would want, if he had a miraculous
power to make anything possible, even contradictions.
(I explained that I hoped this would give us a lead to his
repressed feelings.) He answered that his ideal life would
be to have a secret, very private, very spiritual romance
with me ("with sex five or six times a year"), a romance
totally cut off from the world and from the rest of his life
(as "autistic" a private universe as one could project into
reality)—and, simultaneously, to have a girl of his own

age, as his mistress and companion, who would "mean less" to him than I, but who would share his life in the world. I asked him what she *would* mean to him or what he would expect of her. He answered: "Oh, someone to spend money on, to share my financial success with... someone to go out with... to travel with, and such."

[47] This concludes the evidence relevant to reach the conclusion I have reached. First, some generalized conclusions: it is not possible for a man to reach such a state of intellectual, emotional and moral disintegration—particularly a man of his former stature, intelligence and knowledge—unless the secret he is repressing so fiercely is really something serious and devastating to his self-esteem.

The secret is necessarily an issue of self-esteem; no other issue could be powerful enough to force him to give up or destroy everything he valued.

Our general mistake has been to assume, as an unquestioned absolute, that he is a "good" repressor—i.e., a man who represses some error of knowledge or some misapplied, misidentified virtue. But, to think outside the square, we must consider the question that he might be a "bad" repressor—i.e., a man who represses something actually evil, something that would be shattering to his rational self-esteem and to the entire rational aspect or former part of his character.

[48] I have reached the conclusion that such is the case. No man can live for so long in such *terror of his own emotions and his own subconscious*, without good reason.

I cannot be totally certain of the specific evil which he is repressing and which I shall now name; this specific conclusion has to be regarded by me only as a hypothesis. But until and unless he de-represses and identifies the subconscious root of his trouble, this conclusion will remain as my likeliest hypothesis.

I believe that he is repressing the fact that in the personal-emotional realm, he is a social metaphysician.

I do not know in what form this attitude was acquired by him, nor by what means he is aware of it enough to be in terror and to keep hiding it from himself. Perhaps, it is not fully social metaphysics, but some attitude closely related to it, something in the same category.

My generalized reason for thinking this is the fact that it is not possible for a man to exist without any emotional [49] development, without any kind of code of values in the personal realm. If, for whatever reason, he did not develop his own code, then, by default, he would have had to become a social metaphysician, at least in that realm and to that extent.

(One purely arbitrary "construct" or guess about how this could have happened to him: at 14, reading *The Fountainhead*, he might have recognized some similarity between some of his own feelings and Peter Keating's. This would have terrified him—since all of his conscious mind and better premises admired Roark and he wanted to emulate Roark. His solution was to repress the Keating element fiercely—and to make himself into a Roark by "will power," in the Christophian manner. This might be why the Christophian concept of "health" as the only standard of virtue and of "achievement" as the only virtue appealed to him so strongly. This might also be the reason of the Kantian element in his psychology: the constant, impersonal search for what "one is supposed to be or to do," instead of the normal development of a rational choice of **[50]** personal values, according to rational principles and guided by one's meta-selfishness. His Kantian error in regard to moral issues is probably the most incongruous element in his psychology and has to be motivated by something very powerful; it cannot be an innocent error.)

I cannot even begin to guess about the origins of his problem, but here is some of the evidence to support the hypothesis of social metaphysics in his behavior since the time I met him:

A very small incident in Hollywood: his pleasure at the dinner invitation from [**an older relative of Nathaniel Branden**]. (He said: "People are very seldom nice to me.") I thought that this was charming in him and I took it as a sign of his loneliness, of his frustrated "benevolent universe" premise. But even then I wondered, very slightly, at how he could be touched or pleased by an invitation from a woman whom he had denounced as an evil liberal and whom he despised.

He has always admitted that he wants to like **[51]** people and to be liked by them. So do I—in the rational, "benevolent" sense of the words, and that is what I thought he meant. But there is a very strange ambivalence in his attitude toward people: his bitter, "malevolent" and, today, almost hostile contempt for them does not fit a frustrated "benevolent universer." (And, [Barbara Branden] told me that she sensed that there was something undefinably wrong in his attitude toward people—as if "he wanted something from them," she could never discover *what*.)

Considering his stressed contempt for people, it is strange that he likes giving parties. (Here, an example is [**a friend's**] observation that [Branden] always starts a party as if he expected to enjoy it, then loses interest and withdraws—yet repeats the same pattern at the next party and the next.)

It is strange (again considering his contempt for people) that he enjoys (or used to enjoy) lecturing—in what he described as some undefinably autistic way.

It is strange that he has been drawn more and more [**52**] into activities involving people or dealing with people, particularly since his alleged de-repression, culminating in his desire to be a theatrical producer. (For a man who actually despised people, this last would be the worst kind of martyrdom.)

His peculiar, very subtle or intangible pleasure in giving orders to people has made me call it "the big shot premise," for want of a better name: it is a combination of faint shadings of an autocrat and a show-off.

His "Christophian" role-playing or forced cheerfulness has too many overtones of a "regular fellow" or "life of the party," and is a total contrast to the stylized austerity of the better, rational aspect of his character. (I do not mean his authentic cheerfulness, when he displays it—I mean the false cheerfulness which seizes him at times, almost like an involuntary fit, almost as if he were out of control.)

His too frequent and too inappropriate use of humor has, often, the overtones and/or implications of moral cowardice.

[**53**] I do not mean to imply that such social-metaphysical touches were all there was to him. No, he formed his character and his conscious values by rational means—

and, in regard to his conscious thinking, his writing, his work, he was a fully independent, sovereign consciousness. **[The extent of Branden's deception is still clearly unknown to Rand.]** Some of his rational values were even translated into authentic emotions—such as his love of writing, of scientific discovery, of achievement (in the non-neurotic sense of the word). Some of his conscious values even reached the personal realm; but there, they could not last long nor motivate him permanently in the midst of his massive repression—and of his fear of his own subconscious.

The terrible conflict here was: the sovereign mind of a genius and an enormous intellectual development, on the one side—and, on the other, the inability to apply his conscious, rational standards to himself and to his personal relationships, a pronounced "double standard" in regard to himself and to others, the inability to think *objectively* about people in relation to himself. If, in his own article "Rogues' Gallery," [*The Objectivist Newsletter*, **February and March, 1965**] [54] the superior or morally best type of social metaphysician is the *Ambivalent* type, then I think that he himself was the highest, best, most superior and most tragic kind of *Ambivalent social metaphysician.*

To quote from the article: [**Here, Rand begins an extensive quotation of Branden's article**] "The *Ambivalent* social metaphysician... is the person who, notwithstanding a major psycho-epistemological surrender to the authority of others, has still preserved a significant degree of intellectual sovereignty... The Ambivalent type retains a far greater measure of authentic independence than any other species of social metaphysician.

"His intellectual self-abdication is far more limited; it tends to center on that most sensitive area in which all social metaphysicians are especially vulnerable: the realm of values.

"The Ambivalent type seldom dares to question the fundamental values of his social environment, but he is often indifferent to these values, paying them only perfunctory respect. In the areas of life to which these values [55] pertain, he does not assert counter-values of his own, he merely withdraws, surrendering those aspects of reality to others. He tends to restrict his activity and concern to the sphere of his work, where his self-reliance and sovereignty are greatest." [**at this point Rand quotations of Branden's article come to a pause; ellipses original**]

[Branden's] tragic variant of this pattern was that he was independent enough to choose his own "social environment" or sub-culture. He chose it consciously, by his own rational sovereign judgment, moved by his best premises; but he was unable to apply the values of that social environment to himself: he "merely withdrew, surrendering those aspects of reality to others." That chosen social environment was: *Objectivism.*

I want to stress that he was attracted to Objectivism for proper, rational reasons, that it represented the choice of his independent mind and of his best premises, his best self. But he was unable fully to make Objectivist values his own personal values; the realm of his personal emotions was too tightly closed, i.e., [56] repressed; he struggled very bravely, for years, to live exclusively by Objectivist values; but, eventually, since he would not derepress, he had to let the Objectivist values grow dimmer and slip away from him.

To quote further: [**Rand resumes her quotation of the article**] "His bondage to social metaphysics is revealed in his quietly persistent sense of alienation from reality, in his lack of confidence and freedom with regard to passing value judgments." [**Rand:**] ([Branden] did not lack confidence in passing value judgments in *objective* matters, not related to himself—but he lacked it totally when it came to his personal relationships] [**Branden article:**] "...that others possess a knowledge forever unknowable to him." [**Rand:**] [Branden's] belief that in a romantic relationship, his own terms cannot apply and he must accept the woman's terms while he never even defined any terms of his own], and in his humiliating desire for "approval" and "acceptance" (it is probably this type of desire that [Branden] caught in himself and repressed years ago, because [**57**] it would be totally intolerable to his authentic pride and self-esteem.)

[**Branden article:**] "His superiority to other social metaphysicians is evidenced, not only by his greater independence, but also by his desire to earn, through *objective achievements*, the esteem he longs for, by his *relative inability* to find real pleasure in an admiration not based on standards he *can respect*—and by his tortured disgust at his own fear of the disapproval of others. Often, *he tries to fight his fear*, refusing to act on or surrender to it, exercising immense will-power and discipline—but never winning his battle fully, never setting himself free, because he does not go to the roots of his problem, does not identify the *psycho-epistemological base of his betrayal*, does not accept full and ultimate intellectual responsibility for his own life and goals [in the personal realm]." [**Rand:**] [All italics except first one, are mine.]

[**Branden article:**] "Among this type, one will find men of distinguished achievements and outstanding creative originality—whose [**58**] treason and tragedy lie in the contrast between their private lives and their lives as creators. These are the men who have the courage to challenge the *cognitive* judgments of world figures, but lack the courage to challenge the *value* judgments of the folks next door." [**Rand:**] [in [Branden's] case, I would paraphrase this last to read: but lacks the courage to challenge his personal value-emptiness or to learn how to bring his rational values into a reality where he has to live with the folks next door]...

[**Branden article:**] "The forms which social metaphysics can take are virtually unlimited. But if one grasps the basic principles involved, one will find oneself far less bewildered when contemplating the spectacle of human irrationality... in one's personal encounters." [**this ends Rand's quotation of Branden's article; ellipses original**]

Now, in this context, what was my personal meaning for [Branden]?

His original admiration for me and his devotion to me (in the pre-Toronto period [**i.e., prior to their affair**]) were authentic and rational and based on his best premises. His [**59**] falling in love with me was authentic. But, thereafter, in the post-Toronto period, a terrible conflict began in him, subconsciously, repressed more and more fiercely, never allowed into his conscious mind, experienced by him only in the form of undefinable emotions: to his rational self, I was a woman he loved—but to his social metaphysical (and, *specifically emotional*) repressed self, I was a *moral authority* and he wanted me to remain that, he wanted me to be a superior or a leader, he could not feel a proper masculine superiority to me. (He ascribed this later to his "youth.") He told me once that he felt as if there was an improper element of "surrender" in his love for me—but he never identified what it was.

His constant, unpredictable switches of mood in regard to me and to [Barbara Branden] and to his friends were switches of metaphysics: switches between the rational,

Objectivist universe and the empty, repressed, arid, withdrawn universe of social metaphysics.

Since he did not face the truth about himself (I suspect that he did not even suspect what it was—he [60] knew only that he was repressing more and more), the power of his rational values vanished—and he found himself emotionally exhausted by an unknown inner struggle.

Now, what happened in his alleged de-repression? He did de-repress, in part, not all the way down. He tried to follow the principle of asking himself: "What would give me pleasure?" The terrible result was that nothing really did. What emerged was part of his real emotional self—only there was no such self: repressed for years, it had no personal values, no goals, no standards, only some unattractive reactions, incompatible with his crumbling rational self: defiance, defensiveness, a kind of personal anti-intellectuality (the reluctance to *think* about his problems), and, above all, self-pity. I believe that a lasting self-pity is a social-metaphysical emotion: it implies that "somebody" has been unjust or unfair to him and had treated him badly, while he himself was, somehow, helpless.

[61] Also, this de-repression started to draw him to too many socially-oriented business activities, to "wheeling-dealing."

The most significant symptom of this kind of de-repression was [Patrecia]. **[It must be remembered that Rand is being kept in the dark about his four-year affair with Patrecia.]** I do not know whether his attraction to her was romantic or not. But what was significant was that it represented an attraction based on *mutual flaws*— not mutual *values*: a "Christophian" kind of act, of role-playing, of phony, forced cheerfulness—an act masking an emotional value-emptiness or "value-impoverishment"— a vague rebellion against others (the desire not to let others "get them" in some unspecified way)—an empty "emotionalism," bordering on whim-worship—basic self-doubt—repression—in her case a vague pretentiousness; in his case, an exhausted humility (in comparing himself to her)—in both, an enormous amount of pain and fear— and *autism.*

He could not explain what it was that he enjoyed in her company, except that he could feel [62] "natural," feel "like himself"—*that kind of self.*

A man who does not know his own motivation is run by his subconscious. It was his subconscious self that became determined to get rid of the two opposites of [Patrecia]: [Barbara Branden] and myself. Both [Barbara Branden] and myself were representatives of his rational values, of his rational self—but this rational self was now being equated in his mind with some kind of terrible "pressure" which he talked about, but could not define. It was the pressure of a growing conflict and of a growing repression. [Patrecia] represented to him a self which he did not have to repress *nor to identify*—and thus a temporary escape from the need of facing the nature of his secret, of his "personal realm" problems. Above all, [Patrecia] gave him blind *adulation* (not *admiration,* but he could easily glamorize the first into the second). An unquestioning adulation is what a social metaphysician longs for; a rational admiration was [63] becoming a burden to him. In a rational relationship, he had to think—which made him feel like a "machine." In a social-metaphysical relationship, he could relax and act on undefined emotional "vibrations," which could be interpreted autistically into any fantasy he pleased.

His subconscious got rid of [Barbara Branden] (though his conscious mind is still uneasy about it). But I presented him with a greater problem and conflict—because I appealed to both his selves: to his rational self, I was the symbol of the best within him, of the entire Objectivist "gestalt"; to his social-metaphysical self, I was the *moral authority* whose sanction he needed to retain an illusion of self-esteem. This last is the meaning of his obscene desire to retain me in his life as a kind of "Mother-figure" who would sanction his future mistresses. (Later, he realized how horrible and offensive that notion of his had been; but he never explained how he happened to be unaware of its offensiveness in the first place.)

Thus, both his selves needed me—for opposite reasons. I think the last of his rational self knew [64] that if he lost me, he would lose everything that Objectivism meant to him and in him. This was the cause of his panic, of his violent anxiety, in the early stages of this last 5-month period—while he was grasping the reality of the possibility that I would break with him. Then, gradually, the panic disappeared and a kind of grey, lifeless, indifferent passivity took its place. I think his rational self was giving up and turning to resignation.

The social-metaphysical self won. He could not face the truth—so he wrote his "paper."

Symbolically, this was a battle between my universe and [Patrecia's]. Existentially and objectively, the choice to keep [Patrecia's] and to reject [**mine**] speaks for itself. And for the state of his self-esteem. (And for the state of his value-judgments.) I am sure that he does not see the issue in such terms; but he does not see it in any terms; he has lost his capacity to think in abstractions about himself and his personal [65] relationships—totally and completely.

"Fear is the antonym of thought." He is now totally motivated by fear; he is not moved by the "love of values," he has given them up—he is moved by the desire to escape from fear, the fear that he cannot solve his sex problem. He alternates between the escape through evasion and repression, by evading reality and drowning the fear in frantic activities—and the escape through whim-worship, i.e., acting on the spur and range of the moment. Apparently, he believes that this is de-repression, that he must regain emotional freedom by indulging any chance whim, and that this will bring back his sexual desires which were lost, he thinks, under the "pressure" of a (forced) cold rationality. But, in fact, this is the road by which he will never regain them. The "pressure" which cost him his sexual desires was the pressure of an unresolved inner conflict—of the effort he had to exercise in order to repress it, an effort that took all of his psychological energy and left him drained, unable to enjoy anything; it was the pressure of a growing breach of self-esteem—and [66] he cannot cure it by destroying his self-esteem altogether, which a mindless kind of whim-worship will certainly do.

He seems to believe that there is nothing fundamentally wrong with him, that he would be totally rational "if only he could solve this problem." But so does every other neurotic who places fear above reason. It is precisely the sex problem that requires the use of his reason (and the cure of his self-esteem); he needs to *think* harder than he has ever thought in his life. But "to think" means: to think by the kind of [psycho-epistemology] he uses in the "work realm." There is no double-standard of thought, nor of people, nor of morality, nor of values.

I believe that he has been attempting to cure himself by the primitive, concrete-bound notion of watching his emotions and waiting for some woman to arouse his sexual response somehow. (I believe that this was what he tried in regard to [Barbara Branden], then to me.) But, of course, it did not work and cannot work. And if, by some accident of random factors and evasion, he succeeds [**67**] in desiring some woman and in sleeping with her—it will not last and cannot last; he will lose his sex power again, only with a stronger feeling of hopelessness and despair. A proper sex attitude cannot be regained by chance—nor by a blind combination of subconscious factors. What has been lost by a destructive conceptual conflict, has to be regained by a constructive conceptual harmony. Let him read his own course on "Romantic Love," and say: "and I mean it," and drop the self-delusion that his case is somehow "different." Every neurotic thinks that.

[**68**] If he still intends to save his rational self, the battle is now or never. He has to win by himself, without me or my help. Existentially, he must not have any romantic or even friendship relationship with [Patrecia]—because he cannot cure an evil premise while continuing to act on it. ([Patrecia] herself may not be wholly evil—but the motive of his interest in her, is. Actually, she is the "girl next door.") If he still refuses to come to grips with his actual problem, with his secret self and the root of his repression—then he will have crossed the point of no return on the road to the destruction of his rationality, his mind, his self-esteem, his integrity, even his dignity.

What do I now feel about it all? Only a kind of stunned awe at the magnitude of the horror involved in such a phenomenon—at such an ignominious end for what had been, potentially, such rare and authentic greatness.

[**69**] What do I feel toward him? In his present state (whether the cause of it is social metaphysics or some

other evil premise), I feel the strongest contempt I have ever felt—and I regard him as the worst traitor and the most immoral person I have ever met.

But if he really decides to fight for his life and mind, I would not despise him, even if the secret is social metaphysics. I say this impersonally, not on the ground of any personal hope or love on my part, but on the ground of my "benevolent universe" premise and my estimate of his former greatness. He has (or had) more than a "beach head" of the good, from which to fight his evil premises. If the secret is social metaphysics (or something equally bad), he can start by taking a certain kind of pride in the fact that he loathed it so much that he was willing to wreck himself in the process of repressing it, rather than having to acknowledge it. He does not [**70**] seem to have acquired any "vested interest" in evil— only that exhausted emptiness and the triviality of his present pursuits, which he does not enjoy. He can fight it—and he has a chance to win.

Well, I wish him best premises—in the name of the best within him.

It should be noted, of course, that Rand is still wishing "good premises" to Branden and, in the notes that follow, still dealing with him in personal and professional contexts. Romantic rejection—even the discovery of romantic *deception* lasting for years—was *still* unable to cause a "total" break with Branden.

Her judgments, keen and insightful, are still overly generous to Branden.

Had Rand known the *extent* of Branden's dishonesty, she may well have identified Branden not as the "Ambivalent Type" social metaphysician of Branden's article, but, rather, the "Power-seeking" social metaphysician. Of this type, Branden had written:

While his desire is to control the consciousness of others, he does not necessarily resort to physical force, even when opportunities exist. Manipulation, trickery and deceit are often chosen by him, not as adjuncts to coercion, but as preferred *alternatives*. There are several reasons for this... [T]o some Power-seekers, these non-violent devices represent a *superior* form of efficacy, a more "intellectual" form, so to speak. But what must be recognized is that these devices spring from the same root as the impulse to violence: the desire to by-pass and overcome the *voluntary* judgment of others, to affect others through the imposition of one's own will, *against* their desires, knowledge and interests—to gain a sense of triumph by cheating reason and reality. The desire to manipulate other men [or women] is the desire to manipulate reality and to make one's wishes omnipotent. (97)

In light of all that we know of him, this model fits Branden's description much better, with all due respect to Rand.

Four days after writing this last essay, Rand would write another of the more extensive pieces from these notes. Rand has had time to chew further on Branden's paper and to consider what it means to her—and her opinion of him. The result was not good for Branden, and Rand's anger and pain is even more apparent than before.

Rand has only now begun to fully process the nature and magnitude of Branden's deception. Although she does not yet know of Branden's four-year affair, one thing has become clear: their romance—and Branden's stated feelings for her—had been a fraud for a number of years. The "therapy," too, had been a fraud for some time. Branden was never the man he had claimed to be, his stated values were only that—*stated* values. The psycho-pathological implications are frightening—and the ethical ones are still worse.

Again, the entire essay is reproduced, with little interruption:

[1] July 8, 1968
Additional Notes
I did not think of how all this horror affected me or what it

meant in regard to me, until I had finished the long paper of 7/4/68. I had to bring some order into my mind, i.e., organize the evidence about [Branden], first—to know what had happened, what I was dealing with.

It was not until Saturday (7/6) that I focused specifically on the content of [Branden's] "paper" as it applied to me. Then what I felt was such a revulsion that I felt I would not be able to shake hands with [Branden] without wanting to wash my hand afterward. I mean this literally, and the feeling persists, whenever I think of it, and I think it will remain with me always. I feel as if I had brushed against something so filthy—or, rather, so filthy a soul—that I cannot fully believe it [2] and it takes an effort of will to make it real to myself, because it is outside anything I had ever conceived of as human. It is a Dostoevsky kind of soul. **[Feodor Dostoevsky (1821-1881), the Russian novelist, author of *Crime and Punishment* (1866) among other celebrated works known for their dissection of evil and psychosis.]** I could have believed it, if a potentially great man with an inner conflict had done something tragically wrong, but with some quality of stature about it—like Stadler, who, when he turned against his values, wanted to kill Galt. But [Branden's] history is: a man who thinks and writes at the top of the highest issues and emotions possible to men—Objectivist philosophy, and everything it implies—a man who professes a passion for a "*stylized* universe," and then rejects all of it because he feels a sexual urge for the bodies of chorus girls! (Whether this is true of him or not, this is the meaning of his "paper.")

This is unspeakably filthier than the attitude of the lowest woman-chaser, ..., filthier than the religionists who regard sex as animalistic and evil. At least, all of those people do not degrade man's mind and spirit by placing them *below* their smutty little [3] sex urges; at least, in *their* kind of mindless, foggy view of existence, they split the universe into two dimensions and place man's soul into a *superior* realm, *above* their own gutter—and then they regard their sex lives as an *inferior* realm, a low-grade purely *physicalistic* activity, which they despise, but apologize for by whining that they cannot help it, being only "human" and, therefore, depraved. To that extent, they are closer to reality—and closer to preserving some vestige of respect for the realm of man's soul (of the *mind*). They live by the principle of "church on Sunday"—but at least they *do* go to church once a week, and leave their whorehouse itches at home, to indulge in for the rest of their time. But [Nathaniel Branden's] performance, his way of establishing the mind-body unity, the knowledge that sex is the product of one's values (which he *did* know at one time, in his youth, which he [**says he**] grasped by himself, before he met Objectivism)—is to [**4**] bring a whore into the church, put her up on the altar and proclaim that she is a goddess! (Here, I do *not* mean any specific girl—I mean the nature of his "physical alienation" notion.)

It is this ultimate act of pretentiousness that is so revolting. If a man had some authentic respect for the mind in general and for his own mind specifically, but found himself experiencing physicalistic sex desires, he would identify his own state correctly, then look for an explanation of his conflict—and, if he could not explain it, he would make the choice of either frustrating the desire, in the name of his conscious convictions, or giving in to the desire, consciously, and accepting the fact that he was unable to live up to his ideals and has to lower the level of his self-image and self-esteem. That would be Philip in *Of Human Bondage*. [**This is a reference to the 1915 novel *Of Human Bondage* by W. Somerset Maugham.**] But to solve the conflict by declaring that Mildred is Nora (or "some part" of Nora, or even a cheap carbon copy of

Nora) and then presenting this theory to Nora, with the emphatic [5] declaration that Nora was *not* too much for him and that there's nothing wrong with his self-esteem— is such a depraved performance that Philip (and Somerset Maugham) are clean and innocent by comparison.

I suppose I am still naive if I thought that evil would be expressed by some grand act of treason, like Stadler's. **[Robert Stadler is a character in *Atlas Shrugged*, a brilliant scientist who "sells out" his belief in human greatness.]** And I suppose that this is the ultimate proof of my own theory that evil is not big, but mean, shoddy, smutty and small. But to have to learn it *this* way—and from what had been [Nathaniel Branden]! (The fact that his problem is *not* physical desire, but the lack of *any* desire, does not change the nature of his "paper" or its notion. It merely complicates the issue: it shows what sort of notion he is reaching for, in order to *acquire* some desires.)

I know that [Branden's] "paper" was not the product of his mind, since his mind is in such a disintegrated state, but the product of blind terror, anxiety and the feeling of being cornered—a state which, I understand, consists of feeling that one's self-esteem is being torn away, and reaching blindly, at [6] random, for any weapon to protect it. But it *does* matter what sort of weapon a given man chooses. The nature of the weapon is a clue to his subconscious. And [Branden's] subconscious has become a sewer.

I do not believe the literal content of his "paper"—but before one can study it psycho-pathologically, one has to take it straight and identify its literal ideological meaning, in order to gauge his distance from reality.

Taken straight, it shows his exact [psycho-epistemology] in regard to his problem. He is not trying to think or to understand himself, but to find rationalizations for his desires (or lack of them), to *fit* ideas to his urges—on the exact, *literal* pattern of Hume's "Reason is the slave of the passions." [**David Hume (1711-1776), the Scottish empiricist philosopher best known for his arguments in support of skepticism and ethical subjectivism.**]

His remnant of self-esteem will not even allow him to identify the problem honestly, i.e., to begin by [**6a**] admitting that he feels a purely physical sexual desire for a young body (if this is true)—which clashes with his "Objectivist" self-image. (Or, the same in reverse: that his sexual desire fails to proceed from his values.) Rather than admit the problem, then look for its causes, he perverts his own ideas and the Objectivist view of sex—and pretends that no problem exists. He comes out with the notion that apart from values, reason, reality and his own "visibility principle," there exists another factor, "physical alienation or non-alienation," which supersedes them all—and annihilates them, when it clashes with them. What is significant is that he calls it "physical," and refuses to admit that it is purely a matter of the body, yet still more stubbornly refuses to say that it is a matter of the spirit, of the consciousness inside that body—and keeps insisting that it is some factor of reality against which human beings are helpless.

What made me realize the full extent and rottenness of this sort of rationalization was my focusing on a verbal explanation he gave me Wednesday [**7**] night, when I asked him to define the exact meaning of "physical alienation." He answered very eagerly (and I am certain that his story qua story was true, and that the eagerness was directed at convincing himself, more than me) that he had looked at an attractive 18-year old girl at a swimming-pool, had asked himself whether he felt any sexual desire, but had felt the same "physical alienation," which proved, he said, that this new factor worked both ways, both toward women older than himself and younger than himself, that it was not a matter of desire for a body, and that it pertained, in effect, neither to a body nor to spirit or mind, but somehow both and neither, that it was just a fact of reality, *age*, as an irreducible primary.

I asked him whether this meant that only a woman [8] of 38 would be right for him, and he answered: "No, it means a certain *range*." I remember thinking consciously: "How convenient!" but I did not pursue it any further then, because I saw that the whole thing was insanely irrational. I did, however, believe the story of his reaction to the 18 year-old girl—and postponed till later the attempt to try to understand what was the *actual* meaning of this whole notion in his mind. I knew it was a rationalization, but—as I always do—I thought that I must analyze its meaning in philosophical terms and discover what metaphysical mind-body dichotomy was involved in it. I told him that his notion indicated some sort of mysticism—and, of course, he looked at me blankly and was genuinely unable to see what I meant.

I was still, even then, functioning on the premise that this was [Nathaniel Branden], that he was honest about his philosophical [9] convictions, but in trouble in the emotional realm; I knew that his intellectual realm was affected, but I had no idea of the extent of the corruption. Up to that evening, we had talked in terms of a bad split between his "work-realm [psycho-epistemology]" and his "personal-realm [psycho-epistemology]"—and we regarded as his main assignment, the necessity to bring the latter up to the level of the former. In other words, I believed what he had been assuring me of all along, and had so emphatically assured me of even that last

Wednesday evening: namely, that his mind was intact philosophically and that it would never be possible to him to betray Objectivism in any *intellectual* issue.

It was when I started to analyze his story, Saturday, that I was horrified even more profoundly than I had been Wednesday—because I saw what had happened to his philosophical [psycho-epistemology]. Here is what I realized: if the greatest fear in his mind, in regard to his sex problem, [10] was the fear of admitting to himself that he may be moved by a purely physicalistic desire (which, in fact, he wasn't, since there is no such thing), then he would look at an 18 year-old girl with a wordless emotional attitude which, in effect, if translated into words, would be: "Let me find out whether I am attracted to this girl's body, because, if I am, this will prove that I am a traitor to my own conscious convictions." Then, of course, he would feel nothing—no trace of a sexual attraction—and would feel a great relief, regarding this as proof that his view of sex was *not* physicalistic.

It is inconceivable to me that he would permit this kind of [psycho-epistemological] procedure to the dumbest of his former patients and would not see through it. But this is what he permits himself—and regards it as *"thinking."* *This* is why he has had his problem for [11] years and was unable to solve it. This is why he claims that he is exhausted by years of futile thinking and does not believe that "reason" (!!!) ("reason" as Objectivists understand it) can solve his problem. (This last is not what he has ever actually said; not literally; what he has been saying is that he has exhausted the possibilities of our entire *present knowledge*—and that his problems are caused by some totally new, presently unknown factor, which he is struggling to discover. After which, in the past 5 months of our [psycho-epistemological] discussions, I discovered, by implication, that he had not even tried to apply his own philosophical and psychological knowledge to his own problem—and I encountered a kind of stubborn resistance or passive indifference whenever I tried to analyze his problem by reference to any Objectivist principles.)

[12] Now, to analyze his psychological test literally: there is no conceivable way in which one could feel "alienated"—in *purely physical* terms—from an attractive 18 year-old body. Physically and esthetically, only an adolescent body or an old body (or a crippled, deformed body) may be regarded as outside one's esthetic standards; then, within those rational limits, one may judge which bodies are attractive, which are not—as a sculptor would judge it. And, if a man has crude or repressed sex standards, he will be guided (at least, existentially) by the criterion of physical attractiveness. But [Branden] knows—better than anyone else, since this is *his specialty* in the field of psychology—that *there is no such thing* as a purely physical sex attraction, that even to the crudest woman-chaser it is only a cover-up psychologically, a superficial cover-up caused by poor introspection or guilty repression or evasion. He ([Branden]) cannot evade the story which he gives in his lectures about the "rubber-doll" and the statement: "One [13] wants a consciousness." [**A reference to Branden's own lecture example on the need for psychological visibility, i.e., that a "rubber doll" would not suffice as human companionship, one needs a** *consciousness.*] He knows that the whole issue rests on the question: *"What kind of consciousness?"*

In purely physicalistic terms, I can conceive of how an aging body may be regarded as unattractive—but *not* an 18 year-old body. It is precisely that story of his that makes his rationalization worse, *not* better. If a man is sexually indifferent to an attractive 18 year-old woman, it can be *only* on spiritual grounds, i.e., on the grounds of the fact that an immature *person,* an immature *consciousness,* does not interest him; which is very rational and very proper, unless he meets an exceptional 18 year-old—but then, *and in any case,* it is an issue of *consciousness,* of his *evaluation* of the consciousness involved.

(I could conceivably grant the possibility that my present age is a handicap *physically,* particularly to a physicalistic type of man, and, on purely conventional grounds, even to a better man. But [Branden] was not either (neither physicalistic nor conventional). And, what I do *not* [14] grant, is that this would be true 14 years ago—which, by his own history, it wasn't. Yet his fear of his own youth in regard to my age began then, about 12 years ago, and I did regard it as plausible, in spiritual terms, as he discussed it a few years later. But, today, I do not believe even the spiritual version of that type of age-notion. Besides, none of this "age group" or "certain range" notion applies to [Barbara Branden]—whose case may be different in historical details, but has one crucial similarity with my case: the fact that [Branden's] feeling for her is in exactly the same state of [psycho-epistemological] chaos, evasion, contradiction and vacillation as his feeling for me.)

Why, then, would [Branden] bring such an ugly factor as "physicalism" into the question of his feeling for me— when he knows that this contradicts all of his own theories of sex and love?

Because the physicalistic issue is a smoke-screen to hide something much worse—to hide it [15] from himself, not from me.

I do believe that he *believes* this explanation, that this is how he identifies his feeling for me and the problem of what is missing from his feeling, that he felt he was honest in his "paper"— if one can call it honesty. I do believe that from the time, years ago, when he first became aware of the fact that something was wrong about his feeling for me, he has been telling himself (semi-consciously) that the terror he felt was, perhaps, explicable by the suspicion that there is some physicalistic element in his view of sex and of me, which is caused by my age and which contradicts his spiritual love for me, his conscious evaluation of me, and his own conscious convictions on the subject. (I do believe also that he tried, for years, to "force himself" to feel actual love for me, by the Kantian-Christophian method, which destroyed whatever part of his feeling was authentic, and reduced [16] his love to a purely cerebral issue, cut off almost entirely—except for brief spurts—from his actual emotions.) I do believe that when he formulated his "physical alienation" notion in his own mind, then put it on paper and presented it to me, he *did* believe that he was derepressing a dark secret and that he would now be set free psychologically, even if at the price of tragic unhappiness existentially.

The horror of it is that all of it was a smoke-screen—and that *this* is how far his mind is gone. The smoke-screen was intended, subconsciously, to hide from himself the *spiritual* aspects of his problem—*the fact that the flaw in his love for me was spiritual, not physicalistic.* If he admitted that to himself, the whole structure of the pseudo-self-esteem (which had gradually invaded and replaced the authentic part of his self-esteem) would have collapsed. In the case [17] of [Barbara Branden], he could hide the truth from himself by blaming his indifference on some undefined and undefinable "spiritual" flaws in [Barbara Branden] (with their factual personal history to support his rationalization). In the case of me, his conscious mind knew too well that he could not do it, that no rationalization would stretch far enough to cover the claim that there was a "spiritual" or "*moral*" difference between us (besides, this would have destroyed his ego-value self-image as an Objectivist hero); therefore, the rationalization had to be of a non-spiritual, particularly *non-moral* character: it had to be "fate," reality, a "brute fact" of reality, above and outside his power, choice and volition; there was only one such fact within easy reach: *our age difference*—which, then, had to be translated into physicalistic terms, since he could not claim that my age made a spiritual or intellectual difference to him (yet every variant of what he said on [**18**] this subject implied just that, including the story of the 18 year-old girl.)

The truth (as I see it and fully believe) was, in pattern, as follows: he could never feel that he was fully *himself* either with [Barbara Branden] or with me (for the reasons listed in my paper of 7/4—specifically, for the reason that both [Barbara Branden] and I represented his conscious, rational values, which were cut off from his deeper emotions, from his repressed "self.") So long as the repression of that deeper self was an automatized absolute in his subconscious mind, he was sincerely unable to know what was wrong with his feeling for [Barbara Branden], then later for me; he would only *sense* that something was wrong. He struggled to identify it—by means of a progressively deteriorating [psycho-epistemology], since the more he struggled, the deeper his repression of the hidden self would grow. He had resigned himself to a kind [**19**] of empty, arid, unemotional existence, hiding it from himself and escaping from it into a frantic overload of business "activity"—when he met [Patrecia]. What she gave him was the experience of feeling that *he was himself,* his hidden self which he now proceeded to release or de-repress in part, in terms of feelings and actions, but reinforcing the repression in his intellect, never allowing the truth to be identified by his conscious mind. *This* is the root of his frantic behavior after the so-called [Patrecia]-break: the combination of a superficially greater emotional freedom, an unnatural cheerfulness, a growing intellectual chaos and helplessness, an abnormal tension, a hysterical quality in his behavior, the unattractive new traits listed in my previous paper—and, above all, the combination of growing cheerfulness with a growing undertone of despair. I do not believe that he fell in love with [Patrecia]—because love, on any level of development, is a response to values, to [20] the values one sees in a given person. I do believe that he was sincere when he assured [Barbara Branden] and me that his feeling for [Patrecia] was *not* romantic (sincere as far as a mind in that state can go.) [Patrecia] was not a person to him, but a catalyst: a chance encounter or chance object that made him feel what he had never felt before, that *he was himself.* A "self" without the strain of a cerebrally imposed, "Kantian-Christophian" torture of the self-image of an Objectivist hero (which he had truly loved and wanted at one time, but could not maintain or preserve by his [psycho-epistemological] methods). A "self" freed of the intellect (in the subconscious meaning he had given to the concept and [**used**] here, he might have sincerely thought that he was referring to his work-realm, but what he was referring to was his *emotional realm,* as it involved [Barbara Branden] and me, where an excruciating amount of "thinking" had to be done to keep up [21] the image of an Objectivist hero). *A "self" of which nothing was demanded.* (This is very important: he had complained for years that [Barbara Branden] made some sort of intangible *demands* on him, which he identified under one superficial, inappropriate category after another. He did not speak of "demands" made by me, [**Branden would, of course, in later writings do so**] but the one inexplicable explosion against me, which he himself does not understand to this day, is intelligible in this context and belongs in this category: "I'll be damned if I'll adjust my life to anyone!") That he did not see [Patrecia] as a person at all is proved by his *glamorization* of her, by the fact that he kept insisting that he sees some wonderful qualities in her, which he could not define and which were not seen, nor even sensed, by anyone else (most emphatically not by me). This actually meant that he was not *perceiving* these qualities in her, but was *ascribing* them to her—on the sole ground of the sense of [22] himself which he experienced with her (on the old emotionalist pattern of: "She is tall, blonde and makes me feel free—which proves that she is 'stylized,' idealistic, devoted to and compatible with Objectivism, etc.") Now why was it [Patrecia] that released his repressed "self"? *Because her particular flaws coincided with his*—as I listed them in my previous paper; because she had precisely the kind of act that suited his subconscious: the pretense at something idealistic and "stylized," which was a very crude pretense, but enough to make him tell his conscious mind that he was not a traitor to his values, that he was still responding to the right qualities.

Then there followed four or five years of real psychological torture within him; the conflict between his rational self and this new, subconscious, emotional self must have been ghastly. He knew that something was [23] very wrong with him; but since he would not derepress the truth intellectually, he kept going further away from his rational self and toward the other. And what *did* he get, in exchange for his mind and soul? Nothing. *That* is the grotesque emptiness of evil. Nothing but empty chatter with [Patrecia] at their lunches—as he described them to me—with himself (a mind like his!) keeping silent and listening to the theatrical prattling of a girl who bores much lesser minds within half-an-hour, or else engaging in childish play-acting with her, playing out scenes of being foreign spies, etc. Well, what else was there to do with a girl of that kind? All of the above, as such, may have been innocent enough if it weren't for one thing: during all that time, while his conscious mind was suspended and growing paralyzed, his subconscious was busy planning to get rid of his values: [Barbara Branden] and me.

[24] (If one looks at the above in realistic, existential terms, it becomes pure insanity: why would a man want to give up all the values representing his mind and *his career*, which he truly did love—in exchange for this sort of silly, trashy, vulgar, juvenile nonsense? There is only one answer, and it is *not* directly sexual: he gave it all up for a sense of "personal identity," of his "real self," which he could not hold down forever.)

His terror was that he sensed he preferred [Patrecia] to [Barbara Branden] and me—and since he could not explain this to himself in any rational terms, he began to dread that it was a physicalistic, sexual attraction. (I do not even believe that it was sexual.) *What he could not admit to himself* was the fact that she, [Patrecia], was the "soul-mate" *of his hidden "self."*

(In all of the above, I do not mean to imply that he had no rational self at all—he had, and it had [25] been authentic at one time—I mean that he was surrendering that rational self blindly, by degrees, and moving toward identifying himself with the subconscious, repressed, mindless "self.")

I believe that he made one existential attempt to unite both his selves—symbolically, last New Year's Eve, by trying to enjoy himself with me and [Patrecia] simultaneously. It did not work. I believe that he was sincerely happy, but [Patrecia] was disgustingly phony, and I felt strained:

I wanted to enjoy it, and I liked a few moments of [Branden's] projected enjoyment, but actually I didn't—and ascribed it to my own tension in regard to [Branden]. Thereafter, I told him that the mixture won't work—and I had the impression that he was sad or disappointed, but I cannot be sure.

From about the end of January on, his [psycho-epistemological] progression was one rationalization after another, all aimed at getting rid of me—in an atmosphere of growing intellectual panic. [**In hindsight, it is plain, that this panic had more than one cause.**]

[**26**] Day before yesterday, I pointed out to [Barbara Branden] that his "paper" on "physical alienation" was a symptom of why I feared that he would betray Objectivism: what if he tried to include such a theory in his course on "Romantic Love"? [Barbara Branden] said instantly: "Oh, he wouldn't! He would think it out very carefully before he included it in a lecture."

And *that's* the whole point.

Why didn't he think it out before he used it to destroy me and our relationship? Granted that it is in the nature of his problem that *I* am one of the elements that disintegrates his mind and makes him incapable of thought (not I as such, but his problem in personal relationships)—how long did he expect me to bear it? What can *I* do, if the base of our relationship, *reason*, is gone—and if it is I (*I*, of all people!) who is exempted from the province of reason in his mind? No matter *what* he feels for me, [**27**] *in fact, in reality, on earth* he ended our relationship by means of an offensive, irrational, mindless piece of intellectual trash. And the whole of our past and of its meaning was not strong enough to make him give me the one *courtesy* (if nothing more) that he owed me, and owes every human being he deals with, the one value I had given him so much of in the past: *thought*—the effort of thinking and of a rational decision, even if only a rational way of parting.

If this fact does not make him realize the nature of his psychological state—nothing ever will.

Rand does not consider the possibility that Branden's problems are so profound that he really *would not* be more attracted to the eighteen-year-old, even in purely "physical" terms, that his sexual psychology does not react to values, but to the manipulation and domination of the women in his life. Rather than being made, in his words, the emotional "prisoner" of the soul of a genius or the beauty of an actress, Branden tried to control them through deception, and found his enjoyment in that kind of manipulation.

But Rand does not yet know the extent of Branden's deceptions.

Rand's paper of "July 4" was read by Branden, at least, for he reports to Ms. Branden his reaction which Ms. Branden, in turn, has reported to Rand. The next entry appears to have been written that day or the next and reads:

> [1] [Barbara Branden's] report on discussion of my paper (of July 4)

> [Branden] read my paper yesterday. The discussion covered the notes preceding my conclusions. 1. He said that he was *not* afraid of thinking about people; he chose psychology, in order to learn to understand them. My objections: he was afraid to think about people *in relation to himself*; psychology gave him knowledge which he applied impersonally, but never in regard to *people and himself*. 2. *Important new point*: he said that his fear of believing the full reality of a romantic relationship was the fear of returning to the metaphysical loneliness of his childhood. He also said that, deep down, he believed

that both his relationships ([Barbara Branden] [and] me) were doomed. He admitted that this is an issue of bad premises creating their own metaphysics in reality. 3. Was not discussed any further than originally. 4. He denied this, by repeating some vague, irrelevant things (such as "he didn't mean 'in a vacuum.'") This point, apparently, is still being evaded. 5. He admitted this was wrong. Added nothing new. [2] 6. He said this meant that any woman would be inferior to me—so his fear was caused by making me a "metaphysical absolute." 7. He explained this as the "metaphysical absolute" feeling which he would attach to any relationship important to him. 8. He explained this by saying that he felt at home only in "big issues" (I think this is nearest to the term he used). I pointed out to [Barbara Branden] that he was unable to apply this to *happy* big issues.

Overall impressions or common denominator: motivation by fear. He claims that the cause is autism, leading to the fear of metaphysical loneliness. It may be true, but it does not explain the source and the permanence of his autism. ...

Two important hypotheses: [Barbara Branden] said that he may have felt alienated from me (sense-of-life-wise) by the fact of my stressed *objectivity* versus his *subjectivity*. I said that his autism (i.e., sense of inefficacy in reality) may have been the cause of his over stressed drive for "achievement"—if he felt that "he did not belong on earth." [Barbara Branden] said that this last [3] formulation would be as shocking to him as social metaphysics, since it contradicts all of his conscious values and convictions, and might be the repressed secret which he cannot admit to himself. The words "metaphysical alienation" were used by him so often that it may be a clue to his notion of "physical alienation." (Both mean "alienation from reality"—if that last has any meaning at all.)

Ms. Branden herself knows what else that "secret" involves and is able to simply watch as Rand painfully gropes for theories to explain the unexplainable. Ms. Branden's *continued* desire to keep Rand in the dark about Branden's personal life cannot be part of an effort to "spare her feelings" at this point.

In an entry titled, "Conversation with [Branden]—July 12, 1968" Rand demonstrates that even *after* Branden's disclosure about "age" and "physicalism," and even *after* Rand had shared her "July 4" essay with Branden, Rand is still on speaking terms with Branden, and they are still talking about more than the merely "functional." Rand can actually still dispassionately consider with him even the topic of Branden's "ideal" type of woman.

Female jealousy, in the traditional sense, was alien to Rand, and her ability to remain rational—whatever personal feelings she might have had on the subject—is truly impressive. Rand is demonstrating genuine concern about Branden's romantic happiness—*after* she has been told that his own feelings for Rand had long been a pretense. This degree of concern is inconsistent with Branden claims that it was "over" the minute Branden "rejected" Rand. Such entries prove otherwise and show just how benevolent Rand's feelings for Branden were even at this point.

Rand is, of course, still unaware of Branden's other lies and still (accurately) sees his present excuses as mere rationalizations. Nonetheless, Rand is even able to pay Branden an encouraging compliment. She writes:

[1] [Branden's] mind worked excellently on the editing of the book's chapter.

Then, we talked personally (neither of us wanted to stop, after we finished the editing.)

He said that he will have to solve his problem himself, theoretically—but that [Barbara Branden] was of unusually great help to him, more than he had expected.

I offered my theory that his [sex] problem was caused by his relationship with me, as "conversion hysteria" [**now** called "conversion disorder," this term refers to those who manifest symptoms of neurological disease, such as weakness, paralysis, sensory disorders, or memory loss, in the absence of any physical pathology that could be responsible; or, more generally, the physical manifestation of psychological disorders]... with his fear being the fact that I was "too much for him." He seemed somewhat to agree (with my explanation, not necessarily; but with the origin of the problem, more strongly); he gave me instances of his guilt and tension re: me—going back to start of romance. Later, he said that his pains had disappeared since his "paper.")

I offered the theory that Diana Rigg and "Modesty Blaize" [female action-adventure heroines both originally intended as female James Bond spoofs: Ms. Rigg played "Emma Peel" on the 1960s BBC television series *The Avengers*, and "Modesty Blaise" is the title character of the 1966 film based on the comic book of the same name] were his sense-of-life ideal woman. He agreed very eagerly. We identified the type as an action-woman, intelligent, but not intellectual—not me or [Barbara Branden]. He agreed with the first only as description (she could not be [2] either a philosopher or a novelist)—but he could say nothing about the second part. But he seemed willing even to accept the idea that I was "too much for him," in order to grasp the "himself" [reference to Branden's stated desire to "be himself"].

I mentioned the fact that he had never integrated properly two aspects of himself: the man of thought and the man of action. He said that these two had always felt to him as an indivisible unit. (I suspect that he consigned the first to autism, then left himself value-less and amoral in the second.)

I asked him what I did mean to him. He could not answer. (I had asked why he had not been better in the "Platonic" period; he said he had felt that that was the end of our relationship.) I asked him why he told me (on our date before last) that his love for me was not an ego-value [**in this context, a crutch for his lack of self-esteem**], that he felt close to me "all the way down." He said: "Because it is true." He said it with what seemed, to the best of my knowledge, complete sincerity. (This is an important key to his problem, whatever it is.)

(Smaller things: I told him my decision re: [Patrecia] and the Collective and parties; he agreed—and seemed completely indifferent to the issue. I asked him whether he intended any further friendship with [Patrecia]; he said, No—and was quite firm about it. I explained why I expect or demand this—in regard to therapy, to Objectivism, to the Collective [**the friends and students whom Rand had known while she was still completing** *Atlas Shrugged*], and to myself, i.e., no one of that sort is to profit from this tragedy and from my work.)

Notice that Nathaniel Branden is still claiming a total sexual "freeze" (despite his on-going affair) and is submitting to "conversion hysteria" as its "explanation." The elaborately *psychological* nature of Branden's fraud and manipulation could not be more obvious.

Rand has made certain "demands" which are not fully clear, but which presumably include that Branden no longer socialize with Patrecia, or, at least, not in Rand's presence. It seems that Rand still believes Branden's repeatedly stated claims that he and Patrecia are not involved romantically, for such a demand would otherwise have been impossible (and cruel.) Rand lists these among the "smaller things" they discussed.

Moreover, these demands are almost identical to the social agenda Branden had previously laid out for himself when he said that his relationship with Rand was the only one he would "work on." Recall that, at the time, Rand had been disturbed by Branden's apparent demand that everyone else would have to "adjust" to him. But, by this point, she appears to agree with Branden on the urgent need for radical measures.

On the other hand, it may be that Rand suspects Branden's relationship with Patrecia to be more than he has admitted. One wonders if Rand is, once again, trying to force Branden to come clean about this, for surely if Branden had actually been involved with Patrecia, he would have instantly refused this "demand" and admitted the truth.

But Branden agreed to the demands—and was "quite firm" about it. Branden is, of course, deeply involved with Patrecia, but he will maintain his facade of lies until others inform Rand about his relationship with Patrecia several weeks later.

In other words, Branden has managed to be a complete traitor to *all* of the women in his life—thoroughly, systematically and manipulatively.

Rand herself had made these "demands" while still "officially" accepting his assertions that he was not involved with Patrecia. And she had made them for several reasons—for psychological reasons which we have already seen ("in regard to therapy"), for professional reasons ("...to Objectivism") and for personal reasons ("...and to myself")—which included people other than herself ("...and to the Collective.") All of these motives except the "personal" ones involving Rand herself were completely overlooked in the Brandens' accounts of these events, suggesting that Rand's demands called for inhuman "selflessness" from Branden, although they alone knew the degree of his actual involvement with Patrecia. And Branden "firmly" and immediately agreed to the program.

No, Branden engineered his utter selflessness all by himself.

Rand had named Branden her intellectual heir—because she once had thought that his *mental approach* was "identical" to her own. Rand's endorsement was the main asset of Branden's business ventures—because she once had thought that their *senses of life* were "identical." Branden was even the O'Connors' legal heir—because he had *devoted his life to Rand's work.*

Obviously, the "romance" was already long over between Branden and Rand by July of 1968, and, by then, even Branden had admitted this to Rand. But if Branden could not have retained his "functional" relationship with Rand, as the Brandens allege, then what were these "demands" all about? In fact, he likely could have. It seems that Rand will not have

Branden "drifting" into subjectivist Parts Unknown—nor will she allow Patrecia—"that sort"—to profit from her own efforts and suffering.

One wonders whether Patrecia ever learned the details of Branden's comments and commitments to Rand—and what she would have thought about them. Cut from the same mold as Branden himself, she may have been in total agreement with continued deception and the implicit slap at her which his "firm" promise implied. It is impossible to say. (In either event, Branden sure knew how to treat a lady.)

Branden has not stopped using Rand as his therapist, either, but he was starting to backtrack on some of his previous admissions. In a separate note dated "July 12, 1968," we read:

> [1] Comments on My Comments
>
> [Branden] said: "It would not be alien to him." (The issue of thinking about people impersonally, as psychologist, but not in relation to himself.) Issue of inability to bring me into reality: he said: "Two souls floating in space... As long as everything was right there, he would not think about reality." He could not integrate me with any human relationship. It alienated him from everybody... "Sometimes I think the worst repression is how much it **[his relationship with Rand]** meant to me." "Maybe age would never have been a problem if I was what [Ayn] thought I was."

Notice the safely passive voice here: it is Rand who has "thought" too highly of Branden, not Branden continuously misrepresenting himself to Rand. But, for the first time, Branden has finally admitted the fundamental issue: the *true* nature of his soul.

Rand continues:

> [1] Why [Branden] never took the out of age when I offered it: 1. "He thought it would end our relationship." 2. "He would have been totally morally condemned in his own eyes." In re: his "paper"—he felt he had such unspeakable

psycho[**logical**] problems anyway that one more did not matter (in effect).

He feels terror at how he will adjust to the present situation—he feels the switches and doesn't want to repress or evade. He feels terror at how destructive he is, of suffering and causing suffering, and of terrible inefficacy.

Another crucial admission from Mr. Branden: he could not end just the sexual component—when this was Rand's very offer—because "He thought it would end the relationship." Well, here they are, still talking...

Branden not only demanded that he *not be taken at his literal word*—he never gave Rand the chance to be taken at her word, either. Rand, at this point, was still demonstrating an enormous benevolence and a genuine concern for Branden's well-being—including his romantic happiness. Branden's continued deceptions can only have been an attempt to salvage his practical position and avoid Rand's (justifiable) moral condemnation.

And, there is truth in the second comment: "He would have been totally morally condemned *in his own eyes*" if his feelings were not what he had claimed for so long. One might also add: and in *Rand's eyes*, which, as it turns out, had been pinch-hitting for his own for some time.

Apparently later that same day, Rand is still considering the evidence on the question of Branden's immorality, a subject she no longer shies away from, but about which she is still too innocent and too generous. She has resumed a position of ambivalence—for Rand, the evidence remains "evenly divided" between immorality and severe neurosis at this point.

In a separate note dated "July 12, 1968," Rand writes:

[1] My conclusions (re: conversation with [Branden], 7/11, and phone conversation with [Barbara Branden], 7/12

The evidence, so far, is still evenly divided between an evil explanation and a (perverted) good one—as it has been all during our last 5 months.

The evil one (judging by his existential actions) is that for some hidden, repressed reason (social metaphysics or an equivalent), I was merely an ego-value to him, I was the value chosen by his mind or conscious convictions, but rejected by his "emotional self," which wanted, in reality, the "wheeling-dealing" type of universe; so that I was "too much for him."

The "good" one is that his autism is the real key to everything; i.e., he did love me so much that he had to consign me to his autistic universe—he could not deal with me in any way as part of reality (and could feel no consistent sexual desire), and had to live in reality without me (or his deeper values), by some other kind of standard. [Objectivism as an "impractical" religion.]

[Barbara Branden]'s report on her conversation with him yesterday supports the second explanation. (Also, his discovery of "autism" last Thanksgiving and his subsequent derepression in our "Renaissance" period, support this [2] hypothesis—except that, at the first sign of trouble between us or the first thought of actual, "non-Platonic" reality, he relapsed automatically into all of his "defense-mechanisms.") (I must mention this last to [Barbara Branden].)

Actually, does it matter to me which is the true explanation? I seem to feel that the second one is good (and, by implication, hopeful), but that is probably my greatest mistake at present.

The results, in reality, on earth, are the same. In fact, morally, the second explanation is worse than the first. The first is merely a mind-body split, which is bad enough, but it is less horrible—monstrously, uselessly, wastefully horrible—than the second. The second (the psycho-epistemolog[ical] mechanics of which I do not understand) indicates such an enormous moral cowardice, "malevolent" universe, self-doubt and fundamental motivation by fear, such a moral treason, that my mind stops at this point. I am not able to concretize it and make it even [3] theoretically real to myself.

All I see (and this very strongly and clearly) is that this is the ultimate meaning of what I sensed in my article on "Art and Moral Treason" [*The Objectivist Newsletter,* **March, 1965, reprinted in** *The Romantic Manifesto.*] the deadly enemy I had been fighting all of my life: *not* those who do not see the good, but those *who see it and don't want it* (because they lack the courage for it, and the self-confidence). If "Mr. X," left on his own, would feel guilty if he admired me, and "Mr. Y" would call his own admiration for me "ludicrous"—but then [Branden], on the same pattern, would accept my ideas, but *wipe me out of existence* (i.e., pretend that I am not real). In this sense, [Branden] is the *real* enemy in *Atlas Shrugged*—the man who wanted Rearden Metal without Rearden, in the deepest, metaphysical meaning of that concept, much deeper than I could ever have imagined possible.

A horrible thought struck me just now: this would mean that [Branden] was the *worst* of the people in the *"St. Joan"* [4] Epilogue [**A reference to George Bernard Shaw's 1923 play,** *Saint Joan.*]; he wanted the Saint to exist in heaven, but not on earth—he wanted to be, in effect, a Pope: to serve the Saint, to dream about her, but never to have to live with her, and not because he wanted a Pope's power, not because of any earthly ambition, but because he was too weak (too self-doubting) to fight for the Saint's right to live on earth, yet desired nothing else and solved the conflict by worshiping his values, his ideal, in heaven (in another dimension), "autistically." This is so unspeakably futile, unreal, [**non-rational?**] an attitude that Shaw's characters are rational by comparison: they *preferred* lower grade values on earth; he did not, he was merely

protecting his pseudo-self-esteem (by means of autism),
he was willing to destroy the earth (its reality) *in order not
to discover that he was neither worthy nor able to live on
it.* ("How long, oh Lord? How long?"—is all that's left to
me.) (Show this to [Barbara Branden]).

To her credit, Rand is consciously cautioning herself against allowing
"hope" to distort her judgment about Branden, her innocent desire to see
good in him. She calls this "probably" her "biggest mistake." Even on the
issue of her own objectivity, Rand is insightful—and objective.

But the days of Rand's benevolent "benefits of the doubt" have come
to an end.

The following day, in a note dated, "July 13, 1968," and titled, "Notes:
([Branden's] 'autism')," we read the following:

[1] Re: [Branden's] process of derepression. This is just
a hypothesis: [Branden] began to grasp the enormity of
his problem only after the break [**although they are still
speaking, notice that Rand regards their current state,
at least since Branden's letter about "physicalism," as
a "break"**] with me. Up to then, the meaning and even
the possibility of a break were not fully real to him. When
he grasped (I do not know the details of how) that his
problem was autism, he was deeply disturbed by it. (This
happened, he said, in Atlantic City.) But his main focus
then and up to our break was on his sex problem; he was
stubbornly (and frantically) maintaining the illusion that
it was his only (and [Barbara Branden's] sexual) problem
[**i.e., a problem in his relationship with his first wife**],
that he was repressing some one thing in that realm, and
that his self-esteem was intact.

When he focused on his feeling for me and discovered the
extent to which it was autistic, he concluded that that was
the key to his problem, that some element of reality was
missing from his feeling—and the only rationalization

[2] he could find for that was the age difference. So he pounced on the concept of "physical alienation" to explain it—while he meant (subconsciously) "alienation from reality." Thereafter, he probably tried to explain all his feelings of alienation from people by telling himself that their cause was his "unrealistic" love for me—and that once he had sacrificed me to "realism," he would regain his sense of efficacy in life (which he had never actually had).

Therefore, he could still maintain his self-esteem, he thought, since he had acted in the name of "reason and reality," and had sacrificed his emotions. So he wrote his "paper." The ugliness of it is that he tried to save himself from anxiety by smearing his highest values. (This is one piece of evidence of the [3] fact that if he does not correct his problem *now and to the root*, he will eventually turn *against* me and Objectivism, explicitly and in action. The inner psychological treason has already been forced on him by his problem—and it is more than psychological, it is *existential*, if one considers what it has done to me. This did not stop him; therefore, nothing will stop him from going further *existentially*.)

Now consider the meaning of his [psycho-epistemological] procedure in regard to his "paper." He had split reality (and himself) into two dimensions: his meta-selfishness and his values were consigned to autism—while reason (thinking, creativeness, achievement) were ascribed to the realm of reality, the realm of *other people*, in which he was "invisible." (He said this was true since very early childhood.) He believed that his *mind* could be efficacious in that reality, if he [4] repressed his emotions (i.e., his *personal desires* and values).

When he fell in love with me, he repressed the extent and full meaning of his love—and he kept reinforcing the repression through the years. (The repression caused the inefficacy toward me in reality, which intensified his fear, which reinforced the repression.) (The sex problem was the first major symptom of major trouble; this made him repress on some incredible scale.) As he himself moved away from reality, he moved me and his love for me away from reality, and into his autistic universe. Then, discovering at a first introspective glance, that his love had become largely autistic (*because it represented his own, personal values*), he decided—without further thought—to get rid of me, on the unstated premise that stood between him and reality (!).

Even in his own twisted terms and irrational [5] metaphysics, this meant that he was sacrificing values (that which he regarded as high, great, "stylized") to the world of other people, whom he despised, but whose world he regarded as "*real*" and open to his "efficacy." If this is not abject moral treason—what is?

But, *in fact, in reality*, I was not a wall standing between him and reality, I was his only bridge to reality—the only person (according to his emotions) who was "close to him" and real (and who represented his personal values, his "ideal"). *This* is what he chose to discard—subconsciously, in order not to face the issue of autism and thus preserve his "efficacy" in "reality" and his pseudo self-esteem; existentially, in order *to fit himself into and be accepted by the world of other people.*

If, recently, he identified such a thing as the fact that "he could not integrate *me* with any other relationship," [6] that I (or his relationship with me) alienated him from all other people... [T]his should have given him a clue of the most shattering kind: he should have seen immediately that the only possible meaning of this was the surrender of his highest values to the world of others, the surrender of Galt [**the hero of *Atlas Shrugged***] to the folks next

door. If he did not follow this clue, he is still evading and/
or repressing the basic problem. ([Barbara Branden] must
keep him on this track and not let him stray away from it
for too long.)

It is painful to watch a mind like Rand's laboring in the dark to
construct theories that might help—or, at least, make comprehensible—
Branden's condition and behavior. That such a mind was for so long thus
occupied simply in order for the Brandens to keep their business interests
intact was a tragic waste.

Still, it was *Rand's* mind and, even before learning of the affair with
Patrecia and the multi-layered, multi-year extent of Branden's dishonesty,
Rand has already come to the point where she sees him as the enemy—not
the hero—in *Atlas Shrugged.*

Branden had, at first, play-acted the perfect "mirror" of Rand's
convictions and values. Rand's benevolent optimism had so wanted this
reflection to be honest that she gave it every benefit of every doubt for just
as long as she possibly could.

But, in the end, A remained A, and Rand could no longer ignore her
"stomach-feelings," and the logic they implied. She had accurately inferred
his rationalizations and dishonesty—and had detected the residue of
Branden's deeper lies about his soul—from his *mental method* alone. With
very little assistance—and indeed a great many obstructions from both of
the Brandens—Rand was able to clinically and accurately dissect away any
illusions regarding Branden's character and psychology.

In light of the new insight gained from Rand's notes, we can see
that Rand's anger in July and August of 1968 was the result of nothing
but Branden's *repeated* dishonesty—not the fact that their romance was
over—and not even the dishonesty about just "his feelings" for Rand. On
this matter, too, the Brandens have profoundly misled their readers.

In July, we know Branden told Rand that, for many years, their age
difference *had* mattered to him, despite his many and extreme protestations
"over the years" that age *did not* matter, as we have seen. And, as Rand's
journals confirm, their association, even the counseling, continued.

Also in July, although this is not discussed in her notes, Rand was told
by Branden's cousin, psychiatrist Allan Blumenthal, of Branden's feelings
for Patrecia—but not of their four-and-a-half-year-old affair.

Then, sometime in late August, she learned of this, too. Unfortunately, this is not mentioned in Rand's notes, either.

It can now be revealed, from documentation in the Ayn Rand Archive, that on August 21, 1968, probably just days before their final break, Branden wrote a letter to Rand assuring her that he would devote himself to working on his mental problems with Dr. Blumenthal's professional help. *Even the revelation of Branden's feelings for Patrecia* did not end Rand's association with him—or Branden's dishonest attempts to maintain his position with Rand.

A month later, on September 20, 1968, Branden's attorney wrote Rand to inform her, in legally ominous terms, that Mr. Branden had never given Rand permission to circulate *any* of the letters he had written to her.

Two weeks later, on October 4, 1968, the attorney wrote to suggest a possible libel suit if Rand published "To Whom It May Concern." Rand published it shortly thereafter, but no lawsuit was ever filed. (98) We have seen how the Brandens instead published a tissue of lies about the break in 1968, one they still fervidly insist was the truth—despite the fact that they exhaustively contradict that 1968 statement in their own memoirs.

But after Rand had discovered the scope of Branden's dishonesty in late August, references to Branden in Rand's private journal come to an abrupt end. If these notes are any indication, the state of Branden's mental health was no longer a concern to Rand.

It was only then that Nathaniel Branden's cruel treatment of Rand, and Ms. Branden, and even Patrecia, became clear. It was only then that his denials about Patrecia—as well as his *extreme claims of passionate love for Rand* made well into 1968—were shown to be a fraud. It was only then that it was made clear that the tortuous, senseless and inevitably unproductive counseling—first, the "marriage counseling," then, the "psycho-epistemology" sessions, and, finally, the last several months of grueling psychotherapy—was all an elaborate, extensive and *professional* fraud. His *motive* for prolonging this agony became clear, as well.

In *Judgment Day*, Mr. Branden tells us that he made certain predictions about what Rand would do following their break. He foresaw Rand holding endless discussions of his psychology. And, Branden boasts, his predictions were "precisely what happened." He then reports that he had "heard"—from an unnamed source—that Rand "wrote many papers to herself on my 'psychology' and 'psychoepistemology.'" Nathaniel

Branden claims that after their break, Rand was "obsessed" with the topic of Nathaniel Branden.

In the familiar claim to specialized knowledge that often signals one of Mr. Branden's more dubious assertions, he writes, "Knowing Ayn as well as I did, I knew that in her private notes, not meant for the Collective's eyes, she would be rewriting the history of our relationship in order to explain and justify her own 'errors of knowledge' and my 'collapse into evil.'" (99) Why Rand should rewrite history in notes not meant to be seen by anyone else he does not explain.

Branden repeats these claims in the revised version of his memoir, and even adds what he asks us to believe were his private thoughts in 1968: "God knows what she'll write about me in her journal—she's kept one for years—but I promise you, it will not be primarily governed by considerations of truth." (100)

One can almost see the beads of sweat gathering on Branden's forehead over the prospect of the release of Rand's journals.

However, Rand would not write another word in her journals about Branden after their break. (101) Her readers will be reminded here of the famous scene from *The Fountainhead* where the villain, Ellsworth Toohey, asks the hero, Howard Roark, what Roark thinks of him.

Roark replies, "But I don't think of you."

Branden's predictions and account of Rand's behavior following the break exhibit the essence of his modus operandi.

For example, Branden claims to possess specialized knowledge, his "knowing Ayn as well as he does." Normally, this sort of claim can neither be verified nor rebutted, and we are forced to rely upon our evaluation of Branden's credibility in general. Fortunately, this time, we possess Rand's journals as evidence and can demonstrate Branden's assertion to be false. Far from writing endless essays, she never wrote about him again.

Also, we see Branden exercising his habit of projection, displaying the very traits he criticizes Rand for allegedly possessing: paranoia, suspiciousness, dishonesty, and grandiosity to the point of borderline megalomania.

What precisely he fears from these notes, he does not specify, and he implicitly admits that he does not know their contents ("God knows what she'll write..."). But he *does* know, whatever it is, it's all false.

In classic form, we even see him committing the same sin he accuses Rand of committing, while in the process of making the accusation, when we see him engaging in rewriting history in his memoir—and then rewriting it again a few years later. (He may do it again.)

And we can now see the motive for Branden's unfair accusations against Leonard Peikoff following the publication of Rand's more philosophical journals. It was simply part of a wider fear of what her other notes might contain. It seems that this is a topic about which Branden has himself been obsessing for some time.

His fear of her assessment of him is certainly justified, but his paranoia that Rand's powerful mind would stay focused on his neuroses and vices after the break was not.

Unfortunately for us, but not for Rand, she moved on after learning the truth and stopped writing about him. There was nothing more to discover, no need for theorizing. The very "worst" of Rand's guesses—and more—were all true.

As we have observed, Branden's fraud was not merely a romantic one. He had been Rand's business partner, and Rand's endorsement literally kept him employed. This was the job of teaching Rand's philosophy, including her ethics and such subjects as the virtue of honesty. He had become a role-model and a hero for many of Rand's numerous followers. Rand was by no means Branden's only victim.

Of course, it was a romantic fraud, too, one perpetrated against an artist of exalted romantic vision and hope.

Branden's protestations of romantic, passionate love for Rand, made well into 1968, over four years after his affair with another woman had begun and several years after Branden says that there really was no passion, can only be seen as a cruel (and, simultaneously, selfless) manipulation of the person whom Branden had claimed as his artistic, intellectual and spiritual ideal.

As late as January of 1968, when Rand asked him if he could "project" a life with a hypothetical "Miss X" Branden replied that he could not even project the possibility. He was able, he said, to project a life of "loneliness" but not a life with someone else. By this time, his affair with Patrecia had been going on for four years. We can only assume that Branden's passion for Rand had been absent for at least this same period. Yet as late as 1968, Branden's ideal life, he says at the time, includes occasional sex with the sixty-three year-old Rand.

Branden claims that during the last years of his relationship with Rand the sexual attraction was gone for him. And yet, as we have seen, this did not prevent him from making numerous and extreme claims of enduring passionate love for Rand. Nor did this stop him from making love to Rand—even as late as 1968 he was still kissing her "in a way that was sexual."

For those of us who would be physically incapable of this kind of sexual deception, a degree of psychological explanation is required here.

In his sexual behavior toward Rand, Branden, by his own admission, was motivated not by *lust*, but by *power* and *position*.

As a professional prosecutor with over fifteen years of experience with this category of criminals, this author is able to identify at least one aspect of Branden's character clearly: Branden's psychology shows a striking similarity to *the psychology of a rapist.*

I have interviewed dozens of individuals who have been victims of actual rape. Many physically injured, many threatened with death, some drugged, all brutally wounded. I have seen the terror and the life-enduring trauma distinctive to this crime in its various forms. I have seen the face of rape.

And, obviously, Nathaniel Branden did not commit the crime of rape. He never used physical violence or threats of force against Rand in any way, and he could never have been prosecuted for a sex-crime of any kind for his behavior in this context. Of that violent felony, he was innocent.

However, it is now common-knowledge that rape is not motivated by sexual lust but by the psycho-pathological *need to control*, to dominate, i.e., a kind of *power-lust*. My own experience confirms this, for on two separate occasions, it has been my responsibility to prosecute (successfully through jury-trial) men who had raped quite elderly women. However, even in the cases of younger victims, genuine lust or infatuation appears not to have been the motive, despite the obvious (and twisted) gratification the rapist experiences.

The rapist is merely *using sex* as his chosen instrument of coercion and terror. It is an effective one.

While Branden's *behavior* does not compare, his *motive*—like that of the "Power-seeking" social metaphysician—in his romantic conduct toward Rand was *control and physical gain*, not a sincere passion at all.

Consent can be overcome by fraud as well as by force—Branden himself had written on the relationship between force and fraud as means of manipulation—and what his crime lacked in violence, it made up for in prolonged psychological torment and deception.

And notice the power-relations in Branden's other romantic choices. Barbara and Patrecia were awed and cowed by Branden, as he himself explains in his memoirs. The "Goddess" premise applied to them, too, with Branden as their "Kantian God." But with Rand, a woman of high self-esteem—and whose idea of love was very "un-Kantian"—the only way to achieve some kind of power and control was to *lie*, to attempt to "manipulate her reality," as Branden might have put it himself. Just like the "Power-seeking" social metaphysician, Branden's only way to keep the upper hand of domination was through *deception*. Branden's seeming pleasure in such deception *for its own sake* is hard to otherwise explain. He *enjoyed and prolonged* this kind of domination for years. (102)

In this context, Branden's confessions to becoming sexually excited during "violent quarrels" is noteworthy. We have already seen how Branden, through much of the 1960s, badly used the three women in his life, in one way or another, betraying and slowly inflicting psychological torture on each of them.

Branden was not only able to exploit Rand—intellectually, psychologically, emotionally, professionally and financially—he could do so with an erection.

While his behavior was not, technically, rape, Branden's was nothing less than *the soul of a rapist.*

We have seen that the Brandens' biographies are full of unsupported claims and countless contradictions—not only contradicting each other's accounts, but even repeatedly contradicting themselves. They have exaggerated and distorted the evidence at nearly every opportunity. They have consistently and, obviously, intentionally suppressed vital evidence. Surely they feared that their fabrications would eventually be exposed. Apart from the continued financial exploitation of Rand, something they could have just as easily accomplished with the truth, there must be a reason they took that risk. Why?

The only explanation can be the presence of an even greater fear, one that would make them even willing to face being revealed as liars and frauds.

Fortunately for history, we have Rand's notes, because with them we can fully understand what had previously been inexplicable: we can finally see the underlying motive of the Brandens' contradictory and distorted biographies, where all of the lies and omissions, all of the fabrications, and smears, were aimed at a singular, horrible purpose—the concealment of an act of *spiritual rape.*

Ayn Rand was a unique individual, generations ahead of her time. In the person of Nathaniel Branden, she had sensed the possibility of achieving the complete visibility she had yearned for, something even the husband she loved for over fifty years could not fully give her. This hope, buoyed by Rand's exalted sense of life and concept of romance, is what Branden profoundly undermined in Rand by his prolonged, calculated, and terrible deceit. The full measure of the suffering he caused her can only be guessed.

To whatever extent he ever really appreciated Rand's work, Branden *did* "betray his values." He betrayed them in a way few men ever get the opportunity to do.

However, Rand was never the stereotypical "victim." She was a survivor. No matter what she suffered, neither Rand's philosophy nor her sense of life seems to have been fundamentally altered by the Branden tragedy. As we have seen, her rationality proved to be her greatest weapon, and her self-esteem proved to be her crucial shield.

If Rand had been badly hurt by the events of 1968, it did not take her long to recover. On July 15, 1969, Rand attended the launch of Apollo 11 as an invited VIP. In the September, 1969 edition of *The Objectivist*, she would publish her thrilling account of the day and its meaning—one of the most inspirational essays she ever wrote. (103)

Rand would continue to lecture at the Ford Hall Forum in Boston and elsewhere, and she continued to write, until illness prevented her from doing either. Even in her waning years, she found a renewed enthusiasm for the study of mathematics. Towards the end of her life, she would still take on new projects, such as the writing of a teleplay for a miniseries of *Atlas Shrugged*, which, alas, was never realized.

The source of her strength was best explained, as one might have guessed, by Rand herself. Just six months following her final break with the Brandens, Rand would publish the following in the pages of *The Objectivist*:

> There is a fundamental conviction which some people never acquire, some hold only in their youth, and a few hold to the end of their days—the conviction that *ideas matter*. In one's youth that conviction is experienced as a self-evident absolute, and one is unable fully to believe that there are people who do not share it. That ideas matter means that knowledge matters, that truth matters, that one's mind matters. And the radiance of that certainty, in the process of growing up, is the best aspect of youth.

> Its consequence is the inability to believe in the power or the triumph of evil. No matter what corruption one observes in one's immediate background, one is unable to accept it as normal, permanent or *metaphysically* right. One feels: "This injustice (or terror or falsehood or frustration or pain or agony) is the exception in life, not the rule." One feels certain that somewhere on earth—even if not anywhere in one's surroundings or within one's reach—a proper, human way of life is possible to human beings, and justice matters. (104)

By Rand's own definition of the term, hers was a *stylized* life, one that never ceased to struggle to achieve on earth its own highest values, no matter what obstacles circumstance threw in her way, whether it was Nathaniel Branden or the Russian Revolution. Rand's life was not one of meaningless activity or mere contemplation. Her tireless energy and optimism was the result of one fundamental factor about Ayn Rand—she lived what she believed, a philosophy for living on earth.

FOOTNOTES:

Introduction

1. Even former President Ronald Reagan—despite his later support for the religious politics of the "Moral Majority" and his opposition to abortion rights—described himself in the 1960s as "an admirer" of Ayn Rand, as his recently published correspondence reveals, *Reagan: A Life in Letters*, pp. 281-282.

2. For some examples of such writers and the critical responses to them, see: Chambers, "'Big Sister' is Watching You," pp. 594-596, and Hessen, "Letters: *To the Chambers, Chambers!*" p. 71, and Rothbard, "Letters: The Philosophy of Ayn Rand," p. 95; Vidal, "Comment," *Esquire*, pp. 24-27, and Peikoff, Letter to the Editor, pp. 14 and 20; Nozick, "On the Randian Argument," and Den Uyl and Rasmussen, "Nozick on 'the Randian Argument,'" *Reading Nozick*, pp. 206-269; for Rand's response to such "criticism," see, Rand, "An Open Letter to My Readers," *The Ayn Rand Column*, pp. 43-45.

3. "Rhetorical Incorrectness?" pp. 233-234. Aune also alleges that Rand "has nothing to say to those of us who have children or who are handicapped in some way..." He is apparently unaware of the heroic mother in "Galt's Gulch," *Atlas Shrugged*, pp. 784-785, Rand's comments on parenthood to *Playboy* magazine in 1964, *The Playboy Interview*, vol. II, p. 17, Branden's short essay on the ethics of parental "obligations" in an early edition of *The Objectivist Newsletter*, or Rand's repeated exhortations and demonstrations that the Objectivist ethics are applicable whatever one's native abilities, e.g., *Atlas Shrugged*, pp. 1058-1059. For what one Objectivist would "say" to those with certain disabilities, see Bernstein, *Heart of a Pagan*.

4. In order to avoid any confusion between Nathaniel and Barbara Branden—and in order to avoid the controversy involving the former's academic credentials— Nathaniel Branden is referred to as "Branden" or "Mr. Branden" throughout, while Barbara Branden is always identified as "Ms. Branden," unless the full names are used.

5. "About the Author," *Atlas Shrugged*

6. *Objectivism: The Philosophy of Ayn Rand*, p. 164

7. *Ideas in Action* (television interview)
8. Mr. Branden incorrectly refers to the school where his address was given as "the University of San Diego" in the "Introduction" to the revised edition of his memoir, M.Y.W.A.R., pp. 1.

I. Less Than Zero

1. *The Passion of Ayn Rand* (hereafter, "P.A.R."), p. xiii; Ms. Branden also provides a highly condensed version of Rand's life in "Ayn Rand: the Reluctant Feminist," *Feminist Interpretations of Ayn Rand*, pp. 25-45.
2. *Judgment Day* (hereafter, "J.D."), p. 416
3. P.A.R., pp. 357-358
4. Binswanger, "Ayn Rand's Life," quotes Rand herself—from Ms. Branden's own (1961) taped interviews of Rand—as crediting the influence of Peikoff—at least as much as Branden's influence—on her decision to write her important monograph on epistemology—Rand described one conversation with Peikoff as an "intellectual landmark" in this regard. For his part, Mr. Branden, in the "Prologue" to the first edition of his memoir (J.D., p. 8), may be trying to take credit for getting Rand to write non-fiction in the first place. However, the influences were numerous, and the decision was Rand's. She had also published non-fiction years before meeting the Brandens, for example, Rand's "The Only Path to Tomorrow" which was published in the January, 1944 edition of *Reader's Digest*.
5. For some of the other differences, see Register, "A Kinder, Gentler Judgment Day."
6. "Branden Speaks," *Liberty*, p. 38
7. J.D., p. 381; *My Years With Ayn Rand* (hereafter, "M.Y.W.A.R."), p. 338; the new subtitle some provide in their own citations of this book, "The Truth Behind the Myth," nowhere appears on the first edition as part of the title, but it is a phrase within a description of the book on the cover of the first edition.
8. M.Y.W.A.R., p. 364
9. "Branden Speaks," *Liberty*, p. 43
10. P.A.R., pp. 71-72; in this context, it is interesting to observe that Ms. Branden uniformly names Rand's father "Fronz" while all other sources and scholars are in agreement that his name was "Zinovy." Ms. Branden does not reveal her source for this naming. Perhaps Ms. Branden is attempting to draw more dubious "patterns" between Rand's father and her husband, Frank O'Connor (whose given name was "Francis"), such as those we will see in chapter 2. Ms. Branden also

translates Rand's Russian name as "Alice," while scholars as diverse as Sciabarra and Binswanger normally render it "Alyssa" or "Alisa" in order to convey the Russian pronunciation; see, Sciabarra, *The Russian Radical*, and Binswanger, "Ayn Rand's Life"; at least "Alice" is how her name appeared on her 1926 passport.

11. p. 71, in the book of the film.

12. J.D., p. 73

13. Gotthelf's research is to be included in the revised second edition of his *On Ayn Rand*; the movie Rand saw in Chicago was *The Sheik* with Rudolph Valentino, Rand, *Russian Writings on Hollywood*, p. 202; Rand's DeMille Studio passes are in the possession of the Ayn Rand Archive.

14. Berliner and Ralston, "Something in a Name"; for more on this issue, see Hayes, *Biography "The Passion of Ayn Rand" Is an Inaccurate Chronicle*.

II. Rand and Not Rand

1. P.A.R., p. 7
2. P.A.R., pp. 32-33
3. J.D., p. 214
4. *Journals*, p. 281, and, see Rand, "An Open Letter to My Readers," *The Ayn Rand Column*, pp. 43-45
5. P.A.R., p. 172
6. P.A.R., p. 92; P.A.R., p. 101; P.A.R., p. 99 and p. 172
7. P.A.R., p. 196
8. J.D., p. 64
9. *The Romantic Manifesto*, p. 126
10. P.A.R., pp. 26-27, emphasis original
11. P.A.R., p. 235
12. P.A.R., pp. 237 and 238, emphasis added
13. J.D., p. 111
14. P.A.R., p. 62
15. P.A.R., p. 14
16. *Intellectuals* (hereafter, "I.") p. 218, and pp. 216-217. The current use of *Intellectuals* for biographical contrasts to Rand was not inspired in any way by the very different use made of Johnson's work by Walker in *The Ayn Rand Cult*, p. 256 and p. 265.
17. I., p. 222
18. I., p. 223
19. I., p. 204
20. I., p. 202
21. I., p. 164
22. I., p.165
23. I., p. 302
24. For Rand's own criticism of *Animal Farm*, see *Letters of Ayn Rand*, pp. 310, 337.
25. Peikoff, "My Thirty Years With Ayn Rand," *The Voice of Reason: Essays in Objectivist Thought*, pp. 347-348
26. M.Y.W.A.R., p. 154
27. P.A.R., p. 13; P.A.R., p. 32
28. Sciabarra, "Investigative Report: In Search of the Rand Transcript,"

"The Rand Transcript," and *Ayn Rand: The Russian Radical,* chapters 3 and 4; Mayhew, *Essays on Ayn Rand's We the Living,* chapters 2 and 3. Close scrutiny has been given to Rand's accounts of her own past. Some critics have been so hostile that they have questioned even basic facts that she related about her early life in Russia, e.g., whether she actually took a course from Professor N. O. Lossky—indeed, whether she actually ever attended the University of St. Petersburg (then called "Petrograd," and later "Leningrad," and now "St. Petersburg" again). Sciabarra still questions one or two minor matters, but he acknowledges that nearly all of Rand's autobiographical reports about her life in Russia have been persuasively verified, including her having studied under Lossky.

29. J.D., p. 58
30. J.D., p. 213
31. P.A.R., p. 347
32. P.A.R., p. 153, we revisit the full quotation in the next chapter.
33. P.A.R., p. 169
34. P.A.R., p. 197
35. P.A.R., p. 169
36. *At Random,* pp. 249-253; Cerf's account may have problems of its own: Binswanger, "Ayn Rand's Life," reports that Rand denied a story Cerf related in his memoir, namely, that upon suggesting to Rand that she reduce the length of "Galt's Speech" in *Atlas Shrugged,* Rand allegedly replied, "Would you cut *the Bible?*" Rand told Binswanger that she never would have said such a thing since "the Bible *needs* cutting."
37. P.A.R., p. 370
38. P.A.R., p. 185, and see, Rand, "The Secular Meaning of Christmas," *The Ayn Rand Column,* pp. 111-112
39. P.A.R., p. ix
40. J.D., p. 133; J.D., pp. 193-194 and 252-253
41. J.D., p. 417; in the July, 1962, edition of *The Objectivist Newsletter,* Branden had argued something different in his article, "Benevolence Versus Altruism."
42. M.Y.W.A.R., p. 111
43. J.D., p. 281

44. J.D., p. 296
45. P.A.R., p. 300
46. P.A.R., p. 299
47. P.A.R., p. 268
48. M.Y.W.A.R., p. 2
49. P.A.R., p. 89
50. Peter Schwartz has made similar points in a letter privately circulated to the subscribers of *The Intellectual Activist* following the publication of Ms. Branden's biography.
51. P.A.R., p. 5, emphasis added
52. P.A.R., p. 6, footnote, emphasis added
53. "In Answer to Ayn Rand"
54. "Branden Speaks," *Liberty*, p. 42
55. J.D., p. 74
56. P.A.R., p. 239
57. J.D., p. 54
58. J.D., p. 78; M.Y.W.A.R., p. 67
59. P.A.R. pp. 93-94
60. P.A.R., p. 14; P.A.R., pp. 326-327; P.A.R., p. 5
61. Quoted by Walker, *The Ayn Rand Cult* (hereafter, "T.A.R.C."), p. 243; Walker: the author of the source cited here, apart from his extensive reliance on the Brandens, so grossly misrepresents Rand and Objectivism—for example, calling it a crude form of Nietzsche's philosophy—that his work, as criticism, merits no further comment. Also, Walker's repeated use of empty, personal attack exhibits a degree of hostility towards Rand, her philosophy, and nearly all of her associates, sufficient to suggest significant problems with regard to his objectivity. It is assumed, however, that he has not grossly misquoted persons alive at the publication of his book.
62. J.D., p. 69
63. J.D., p. 65
64. J.D., p. 65; P.A.R., p. 187
65. P.A.R., p. 219; it is also worth recalling that Rand lived the last three decades of her life in Manhattan where driving is not essential.
66. P.A.R., p. 187
67. P.A.R., p. 153

68. P.A.R., pp. 326-327

69. P.A.R., pp. 54, 239-240; J.D., p. 83

70. P.A.R., p. 137; J.D., p. 290

71. J.D., p. 65; P.A.R., p. 326

72. J.D., p. 218

73. P.A.R., pp. 192, 240

74. P.A.R., p. 318; J.D. p. 142

75. J.D., p. 347, emphasis added

76. J.D., p. 347

77. In Rand's private journals, an entry dated June 19, 1958, reads succinctly, "*'Cosmology' has to be thrown out of philosophy*," and see the discussion which follows, *Journals*, pp. 698-699 (italics original); this passage is cited by Ms. Branden in P.A.R. at pp. 322-323.

78. Rand's private notes, July 4, 1968, p. 53

79. J.D., p. 119

80. J.D., p. 223

81. J.D., pp. 212-213

82. J.D., p. 252; P.A.R., p. 194

83. P.A.R., p. 194

84. J.D., p. 215; J.D., p. 83

85. *At Random*, p. 252

86. J.D., p. 213; J.D., p. 157; cf. J.D., p. 165

87. J.D., p. 63

88. *Atlas Shrugged*, "About the Author"

89. *Who Is Ayn Rand?* pp. 170-171, p. 172, p. 204

90. P.A.R., p. 60, p. 72, p. 76

91. *Letters of Ayn Rand*, p. 11, p. 13, p. 27, p. 28, p. 64, pp. 70-71

92. *The Fountainhead*, Introduction to the Twenty-fifth Anniv. Edit., p. ix

93. J.D., p. 136; Ms. Branden, however, does report that they once argued rather intensely, although they did not part even from that discussion as foes, see P.A.R., p. 253.

94. *Ayn Rand's Marginalia*, edit. Robert Mayhew, esp. pp. 105-144

95. P.A.R., p. 293

96. "Foreword," 1959, *We the Living*, p. xviii

97. *We the Living*, New York, 1936, Macmillan, and, revised edition,

New York, 1959, Random House. For the view that Rand had a real "Nietzschean Phase" which included the period during which she wrote *We the Living*, see Merrill, *The Ideas of Ayn Rand*, ch. 3, esp. pp. 37-40, but for a more complete discussion of the issues raised in this section see Mayhew, *Essays on Ayn Rand's We the Living*, chapters 1 and 9. Scholars have repeatedly shown that Nietzsche himself was no prototype Nazi, despite the claims and assumptions still made by some: he opposed socialism along with contemporary German nationalism and what he saw as its tendency to be anti-Semitic—and he even had a falling out with Hitler's favorite composer Richard Wagner. But Nietzsche's praise for figures like Alcibiades and the Borgias—among many other indicators—suggests that he possessed nothing resembling the political values of Jefferson and Madison, either.

98. In notes dated May 9 and 15, 1934, Rand explicitly rejected the need for a "history" or "genealogy" of morals, only a very un-Nietzschean "system" of ethics, and, in explicitly rejecting the notion that she was simply trying to "impose" her "own peculiarities" on philosophy, she had rejected the concept of knowledge as subjective "interpretation," see, *Journals*, notes for "The Little Street," pp. 23-48 and "First Philosophic Journal," pp. 66-73. On the subsequent development of Rand's fiction, see *The Early Ayn Rand*. Whatever Nietzsche's early influence on Rand, un-Nietzschean tributes to Aristotle's metaphysics and logic can also be found as early as *We the Living*, as when Kira, Rand's heroine praises the honesty of engineering by saying, "Steel is steel." This is, perhaps, Rand's earliest literary use of the formula "A is A," *We the Living*, (1995 edition, p. 25, but also found in the earliest edition.)

99. P.A.R., p. 271; P.A.R., p. 311

100. *Who Is Ayn Rand?*, pp. 165-166; for an analysis of Nietzsche's ideas from the Objectivist perspective, see Bernstein, "Friedrich Nietzsche—His Thought, His Legacy; His Influence on Ayn Rand."

101. "Introduction," *The Fountainhead*, Twenty-fifth Anniversary Edition

102. "About the Author," *Atlas Shrugged*

103. Rand, "Review of *Aristotle* by John Herman Randall, Jr.," *The Voice of Reason: Essays in Objectivist Thought*, pp. 6-12

104. *Capitalism:The Unknown Ideal,* "Theory and Practice," p. 134

105. Kaufmann, "Editor's Introduction," 2, *Ecce Homo;* in *Antichrist* 8, Nietzsche does credit Aristotle for his critique of pity, but is elsewhere highly critical of Aristotle; Sciabarra, *Ayn Rand: the Russian Radical,* also contends that Rand may have acquired what he calls her "dialectical" method of thinking from Hegel and Marx, two of the architects of modern collectivism, via her professors at university; however, a similar response can be made: what supposed value may be culled from Hegel's (or Marx's) use of a valid "dialectical" logic can be traced directly to the influence of Aristotle—whose own logic does not come packaged with Hegel's profound errors—including his "dialectical" assaults on logic itself.

106. J.D., p. 226; P.A.R., p. 295

107. P.A.R., p. 295; J.D., p. 226

108. *At Random,* pp. 249-253

109. Mary Ann Sures and Charles Sures, *Facets of Ayn Rand,* pp. 87-88

110. P.A.R., p. 70

111. P.A.R., pp. 70-71

112. P.A.R., p. 190

113. P.A.R., p. 173

114. J.D., 348; cf. M.Y.W.A.R., p. 306

III. Mullah Rand?

1. P.A.R., pp. 190-191
2. J.D., p. 288
3. P.A.R., p. 271, emphasis added
4. J.D., pp. 255-256
5. J.D., p. 256. Despite Branden's "best not to say openly" remark, Jerome Tuccille actually cites Branden as his source for the proposition that to remain in Rand's favor one was *required* to "believe and state openly" the most bizarre of these premises. This is a good example of Tuccille's methodology and shoddy scholarship when discussing Rand, and it is but one example of how the Brandens' dubious histories are used and built upon in still more dubious ways, see Tuccille, *Alan Shrugged*, pp. 73-74. In fairness to Tuccille, it must be acknowledged that many of his errors stem from his extensive (and uncritical) reliance on both Rothbard and the Brandens. (In Rand criticism, it usually begins with the Brandens.) However, given the repeated stress placed on the "implicit" nature of these demands in both Brandens' books and the sheer number of other Branden-like contradictions in Tuccille's histories of Rand, one suspects that a hostile dishonesty—comparable to the Brandens'—is at work.
6. J.D., p. 352, emphasis added
7. J.D., p. 172; Branden is here echoing an identical claim made to *Reason* in 1971, but—in sharp contrast to his later accounts—Branden then claimed that this "demand for loyalty" was made "during an argument" and that it explicitly pertained only to his relationships with Ms. Branden and Rand and potential "conflicts" among those personal relationships. Whether his marriage was already falling apart yet or not was not revealed, and, of course, Rand's actual words were not reported.
8. J.D., p. 291
9. "To Whom It May Concern," (*The Objectivist* bound volume p. 454)
10. J.D. pp. 236-237; Ms. Branden suggests that—at least initially—Rand was "dubious" of NBI-type courses *as such*, saying that "Ayn was dubious about the presentation of such a course [on Objectivism.]" P.A.R., p. 306.

11. J.D., p. ix

12. Rand's private notes, July 4, 1968, pp. 45-46

13. Bennett Cerf quotes George Axelrod, who wrote the screenplay for the 1962 film version of *The Manchurian Candidate*, as saying, "[Ayn Rand] knows me better after five hours than my analyst does after five years," *At Random*, p. 250, and Mr. Branden himself says that he "marveled at [Rand's] insight" into masculine psychology. J.D., p.85; "Psychology of 'Psychologizing,'" *The Objectivist*, reprinted in *The Voice of Reason*, p. 23-31.

14. P.A.R., p. 270

15. P.A.R., p. 271

16. P.A.R., p. 269

17. J.D., p. 264

18. *ibid*

19. J.D. p. 265

20. J.D., p. 264

21. J.D., p. 116; M.Y.W.A.R., p. 97

22. B. Branden, *Liberty* Interview; "Interview: Barbara Branden," *Full Context*

23. J.D., p. 131; J.D., p. 297

24. P.A.R., pp. 242-243

25. P.A.R., p. 268

26. J.D., p. 348; J.D., p. 241; cf. P.A.R., p. 268

27. J.D., p. 252; P.A.R., p. 243

28. *Facets of Ayn Rand*, pp. 81-82

29. "My Thirty Years With Ayn Rand," *The Voice of Reason*, p. 349; it is also worth noting that such a spiritual "wall" did not prevent Rand from designating Leonard Peikoff, a lover of jazz music, her heir.

30. P.A.R., p. 304

31. P.A.R., p. 255

32. J.D., p. 346

33. quoted in Walker, T.A.R.C., p. 151

34. I owe this point to Casey Fahy.

35. "The Psychology of 'Psychologizing,'" *The Objectivist* (and *The Voice of Reason*, pp. 23-31); *Atlas Shrugged*, p. 1059

36. Rand's private notes, January 25, 1967, p. 9

37. "Books in Review: 'Big Sister' Is Watching You," *The National Review*; that magazine's editor did not assign the review to either John Chamberlain or Murray Rothbard—two of its most frequent and popular book reviewers at this time—either of whom would have positively reviewed the novel, see Chamberlain, *A Life with the Printed Word*, p.136 and p.150, and Rothbard, "Letters: the Philosophy of Ayn Rand," p. 95. The magazine has continued to published articles highly critical of Rand but of little substance. Its founder, William F. Buckley, relies heavily on the Brandens in his own attacks on Rand, see *Getting It Right*. The Objectivists have not publicly responded to these attacks since the 1950s.

38. J.D., p. 47; J.D., p. 89; J.D., p. 201; and, J.D., p. 261. Ayn Rand's many friends included the celebrated writer Morrie Ryskind and prominent business figures like William Mullendore of Consolidated Edison of California and Herbert Corneulle of Dole Pineapple. In the 1940s and 1950s, Rand also had a number of friends and associates among the writers then advocating a free market, and even had a limited degree of influence on them. For example, John Chamberlain revealed that *The Fountainhead* and *Atlas Shrugged* were two of the four books that finally converted him from socialism (*A Life with the Printed Word*, p. 136). After meeting with Rand in early 1953, Max Eastman appears to have been favorably impressed by their agreement on the "momentous" (but unspecified) issue they had discussed, according to the letter he sent her, dated February 27, 1953, and now in the Ayn Rand Archive. And Ludwig von Mises once referred to Rand as "the most courageous man in America." (Rand is said to have been pleased when Henry Hazlitt confirmed that Mises had indeed said "man," P.A.R., p. 189. Since Hazlitt was alive at the time of this report, it must be regarded as credible.)

39. J.D., p. 63 and p. 281

40. P.A.R., p. 154

41. See, Peter Schwartz, "Libertarianism: The Perversion of Liberty," *The Voice of Reason: Essays in Objectivist Thought*, pp. 311-333

42. P.A.R., p. 391

43. Murray Rothbard: No attempt here is made to address the Rothbard critique. When I asked him about it in 1982, Professor Rothbard

himself told me that his "Sociology of the Ayn Rand Cult" was "highly fictionalized." For example, no one was ever "excommunicated" from Rand's circle for not liking the music of Rachmaninoff as Rand did. Rothbard was himself explicitly aware of the dishonesty of his attack.

44. On Rothbard's use of Rand, see, especially, *The Ethics of Liberty*, 1982, pp. 3-31, esp. p. 31, where he discusses "the fusion of matter and spirit" in production, and Rothbard, "Individualism and the Methodology of the Social Sciences," especially the validation of free will.

45. P.A.R., p. 324; J.D., pp. 308-309

46. Hospers, "Conversations with Ayn Rand," pp.42-52, "Memories of Ayn Rand"

47. J.D., p.308; *Letters of Ayn Rand*, pp. 502-563

48. J.D., p. 309; Branden was no more specific about the details of the Efron break even in 1971, although he was then claiming no inability to remember, see "Break Free," *Reason*, p. 14. The most detail on the cause of Efron's departure with Rand has so far been provided by Tuccille, who mentions only a personal and "biting remark" Efron had made about Rand—within earshot of Rand. We are still curiously not given the content or nature of this personal insult, or its surrounding context, see Tuccille, *Alan Shrugged*, p. 73.

49. See Peikoff, "Fact and Value," for a fuller discussion of this.

50. P.A.R., pp. 241, 328, cf. 311

51. J.D. pg. 199; P.A.R. p. 205

52. See *Sweet Land of Liberty?*, esp. pp. 100-101, how the High Court created the privacy right "out of whole cloth."

53. See, *Ayn Rand's Marginalia*, esp. pp. 203-205; Binswanger, "The Hardwick Decision," cf. Macedo, *The New Right v. the Constitution*.

54. quoted by Walker, T.A.R.C., p. 247

55. T.A.R.C., pp. 35-36 and p. 37

56. T.A.R.C., p. 341; J.D., pp. 309-310

57. T.A.R.C., p. 35, Miss. Smith refused the author's request to be interviewed in 1983.

58. T.A.R.C., p. 248

59. T.A.R.C., p. 250

60. P.A.R., p. 329

61. J.D., p. 237; J.D., p. 244
62. J.D., p. 243
63. P.A.R., p. 329
64. *ibid*
65. *ibid*
66. *The Phil Donahue Show*, May 15, 1979; P.A.R., pp. 391-392
67. J.D., pp. 243-244, emphasis original
68. *ibid*
69. J.D., p. 213
70. *ibid*
71. *The Virtue of Selfishness*, p. ix
72. J.D., p. 335
73. *ibid*
74. "My Thirty Years With Ayn Rand," *The Voice of Reason*, pp. 350-351
75. *Facets of Ayn Rand*, p. 110
76. *ibid*

IV. Exploiters and Exploited

1. J.D., pp. 327 and 338
2. J.D., p. 404
3. I have heard a portion of this taped interview material at the home of Leonard Peikoff. While Jesus and Rand are, of course, opposites in nearly all respects, it is probably not too much of an exaggeration to compare the Gospels and the Branden biographies in respect to their accuracy and reliability.
4. "To Whom It May Concern" (hereafter, "T.W.I.M.C."), *The Objectivist*, p. 1, bound volume p. 449; "In Answer to Ayn Rand" (hereafter, "I.A.A.R."), pp. 1 and 6; all further references in this chapter are these two statements unless otherwise indicated.
5. J.D., p. 91
6. J.D., p. 252
7. J.D., p. 352
8. J.D., p. 331
9. J.D., p. 420; J.D., p. 245, emphasis added
10. J.D., p. 347; the speech was "The Benefits and Hazards of the Philosophy of Ayn Rand."
11. "Break Free," *Reason*, October 1971, p. 12
12. "Break Free," *Reason*, p. 15, emphasis added
13. *ibid.* Rand quite obviously did not intend Dominique to be one of the "folks next door," or even a typical personality type, and, literally, the question is simply whether the character's psychology is plausible in the context of the story and consistent with its theme. The author's own stated affinity to the character (at least while "in a bad mood") perhaps helps to explain how Rand could render her readers able to suspend their disbelief regarding Dominique's unusual qualities. Rearden's mental anguish, though significant and acknowledged in the text, cannot compare to the potential dangers to the strikers if they are discovered, as Galt's later fate demonstrates.
14. Branden, "Break Free," *Reason*, p. 11
15. N. Branden, *The Basic Principles of Objectivism*, esp. Lectures 1 through 5
16. "Break Free," *Reason*, p. 12, emphasis added

17. J.D., p. 347
18. J.D., p. 308
19. J.D., p. 335
20. "Break Free," *Reason*, p. 10, emphasis added
21. J.D., p. 285, emphasis added
22. "Break Free," *Reason*, p. 10
23. Branden, "The Benefits and Hazards of the Philosophy of Ayn Rand"
24. "Branden Speaks," *Liberty*, p. 44
25. J.D., p. 375
26. "Break Free," *Reason*, p. 11
27. J.D., p. 434
28. J.D., p. 340
29. J.D., p. 374; ten years later, in his revised memoir, Branden removes his earlier admission that at the time he thought Ms. Branden and himself to be "operators." (M.Y.W.A.R., p. 331.)
30. T.W.I.M.C., pp. 4-5
31. I.A.A.R., p. 3
32. I.A.A.R., p. 4; J.D., p. 291
33. J.D., p. 368
34. J.D., p. 362
35. J.D., p. 368
36. *Liberty*, Jan. 1990, pp.49-76; Joan Blumenthal is quoted by Walker in T.A.R.C., p.153.
37. T.W.I.M.C., pp. 1-2I; I.A.A.R., p. 2
38. J.D., p. 370)
39. I.A.A.R., p. 2; J.D., p. 370
40. J.D., p. 370
41. IAAR, p. 2; Branden, "The Basic Principles of Objectivism"; it was David Hayes who first pointed out the actual extent of the "updates" of the course.
42. T.W.I.M.C., p. 3; I.A.A.R., p. 5
43. I.A.A.R., p. 5; J.D., p. 346; J.D., p. 339; Ms. Branden writes in P.A.R. that it was Rand who offered her help to Branden at this time, P.A.R., p. 333, but it is highly unlikely that Mr. Branden would make such an admission if it were not the case. Moreover, Branden's solicitation of Rand may simply have been outside of Ms. Branden's knowledge.
44. M.Y.W.A.R., p. 250; cf. J.D., p. 286 and pp. 110-111
45. "Branden Speaks," *Liberty*, p. 42

46. *ibid*
47. J.D., p. 340
48. P.A.R., p. 335
49. J.D., p. 372; J.D., p. 364
50. Rand's private notes, November 27, 1967, p. 2
51. I.A.A.R., p. 6
52. T.W.I.M.C., p. 4
53. P.A.R., pp. 332-333; J.D., p. 327; J.D., pp. 325-327
54. J.D., p. 375
55. J.D., p. 378; P.A.R., p. 341
56. J.D., p. 359
57. P.A.R., p. 350; a copy of what appears to be Ms. Branden's business plan is in the possession of the Ayn Rand Archive.
58. P.A.R., p. 351; I.A.A.R., p. 10
59. T.W.I.M.C., pp. 6-7
60. T.W.I.M.C., p. 7
61. P.A.R., p. 350
62. J.D., p. 398, emphasis original
63. Copies of these letters are with the Ayn Rand Archive.
64. I.A.A.R., p. 4
65. J.D., p. 391; P.A.R., p. 349
66. J.D., pp. 400-401; certain of Rand's papers in the possession of the Ayn Rand Archive make clear that Branden's copyrights were indeed the subject of legal discussion during the break; while these papers are mostly limited to items like lists of Branden's articles, they appear to assume a willingness on Rand's part to provide Branden with the release he sought.
67. I.A.A.R., p. 4
68. *ibid*; P.A.R., p. 349
69. Rand's private notes, July 4, 1968, pp. 13-14
70. J.D., p. 391

V. Something Between Them

1. "The Objectivist Ethics," *The Virtue of Selfishness*, p. 29
2. *ibid*
3. "Of Living Death," *The Voice of Reason*, p. 54
4. For more on Rand's ethics, see Rand, "The Objectivist Ethics", *The Virtue of Selfishness*, pp. 1-34 (pb. pp.13-39), Peikoff, *Objectivism: the Philosophy of Ayn Rand*, pp. 187-349, and Smith, *Viable Values*.
5. *The Playboy Interview*, p. 18
6. "Censorship: Local and Express," *Philosophy: Who Needs It*, pp. 210-230
7. But see, "The Psychology of 'Psychologizing,'" *The Voice of Reason*, pp. 23-31; *The Objectivist*, March 1971, pp. 5-6. Although repeatedly attacked for her "published" views on homosexuality, by Tuccille and others, Rand never discussed them in any of her published writings, perhaps indicating a lack of certainty on the topic. Following a lecture at the Ford Hall Forum in 1971, responding to a question about homosexuality —while Rand was quick to point out that it should, of course, not be a legal issue—she also said that it is the result of not only "unfortunate premises" but also psychological "flaws" and "corruptions." She stated that its practice was not only personally "disgusting" to her but also "immoral." Quite understandably, her response deeply hurt many of her (perfectly moral) admirers. Rand's published remarks on emotion and morality, and especially in light of her opposition to "Platonic" love—in the author's view— contradict this interpretation. Had Rand's views on homosexuality been part of her system of thought, one which dealt explicitly with human sexuality, one would have expected them to have been included, in some form, in her published work. As with some of her statements regarding feminism—such as when Rand called herself "a male chauvinist, proudly," while, in the common meaning of the term, this is hardy a fair description of her position—we must be cautious in our interpretation of Rand. Her anger at Gay Activists and the "ideological" lesbianism of some radical feminists is the likely motive for her attack here. Of interest, Ms. Branden relates that Rand was herself quite close to her brother-in-law Nick O'Connor—who,

according to Ms. Branden, Rand believed was gay. (P.A.R., pp. 100-101) Unlike Libertarians, Rand usually focused on that which she considered the *ideal*—never merely the *permissible*; for a contrary view, see Sciabarra, *Ayn Rand: the Russian Radical,* pp. 200-201.

8. J.D., p. 205
9. *The Playboy Interview,* p. 18
10. *Atlas Shrugged,* p. 491
11. *Journals,* p. 607
12. "Through Your Most Grievous Fault," *The Voice of Reason,* p. 160
13. P.A.R., p. 263
14. P.A.R., p. 262
15. J.D., p. 160
16. P.A.R., pp. 263-264
17. J.D., p. 156
18. P.A.R., p. 260
19. Of course, Rand, in her writings and in person, also had a profound impact on mature minds, including, among others, the previously mentioned John Hospers and Charles Sures.
20. P.A.R., p. 260
21. J.D., p. 60; J.D., p. 102
22. J.D., p. 345. There is only one instance that either of the Brandens can produce that even comes close to a denial of the affair by Rand. Branden's oldest sister, Florence, was the first of his sisters to actually side with him after his break with Rand, and he twice describes her as being "very protective" of her younger brother. (J.D., p. 28 and p. 392; M.Y.W.A.R., p. 22 and p. 350.) According to Branden's report, based on what Florence told him, big sister can only be described as having soon confronted (if not assailed) Rand about her break with Branden. Florence reported to him that after "*several hours of evading questions*" about the affair with Branden, Rand angrily admitted it (J.D., p. 393, M.Y.W.A.R., p. 350, emphasis added; cf. "Interview with Nathaniel Branden," *Full Context.*) According to Objectivism, auch (intense) prying into another's personal affairs could have justified an outright denial on Rand's part, but, even in this instance, Rand did not leave the other party in ignorance. From the beginning of the conversation, it must have been quite clear that Branden had already

told his sister something. Only Rand's unwillingness to discuss her feelings with this individual is indicated here, in any event. The report itself, of course, must also be treated skeptically.

23. J.D., p. 99, p. 107, and pp. 145-147
24. J.D., pp. 151-153
25. J.D., p. 158
26. J.D., p. 159
27. J.D., p. 268
28. J.D., p. 365, emphasis added.
29. J.D., p. 221
30. J.D., p. 371
31. *ibid*
32. P.A.R., p. 340
33. J.D., p. 371; J.D., pp. 352-353, emphasis added
34. P.A.R., p. 272
35. *ibid*
36. *ibid*
37. *ibid*
38. P.A.R., p. 384
39. *ibid*
40. Ms. Branden's preposterous assertion that O'Connor "once" struck Rand is not addressed. Ms. Branden brazenly cites no source whatsoever for this serious charge, and it would have been highly out of character, even by the Brandens' accounts, either for Rand to have tolerated this, or for the gentle O'Connor to have been capable of this.
41. P.A.R., p. 366
42. This is the author's best recollection of Leonard Peikoff's statement in response to a question on the subject given during a conversation at his home in California in 1991, and it echoes comments made by Peikoff in the question and answer period following his speech "My Thirty Years With Ayn Rand" which was delivered at the Ford Hall Forum in Boston on April 12, 1987; "Interview: Nathaniel Branden," *Full Context*; however, the author's grandmother painted in oils, and did, indeed, use narrow necked bottles (somehow) in her work—and she was religiously abstentious.

43. "Interview: Barbara Branden," *Full Context*, 1992

44. J.D., p. 373

45. M.Y.W.A.R., p. 143, cf. J.D., p. 166

46. P.A.R., p. 334

47. P.A.R., pp. 272-273

48. .A.R., p. 258

49. P.A.R., p. 262

50. J.D., p. 155

51. J.D., p. 157

52. M.Y.W.A.R., p. 145

53. J.D., p. 156

54. J.D., p. 157

55. Being the most culpable and the least victimized in the situation, Branden says that he does not believe in "victims" in situations of this kind, and then continues to complain of Rand's unfeeling indifference to her husband's feelings. (J.D., p. 166) As we have seen, Branden is as much a master of misdirection as any magician.

56. P.A.R., p. 259

57. P.A.R., p. 261, emphasis added

58. P.A.R., p. 263; P.A.R., p. 338

59. P.A.R., p. 26

60. J.D., p. 160

61. P.A.R., p. 282, emphasis added

62. P.A.R., pp. 262-263

63. J.D., p. 67

64. P.A.R, p. 248

65. J.D., p. 101; J.D., p. 109

66. J.D., p. 218

67. P.A.R., p. 185

68. J.D., p. 218

69. J.D., p. 218-219

70. J.D., p. 161

71. J.D., p. 68

72. This and other evidence tends to contradict Branden's assertion that Rand had once told Branden in private that she had always been the "initiator" of all of the sex during her marriage; Branden's claim is

based on yet another of those "private" and unverifiable conversations which seem to contradict other evidence.

73. P.A.R., p. 153
74. *The Phil Donahue Show*, April 29, 1980
75. J.D., p. 46
76. P.A.R., p. 96; P.A.R., p. 218; J.D., p. 79; P.A.R., p. 291; P.A.R., p. 282
77. P.A.R., p. 172; P.A.R., p. 170, and Rand, "Introduction," Twenty-fifth Anniv. Edition, *The Fountainhead*, p. vii
78. P.A.R., pp. 235-236
79. P.A.R., p. 88
80. *ibid*
81. P.A.R, pp. 87-88
82. *ibid*
83. J.D., p. 66
84. *Letters of Ayn Rand*, p. 418
85. J.D., p. 66; J.D., p. 67; J.D., p. 135
86. "Introduction," *The Fountainhead*, Twenty-fifth Anniv. Edit., p. vii-ix
87. J.D., p. 76
88. P.A.R., p. 171; J.D., p. 76; *Who is Ayn Rand?*, p. 202.
89. P.A.R., p. 338
90. *Letters of Ayn Rand*, p. 437
91. *Letters of Ayn Rand*, pp. 661-662, half of the quoted portion of this letter is translated from the original Russian in that edition.
92. P.A.R., p. 137
93. J.D., p. 207
94. *Atlas Shrugged*, p. 798; Rand also discusses this principle at greater length in "The 'Conflicts' of Men's Interests," *The Virtue of Selfishness*, pp. 57-67 (pb. pp. 57-65.)
95. *Journals*, p. 609
96. *Journals*, p. 605, emphasis added.
97. Pronounce the names "Francisco d'Anconia" and "Frank O'Connor" or "Francis O'Connor" aloud to get this point concretely, and my thanks to Lee Pierson for this observation.
98. *Atlas Shrugged*, p. 643
99. *Atlas Shrugged*, p. 808
100. *Journals*, p. 553, emphasis added

VI. School or Cult?

1. P.A.R., p. 352
2. Rand's enemies began the construction of a hostile mythology about her life quite early. The Ayn Rand Archive possesses a letter—unfortunately bearing no date, but apparently written in the 1950s—Henry Hazlitt wrote to Russell Kirk in order to vigorously refute the (frequently repeated) story that Ludwig von Mises once accused Rand of behaving "just like a little Jewish girl" during a heated argument. Hazlitt explained that he had introduced the two and was an eyewitness to the conversation in question. Despite this, the legend is still in circulation.
3. Peikoff, *Objectivism: the Philosophy of Ayn Rand*, pp. 163-171
4. *The Passion of Ayn Rand* (movie); Ms. Branden's enthusiasm for the movie version of her book can be found at http://www.barbarabranden.com/movie.html
5. J.D., p. 185
6. For a detailed outline of Rand's life (while not yet the complete biography that the subject deserves), one using material from the recorded autobiographical interviews and the extensive documentation housed at the Ayn Rand Archive, see Britting, *Ayn Rand.*

PART II: The Rape of Innocence

1. Rand's private notes on the Brandens (hereafter, "R.P.N."), January 25, 1968, p. 13.
2. R.P.N., July 4, 1968, pp. 38-39
3. J.D., p. 340, pp. 368-369, p.371, p. 377; P.A.R., p. 340
4. J.D., p. 349 and p. 369
5. P.A.R., 346, but, cf. J.D., pp. 383-387 and M.Y.W.A.R., pp. 342-345, where this assertion is noticeably *not* related in Branden's own depiction of the event.
6. For example, J.D., p. 352
7. R.P.N., July 8, 1968, p. 16, emphasis original.
8. R.P.N., July 4, 1968, p. 44
9. R.P.N., July 8, 1968, p. 13
10. R.P.N., July 8, 1968, p. 13, emphasis original.
11. R.P.N., July 4, 1968, p. 24
12. R.P.N., November 27, 1967, pp. 6-8 and p. 2
13. R.P.N., January 25, 1968, p. 7
14. R.P.N., July 4, 1968, p. 45
15. R.P.N., February 14, 1968, p. 6
16. R.P.N., July 4, 1968, p. 40
17. R.P.N., January 25, 1968, p. 17
18. R.P.N., July 8, 1968, p. 27
19. R.P.N., July 4, 1968, pp. 6-7
20. R.P.N., July 4, 1968, p. 15
21. R.P.N., July 4, 1968, p. 7
22. *ibid.*
23. R.P.N., July 4, 1968, pp. 29-30
24. R.P.N., July 8, 1968, p. 24
25. R.P.N., "BB's Report on discussion of my paper (of July 4)," p. 2
26. R.P.N., July 4, 1968, p. 35
27. R.P.N., July 4, 1968, p. 3
28. R.P.N., July 4, 1968, p. 52
29. *ibid.*
30. R.P.N., July 4, 1968, pp. 50-51
31. R.P.N., July 4, 1968, p. 49

32. R.P.N., July 4, 1968, pp. 4-5
33. R.P.N., July 4, 1968, p. 8
34. R.P.N., July 4, 1968, pp. 30-31
35. R.P.N., July 4, 1968, pp. 32-33
36. R.P.N., November 27, 1967, pp. 10-11
37. R.P.N., January 25, 1968, p. 7, emphasis added
38. R.P.N., November 27, 1968, p. 7
39. R.P.N., January 25, 1968, p. 19
40. For a complete discussion of the syndrome Objectivism refers to as "rationalism," see Peikoff, "Understanding Objectivism."
41. R.P.N., January 25, 1968, p. 8
42. R.P.N., January 28, 1968, p. 1
43. R.P.N., January 28, 1968, unpaginated, single-page entry
44. R.P.N., February 10, 1968, unpaginated, single-page entry
45. R.P.N., January 25, 1968, p. 9, emphasis original
46. R.P.N., February 17, 1968, unpaginated, single-page entry
47. R.P.N., July 4, 1968, pp. 13-14
48. For the Objectivist theory of history, see, Peikoff, *The Ominous Parallels*, and Rand, *For the New Intellectual*, title essay.
49. Bronowski, *The Ascent of Man*, p. 437
50. For a comprehensive glossary of Objectivism's distinctive lexicon, see Binswanger, *The Ayn Rand Lexicon*.
51. Rand, "Introduction," *The Fountainhead*, Twenty-fifth Anniv. Edit., p. xi
52. See Rand, "The Goal of My Writing"
53. J.D., pp. 18-20
54. See Branden, "Self-Esteem and Romantic Love," especially, Parts I and II
55. On psycho-epistemology, generally, see Binswanger, *The Ayn Rand Lexicon*, pp. 392-394, and Branden, "Psycho-Epistemology"; on Rand's distinctive psycho-epistemology, see Peikoff, "My Thirty Years With Ayn Rand."
56. J.D., pp. 42-52, esp. p. 48
57. *Love Letters*, Hal Wallis Productions, 1945 (screenplay)
58. Peikoff, *Objectivism: the Philosophy of Ayn Rand*, pp. 342-349
59. M.Y.W.A.R., p. 316
60. *Reason* interview, p. 14

61. See Rand, "Philosophy and Sense of Life," *The Objectivist*, February, 1966, reprinted as Chapter 2 of *The Romantic Manifesto*

62. M.Y.W.A.R., p. 319

63. M.Y.W.A.R., p. 325

64. P.A.R., p. 332

65. R.P.N., November 27, 1967, p. 8

66. R.P.N., July 8, 1968, p. 20

67. J.D., p. 325 and M.Y.W.A.R., p. 286, this assertion, it must be pointed out, was made years after Patrecia's death.

68. J.D., p. 221

69. J.D., p. 346

70. P.A.R., p. 333 and J.D., pp. 354-361

71. J.D., p. 350

72. P.A.R., p. 334

73. J.D., p. 355

74. J.D., p. 356

75. P.A.R., p. 334

76. J.D., p. 368

77. J.D., p. 352, emphasis added.

78. P.A.R., p. 335, emphasis added.

79. R.P.N., July 4, 1968, pp. 31-32

80. P.A.R., p. 337

81. J.D., p.371; *ibid*; J.D., p. 366

82. J.D., p. 371

83. P.A.R., pp. 335-336

84. J.D., p. 372

85. J.D., p.365, emphasis added.

86. R.P.N., July 4, 1968, pp. 35-36

87. R.P.N., July 4, 1968, p. 46

88. J.D., p. 365-366

89. R.P.N., July 4, 1968, p. 9

90. P.A.R., p. 299 and p. 300

91. R.P.N., January 25, 1968, p. 16

92. See Branden, "Emotions and Values," and "Self-Esteem," Parts I-V

93. J.D., pp. 325-326

94. J.D., p. 349 and p. 369

95. Rand, "Causality Versus Duty," *Philosophy: Who Needs It*, pp. 115-122

96. Jones, *A History of Western Philosophy*, vol. 4, chapters 2-4, esp. pp. 14-99

97. Branden, "Rogues' Gallery," p. 3

98. Copies of all of these letters are with the Ayn Rand Archive. No lawsuit was ever filed, according to Branden, because he wanted to avoid living in the "sewer" of a libel action for two years, and he says that he just wanted to get on with his life, J.D. p. 404-405, M.Y.W.A.R., p.360; Ms. Branden says much the same, P.A.R., p.356.

99. J.D., p. 407

100. M.Y.W.A.R., pp. 363-364

101. Rand's notes are dated and represent a contemporaneous account of the progression of her developing understanding of Mr. Branden's psychology. An obvious effort has been made to preserve all of Rand's notes. When a specific inquiry was made, Leonard Peikoff confirmed that he knows of no later journal entries referring to Branden.

102. On this phenomenon, see Peikoff, "What To Do About Crime," esp. sections 3, 4 and 5.

103. See Rand, "Apollo 11"

104. Rand, "The 'Inexplicable Personal Alchemy,'" *Return of the Primitive*, p. 122

REFERENCES:

Aune, James Arnt
- "Rhetorical Incorrectness?" *The Journal of Ayn Rand Studies*, volume 4, number 1, Fall 2002, 231-234

Berliner, Michael and Ralston, Richard
- "Something in a Name," *Impact: The Ayn Rand Institute Newsletter*, May 1997, Scott McConnell, editor

Bernstein, Andrew
- *Heart of a Pagan: The Story of Swoop*, 2002, Cresskill, New Jersey: The Paper Tiger
- "Friedrich Nietzsche—His Thought, His Legacy; His Influence on Ayn Rand," 1999, New Milford, Connecticut: Second Renaissance Books (6 audio recorded lectures, now available through the Ayn Rand Bookstore)

Binswanger, Harry
- "Ayn Rand's Life: Highlights and Sidelights," 1994, Oceanside, California: Second Renaissance Books (2 audio recoded lectures, now available through the Ayn Rand Bookstore)
- "The Hardwick Decision," *The Objectivist Forum*, volume 7, number 5, October 1986
- *The Ayn Rand Lexicon: Objectivism From A to Z*, Binswanger, editor, 1986, New York: New American Library

Branden, Barbara
- *The Passion of Ayn Rand*, 1986, Garden City New York: Doubleday
- "Ayn Rand: the Reluctant Feminist," in *Feminist Interpretations of Ayn Rand*, Gladstein and Sciabarra, editors, 1999, University Park, PA: The Pennsylvania State University Press, 25-45
- *Liberty* Interview, *Liberty*, January 1990
- "Interview: Barbara Branden," *Full Context*, October, 1992
- *The Passion of Ayn Rand*, 1999, Showtime (movie)

Branden, Nathaniel
- *Judgment Day: My Years With Ayn Rand*, 1989, Boston: Houghton-Mifflin
- *My Years With Ayn Rand*, 1999, San Francisco, California: Jossey-Bass
- "What are the respective obligations of parents to children, and children to parents?," *The Objectivist Newsletter*, December, 1962
- "Nathaniel Branden Speaks," *Liberty*, Sept. 1999
- "Benevolence Versus Altruism," *The Objectivist Newsletter*, July 1962
- "The Benefits and Hazards of the Philosophy of Ayn Rand," *The Journal of Humanistic Psychology*, Fall 1984
- "Break Free:An Interview With Nathaniel Branden," *Reason*, October 1971, 4-9
- "The Basic Principles of Objectivism," Nathaniel Branden Institute; vinyl LPs of the lectures bearing only the copyright 1960 were made available through Academic Associates after 1968 (audio recording).
- *The Psychology of Self Esteem*, 1969, Los Angeles: Nash
- "Interview with Nathaniel Branden," *Full Context*, Sept.-Oct. 1996.
- "Psycho-Epistemology," Parts I and II, *The Objectivist Newsletter*, October and November, 1964
- "Self-Esteem and Romantic Love," Parts I, II and III, *The Objectivist*, December, 1967, January and February 1968
- "Emotions and Values," *The Objectivist*, May, 1966
- "Self-Esteem," *The Objectivist*, Part I, March, 1967, Part II, April, 1967, Part III, May, 1967, Part IV, June, 1967, and Part V, September, 1967
- "Rogues' Gallery," *The Objectivist Newsletter*, Part II, March, 1965

Branden, Barbara, and Branden, Nathaniel
- "In Answer to Ayn Rand," 1968, privately circulated, now available on their respective websites.
- *Who Is Ayn Rand?*, 1962, New York: Random House

Britting, Jeff
- *Ayn Rand*, (forthcoming) Woodstock, N,Y.: Overlook Press

Bronowski, Jacob
- *The Ascent of Man*, 1973, Boston, Mass.: Little, Brown and Company

Buckley, William
- *Getting It Right*, 2003, Washington, D.C.: Regnery

Cerf, Bennett
- *At Random*, 1977, New York: Random House

Chamberlain, John
- *A Life with the Printed Word*, 1982, Chicago: Regnery Gateway

Chambers, Whittaker
- "Big Sister Is Watching You," *The National Review*, December 28, 1957

Den Uyl, Douglas and Rasmussen, Douglas
- "Nozick on 'the Randian Argument'" *The Personalist*, Spring 1978, reprinted along with Nozick article in *Reading Nozick: Essays on Anarchy, State and Utopia*, J. Paul, editor, 1981, Totowa, New Jersey: Rowman and Littlefield, 206-269.

Gotthelf, Allan
- *On Ayn Rand*, revised second edition (forthcoming), Belmont, Calif.: Wadsworth Philosophers Series

Hayes, David
- "Biography, 'The Passion of Ayn Rand' is An Inaccurate Chronicle" http://arname.davidhayes.net and http://arbio.davidhayes.net

Hessen, Robert
- "Letters: *To the Chambers, Chambers!*" *National Review*, January 18, 1958, 71

Holzer, Henry Mark
- *Sweet Land of Liberty?*, 1983, Costa Mesa, California: Common Sense Press

Hospers, John
- "Conversations With Ayn Rand," *Liberty*, July, 1990, 23-36, and September, 1990, 42-52

- "Memories of Ayn Rand," *Full Context*, May, 1998, and http://www.fullcontext.org/backissues/Memories_of_Ayn_Rand.htm

Johnson, Paul
- *Intellectuals*, 1988, New York: Harper & Row

Jones, W.T.
- *A History of Western Philosophy*, volume 4, 1952, New York: Harcourt, Brace Jovanovich

Kaufmann, Walter
- "Editor's Introduction" to *Ecce Homo, The Basic Writings of Nietzsche*, translated and edited by W. Kaufmann, 2000, New York: Modern Library, Random House.

Macedo, Stephen
- *The New Right Versus The Constitution*, 1987, Washington, D.C.: Cato

Mayhew, Robert, editor
- *Essays on Ayn Rand's We the Living*, 2004, Lanham, Maryland: Lexington Books

Merrill, Ronald
- *The Ideas of Ayn Rand*, 1991, LaSalle, Illinois: Open Court

Mises, Ludwig von
- *Human Action*, 1949, New Haven, Conn.: Yale University Press, but more accessible is the third revised edition, 1966, Chicago: Contemporary Books.

Nozick, Robert
- "On the Randian Argument," *The Personalist*, Spring 1971, reprinted, along with critical response, in *Reading Nozick: Essays on Anarchy, State and Utopia*, J. Paul, editor, 1981, Totowa, New Jersey: Rowman and Littlefield, 206-269.

Paxton, Michael
- *Ayn Rand: A Sense of Life*, 1998, Layton, Utah: Gibbs-Smith

Peikoff, Leonard
- Letter to the Editor, "Atlas Shrieked," *Esquire*, October 1961
- *Objectivism: The Philosophy of Ayn Rand*, 1991, New York: Dutton
- *Ideas in Action*, interview with James Valliant, 1995, WJM Productions (television interview)
- "My Thirty Years With Ayn Rand," *The Voice of Reason: Essays in Objectivist Thought*, 334-353
- "Fact and Value," *The Intellectual Activist*, volume v, number 1, May 18, 1989
- "Understanding Objectivism," 1983, Oceanside, CA: Lectures on Objectivism (12 audio recorded lectures)
- *The Ominous Parallels*, 1982, Stein and Day: New York
- "What To Do About Crime," *The Intellectual Activist*, vol. ix, no. 5, September, 1995 (lecture originally given at Ford Hall Forum, April 23, 1995)

Rand, Ayn
- *Atlas Shrugged*, 1957, New York: Random House
- "An Open Letter to My Readers," *The Los Angeles Times*, August 26, 1962, reprinted in *The Ayn Rand Column*, 43-45.
- *The Fountainhead*, 1943, New York: Bobbs-Merrill, and Twenty-fifth Anniversary Edition, with "Introduction," 1968, New York: Bobbs-Merrill
- "The Only Path to Tomorrow," *Reader's Digest*, January, 1944, reprinted in *The Ayn Rand Column*, 105-108.
- *We the Living*, 1936, New York: Macmillan; new edition with "Introduction," 1959, New York: Random House, 1995, New York: Dutton
- *Russian Writings on Hollywood*, Michael Berliner, editor, 1999, Marina del Rey, California: The Ayn Rand Institute Press
- *Love Letters*, 1945, Hal Wallis Productions (screenplay)
- *The Journals of Ayn Rand*, David Harriman, editor, 1997, New York: Dutton

- *The Ayn Rand Column*, Peter Schwartz, editor, 1991, Oceanside, California: Second Renaissance Books
- *The Romantic Manifesto*, Expanded 2nd Edition, 1975, New York: New American Library
- *Anthem*, 50th Anniv. Edition, with "Introduction" by Leonard Peikoff, 1995, New York: Dutton
- *The Night of January 16th*, 1968, New York: New American Library
- *The Voice of Reason: Essays in Objectivist Thought*, Leonard Peikoff, editor, 1988, New York: New American Library
- *For the New Intellectual*, 1961, New York: Random House
- "The Secular Meaning of Christmas," *The Objectivist Calendar*, December, 1976, reprinted in *The Ayn Rand Column*, 111-112
- *Letters of Ayn Rand*, Michael Berliner, editor, 1995, New York: Dutton
- *Ayn Rand's Marginalia*, Robert Mayhew, editor, 1995, New Milford, Connecticut: Second Renaissance
- "Review of *Aristotle* by John Herman Randall, Jr.," *The Objectivist Newsletter*, May 1963, reprinted in *The Voice of Reason: Essays in Objectivist Thought*, 6-12.
- *Capitalism: The Unknown Ideal*, 1966, New York: New American Library
- *The Early Ayn Rand*, Leonard Peikoff, editor, 1984, New York: New American Library
- "To Whom It May Concern," *The Objectivist*, May, 1968
- "The Psychology of 'Psychologizing,'" *The Objectivist*, March 1971, reprinted in *The Voice of Reason*, 23-31
- *The Phil Donahue Show*, May 15, 1979 (television interview)
- *The Virtue of Selfishness*, 1964, New York: New American Library
- *Introduction to Objectivist Epistemology*, expanded 2nd edition, Leonard Peikoff and Harry Binswanger, editors, 1990, New York: New American Library
- "Of Living Death," *The Objectivist*, September, October and November 1968, reprinted in *The Voice of Reason*, 46-63.
- "Interview With Ayn Rand," *Playboy*, March 1964, reprinted in *The Playboy Interview, Volume II*, B. Golson, editor, New York, N.Y.: Wideview/Perigee, 13-27
- *Philosophy: Who Needs It*, 1982, New York: Bobbs-Merrill

- "Censorship: Local and Express," *The Ayn Rand Letter*, volume II, number 23-25, August 13 through September 10, 1973, reprinted in *Philosophy: Who Needs It*, 211-230.
- "Through Your Most Grievous Fault," *The Los Angeles Times*, August 19, 1962, reprinted in *The Voice of Reason*, 158-160.
- *The Phil Donahue Show*, April 29, 1980 (television interview)
- "The Goal of My Writing," *The Objectivist Newsletter*, in two parts, October and November, 1963, and reprinted as chapter 11 of *The Romantic Manifesto*
- "Philosophy and Sense of Life," *The Objectivist*, February, 1966, reprinted as Chapter 2 of *The Romantic Manifesto*.
- "Art and Moral Treason," *The Objectivist Newsletter*, March, 1965, reprinted in *The Romantic Manifesto*.
- "Apollo 11," *The Objectivist*, September, 1969, reprinted in *The Voice of Reason*, 161-178.
- "The 'Inexplicable Personal Alchemy,'" *The Objectivist*, January, 1969, reprinted in *Return of the Primitive: the Anti-Industrial Revolution*, 119-121, Peter Schwartz, editor, 1999, New York: Meridian.

Register, Bryan
- "A Kinder, Gentler Judgment Day," *Liberty*, August, 1999

Rothbard, Murray N.
- "Letters: The Philosophy of Ayn Rand," *National Review*, January 25, 1958, 95
- *The Ethics of Liberty*, 1982, Atlantic Highlands, New Jersey: Humanities Press
- "Individualism and the Methodology of the Social Sciences," Cato Paper Number 4, 1979, Washington, D.C.: Cato
- "The Sociology of the Ayn Rand Cult," 1987 (but privately circulated much earlier), Port Townsend, Washington: Liberty Publishing, reprinted 1990, Burlingame, CA: The Center for Libertarian Studies.

Schwartz, Peter
- "Libertarianism: The Perversion of Liberty," in *The Voice of Reason*, Leonard Peikoff, editor. 1988, New York: New American Library, 311-333

Sciabarra, Chris Matthew
- "Investigative Report: In Search of the Rand Transcript," *Liberty*, October 1999
- "The Rand Transcript," *Journal of Ayn Rand Studies*, Fall 1999, and http://www.nyu.edu/projects/sciabarra/essays/randt2.htm
- *Ayn Rand: The Russian Radical*, 1995, University Park, Pennsylvania: Pennsylvania State University Press

Skinner, Kiron K., Anderson, Annelise, and Anderson, Martin, editors
- *Reagan: A Life in Letters*, 2003, New York: Free Press

Smith, Tara
- *Viable Values*, 2000, Lanham, Maryland: Rowman and Littlefield

Sures, Charles and Sures, Mary Ann
- *Facets of Ayn Rand*, 2001, Irvine, California: Ayn Rand Institute Press

Tuccille, Jerome
- *Alan Shrugged*, 2002, Hoboken, New Jersey: John Wiley & Sons

Vidal, Gore
- "Comment," *Esquire*, July 1961

Walker, Jeff
- *The Ayn Rand Cult*, 1999, Chicago and LaSalle, Illinois: Open Court

About The Author

James S. Valliant is an attorney and the host of the award-winning interview program, *Ideas in Action*. He lives in San Diego with his wife Holly and their two small dogs, Marcus Antonius and Cleopatra.

Index